Paddling
Minnesota

Greg Breining
With support from the Minnesota Conservation Volunteer, *bimonthly magazine of the Minnesota Department of Natural Resources*

FALCON®

HELENA, MONTANA

A FALCON GUIDE®

Falcon® Publishing is continually expanding its list of guidebooks. All books include detailed descriptions, accurate maps, and all the information necessary for enjoyable trips. You can order extra copies of this book and get information and prices for other Falcon® guidebooks by writing Falcon, P.O. Box 1718, Helena, MT 59624, or calling toll-free 1-800-582-2665. Also, please ask for a free copy of our current catalog. Visit our website at www.FalconOutdoors.com or contact us by e-mail at Falcon@falcon.com.

Library of Congress Cataloging-in-Publication Data.
Breining, Greg.
    Paddling Minnesota / by Greg Breining.
       p.   cm. — (A FalconGuide)
    Includes index.
    ISBN 1-56044-690-0 (pbk. : alk. paper)
      1. Canoes and canoeing—Minnesota Guidebooks. 2. Minnesota Guidebooks.
I. Title. II. Series.
GV776.M6B74 1999
797.1'22'09776—dc21   99-14402
                                                                             CIP

CAUTION

Outdoor recreational activities are by their very nature potentially hazardous. All participants in such activities must assume responsibility for their own actions and safety. The information contained in this guidebook cannot replace sound judgment and good decision-making skills, which help reduce risk exposure, nor does the scope of this book allow for disclosure of all the potential hazards and risks involved in such activities.

Learn as much as possible about the outdoor recreational activities in which you participate, prepare for the unexpected, and be cautious. The reward will be a safer and more enjoyable experience.

 Text pages printed on recycled paper.

Contents

Lake Superior and the North Shore

Northwest

Mississippi River

Central

Crow Wing River

Kettle River

North Fork of the Crow River

Pine River

Rum River

Sauk River

Snake River

St. Croix River

Acknowledgments

The author would like to thank the staff of the Minnesota Department of Natural Resources, especially Steve Mueller and Steve Johnson, for reviewing the manuscript, and the folks with Trails and Waterways Unit, who promote paddle sports and share their detailed knowledge of Minnesota rivers.

This book was written with funding from the *Minnesota Conservation Volunteer,* bimonthly magazine of the Minnesota Department of Natural Resources.

Minnesota's Rivers

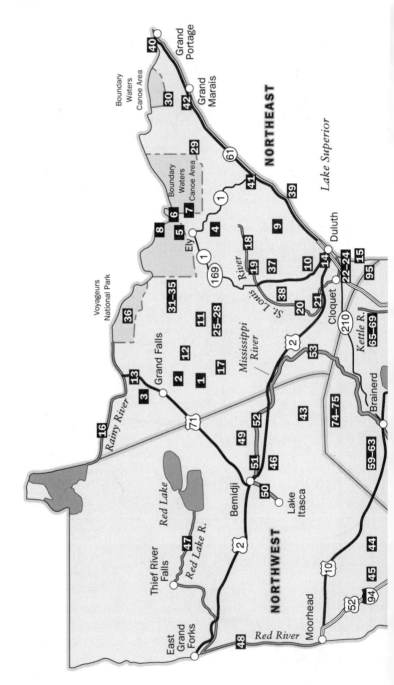

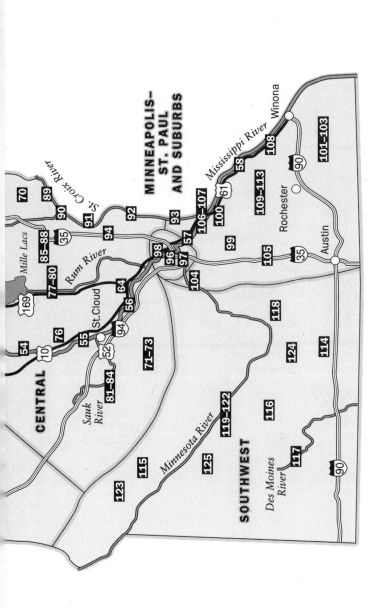

MINNEAPOLIS–
ST. PAUL
AND SUBURBS

CENTRAL

SOUTHWEST

Mille Lacs

St. Croix River

Mississippi River

Rum River

Sauk River

Minnesota River

Des Moines River

St. Cloud

Rochester

Austin

Winona

54

169

76

70

89

90

91

92

93

85–88

35

94

77–80

55

64

56

94

52

71–73

81–84

123

115

125

119–122

116

117

90

124

118

114

90

35

105

99

104

97

96

98

57

100

106–107

61

58

108

101–103

90

109–113

35

10

Map Legend

Interstate		County Line Boundary	
US Highway		State Boundary	MINNESOTA
State or Other Principal Road		Campground	
Forest Road	4165	City/Town	
Interstate Highway			
Primary Road		Dam	
Secondary Road		Put-in/Take-out	
Route(s)		Carry-in/Carry-out	
Portage			
Parking Area		Map Orientation	N
River/Creek/Rapids			
		Scale	0 0.5 1 Miles
Lake			
		Locator	

Introduction

LAY OF THE LAND

Minnesota and its rivers are the product of the glaciers that rolled over most of the state as recently as 10,000 years ago. In places, the glaciers, up to a mile thick, scraped clear down to the bedrock. In other regions, the slow-moving ice dumped sand and gravel as a conveyor belt would, forming hills and ridges. Ice dams and meltwater created glacial lakes, whose dried-up beds form vast flatlands.

In the northeast, forests of aspen, birch, and conifers grace a rugged land of thin soils and bare rock. Overall, the region is flat, but locally rugged. Streams follow faults and tumble over cliffs. They have low gradients but often run through widely spaced rapids.

The rocky, browlike ridge that forms the North Shore of Lake Superior is still rising imperceptibly slowly as it rebounds from the crushing weight of glacial ice. Rivers scream off the hill toward the lake. Some runs drop more than 200 feet per mile with difficult and potentially dangerous whitewater.

In the northwest, bogs, marsh, and the utterly flat prairie formed in the former bed of Glacial Lake Agassiz. The streams of this region are mostly sluggish and meandering, except where they rush from one flatland to another at a lower elevation.

In central Minnesota, glaciers left behind rolling hills of gravel, sand and boulders. Streams of this region are often swift and rocky, though rapids are pretty tame.

Southwestern Minnesota takes in broad regions of sloping prairie (now farm fields), dominated by the wide valley of the Minnesota River. In geological terms, the river is underfit, a puny inheritor of the vast trench carved through southern Minnesota by the mighty Glacial River Warren. Rivers run swiftly from the uplands into the Minnesota Valley with generally easy rapids.

The southeast is the only region of Minnesota to have escaped the most recent round of glaciation. While the rest of Minnesota was crushed, bulldozed, and rearranged, the southeast retained a visage that had been carved deep by rivers. Today, the streams, flanked by limestone and dolomite cliffs and bluffs, are swift, riffly, and generally easy to paddle.

Many visitors would argue that the glaciers never really left Minnesota. We're famous for cold weather. Peak stream flows occur as the last of the snow melts and spring rains begin—usually in early April in southern Minnesota, and late April or early May in northern Minnesota. Flows decline through the summer but often have a secondary peak with cooler weather and rain in the fall.

HOW TO USE THIS GUIDE

Paddling Minnesota is written to help you to sort through the state's myriad waters to find a route to your liking. Each trip description is organized to make it easy to choose on the basis of scenery, difficulty, location, and other factors.

We have included major streams of interest to paddlers, as well as a few oddballs that have something special to offer, such as historic sites, good fishing, or difficult whitewater.

Paddling Minnesota also highlights a few lakes. We can't include them all—not in a state that has, according to the Minnesota Department of Natural Resources, 11,842 that are 10 acres or larger. We have highlighted a few with something special to offer: an unusual landscape, the opportunity to travel lake to lake, historical significance, or the chance to see wildlife.

The book divides longer streams into several "trips" on the basis of character, access, and difficulty—separating the flatwater from the whitewater sections, for example.

Each trip begins with capsulized bits of information, meant to be read at a glance to help determine if the entire river description is of interest to you. The information includes:

Character: A short description of the river and what makes it worth including in a book on Minnesota's waters.

Length: Distance of the run in miles.

Average run time: The time it takes to paddle the run at an average pace. Generally we calculated that time on a floating speed of about 2 to 3 miles per hour. Plan to travel more slowly if there are difficult rapids to scout or portage. Double your travel time if you plan to fish seriously.

Class: The difficulty level of the water, based on the International Scale of River Difficulty. Where sufficient information is available, the difference in difficulty between low water and high flows has been noted. Generally, difficult rapids get more difficult as flow increases. The scale runs from classes I to VI, with a newly modified class 5, which differentiates degrees of difficulty by adding a decimal number, as rock climbers and mountaineers describe the difficulty of a certain climb—5.1 or 5.7 or 5.9. On lakes and on rivers where the current is very slow or almost imperceptible, we call the water "quiet."

Sheer cliffs tower above the St. Croix at Taylors Falls. MINNESOTA DEPARTMENT OF NATURAL RESOURCES

The six difficulty classes

Class I: Easy. Fast-moving water with riffles and small waves. Few obstructions, all obvious and easily missed with little training. Risk to swimmers is slight; self-rescue is easy.

Author's note: *Good for beginners who know basic strokes.*

Class II: Novice. Straightforward rapids with wide, clear channels which are evident without scouting. Occasional maneuvering may be required, but rocks and medium-sized waves are easily missed by trained paddlers. Swimmers are seldom injured and group assistance, while helpful, is seldom needed.

Author's note: *Go with a more experienced paddler to give advice and pick up paddles after you dump.*

Class III: Intermediate. Rapids with moderate, irregular waves which may be difficult to avoid and which can swamp an open canoe. Complex maneuvers in fast current and good boat control in tight passages or around ledges are often required; large waves or strainers may be present but are easily avoided. Strong eddies and powerful current effects can be found, particularly on large-volume rivers. Scouting is advisable for inexperienced parties. Injuries while swimming are rare; Self-rescue is usually easy but group assistance may be required to avoid long swims. Rapids that are at the lower or upper end of this difficulty range are designated "class III-" or "class III+" respectively.

Author's note: *Experienced paddlers only.*

Class IV: Advanced. Intense, powerful, but predictable rapids requiring precise boat handling in turbulent water. Depending on the character of the river, it may feature large, unavoidable waves and holes or constricted passages demanding fast maneuvers under pressure. A fast, reliable eddy turn may be needed to initiate maneuvers, scout rapids, or rest. Rapids may require "must" moves above dangerous hazards. Scouting may be necessary the first time down. Risk of injury to swimmers is moderate to high, and water conditions may make self-rescue difficult. Group assistance for rescue is often essential but requires practiced skills. A strong Eskimo roll is highly recommended. Rapids that are at the upper end of this difficulty range are designated "class IV-" or "class IV+" respectively.

Author's note: *Very tough and hazardous water in an open canoe, even for an expert.*

Class 5: Expert. Extremely long, obstructed, or very violent rapids which expose a paddler to added risk. Drops may contain large, unavoidable waves and holes or steep, congested chutes with complex, demanding routes. Rapids may continue for long distances between pools, demanding a high level of fitness. What eddies exist may be small, turbulent, or difficult to reach. At the high end of the scale, several of these factors may be combined. Scouting is recommended but may be difficult. Swims are dangerous, and rescue is often difficult even for experts. A very reliable Eskimo roll, proper equipment, extensive experience, and practiced rescue skills are essential. Because of the large range of difficulty that exists beyond class IV, class 5 is an open-ended, multiple-level scale designated by class 5.0, 5.1, 5.2, etc. Each of these levels is an order of magnitude more difficult

than the last. Example: Increasing difficulty from class 5.0 to class 5.1 is a similar order of magnitude as increasing from class IV to class 5.0.
Author's note: *Only experts in decked canoes, kayaks, or rafts need apply.*

Class VI: Extr eme and Explorator y. These runs have almost never been attempted and often exemplify the extremes of difficulty, unpredictability, and danger. The consequences of errors are very severe and rescue may be impossible. For teams of experts only, at favorable water levels, after close personal inspection, and taking all precautions. After a class VI rapids has been run many times, its rating may be changed to an appropriate class 5.x rating.
Author's note: *There's a real chance you'll die if you mess up.*

Reprinted with permission, American Whitewater Affiliation
Revised, May 1998

The italicized author's notes are comments made by Greg Breining and are not ascribed to the official AWA version, shown in non-italic type.

Skill level: beginner, intermediate, or expert—based largely on difficulty and perceived hazard. The remoteness of a particular stretch is also taken into consideration. The different levels of paddling skill are an approximation, based on the following parameters:

Beginner: Knows the basic strokes and can handle craft competently in smooth water. Knows how to bring the boat to shore safely in fast current, can negotiate sharp turns in fast current, can avoid strainers and other obstacles, and understands the difficulties of the stream to be floated. A beginner is not a person who is picking up a paddle for the first time. Novices should get some practice on a lake or with an experienced floater before taking their first trip.

Intermediate: Knows basic strokes and uses them effectively. Can read water well, can negotiate fairly difficult rapids with confidence, and knows how to safely catch an eddy. Won't panic and knows what to do in the event of an upset. Can come to shore quickly to inspect dangerous spots and knows when to portage. The tandem paddler knows how to coordinate strokes between bow and stern and can paddle at either end.

Expert: Has mastered all strokes and uses them instinctively. Confident of own ability even in very difficult situations. Skillful in heavy water or complex rapids. Knows when a rapid is unrunnable and has a deep respect for all safety precautions.

Optimal flow: Included in trip descriptions where it's relevant, this is sometimes an inexact term. At the very least, it indicates a level with enough water to float over most obstructions. Anglers may prefer lower flows, when fish are concentrated in pools. On the other hand, die-hard whitewater paddlers may salivate over much higher water levels, when rapids are at their waviest and toughest. For this reason, we generally haven't included upper limits, but be advised that all rivers are hazardous in flood. "High water," as it is used in several trip descriptions, refers to a stream that is bank full or with water into the terrestrial vegetation.

Average gradient: The steepness with which the river falls, calculated as vertical feet per mile.

Hazards: Any risks that require your attention. You can pay attention now (before you paddle through the hazardous waters) or pay later (at the hospital, the chiropractor's, dentist's, physical therapist's office, or worse).

Maps: A list of the detailed maps you will need to navigate your way to and along a waterway. The maps in this book are designed to give you a general idea of the water route. They are meant to be used for trip planning, not as navigational tools.

After these capsules of information, **The paddling** gives a narrative description of the run—what you're likely to see and experience.

The information that follows the narrative description of the river includes:

Access: Included for most descriptions, provides directions to developed carry-in canoe landings or boat landings. Often, however, you'll gain access to a stream by way of a bridge crossing. If an access is described as developed, there is parking. If not, assume you'll be parking by the side of the road.

Shuttle: Tells how to reunite your car and boat at the end of the trip. The most common way is to use two vehicles to "run a shuttle," that is, spot a vehicle at the take-out and drive back up to the put-in with your gear. *Paddling Minnesota* includes approximate distances and estimated times for running the shuttle with a car. But there are more creative ways to set up a shuttle. Fitness buffs can walk, jog, bike, or even skate (on wheels) from the take-out back to the put-in. Others hire an outfitter to shuttle the vehicle for them.

MA&G: The page and map coordinates to turn to in the *Minnesota Atlas & Gazetteer* to find the waterway in question. The atlas is published by and available from DeLorme Publishing, P.O. Box 298, Yarmouth, ME 04096; 800-452-5931. We recommend its use in conjunction with *Paddling Minnesota.*

Camping: Provides both public riverside campsites and nearby public campgrounds. Often, private campgrounds are available, but because of the difficulty of finding all private sites and evaluating them, we generally have not included them in this guide.

Food, gas, and lodging: Lists nearby communities where those essentials can be found.

Rocky shores characterize waterways in the Boundary Waters Canoe Area Wilderness and Voyageurs National Park. Bring a good air mattress. MINNESOTA OFFICE OF TOURISM

For more information: Gives the names of offices or agencies that can provide greater detail and may be able to answer questions that have not been answered in this book.

PLANNING YOUR TRIP

Paddling Minnesota will help you pick a river to run, but we encourage you to consult additional sources of information.

You can obtain detailed maps for many Minnesota streams from the Minnesota Department of Natural Resources (MDNR). Free canoe route maps show accesses, campsites, and rapids on about two dozen rivers around the state. Order from the MDNR Information Center: 651-296-6157 or toll-free in Minnesota, 888-646-6367. (TTY for the deaf: 651-296-5484 or toll-free in Minnesota, 800-657-3929.)

The MDNR also publishes Public Recreation Information Maps (PRIM), which cover the entire state and show public lands and recreational sites. PRIM maps, as they are called, are helpful if no canoe route map is available for a particular stream. PRIM maps cost $4.95 apiece. Order from the DNR Gift Shop, 500 Lafayette Road, St. Paul, MN 55101; 651-228-9165. Allow four to six weeks for delivery.

The USDA Forest Service has free maps of many of the canoe routes through national forests. Contact either the Chippewa or Superior National Forests in Minnesota.

The most detailed maps available are topographic quadrangles published by the U.S. Geological Survey, Reston, VA 22092; call 800-USA-MAPS. These show land contours, among other information, and are especially useful in scouting out steep whitewater runs. By calculating the foot-per-mile gradient of a run, you can hazard a reasonable guess at the difficulty of whitewater. Generally speaking, gradients in excess of 20 feet per mile suggest class II water or something even more difficult. Gradients over 100 feet per mile mean some deadly stuff indeed. Looking at the gradients given in the trip descriptions will help you figure out how gradient relates to difficulty.

Before you leave on your trip, get up-to-date water level information. Some streams, especially small, steep creeks, are runnable only under certain circumstances. The MDNR Information Center provides gauge readings and interpretations for more than two dozen favorite rivers around the state. Regularly updated river level readings are also available on the MDNR website: www.dnr.state.mn.us.

For additional water-level information, including current readings and hydrographs, check the following websites:

- MDNR Division of Waters site on the MDNR website: www.dnr.state.mn.us/water.html
- U.S. Geological Survey at http://mn.water.usgs.gov/wrd/stream.html
- U.S. Army Corps of Engineers at www.mvp.usace.army.mil

Hydrographs—a record of a stream's ups and downs over time—have been provided for the river sections where such information is available. Most of this information comes from the U.S. Geological Survey website. Hydrographs indicate the size of a river (the greater the flow, the larger the stream), its "flashiness" (that is, the extent of its peaks and valleys), and the times water flows are greatest and least. In most cases, an **estimated minimum runnable flow** has been indicated on the hydrographs; flows below this level mean you'll be bumping and dragging down the river. When you're on the U.S.G.S. website, use the **station number** provided with each hydrograph to quickly find the present-time flow for a particular site.

Outfitters rent paddling and camping equipment that will enable you to travel along rivers or lakes at almost any level of comfort you choose. To find out about outfitters near the river you're running, call the MDNR Information Center.

SAFE PADDLING

Water sports such as canoeing and kayaking are inherently risky. That's especially true of paddling whitewater or wilderness streams. Stay out of trouble by taking the following precautions.

- Most important, wear a life vest. Minnesota law requires that at the very least you have a Coast Guard–approved life jacket for every person on board and that it be handy. Lashed under a canoe seat is not handy!
- Stow a spare paddle.

- Bring adequate food and water to tide you over if your trip takes longer than planned. Pack warm clothes, rain gear, and matches or a lighter. Wear or bring good footwear in case you have to portage or walk for help. On remote streams, bring a map and compass in case you have to walk out of the river.
- If you're paddling difficult water in early spring or late fall when the water is cold, wear a wetsuit or drysuit to stay warm in case you capsize.
- Whitewater requires some special gear, no matter what the season. Wear a helmet to protect your noggin if you flip. Make sure your boat, whether a kayak, decked canoe, or open canoe, has enough flotation to keep it riding high if you dump and have to bail out. A low-riding boat tends to wrap around rocks and is difficult to fish out of the river.
- Bring a throw rope. Not only is it handy for rescues, you can use it for hauling wrapped canoes off rocks and for raising and lowering boats on steep bluffs.
- Other than difficult rapids, two kinds of hazards warrant special caution. The first are "strainers," such as downed trees in the current that trap boats and paddlers while water flows through. The second are low-head dams, which can form a recirculating "hole" (hydraulic) that can hold on fast to boats and paddlers. They can be so deadly they're sometimes called "drowning machines."
- Finally, don't paddle alone on difficult water. Go with a group of paddlers who are up to the task. If a boat flips, rescue paddlers first. Go for gear later, after people are safely on shore.

Except for the life vests and ball caps, these might be the voyageurs that plied Minnesota water two centuries ago. MINNESOTA OFFICE OF TOURISM

CAMPING

Public campsites are found along many waters in the state. Even if there are no developed sites, you can camp on most state and federal forest land. Look for a level spot, out of the mud and several feet above the river, so a hard rain that raises the river won't flood your site. If there is no outhouse, relieve yourself well away from the river and any trails. Dig a shallow "cat hole" and bury your waste.

If you build a campfire, gather only deadwood. Build your fire in an established fire ring or on rock or mineral soil. Pack out your garbage.

On all canoe trips, bring water or filter it. None of the waters in this book are suitable for drinking if untreated. Even Lake Superior, as clear as it is, may contain *Giardia,* an organism that can cause severe and long-lasting gastrointestinal distress.

STEWARDSHIP

If you want to roll up your sleeves and help out the streams you enjoy, check out the MDNR's Adopt-A-River Program. The program furnishes volunteers with free rubbish bags, gloves, and recognition for collecting trash along streams. Call 651-297-5476 or check out the MDNR website.

Several streams in this guide have been designated state wild and scenic rivers. For more information on this conservation program, go to the MDNR website.

The common loon lives on many medium to large lakes in central and northern Minnesota. MINNESOTA OFFICE OF TOURISM

FISHING

Many Minnesota streams provide great fishing. Large rivers with deep holes fish well throughout the warm-weather season. Small streams often lack the depth and cover to hold fish year-round but provide good fishing during the spring and early summer.

It's helpful to split Minnesota's streams into two categories, each with distinct fish communities. Coldwater streams make up the smaller group. With ample sources of groundwater from springs, these streams remain cold and well-oxygenated (since cold water holds more dissolved oxygen that warm water does) throughout the year. They don't flood often. Trout are the most common game fish. The best places to fish are the "runs," that is, the places where a riffle gives way to a deep hole. Fish this transition with tiny spinners, jigs, or plugs. Flies are also effective. Because these streams are small, beach your craft and fish downstream.

Warmwater streams make up the second group and include most floatable streams in Minnesota. These rivers receive little groundwater, but instead rise and fall depending on rain. Their temperature may rise to more than 80 degrees F in midsummer. Most warmwater streams harbor northern pike, walleyes, smallmouth bass, and channel catfish. Some have muskies. Warmwater streams that link a chain of lakes often hold species more typical of still water, such as largemouth bass and bluegills.

Because warmwater streams tend to be larger than coldwater streams, you can fish them as you drift downstream. For northern pike (and muskies, where they occur), fish deep eddies along shore with spinners, plugs, or large flies. Catch walleyes in deep holes with jigs or deep-running plugs. Smallmouth bass hold in deep water below riffles and along deep banks with a bit of current and exposed rock. Catch them on spinners, small plugs, jigs, or fly-rod poppers and streamers. Channel cats occupy deep holes, moving up below riffles when they are actively feeding. At these times, you may catch them on artificial lures. But the tried-and-true method is to bait a hook with cut fish, worms, or "stink bait" and fish it on the bottom with a heavy sinker.

Some Minnesota streams are subject to special regulations, such as length limits. Be sure to check state regulations before packing your fishing rod.

The Minnesota Department of Health has issued advisories about eating fish from many state lakes and streams because of pollutants such as mercury and PCBs. The advisories are too complicated to summarize here; if you're planning to fish, ask for the printed advisory by calling 612-215-0950 or 800-657-3908.

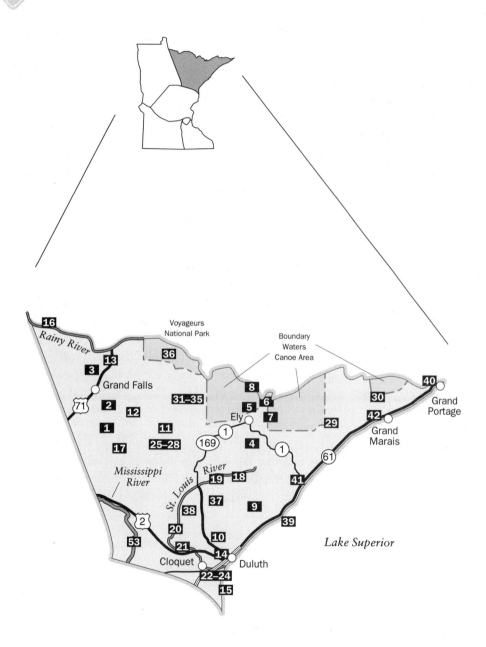

Northeast

16

Rainy River

13

3

Grand Falls

71

2

12

1

17

Mississippi
River

Voyageurs
National Park

36

31–35

Ely

5

11

25–28

169

Boundary
Waters
Canoe Area

8

6

7

29

4

1

1

St. Louis River

18

19

37

38

20

53

21

10

14

Cloquet

22–24

15

Duluth

9

41

39

61

30

40

Grand
Portage

42

Grand
Marais

Lake Superior

2

BIG FORK RIVER

1 Dora Lake to Minnesota Highway 6

Character: The Big Fork provides the occasional wild ride as it flows past a mix of forest land and farms. With many developed campsites, it's a good choice for an overnight trip.
Length: 77 miles.
Average run time: Three to four days.
Class: I–II, with one class IV falls.
Skill level: Intermediate, with wilderness camping skills.
Optimal flow: 5.5 feet or higher on the gauge at Minnesota Highway 38 in the town of Bigfork.
Average gradient: 1.3 feet per mile.
Hazards: No particular hazards.
Maps: MDNR *Big Fork River Canoe Route.*

The paddling: Two things in particular recommend the Big Fork, the wild character of the surrounding forest and the presence of large muskies in the river. To appreciate the wild country around you, plan an overnight trip. If you're lucky, you may hear the howls of timber wolves. To catch a muskie, cast a large spinner, spinnerbait, or plug to deep shorelines, eddies, and pools as you drift downstream.

Despite its name, the Big Fork is similar in size to its neighbor, the Little Fork. It is similar, too, in the wildness of the surrounding terrain, the difficulty of its rapids, and its fisheries. Because of its surficial geology and the many lakes in its upper reaches, the Big Fork is less prone to turn cloudy with runoff than the Little Fork.

The trip down the upper Big Fork begins at the Forest Service picnic area at Dora Lake. An interesting side trip is the so-called Lost Forty, about 4 miles to the northwest, an area of virgin red and white pine missed by loggers because early maps showed the area to be underwater. A half-mile trail loops beneath the canopy of pines.

Leaving Dora Lake, the fledgling Big Fork flows quietly eastward, running through only two rapids (**Robb's Rapids** and **Hauck Rapids,** both class I) en route to the town of Bigfork. Four miles downstream from town, the river flows through **Rice Rapids,** a long, bouldery class I rapids that washes out in high water. The river then flows quietly for several miles.

Just above Minnesota Highway 1, the river again runs through a long, bouldery class I section. After several miles more of quiet water, the Big Fork speeds through another class I stretch and then comes to **Muldoon Rapids,** a half-mile-long class II pitch with 2-foot-high waves in high water.

Two miles after the little settlement of Craigville, the Big Fork spills over the largest rapids of the upper river, Little American Falls, a 6-foot-high ledge that drops into a large pool flanked by 60-foot bluffs. This class IV–5 pitch is easy to bypass with a short portage on the left.

1 Dora Lake to Minnesota Highway 6

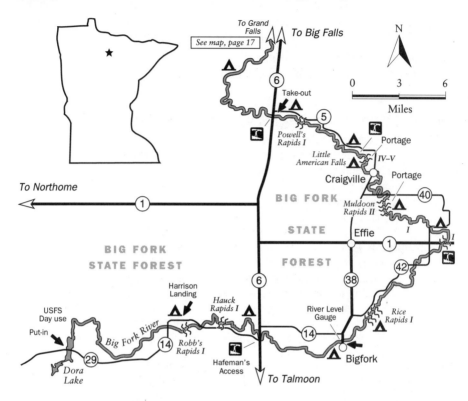

Several miles after **Little American Falls,** the Big Fork races through a final class I pitch, **Powell's Rapids,** before the take-out at Minnesota Highway 6.

Access: Dora Lake put-in: From Bigfork, drive west 23 miles, first on County Route 14 and then on County Route 29 to Dora Lake. **MN 6 take-out:** From Bigfork, drive north 6.5 miles on MN 38 to Effie; 6 miles west on MN 1 to MN 6; and then north 9 miles to the bridge and access. Note that MN 6 crosses the Big Fork in two other locations.

Alternate accesses are located at Harrison Landing, MN 6 near Bigfork, MN 38 in Bigfork, MN 1 east of Effie, and County Route 5 at Little American Falls.

Shuttle: 33 miles. About 1.5 hours.

ADDITIONAL HELP

MA&G: 73, A7–9; 74, A1; 85, E9.
Camping: Riverside camping is possible at several sites, including Harrison Landing Campground at the County Route 14 bridge, Little Minnow Campsite 2 miles upstream from the MN 6 bridge near Bigfork, at a park in Bigfork, Rice Rapids

Campsite, Busticogan Campsite a mile downstream from the MN 1 bridge, Muldoon Campsite, Little American Falls, and Old Hudson Bay Farm Campsite 2 miles upstream from the take-out. Auto camping is possible in Big Fork State Forest, George Washington State Forest, and McCarthy Beach and Scenic State Parks.

Food, gas, and lodging: Big Falls, Bigfork, Grand Rapids.

For more information: MDNR Information Center.

2 | Minnesota Highway 6 to Big Falls

Character: The Big Fork travels placidly across the boggy and forested northern Minnesota landscape. This section affords a lazy paddle and remote camping.

Length: 38.5 miles.

Average run time: Two to three days.

Class: Quiet water.

Skill level: Beginner, with wilderness camping skills.

Optimal flow: 5.5 feet or higher on the gauge at Minnesota Highway 38 in the town of Bigfork, or 1.5 feet or higher according to the gauge on the railroad trestle above the falls in Big Falls. With few rapids in this stretch, water level isn't critical.

Average gradient: 0.9 foot per mile.

Hazards: Don't miss the take-out above the falls at Big Falls.

Maps: MDNR *Big Fork River Canoe Route.*

The paddling: This quiet and often sandy stretch of river flows unhurriedly past a dense forest of birch, aspen, spruce, and fir. The first half of the run, from MN 6 to the next MN 6 bridge, is quite remote, surrounded by the dense forest and bog of Pine Island and Koochiching State Forests. The second half of the segment frequently loops back to within earshot of MN 6.

The remote reaches of these northern forests are home to animals such as black bears, moose, otters, bobcats, and timber wolves. Keep an eye out as you round each bend and look for tracks along the shoreline.

A century ago, loggers cut vast stands of white and red pine in the Big Fork watershed and floated the logs to mills along the Canadian border. Logging continues to be an important industry of the region. These days, however, the most important forest products are not saw logs of virgin pine, but pulpwood of aspen, spruce, and other species for use in making paper.

Access: MN 6 put-in: From Bigfork, drive north 6.5 miles on MN 38 to Effie; 6 miles west on Minnesota Highway 1 to MN 6; and then north 9 miles to the bridge and access. **Big Falls take-out:** From the put-in, follow MN 6 north 20 miles to the town of Big Falls; the access lies above the cataract also known as Big Falls on the left side of the river by the railroad trestle upstream from the U.S. Highway 71 bridge.

2   Minnesota Highway 6 to Big Falls

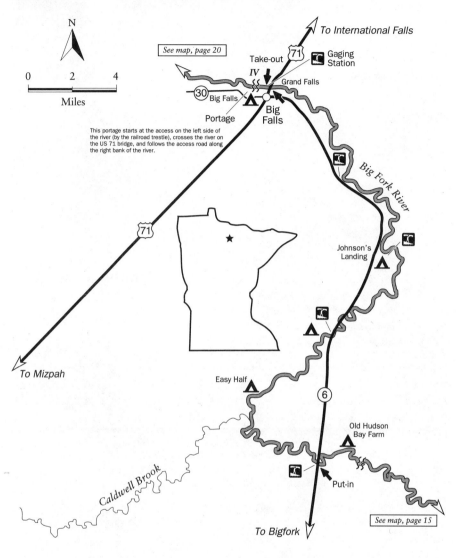

N

0   2   4
Miles

To International Falls

See map, page 20

71

Take-out

IV

Gaging Station

Grand Falls

30 Big Falls

Portage

Big Falls

This portage starts at the access on the left side of the river (by the railroad trestle), crosses the river on the US 71 bridge, and follows the access road along the right bank of the river.

71

★

Big Fork River

Johnson's Landing

To Mizpah

Easy Half

6

Old Hudson Bay Farm

Caldwell Brook

Put-in

See map, page 15

To Bigfork

Access is also possible at the MN 6 bridge 6 miles north of the put-in, Johnson's Landing, and an unnamed landing midway between Johnson's Landing and Big Falls (see map).

Shuttle: 20 miles. About 50 minutes.

ADDITIONAL HELP

MA&G: 85, E–C8.

Other than a few rapids, the Big Fork River is largely placid. MINNESOTA
DEPARTMENT OF NATURAL RESOURCES

Camping: Three campsites are located along this stretch—Easy Half Campsite, 2 miles downstream from the mouth of Caldwell Brook; a campsite at the second MN 6 bridge; and Johnson's Landing. Camping is also possible in Big Falls, and at McCarthy Beach and Scenic State Parks.

Food, gas, and lodging: Bigfork, Big Falls.

For more information: MDNR Information Center.

3 Big Falls to Rainy River

Character: After a tumultuous falls at Big Falls, the Big Fork meanders placidly to its meeting with the Rainy River. It's a good stretch for canoe camping or fishing.

Length: 51 miles.

Average run time: Two to three days.

Class: Quiet.

Skill level: Beginner, with wilderness camping skills.

Optimal flow: 1.5 feet or higher (about 500 cfs) according to the gauge on the railroad trestle above the falls in Big Falls. With few rapids in this stretch, water level isn't critical.

Average gradient: 1.5 feet per mile, not including the series of falls at Big Falls, where the river drops about 35 feet in a quarter mile.

Hazards: The falls at Big Falls.

Maps: MDNR *Big Fork River Canoe Route.*

The paddling: The major scenic attraction in this stretch is the series of falls and rapids in Big Falls, where the Big Fork, a sizable river at this point, plunges over a series of rocky ledges. The falls rate class IV in low water, but soon become much more difficult as the water rises and the drops fill with 6-foot-high backrollers and big souse holes. At exceptionally high water, the turbulence and mayhem is breathtaking. The portage around the falls starts at the access on the left side of the river (by the railroad trestle), crosses the river on the U.S. Highway 71 bridge and follows the access road along the right bank of the river.

Once you launch downstream of the falls, things settle down. The river runs through a short burst of class I rapids immediately downstream of the put-in, but then turns quiet for the rest of its length. Many people fish the lower river by small fishing boat instead of canoe. Land along the river is almost continuously forested.

At the mouth of the Big Fork, within easy walking distance of the take-out, sits Grand Mound Center, managed by the Minnesota Historical Society. The center tells the story of the people who

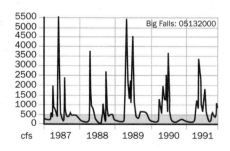

500 cfs = minimum for good paddling

3 Big Falls to Rainy River

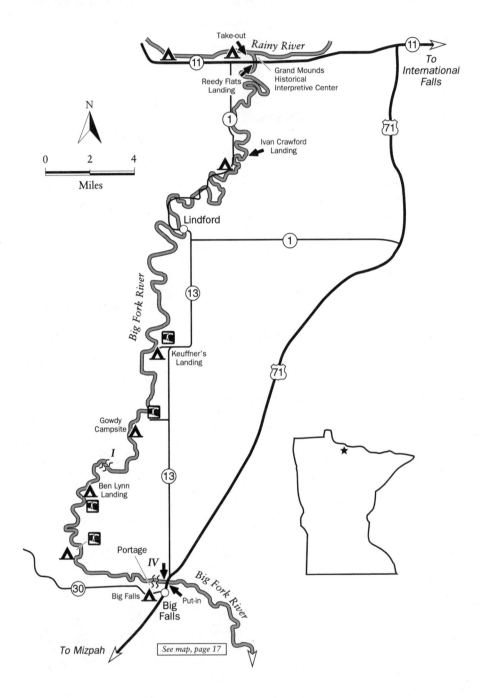

N

0   2   4
Miles

Take-out

Rainy River

11

To
International
Falls

Reedy Flats
Landing

Grand Mounds
Historical
Interpretive Center

71

1

Ivan Crawford
Landing

Lindford

1

Big Fork River

13

71

Keuffner's
Landing

Gowdy
Campsite

I

Ben Lynn
Landing

13

Portage

IV

30

Big Falls

Put-in

Big
Falls

Big Fork River

To Mizpah

See map, page 17

built the prehistoric burial site known as Grand Mound. Measuring 25 feet high and 100 by 140 feet at the base, the hill is the largest prehistoric man-made structure in Minnesota. The remains of an estimated 2,000 to 5,500 people are buried there, the population of a sizable town.

Grand Mound and several smaller burial mounds were constructed during the period 500 B.C. to A.D. 800 by a group of Indians known as the Laurel Culture. They lived in small villages on the river banks and fished the Rainy and Big Fork Rivers for lake sturgeon with toggle-headed harpoons that resembled those of subarctic tribes. The very abundance of food supported a population large enough to require or construct the mounds. By appearances, corpses were set on platforms to decay or were buried and then unearthed. The large bones were bundled for burial in the Grand Mound and smaller nearby mounds.

After A.D. 800, the habits and artifacts of the inhabitants shifted. Pottery changed. The bow and arrow replaced the atlatl and spear. Wild rice became an important food. The new culture, known as the Blackduck, interred their dead whole soon after death, placing them in smaller mounds or simply adding to the Laurel mounds. They often placed pots, tools, copper jewelry, shell necklaces, and clay masks in the graves. Did the Laurel evolve to become the Blackduck? Or did the Blackduck drive the Laurel from the region? We don't know. For that matter, what might have become of the Blackduck? When French explorers such as Jacques de Noyon passed through the area in the late 1600s, the area was only sparsely settled by Dakota and Cree. The Blackduck might have become any of these tribes, or for that matter Assiniboin, Cheyenne, Blackfoot, or Arapaho.

Since the late 1800s, Grand Mound has attracted archaeologists and grave robbers. In 1933, Albert Jenks of the University of Minnesota completely excavated one of the smaller mounds. In 1991, as sensitivity over the sanctity of the graves has superseded our curiosity about their contents, all human remains were reinterred, with a ceremony by Ojibwa and Dakota.

Access: **Big Falls put-in:** In town, below the falls on the right side of the river and downstream from the US 71 bridge. **Rainy River take-out** (known as Reedy Flats Landing): From Big Falls, follow County Route 13 north 16 miles to Lindford; cross the Big Fork on County Route 1 and follow the river generally northward to Minnesota Highway 11 for 9 miles; turn east and drive 1 mile to the landing.

Access is also possible at Sturgeon River Landing, Ben Lynn Landing, an unnamed landing off County Route 13, Keuffner's Landing, and Ivan Crawford Landing (see map for locations).

Shuttle: 28 miles one way. About 1.25 hours.

ADDITIONAL HELP

MA&G: 85, C–A8; 95, E9.

Camping: Riverside camping is possible at Sturgeon River Landing, Ben Lynn Landing, Gowdy Campsite, Keuffner's Landing, and on river left about 2 miles upstream from Ivan Crawford Landing. River campsites are also located on the Rainy River, about a mile below the mouth of the Big Fork, and at Loman Park, about 3.5 miles below the confluence. Auto camping is possible in Big Falls, Koochiching and Pine Island State Forests, and Franz Jevne and Scenic State Park.

Food, gas, and lodging: Big Falls, International Falls.

For more information: MDNR Information Center.

4 Birch Lake

Character: Here's a way to experience the rugged, rocky lakes of the Superior National Forest, complete with primitive campsites without having to portage.

Paddling time: Day trip or overnight.

Hazards: Take precautions against bears in camp.

Maps: Superior National Forest map and *Birch Lake Backcountry Sites,* a photocopied hand-out.

The paddling: Birch Lake is an excellent lake to explore with a canoe or kayak. It winds through the rock outcrops and forests north of Babbitt. It stretches more than 20 miles and totals 7,800 acres. The 80-mile shoreline is jagged, with many bays and islands. Because of its serpentine shape, it is relatively well protected from strong winds. Fishing is good for walleyes, northern pike, smallmouth bass, and lake trout.

Access: There are several public accesses on the lake. From Babbitt, drive east 3 miles on Forest Road 112, or north 2 miles on County Road 407. An access is located at the north end of the lake at Minnesota Highway 1. Finally, from the north end of the lake, drive south 5 miles on Forest Road 429 to the access at Birch Lake Campground.

ADDITIONAL HELP

MA&G: 76, A5.

Camping: 16 backcountry campsites are located at various points along the shoreline. Camp by car at Birch Lake Campground.

Food, gas, and lodging: Virginia, Babbitt.

For more information: Superior National Forest.

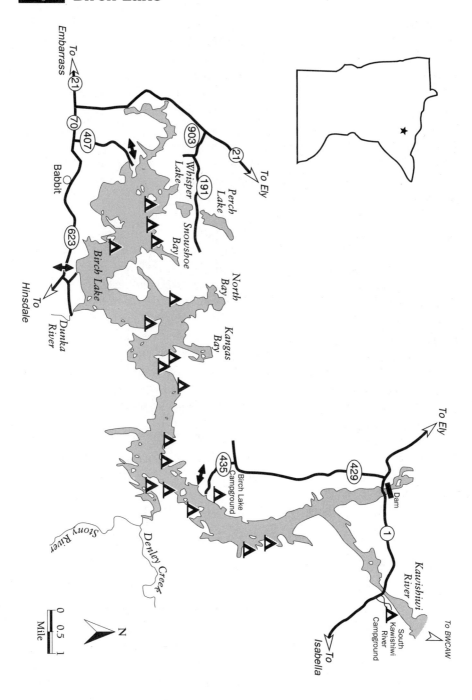

BOUNDARY WATERS CANOE AREA WILDERNESS

The Boundary Waters Canoe Area Wilderness is a brooding, eternal land of elemental rock and water, with ancient trails trod deep by the moccasins of countless generations. It is a land where the call of a loon drifts across an open bay and fades into eternity, where ochre men and animals dance on black cliffs. It is still quite possible to lose oneself on a web of rivers and lakes that reaches back to the days of voyageurs and unnamed Indian tribes and beyond.

It is a land for which canoes were made. For thousands of years, Indians traversed these waters, hunting moose and caribou, harvesting wild rice, and netting whitefish. French-Canadian voyageurs paddled and portaged 25-foot birch-bark canoes down these same lakes in a determined quest for furs. It is not by accident that it is called the Boundary Waters, for the border between the United States and Canada was set along the traditional route of the fur traders.

The Boundary Waters calls to canoeists still with the promise of wilderness and solitude, the sight of a moose on a portage, a glimpse of a bald eagle gliding watchfully over a lake, and the sound of gray wolves howling at night.

Stretching more than 100 miles along the Canadian border, the Boundary Waters is a federal wilderness within Superior National Forest. It is a land of 1.1 million acres of unbroken forest and some 2,500 lakes, where, with the exception of a handful of lakes, motors are not allowed and progress is measured by the firm bite of a paddle in clear water and the weight of a canoe and pack on your shoulders. Canoe travel is possible over an infinite combination of water routes and portages that might require a part of a day to more than a week. When you come to the Boundary Waters, you'll discover there are plenty of ways to approach the wilderness.

Some visitors delight in traveling. They are the inheritors of the voyageur tradition. They pack light and travel fast. Each morning, they rise early, make breakfast quickly, strike camp, and put on the water. Rarely does the tent stand in the same camp for two nights.

Others prefer to establish a base camp. Then, each day they pack a lunch, jacket, and lighter or matches for an emergency fire, and head out to explore for the day. The portages are a breeze—no packs to carry—and they return to their comfortable camp at the end of the day. Since they're not packing up gear and carrying every day, they can afford to two-trip the portages on the way in and stock up on luxuries: a reflector oven or Dutch oven for baking and lawn chairs for lounging around camp. (If you camp in the Boundary Waters Canoe Area Wilderness, be sure to hang your food high between trees to keep it safe from bears.)

Just getting started? Try a day trip. Plenty of interesting lakes lie just inside the wilderness. Paddle in during the morning and come out before nightfall. You'll have little gear to portage and no need for voluminous packs, cook kits, lightweight food, tent, or sleeping bags. No need either to learn how to sling a food pack between trees to keep it from hungry bears while you sleep or travel. Spend each evening in a campground. Or, if you really want it soft, in a resort.

How to pick a route through the wilderness? If you're unfamiliar with the Boundary Waters, call an outfitter and work together to plan a route. Or look over the Forest Service map of the wilderness to find an area that interests you. Then order more-detailed maps of that area from an outfitter or sporting goods store. Find a route of lakes joined by portages, taking into account the length of portages and size of lakes. Big lakes may force you to take shelter from the wind, though a string of small lakes may wear you down from all the portaging. You'll be required to stay in designated sites. Then apply to the Forest Service for a permit, necessary for all overnight trips. You'll be asked to detail your route, but once you are underway, you can change your plans as you wish.

To help in your decision, here are four trips through the Boundary Waters. You can tailor them to your wishes and abilities.

Whenever you venture very far into the Boundary Waters, remember you're a long way from help. Don't take foolish risks. Black bears are campsite pests, even on some islands; hang food at night and during the day, if you leave camp.

Best time: Late May to mid-September. Fishing is generally best early in the season (even mid-May for lake trout). Black flies can be bad in spring. Mosquitoes take over in early summer. In spring and early fall, be prepared for frost.

Outfitters: Wilderness canoe travel requires some specialized camping equipment. If you don't want to invest in your own, work with an outfitter who can help plan your trip and supply everything you'll need, including food.

Canoe: The best canoe is fast, light, and large enough to carry packs and two or three people safely. Best are streamlined canoes at least 18 feet long and made of the strong, lightweight material called Kevlar.

Packs: A Duluth pack, a voluminous canvas envelope with leather straps, holds lots of gear and stows easily in a canoe. It has no frame to stick up over your shoulders, so you can carry a Duluth pack and a canoe at the same time—if your legs hold out. Pack sleeping bags, food, and warm clothes in waterproof, roll-top bags.

Cooking gear: A reliable gas stove saves the day during rainy weather when a wood fire is hard to start, or during drought when wood fires may be banned.

Supreme synthetics: Polypropylene long underwear, polyester fleece pullovers, and high-quality rain gear (such as Gore-Tex) are best for cold, rainy weather.

Bugs: Bring insect repellent to protect against mosquitoes, black flies, and ticks. If you really are bothered by insects, bring a head net for use around camp.

Bears: Though they rarely hurt anyone, bears are tireless in their pursuit of food. At night you must hang every last candy bar and pack of gum (and all the rest of your food) between two trees, at least 10 feet off the ground. Use 100 feet of 0.25-inch rope. Tie a chunk of wood to one end of the rope and toss it over a branch 20 feet off the ground. Tie the middle of the rope to the pack. Pull on the free ends of the rope to hoist the pack off the ground and away from the trees. Tie each end securely.

Information and permits: To prevent crowding in this popular wilderness area, the USDA Forest Service limits access through a permit system. You will need to reserve a permit for overnight/multi-day trips by calling toll-free 877-550-6777. You will pay a fee to register ($9 per party) and camp ($10 per adult per trip and $5 for each youth under 18). To get additional information about the Boundary Waters, call 218-626-4300. Party size is limited to nine people and four canoes. Also, no disposable cans or bottles are allowed, though disposable plastic and cardboard containers are fine.

Maps: Good maps are a must to negotiate the confusing web of water. Two companies—McKenzie Maps and W.A. Fisher Company—publish detailed, waterproof maps that show waterways, portages, and campsites. The Fisher maps come in different scales. Listed here is the larger, more detailed, scale: 1.5 miles = 1 inch. Buy them from outfitters or order from the companies. You'll also want a compass when navigating among islands and bushwhacking where portage trails give out.

5 Hegman Lake

Character: This is a great short trip—perfectly suited for beginners—with a short portage and a surprise at the end.
Distance: 4 miles round trip.
Paddling time: About 2 hours.
Hazards: No particular hazards.
Maps: McKenzie Maps No. 11 and W.A. Fisher Co. F-9.

The paddling: From the South Hegman Lake access on the Echo Trail, carry your canoe about 80 rods (440 yards) to the lakeshore. (Traditionally, portages in the Boundary Waters are measured in rods. One rod equals 5.5 yards. We've continued that practice in this book.) Paddle about 5 rods north about 1 mile to the thin isthmus of rock that separates South Hegman Lake from North Hegman. Portage into North Hegman and paddle to the narrows at the far end of the lake to view the collection of dark red figures and symbols on the left side of the long bay, several feet above the waterline. The figure of a man stands as if in surprise, with arms outstretched and fingers spread apart. Standing with him are a moose and a dog (or wolf). Crescent-shaped canoes float on the rock face. This tightly composed picture is one of the clearest of the many Indian pictographs scattered throughout

5　Hegman Lake

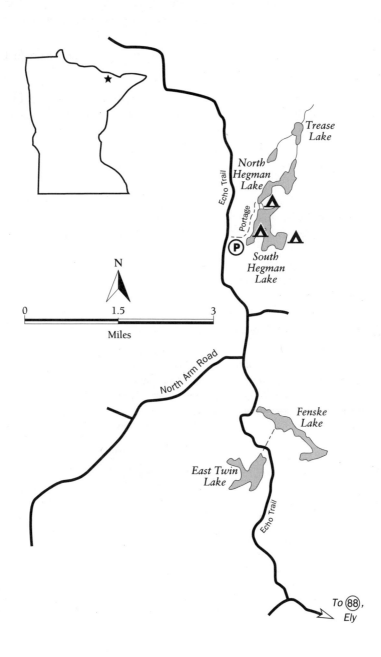

the Great Lakes region of United States and Canada. Their ages are difficult to determine. Their meanings are similarly vague, though they apparently speak of the many spirits that animate the world of the Ojibwa.

If you wish to extend the trip, paddle north on the narrow creek into Trease Lake before returning to the put-in.

None of these lakes is renowned for fishing, though South Hegman holds walleyes, northern pike, and smallmouth bass.

Access: From Ely, drive east and then north on County Route 88 and then the Echo Trail (County Route 116) a total of about 14 miles to the parking area. Portage to South Hegman Lake.

ADDITIONAL HELP

MA&G: 88, D4.
Camping: Auto camping is possible at Fenske Lake (also on the Echo Trail) and several other Forest Service sites nearby. If you wish to canoe camp, there are three sites on South Hegman Lake.
Food, gas, and lodging: Ely.
For more information: Superior National Forest.

6 Basswood Lake

Character: A trip to Basswood Lake doesn't require much portaging but puts the paddler into some of the best fishing in Minnesota.
Distance: Varies greatly, depending on route.
Paddling time: Three days to more than a week.
Hazards: No particular hazards.
Maps: McKenzie Maps Nos. 9, 10, 17, 27 and W.A. Fisher Co. F-10.

The paddling: With hundreds of lakes and few serious anglers at work, the Boundary Waters offers remarkable fishing for northern pike, walleyes, lake trout, and smallmouth bass. Some anglers will want to take plenty of tackle, including depthfinders and fishing boats with outboard motors. As a result, they'll stick to the larger lakes were motors are allowed. Other anglers will be satisfied to fish from a canoe, using a minimum of gear. They are free to paddle and portage to remote lakes that are fished only lightly.

The best fishing for walleyes, northern pike, and smallmouth is generally found in the large lakes. One of the best of all is Basswood, a large, convoluted, island-studded basin straddling the border with Canada. A trip to Basswood provides a great introduction to the Boundary Waters and its fishing, with a minimum of portaging.

Begin your trip at Moose Lake. Paddle northeastward down the long channel formed by Moose, New Found, and Sucker Lakes. Take 40-rod (220 yards) Prairie

6 Basswood Lake

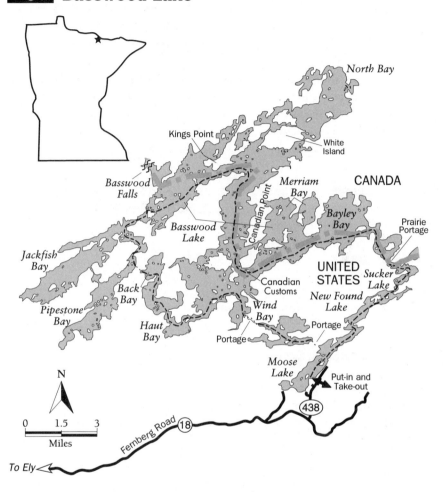

North Bay

Kings Point

White Island

Basswood Falls

Merriam Bay

CANADA

Canadian Point

Bayley Bay

Prairie Portage

Basswood Lake

Jackfish Bay

UNITED STATES

Sucker Lake

Back Bay

Canadian Customs

New Found Lake

Pipestone Bay

Wind Bay

Haut Bay

Portage

Portage

N

0   1.5   3
Miles

Moose Lake

Put-in and Take-out

438

Fernberg Road 18

To Ely

Portage into Basswood. At this point, if you have an Ontario fishing license and have completed a Remote Area Border Crossing Permit from Citizenship and immigration, you can paddle the less-traveled Canadian bays to fish for walleyes, northern pike, and smallmouth bass. Otherwise, you'll have to limit your fishing to the Minnesota side of the lake. (For information about clearing customs, call Canada Immigration, 807-274-9780.)

In spring and early summer, you will probably have your greatest success casting to rocky shallows for bass and weedy areas for northern pike. Try poppers, minnow lures, spinners, and jigs. For walleyes, work jigs along drop-offs and long points. If you're really serious about this, bring a portable depth-finder to locate underwater humps, drop-offs, and deep weed beds. In late summer and fall, this "structure"—sometimes 15 to 25 feet deep—will hold most of the fish.

Lake trout are most accessible at the beginning of the season, especially if spring is late and the ice is just off the lakes. Then trout are in shallow water. Fish for them with spoons or plugs that imitate minnows. As the season progresses and water warms, however, trout will drop into deep water, often 50 feet or more. It's tough to fish effectively at that depth from a canoe.

If you're an ambitious traveler, you can take a loop to get back to your put-in. From Pipestone Bay (at the far southwestern end of Basswood), portage to Back Bay. Follow the winding channel to Wind Bay, portage 160 rods (880 yards) into Wind Lake, and then take another 160-rod (880 yards) portage back into Moose Lake. Otherwise, retrace your path back across Prairie Portage to the access on Moose Lake.

Access: From Ely, drive northeast 20 miles, first down Minnesota Highway 169 and then down the Fernberg Road (County Route 18). Turn left (north) on Forest Road 438 to the Moose Lake put-in.

ADDITIONAL HELP

MA&G: 8, 9.
Camping: Dozens of campsites are scattered about the shores of Basswood Lake. Auto camping is possible at the Forest Service site at Fall Lake near Ely.
Food, gas, and lodging: Ely.
For more information: Superior National Forest.

7 Louse River

Character: If you like the idea of paddling and portaging deep into the woods, here's a trip for you.
Distance: 35 miles and 35 portages, including a monster carry of 1.5 miles near the end.
Paddling time: Two to five days, depending on your determination to travel.
Hazards: No particular hazards except getting lost and losing your shoes in muddy portage trails.
Maps: McKenzie Maps Nos. 21, 20 and W.A. Fisher Co. F-5, F-11, F-12.

The paddling: Here's a trip to test your ability to travel light. You'll do okay if you can pare your gear to the essentials so that you need to take only a single trip down each portage trail. If you have to two-trip the portages (and thus actually triple your walking distance), this will be a tough trip indeed.

Launch your canoe on Sawbill Lake, at the end of the Sawbill Trail. After a 1-mile paddle north, take the short portage into Alton Lake. Scoot south on Alton about 3 miles and portage 140 rods (770 yards) into Beth Lake. The portage into Grace Lake, 285 rods (1,568 yards), will give you a sample of what is to come.

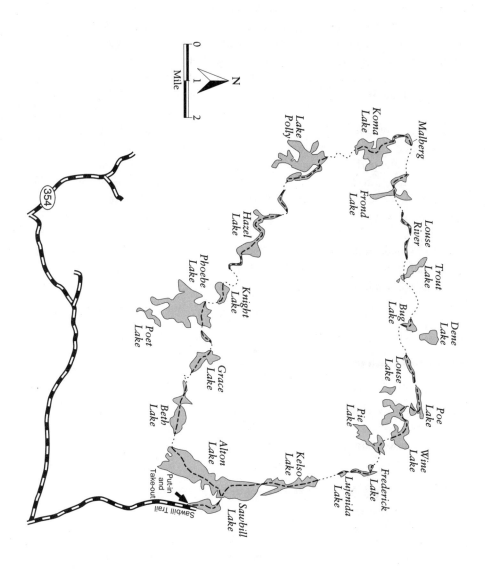

The route follows a string of portages and lakes that loops generally to the northwest through Phoebe, Knight, Hazel, Polly, Koma, and Malberg Lakes. These portages range from 5 to 140 rods (28 to 770 yards). Campsites are plentiful.

From Malberg, the route turns abruptly to the east. The character of the waterway changes as well. Lakes give way to a narrow channel that eventually becomes the Louse River. In places the channel is so choked with water lilies, you may have to pole your way through to open water. Occasionally a tributary branches to one side. Consult your map to make sure you stay on the right route. Shallow, rocky stretches occasionally block the stream. Several short portages are necessary. Many of the trails are faint; some are partly blocked by deadfalls.

After about 5 miles, the view begins to open. Bug Lake, Louse Lake, Poe Lake, Wine Lake, and Frederick Lake are not exactly expansive. In fact, they are small, with densely wooded shores—but they are considerably less cloistered than the Louse River. They are connected by portages of up to 135 rods (743 yards).

Then comes perhaps the single greatest challenge of the trip: the 480-rod (2,640 yards) portage into Lujenida Lake. It rises slowly over the gentle divide between the two lakes and then slogs through saturated quagmires, before heading down again to the water. From there, follow Lujenida, Kelso, and Alton Lakes back to Sawbill and your put-in.

Sawbill Lake holds walleyes, northern pike, and smallmouth bass. Alton holds those species and lake trout, too. The other lakes, which are smaller, hold northern pike and some harbor walleyes.

Access: From Tofte, drive north on the Sawbill Trail (County Route 2) about 23 miles to where the road ends on Sawbill Lake.

ADDITIONAL HELP

MA&G: 67, D8 (inset); 78, D–E2.
Camping: Canoe campsites dot the route. Camp by car at Sawbill Lake.
Food, gas, and lodging: Tofte, Beaver Bay, Grand Marais.
For more information: Superior National Forest.

8 Crooked Lake–Basswood River

Character: Here's a trip that provides great fishing and backwoods travel—if you're ready to portage.
Distance: 36 miles.
Paddling time: Two to five days (longer if the fishing is good).
Hazards: No particular hazards.
Maps: McKenzie Map No. 11 and W.A. Fisher Co. F-9, F-10, F-11.

The paddling: Put in on the small creek leading to Mudro Lake. Paddle to the northern corner of the lake and follow a 30-rod (165 yards) portage and 140-rod

Portaging into Fourtown Lake, one of the links in the trip to Crooked Lake and Basswood River.

(770 yards) portage into Fourtown Lake. Head into the western bay and portage and paddle through Boot, Fairy, and Gun Lakes. From the long bay at the northeast corner of Gun Lake, portage 300 rods (1,650 yards) into Wagosh Lake. Cross this small lake and take a short portage into Niki Lake. Paddle through a marshy creek through Chippewa and Papoose Lakes, and then take a swampy portage of 90 rods (495 yards) into Friday Bay.

Friday Bay is part of Crooked Lake, a large lake with shallow bays, rocky cliffs, and plummeting depths. Like many of the large border lakes, Crooked provides outstanding fishing for large northern pike, walleyes, and smallmouth bass. Fish the shallow, rocky bays and shorelines early in the year. As summer progresses and turns to falls, look for deep weedlines, drop-offs, and humps.

Several routes lead back to the put-in. One pleasant route runs along the international border eastward through Crooked Lake and then south, up the Basswood River. Portage Lower Basswood Falls and head up the Horse River. Three short portages will put you in Horse Lake. Head south through Tin Can Mike, Sandpit, and Mudro Lakes to the access.

Crooked Lake holds a variety of fish including walleyes, smallmouth bass, northern pike, largemouth bass, crappies, and sunfish. The other, smaller lakes can be counted on for northern pike and walleyes. Mudro is notable for harboring lake trout.

8 Crooked Lake–Basswood River

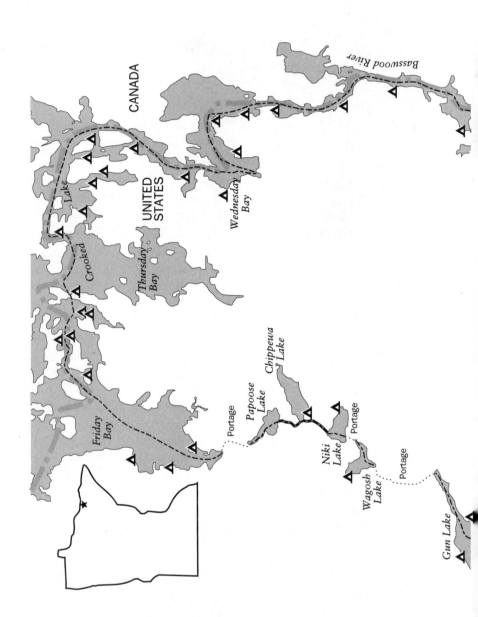

Access: From Ely, drive east and then north on County Route 88 and then the Echo Trail (County Route 116) a total of about 11 miles to Fenske Lake. Turn right (east) and drive 5 miles on Forest Road 459 and then Forest Road 457 to the access.

ADDITIONAL HELP

MA&G: 88, D–C5.
Camping: Canoe campsites dot the route. Camp by car at Fenske Lake.
Food, gas, and lodging: Ely.
For more information: Superior National Forest.

CLOQUET RIVER

9 Indian Lake to Island Lake

Character: The wild upper stretch of the Cloquet makes a two-day canoe trip with enough rapids to keep the paddling interesting.
Length: 35 miles, including a 1.5-mile paddle across Island Lake to the take-out.
Average run time: Two days.
Class: II.
Skill level: Intermediate to expert. Beginners will probably portage a few rapids.
Optimal flow: Above 3.5 feet on gauge on the County Route 44 bridge near Rollins
Average gradient: 3.3 feet per mile.
Hazards: The height of the waterfall where the river enters Island Lake Reservoir depends on the reservoir level. High water in the reservoir may completely cover the waterfall; low water may create an unrunnable falls several feet high. Scout first.
Maps: MDNR *Cloquet River Canoe Route, 1.*

The paddling: The Cloquet River slides down the backside of the crest that runs along the North Shore, through the sparsely settled territory north of Duluth and Two Harbors. From Indian Lake (near Brimson and Rollins) to Island Lake, the Cloquet provides a two- to three-day wilderness outing, with several class I and class II rapids to run or portage. Appropriately, Major Stephen Long's map from his expedition of 1823 labeled the stream the Rapid River. On an 1843 map, Joseph Nicollet called the river the Cloquet, probably for a French trader.

Forest wildlife that you might see includes ospreys, bald eagles, black bears, moose, and even timber wolves. Northern pike and walleyes are common in the deeper holes of this stretch. A few smallmouth bass and channel catfish are present. Brook trout live in some coldwater tributaries.

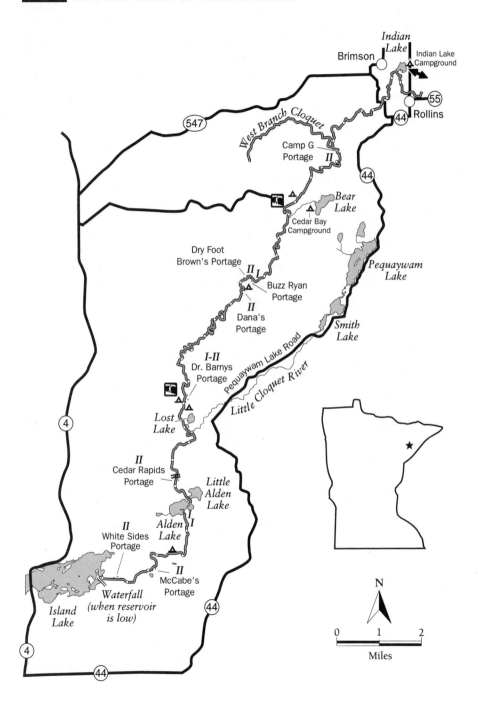

Leaving Indian Lake as a rather small stream, the Cloquet flows past banks forested with spruce, fir, birch, and aspen. The river glides quietly for about 6 miles before turning sharply right and plunging down **Camp G Rapids,** a straightforward class II drop most easily run toward the left side. Portage left about 300 yards.

The river runs quietly again and turns through some loopy meanders for about 8 miles before coming to **Buzz Ryan Rapids,** named for J.C. Ryan, district ranger of the Cloquet River Valley State Forest for more than 40 years and noted logging historian. The rapids is a wavy class I drop. Avoid the ledge located on the left. Portage left 150 yards.

A tougher rapids is right around the corner: **Upper Britton,** also known as **Dry Foot Brown's Rapids,** a class II rapids that kicks up 2-foot waves in high water. Portage right 400 yards.

A half mile downstream is **Lower Britton,** also known as **Dana's Rapids,** a long series of rocks and standing waves that curves to the left. Portage this class II drop on the left, 200 yards.

After about 6 miles of slow meanders and backwaters, the Cloquet runs through **Dr. Barny's Rapids,** a long series of small waves and boulders that rates class I. Portage either side, about 1,300 yards. The Carrol State Forest Road meets the river from the west, providing a convenient access to this stretch.

After another 3.5 miles of quiet water, the Cloquet plunges over **Cedar Rapids,** a class II stretch. Run the ledge on the far right and pick your way through the boulders. Portage left about 800 yards.

A mile later, the Cloquet dumps into Alden Lake. Paddle south, west, and then south again about a half mile to pick up the river again. The Cloquet runs through a couple short, nondescript class I rapids and then flows quietly again for a couple of miles before coming to **McCabe's Rapids.** This short class II pitch consists of three ledges, each about 2 feet high with offset chutes that require a bit of maneuvering. Portage left about 100 yards.

After another mile, the Cloquet roars through its most difficult drop, **White Sides Rapids.** It's long, steep, and wavy, with plenty of boulders to pin and bend a canoe. In high water, waves may reach 2 to 3 feet. It's a tough class II that requires careful maneuvering, especially near the top of the rapids.

Just downstream from the end of White Sides, the Cloquet enters Island Lake Reservoir. A waterfall forms when the reservoir is drawn down and a natural ledge is exposed. Most canoeists never see the falls because the reservoir is high and the ledge covered in late spring and summer, when the river is usually run. But in early spring or during dry years, the reservoir may be low enough to reveal an unrunnable series of drops 15 feet high. The falls is runnable when only a few feet high. Scout carefully and decide for yourself.

From the mouth of the river, paddle about 1.5 miles to the access on the north shore of the lake.

The Cloquet Valley was the stomping ground of lumberjacks early in the century, and many of the places still ring with names from the era of white-pine logging. There were an estimated 8 billion board feet of pine in the Cloquet River Valley. It was in this area that the largest section of timber ever recorded was cut—33 million board feet from a square mile near Little Alden Lake, cut by the Brooks-Scanlon Lumber Company, which had the biggest white-pine mill in the world from 1901 to 1909. Lumbering diminished steadily after a record season in 1902.

Access: Indian Lake put-in: From Rollins, drive 1 mile north on County Road 44 to the state forest campground and access. **Island Lake take-out:** From Duluth, drive north on County Route 4 to the community of Island Lake on the north shore of the reservoir. Follow County Route 4 eastward along the north shore about 1.5 miles to the access.

Alternate accesses are located off County Route 44 a mile east of Cedar Bay campground, and at the end of the Carrol State Forest Road at Dr. Barny's Rapids.

Shuttle: 38 miles one way. About 2 hours. The long shuttle on many miles of dirt roads is the big drawback of this trip. Roads can be bad in early spring, with soft spots created by frost.

ADDITIONAL HELP

MA&G: 76, E4; 66, A4–B3.
Camping: Most land along The Cloquet is public, where camping is allowed. Two river campsites are located near Cedar Bay Campground (see map). Campsites are also located at Buzz Ryan Rapids (river left), on river right at Dr. Barny's Rapids (at the end of the Carrol State Forest Road), and about a half mile downstream on river left. Another river campsite is located on the right bank about 2 miles downstream of Alden Lake. Auto camping is possible at Indian Lake Campground, Cedar Bay Campground, and at the end of the Carrol State Forest Road.
Food, gas, and lodging: Duluth.
For more information: MDNR Information Center.

10 Island Lake Dam to St. Louis River

Character: The Cloquet races through a series of pools and easy rapids to its confluence with the St. Louis. The lower Cloquet provides good fishing for smallmouth bass, brown trout, and other species.

Length: 29 miles.

Average run time: 10 to 15 hours. Make it an overnight trip or use an alternate access for a shorter day trip.

Class: I with a class II stretch near the confluence with the St. Louis River.

Skill level: Beginner to intermediate.

Optimal flow: Above 1.4 feet on gauge on U.S. Highway 53 bridge, or more than 350 cfs as measured below the Island Lake Dam. Discharge in this section depends on releases from the Minnesota Power dam at the outlet of Island Lake Reservoir. Call Minnesota Power at 800-582-8529 for a recording of water-level information on the Cloquet and other rivers and reservoirs in its system. Minnesota Power is required to provide a minimum flow of 350 cfs (if available) in May and June and 175 for the rest of the summer (if available), enough to scrape down the rapids if you're willing to get out and push occasionally.

Average gradient: 4.1 feet per mile.

Hazards: No particular hazards, though rapids get markedly more difficult near the river's mouth.

Maps: MDNR *Cloquet River Canoe Route, 2.*

The paddling: This stretch of the Cloquet varies between wild and bucolic. A riverside forest of pine, fir, spruce, aspen, and birch occasionally is broken by farmland and a few homes and cabins. Several bridges cross this stretch, but there are no large towns or cities.

From the access below the power dam at the outlet of Island Lake Reservoir, the river flows slowly through largely undeveloped country for more than 10 miles. After the Us-Kab-Wan-Ka River joins the Cloquet, the larger river begins dropping through increasingly long sections of bouldery rapids, including a nearly continuous stretch of whitewater that begins about 1.5 miles above the US 53 bridge and continues for more than half a mile downstream from the bridge. Further along, the Cloquet flows through other nondescript rapids. All these rapids rate class I, forcing paddlers to dodge a few rocks and ride long chains of small waves.

Finally, after the Cloquet passes beneath the County Route 7 bridge, it enters a stretch of frequent rapids in the final 4 miles to the river's confluence with the St. Louis. This stretch rates predominantly class I. In the final mile before its confluence with the St. Louis River, the Cloquet falls about 20 feet and rates class II. To reach the take-out, paddle onto the St. Louis and about a mile downstream to the U.S. Highway 2 bridge, river left.

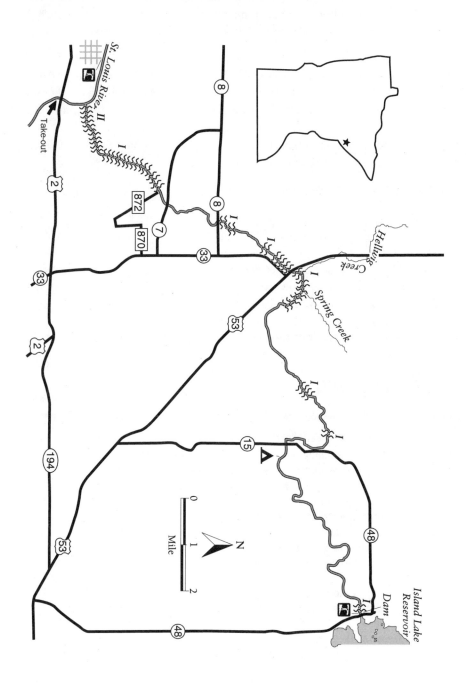

This lower reach of the Cloquet provides excellent fishing. Smallmouth bass are plentiful, but most run small. Light spinning and fly-fishing gear works well. Brown trout are found in this stretch, mostly near coldwater tributaries such as Hellwig and Spring Creeks. Other popular game fish include northern pike, walleyes, and channel catfish.

Access: Island Lake Dam put-in: From US 53 northeast of Duluth, drive north on County Route 48 about 11 miles to the dam and access. **St. Louis River take-out:** From US 53 northeast of Duluth, drive west on Minnesota 194 until it joins US 2; continue west to river and access.

Access is possible at several bridge crossings: County Route 48, US 53, County Route 15, County Route 8, County Route 7, and County Road 694.

Shuttle: 27 miles one way. About 1.25 hours.

ADDITIONAL HELP

MA&G: 66, C1; 65, C9.
Camping: Most land along the river is public, where camping is allowed. A river campsite is located a half mile upstream of the County Route 15 bridge, river left. Camp by auto at Jay Cooke State Park.
Food, gas, and lodging: Duluth, Cloquet.
For more information: MDNR Information Center.

LITTLE FORK RIVER

11 Cook to Samuelson Park

Character: Running through woods and past open pastures, the Little Fork descends through many runnable rapids and one that is unrunnable to all but the most experienced paddlers.
Length: 40 miles.
Average run time: Two days.
Class: I–II, except Hannine Falls, which rates at least class IV.
Skill level: Intermediate.
Optimal flow: Above 1.9 feet on the gauge on the railroad trestle in Cook.
Average gradient: 2.6 feet per mile.
Hazards: The upper reaches are narrow. Watch for downed trees blocking the channel.
Maps: MDNR *Little Fork River Canoe Route.*

The paddling: From Cook, the Little Fork flows slowly and quietly for about 4 miles. Then it begins to tumble through the easy to moderate rapids that characterize

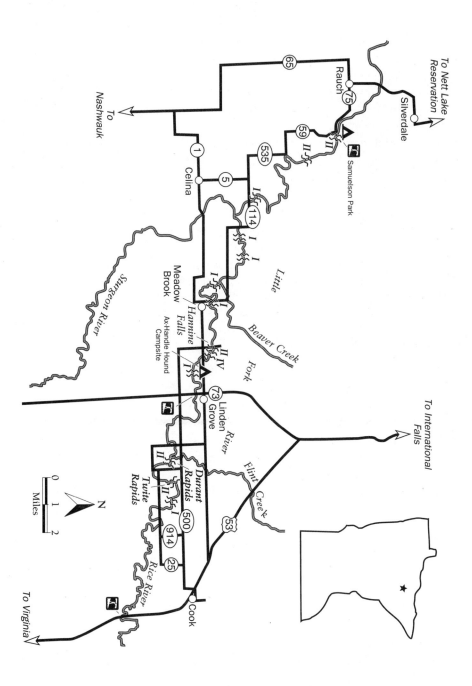

this upper stretch. The first rapids, just above the Rice River confluence, rates class I.

Just downstream from the confluence, the Little Fork flows through a 50-yard-long rapids, flanked by outcrops, which bends sharply left and throws 2-foot waves in high water. It rates class II, but there is no developed portage.

After a few hundred yards, the river runs through a short class I rapids. Then, quickly, comes **Twite Rapids,** class II. The river drops about 8 feet in 300 yards. Scattered boulders create 2-foot waves in high water. Scout from the right. There is no developed portage.

Two miles downstream, the Little Fork slides through **Durant Rapids,** a 100-yard-long class II stretch that bends right and then left. Two-foot waves fill the drop in high water. There is no developed portage.

The river is quiet again for 6 miles. Just above the Minnesota Highway 1 bridge, the Little Fork tumbles through a class I rapids. But a mile later, the river does something to make you take notice: It roars through **Hannine Falls,** a sloping, 15-foot drop, rated class IV. Though conceivably runnable at low water levels by an expert in a kayak or decked canoe, this falls is filled with big holes in high water. The waterfall is followed by 150 yards of class II rapids. There is no developed portage.

Two miles downstream lies another class I rapids, and 2 miles after that there's a 100-yard-long class II section; 2-foot-high waves form in high water. High clay banks flank the river on the right.

After 2 miles more comes a class I and a mile after that, a big, flat outcrop on the right pinches the river, kicking up waves. The 100-yard-long drop tails off into scattered boulders. There is no developed portage.

The Little Fork joins the Sturgeon River, one of its major tributaries and an interesting canoe stream in its middle reaches, where it runs through several class II–III rapids. The Sturgeon's lower reaches, though less difficult, are often blocked by deadfalls.

A mile after the confluence, at the County Route 114 bridge, is a class I rapids. For 6 miles, the river flows quietly. But then, its smooth surface is broken by a 150-yard-long pitch of class II water. In high water, the rapids throws up 3-foot waves. In low water, the rapids is bouldery and ledgy.

Two miles later, at Samuelson Park, the river slides over a 4-foot high ledge with a well-formed backroller. It rates class II at most water levels.

Throughout this stretch, low forested banks and an occasional hayfield flank the river. Wildlife you may encounter includes black bears, white-tailed deer, and timber wolves.

The Little Fork is notable for its fishing. Smallmouth bass, northern pike, and walleyes are all present. Most notable, however, are the river's muskies, which can exceed 20 pounds. Fish the deep bank, holes, and eddies with large plugs, bucktails, or spinnerbaits.

Looking down the Little Fork from Hannine Falls. MINNESOTA DEPARTMENT OF
NATURAL RESOURCES

Access: Cook put-in: No developed access exists near Cook. Put in at one of the county roads just west of town, such as County Road 500 or County Road 914. **Samuelson Park take-out:** From the town of Rauch, drive east about 2.5 miles on County Route 75 to the bridge at the park.

There's a developed access at Minnesota Highway 73. To start here, however, requires an almost immediate portage of Hannine Falls. By putting in at one of the county roads just downstream, you can pick up several class II rapids on your way to the take-out.

Shuttle: 36 miles one way. About 1.5 hours.

ADDITIONAL HELP

MA&G: 74–75; 86–87.
Camping: Riverside camping at Ax-Handle Hound Campsite a mile above Hannine Falls and Samuelson Park. Auto camping at McCarthy Beach State Park.
Food, gas, and lodging: Cook, Virginia.
For more information: MDNR Information Center.

12 Samuelson Park to Dentaybow

Character: This stretch of the Little Fork is isolated and wild, and will appeal to paddlers who want to get away from it all.
Length: 53 miles.
Average run time: Two to three days.
Class: I–II, though the stretch is predominantly quiet.
Skill level: Intermediate, with wilderness camping skills.
Optimal flow: Above 1.7 feet (estimated 500 cfs) on gauge on the U.S. Highway 217 bridge at Little Fork. The river rises quickly after a heavy rain and turns cloudy from clay in the watershed, remnant of glacial lake beds.
Average gradient: 1.2 feet per mile.
Hazards: You'd better bring everything you need, because it's a long walk back to town.
Maps: MDNR *Little Fork River Canoe Route.*

The paddling: Once the Little Fork slips under the Minnesota Highway 65 bridge near Silverdale and Rauch, the river flows unfettered and undeveloped for more than 40 miles before it hits another bridge. A few trails and four-wheel-drive tracks touch the river, but for much of that length, no real roads parallel the river. The riverside scenery isn't spectacular—it consists largely of low-lying hardwood and conifer forest and peat bog—but it shows little evidence of human activity. The river is flanked, for the most part, by state forest land or tribal lands of the Ojibwa Nett Lake Indian Reservation.

12 Samuelson Park to Dentaybow

The gradient of this stretch is slight; there are only three rapids of note. The first, class I **Nett Rapids,** lies along the upstream boundary of the reservation. Some 16 miles later, the river plunges into **Seller's Rapids,** a quarter mile of class II boulder bed. The rapids washes out in high water and becomes somewhat easier. Portage left, 700 yards.

Deadman's Rapids is less treacherous than its name implies. This class II washes out in high water. Portage right about 450 yards.

This section of river, like the stretch upstream, is particularly noted for its muskie fishing. Other game fish include northern pike, walleyes, and smallmouth bass. To fish within the borders of the Nett Lake Indian Reservation you'll need a permit from the tribal office.

Magnificent stands of white and red pine near the Little Fork's headwaters were logged in the late nineteenth and early twentieth centuries. Logs choked the river and its tributaries as loggers drove the timber to nearby mills. A log drive down the Little Fork Rivers in 1937 was the last major drive in the region. Rare movie footage of the event is shown at the Forest History Center in Grand Rapids. It shows "whitewater men" walking logs as they fly through fast water. Wanigans, floating bunkhouses and cook shacks, slam down the rollicking rapids of the river. The drive began with spring melt and ended in midsummer on the Rainy River, where the logs were loaded on railcars and hauled overland to mill in International Falls.

Access: Samuelson Park put-in: From the town of Rauch, drive east about 2.5 miles on County Route 75 to the bridge at the park. **Dentaybow take-out:** From the put-in, drive northwest 33 miles on MN 65 until the road crosses the Little Fork; after about a half mile, turn right on County Route 31 to the access.

Shuttle: 33 miles. About 1.25 hours.

ADDITIONAL HELP

MA&G: 86.

Camping: River camping is possible at Samuelson Park and a site on river right about 2 miles above the upstream boundary of the Nett Lake Indian Reservation. Camp by car at McCarthy Beach State Park or several campgrounds in George Washington State Forest.

Food, gas, and lodging: Hibbing, Orr, Little Fork.

For more information: MDNR Information Center.

13 Dentaybow to Rainy River

Character: The Little Fork continues its quiet way northward through largely wild country.
Length: 56 miles.
Average run time: Two to three days.
Class: Quiet, with one class II rapids.
Skill level: Intermediate, with wilderness camping skills.
Optimal flow: Above 1.7 feet (estimated 500 cfs) on gauge on the U.S. Highway 217 bridge at Little Fork. The river rises quickly after a heavy rain and turns cloudy from clay in the watershed, remnant of glacial lake beds.
Average gradient: 1 foot per mile.
Hazards: No particular hazards.
Maps: MDNR *Little Fork River Canoe Route.*

The paddling: Past Dentaybow, the Little Fork continues its way past a dense forest of aspen, birch, spruce, and fir. As the river approaches the town of Little Fork, a few roads and houses close in on the river. Below town, the river continues through largely unsettled country to its confluence with the Rainy River.

13 Dentaybow to Rainy River

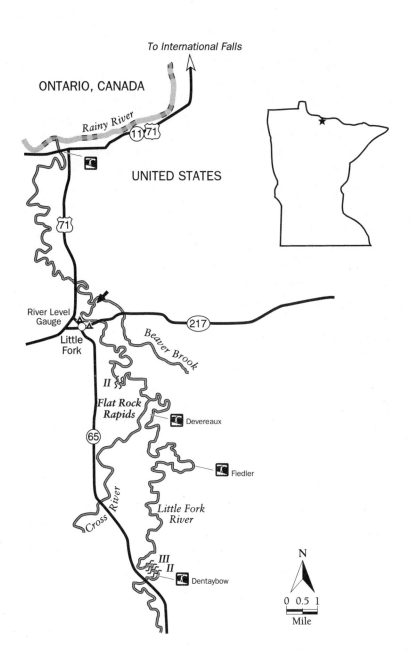

To International Falls

ONTARIO, CANADA

Rainy River

11 71

UNITED STATES

71

River Level Gauge

Little Fork

217

Beaver Brook

II

Flat Rock Rapids

Devereaux

65

Fiedler

Cross River

Little Fork River

III

II

Dentaybow

N

0 0.5 1

Mile

This stretch of the Little Fork contains only one notable rapids, **Flat Rock Rapids,** an easy class II stretch about 9 miles upstream from Little Fork.

This lower stretch of the Little Fork harbors a variety of game fish, including walleyes, northern pike, smallmouth bass, and muskies. Anglers who fish bait along the bottom may also catch lake sturgeon, a primitive fish that may ex-

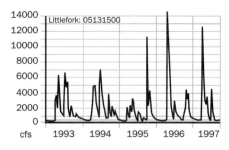

500 cfs = minimum for good paddling

ceed 100 pounds. By now, the river is large enough for small fishing boats, which provide a more effective fishing platform than a canoe.

Access: Dentaybow put-in: From the put-in, (see previous trip) drive northwest 33 miles on Minnesota Highway 65 until the road crosses the Little Fork; after about a half mile, turn right on County Route 31 to the access. **Rainy River take-out:** From the town of Little Fork, drive north 9 miles on U.S. Highway 71 to the intersection with Minnesota Highway 11; the access is on the left, about a half mile upstream from the confluence with the Rainy River.

Shuttle: 23 miles. About one hour.

ADDITIONAL HELP

MA&G: 86, B–A1; 85, A9; 95, E9.
Camping: River camping is possible at the Lofgren Park city campground in Little Fork. Camp by car at several campgrounds in Koochiching State Forest and Voyageurs National Park.
Food, gas, and lodging: International Falls, Orr, Little Fork.
For more information: MDNR Information Center.

14 Midway River

Character: The Midway is a short, rocky run with several challenging rapids and a surprise at the end.
Length: 4 miles.
Average run time: Two hours.
Class: II.
Skill level: Intermediate.
Optimal flow: No gauge readings available. Water must be high. If you scrape through the first rapids near the bridge, pack up and go home.
Average gradient: 20 feet per mile.
Hazards: Watch for deadfalls and the difficult rapids at the end of the run.
Maps: PRIM *Duluth*.

14 Midway River

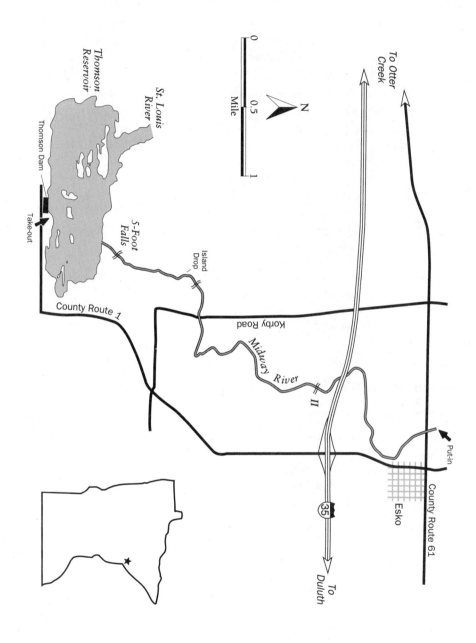

The paddling: The Midway is a small stream, sometimes less than 20 feet wide. Because it's narrow, watch for sweepers, though they don't seem to be particularly common.

Near Esko the Midway is flanked by houses, but as you drift downstream, the houses disappear and the river runs by woods and occasionally by rocky cliffs.

The river runs through some riffles from the beginning, but the first class II drop occurs not far below Interstate 35. The Midway settles down again until the Korby Road bridge. Then it begins to rush through long, rocky class II drops. At one point, the river splits around a rocky island, the right half going over a narrow, rocky, uninviting drop. Take the left channel, which drops more gradually. The final half mile to the reservoir drops about 30 feet and really screams in high water.

The surprise is a 5-foot-high falls right before the reservoir. The river runs through a boulder-bed pitch before narrowing to about 6 feet and plunging over a nearly vertical ledge. Watch out for a big hole in high water.

Paddle across the reservoir to the same take-out used to finish the popular stretch of the St. Louis River above the Thomson Reservoir.

Access: The Esko put-in is located at the County Route 61 bridge on the west edge of town. The **Thomson Reservoir take-out,** owned by the University of Minnesota–Duluth, is located less than a mile west of the town of Thomson, on the east side of the Thomson Dam.

Shuttle: 5 miles one way. About 15 minutes.

ADDITIONAL HELP

MA&G: 65, E9; 66, E1
Camping: No developed campsites along the river. Camp by car at Jay Cooke State Park.
Food, gas, and lodging: Carlton, Duluth.
For more information: Unavailable.

15   North Fork Nemadji River

Character: The Nemadji makes a pleasant day trip through wild and rather strange country with dramatic clay banks, murky water, and the clear voice of timber wolves.

Length: 13 miles.

Average run time: Five to seven hours.

Class: I.

Skill level: Beginner to intermediate.

Optimal flow: This stretch should be runnable above about 300 cfs on USGS gauge near South Superior, Wisconsin.

Average gradient: 10.7 feet per mile.

Hazards: Watch out for deadfalls. The steep, clay banks continually slump, constricting and changing the channel.

Maps: PRIM *Duluth* (for Minnesota portion only).

The paddling: The Nemadji heads up in the clay hills north of the St. Croix River and flows through a weird kind of no man's land into Wisconsin and Lake Superior. The Minnesota portion of the stream is contained in Nemadji State Forest, a rugged and largely uninhabited corner of the state. Steep, high, clay banks flank the river and its tributaries. The clay is unstable and constantly slumping, forcing roads to be moved and clogging rivers with living trees, boulders, and other debris. With so much fine clay in the watershed, the river runs murky after rains.

This stretch of the Nemadji trips through several stretches of fast water and class I rapids. Each trip down the Nemadji can be a new experience. Round a bend and you may find that a new landslide has forced the river into a narrow, swift chute. In particular, watch out for slides that have brought a stand of trees into the channel.

You're likely to see all kinds of wildlife in this unsettled country. White-tailed deer and black bears are common. Timber wolves and bobcats frequent the area, but they are a rare sight.

The canoeable portion of the river, because it is so muddy, is a marginal trout stream. It does receive a run of steelhead in the spring.

Access: The **Minnesota Highway 23 put-in** is located about 16 miles northeast of Kerrick. You'll have to park along the road and carry down to the river. To reach the **County Route W take-out,** follow County Route 8 through Holyoke and across the state line, where the road changes to County Route B in Wisconsin at the intersection with County Route W, drive north 2.5 miles to the river.

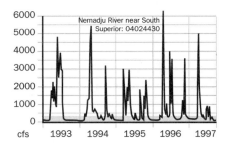

300 cfs = minimum for good paddling

15 North Fork Nemadji River

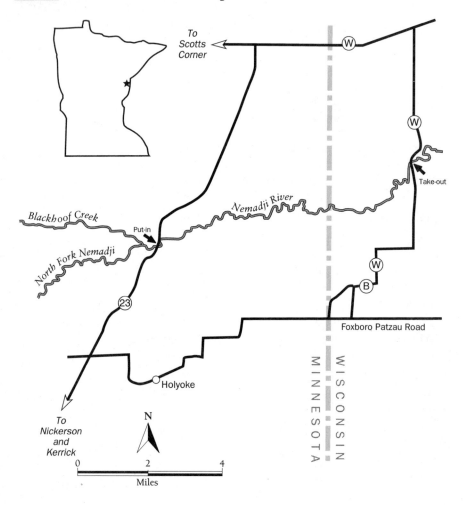

To
Scotts
Corner

W

W

Take-out

Nemadji River

Blackhoof Creek

Put-in

North Fork Nemadji

W

B

23

Foxboro Patzau Road

Holyoke

MINNESOTA

WISCONSIN

N

To
Nickerson
and
Kerrick

0   2   4
Miles

Shuttle: 20 miles one way. About 50 minutes.

ADDITIONAL HELP

MA&G: 58, A1; Wisconsin A&G: 100, D2.
Camping: There are no developed campsites along the river. Camp by car at Moose Lake State Park or the Nemadji State Forest campground east of Nickerson.
Food, gas, and lodging: Duluth, Carlton, Sandstone.
For more information: DNR. Ask for information about Nemadji State Forest.

16 Rainy River

Character: The Rainy is a wide and generally calm river of interest to canoeists primarily for its history and the fishing it offers.
Length: 78 miles.
Average run time: Three to six days for the whole stretch.
Class: I.
Skill level: Beginner, with wilderness camping skills.
Optimal flow: Any level.
Average gradient: 0.26 feet per mile.
Hazards: No particular hazards.
Maps: PRIM

The paddling: Though early traveler Sir Alexander Mackenzie had called the Rainy "one of the finest rivers in the N.W.," from a canoeist's standpoint, the Rainy is long, wide, and rather boring, with Minnesota Highway 11 flanking the river to the south for nearly its entire length. On the Minnesota side, the river is screened from the road by a fringe of aspen woods and occasional hayfields flank the river at times. On the Canadian side, the highway strays farther from the river. The river passes through sections of fast water and some rapids, but nothing especially difficult.

The Rainy River has a long history of human use. Undoubtedly it was a major transportation route for Indians of the region. European explorers followed these same routes, and the Rainy River became an important avenue of the fur trade during the eighteenth and early-nineteenth centuries. Voyageurs traveling from Lake Superior would travel what is now the international border, paddling and portaging through the area we now know as the Boundary Waters, into the large lakes that make up Voyageurs National Park and down the Rainy River to Lake of the Woods and northwestward to Lake Athabasca in far northern Canada. Hudson's Bay Company and later the American Fur Company established posts along the Rainy. In the early 1900s, a dam was built at the site of Koochiching Falls in International Falls to harness power for paper mills on both sides of the international border.

Put in about 3 miles below the dam in International Falls. The bedrock punctuates the shoreline and forms a few islands. The streambed ranges from rock to boulder to silt and clay. It is a large stream, having gathered the many waterways of the Boundary Waters and Voyageurs National Park region. It makes few bends and affords long vistas downstream.

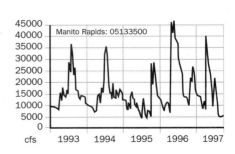

Always runnable

16 Rainy River

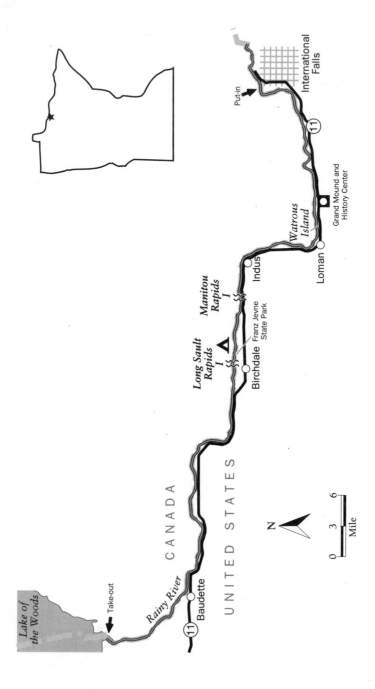

As the Rainy River approaches Lake of the Woods, it passes Wheeler Point.
MINNESOTA OFFICE OF TOURISM

At Pelland, the Rainy joins one of its major tributaries, the Little Fork. Seven miles downstream, it picks up another tributary, the Big Fork. At the confluence sits the Grand Mound Center, a Minnesota Historical Society site that protects and interprets one of Minnesota's most notable prehistoric burial sites (see the Big Fork trip description).

About 2 miles downstream from the mounds, the river splits around Watrous Island and another island. At Loman, the river turns abruptly north. Several miles downstream from Loman, the river splits around several more islands.

At Indus, the river turns sharply west again. Three miles downstream, a dramatic point juts into the river from the left (south). This marks the location of **Manitou Rapids,** a short class I burst of rapids.

At Franz Jevne State Park (a small wayside with camping) the Rainy runs through **Long Sault Rapids,** a bouldery class I stretch that stretches about a mile. The banks, at this point, are wooded and steep.

Baudette is, other than International Falls, the only sizable town on the banks of the Rainy. Willy Walleye, a roadside icon about 20 feet long, stands near the river, a symbol of what many people find of value in the Rainy. The river provides excellent fishing for walleye and smallmouth bass. Northern pike and the occasional muskie are also caught. Lake sturgeon, some exceeding 50 pounds, are caught on hook and line.

The Rainy has grown to a quarter-mile wide by the time it empties into Lake of the Woods. In the lake, just beyond the river's mouth, is the Pine and Curry Island Scientific and Natural Area. The 4-mile-long sand spit with open beach, dunes, and marsh provides a home for a couple of unusual species in Minnesota: white-tailed jackrabbits and the only remaining nest population of piping plovers in the state. Many other bird species, including bald eagles, ravens, spotted sandpipers, and common terns also nest on the island. In addition, the woods and fields in this region harbor another unusual resident to Minnesota, the black-billed magpie.

Access: The **International Falls put-in** is located about 3 miles downstream of the bridge to Fort Frances and paper mill dam. Take Minnesota Highway 11/U.S. Highway 71 to the west edge of town and follow the small road along the river about a mile to the access. The **Lake of the Woods take-out** is located on the west side of the river, on the upstream side of Wheelers Point.

Alternative accesses are located at the mouth of the Big Fork, near Loman, Franz Jevne State Park, Frontier, near the Lake of the Woods–Koochiching county line, and Baudette.

Shuttle: 80 miles one way. About 3 hours.

ADDITIONAL HELP

MA&G: 94–95.
Camping: Check PRIM. A small campground is located at Franz Jevne State Park.
Food, gas, and lodging: International Falls, Baudette.
For more information: For additional information call DNR Fisheries in International Falls or Baudette.

17 Rice River

Character: A lazy stream with several small lakes along its course, the Rice tells a tale of the big-pine logging that once took place in this region.
Length: 18 miles.
Average run time: Six to nine hours.
Class: Quiet.
Skill level: Beginner.
Optimal flow: Gauge readings and water level information are not available. Levels are usually best in late spring or early summer.
Average gradient: 2.3 feet per mile.
Hazards: No particular hazards.
Maps: Chippewa National Forest, *Rice River Canoe Tour.*

The paddling: From a cluster of lakes in Chippewa National Forest, the Rice River winds slowly northward to join the Big Fork River. Launch your canoe at Club-house Lake and follow the waterway through Mikes Lake to the junction of East

17 Rice River

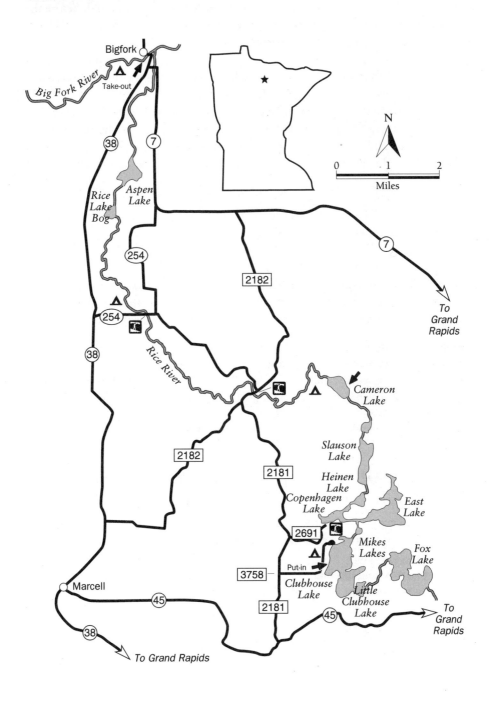

Bigfork

Big Fork River

Take-out

38

7

Rice Lake Bog

Aspen Lake

254

254

38

Rice River

N

0   1   2
Miles

2182

7

To Grand Rapids

Cameron Lake

Slauson Lake

2182

2181

Heinen Lake

Copenhagen Lake

East Lake

2691

Mikes Lakes

Fox Lake

Put-in

3758

Clubhouse Lake

Little Clubhouse Lake

To Grand Rapids

Marcell

45

2181

45

38

To Grand Rapids

Lake and Copenhagen Lake. You can take an interesting side trip by turning east (right) into East Lake to see a grove of pines more than 200 years old. Before the heyday of big-pine logging in this area during the late 1800s, large groves such as these spread across much of northern Minnesota.

Head back west into Copenhagen Lake, named of course for the popular brand of "snoose" the lumberjacks used. This lake, a widening of the river channel, was once flooded by a logging dam just downstream.

Paddle north through Heinen Lake, Slauson Lake, a small unnamed lake, and a short segment of river into Cameron Lake. At the outlet are the remains of a "splash" dam built to temporarily raise the water level and carry stored logs through the shallows downstream on a sudden surge of water. The dam was used until 1907.

Just north of the river at the Forest Road 2182 bridge stood a large logging camp in 1900. The bunk house stood four stories. Farther downstream is the Skunk Farm, an old logging camp that later became a small farm.

About a half mile downstream from County Road 254 are the remnants of the third of several dams built by Keewatin Lumber Company.

For the last several miles, the Rice River broadens and winds through marsh and small lake-like stretches until it joins the Big Fork River. To reach the take-out, turn west (left) and paddle less than a quarter mile up the larger river.

Access: The **Clubhouse Lake put-in** is located at the west end of Clubhouse Lake, about 5 miles east of Marcell on County Route 45, 1.5 miles north on Forest Road 2181, and 1.5 miles east on Forest Road 3758. The **Bigfork take-out** is located on the Big Fork River next to the Minnesota Highway 38 bridge in the town of Bigfork.

Shuttle: 20 miles one way. About one hour.

ADDITIONAL HELP

MA&G: 73, B9.
Camping: Developed campsites are located on Clubhouse Lake, about a mile downstream from Cameron Lake, about a half mile downstream from the CR 254 bridge, and in Bigfork.
Food, gas, and lodging: Bigfork, Grand Rapids
For more information: Chippewa National Forest, Marcell Ranger District.

ST. LOUIS RIVER

18 Round Lake to Aurora

Character: At high water, the uppermost stretch of the St. Louis River provides a wild ride and real wilderness experience. At anything less than high water, it makes a really terrible hike down long stretches of boulders.

Length: 40 miles. Shorter runs are possible.

Average run time: Two days.

Class: I–II.

Skill level: Intermediate.

Optimal flow: No water-level readings are available for this stretch. Gauge readings available for the lower reaches of the St. Louis won't necessarily tell you what this upper stretch is like. Generally speaking, don't try this stretch unless the USGS gauge at Aurora exceeds 400 cfs (check the USGS website), and nearby streams such as the Cloquet, are high. Then eyeball the river at County Road 346, Forest Road 130, and Forest Road 128 to see if there's enough water to run.

Average gradient: 8.1 feet per mile (not counting the lake portion at the beginning of the run).

Hazards: No particular hazards except the aforementioned problems with low water and long, rocky rapids.

Maps: Superior National Forest map.

The paddling: Like much of northern Minnesota, the upper St. Louis basin is flat and underpinned by rock. So the upper St. Louis spends much of its time going nowhere at a leisurely pace. But when it decides to go, it goes in a hurry. You'll have to dodge boulders while riding long chains of waves. Near the take-out south of Aurora, the character of the river changes abruptly. It enters a flat plain and meanders slowly.

The upper reaches of the St. Louis are inaccessible except by a few forest and logging roads. and except for clear-cuts, there is little sign of economic activity along the river. In such wild and unpopulated country, you'll have to come prepared to be self-reliant. As a reward, you'll paddle through often beautiful country and stand a chance of seeing moose, black bears, and even timber wolves. Northern pike and walleyes inhabit the upper St. Louis.

From the put-in, paddle across Round Lake and through Seven

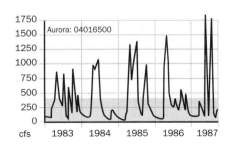

400 cfs for good paddling above Aurora

18 Round Lake to Aurora

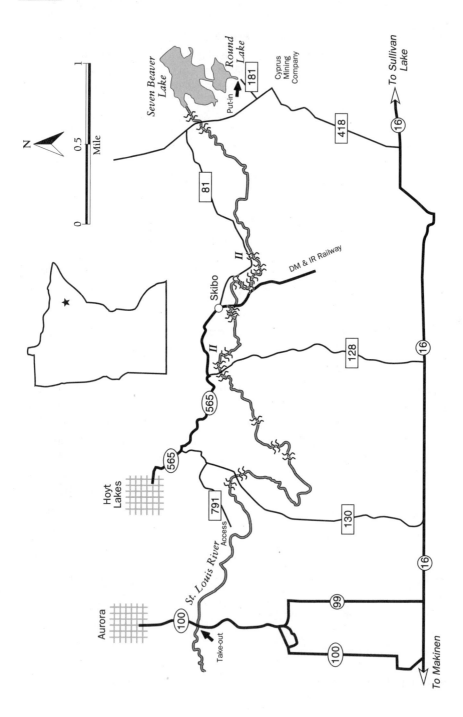

Beaver Lake to the river. Several short, easy class I rapids lie between Seven Beaver and Skibo Mill.

Just downstream from Skibo Mill, the river takes off, falling 40 feet in about a mile. This section rates class II. The river hits a long pool and then falls through a similar long class II section.

After another long pool, the rivers runs through sporadic class I rapids to the take-out.

Access: Round Lake put-in: From Aurora, drive south 6 miles on County Route 100 to County Route 99 and continue south 6 miles to County Route 16; head east 17 miles on County Route 16 past Cadotte Lake Campground to Forest Road 418; drive northeast 6 miles on Forest Road 418 to FR 181 and then on Forest Road 181 for 2 miles to the put-in. **Aurora take-out:** From Aurora, drive south 3 miles on County Route 100.

Alternate accesses are at CR 346, FR 130, FR 128, and FR 791.

Shuttle: 18 miles one way. About one hour

ADDITIONAL HELP

MA&G: 76, D1–5.
Camping: The upper St. Louis is surrounded by the Superior National Forest. Camp anywhere you like so long as the land is not obviously private. Auto camping is possible at Forest Service campgrounds at Cadotte Lake and Whiteface Reservoir.
Food, gas, and lodging: Aurora, Virginia.
For more information: Superior National Forest Laurentian Ranger District.

19 Aurora to Forbes

Character: This section of the St. Louis is peaceful, meandering, and wooded. It's not heart stopping, but it makes a pleasant trip.
Length: 38.5 miles.
Average run time: Two days.
Class: Quiet.
Skill level: Beginner.
Optimal flow: Above 2.1 feet on the gauge on the County Route 7 bridge at Forbes.
Average gradient: 1.8 feet per mile.
Hazards: In high water, watch out for trees on the outside of river bends. Take out before the dam at Forbes.
Maps: MDNR PRIM.

The paddling: Not much here to raise your blood pressure. In fact, this stretch of the St. Louis is practically the definition of soothing. The river speeds through a

19 Aurora to Forbes

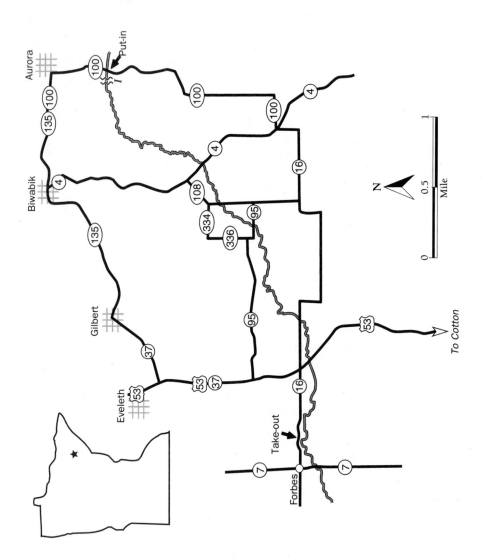

short class I rapids just downstream from the put-in, but then crosses the bed of Glacial Lake Upham, where there's not much topography to speed the river along. Narrow and intimate, the river gently winds—and winds and winds—between low banks forested by spruce, fir, birch, and aspen. For the first half of the run, the river meanders incredibly. Many of the poorly drained lowlands have filled with peat, a soggy, acidic, organic soil that has accumulated over the thousands of years since the last ice age. At the end of the reach, the river backs up behind the inflatable dam at Forbes. The dam, owned by Eveleth Mines, stores water for taconite processing. Take out on river right before the dam.

Northern pike and walleyes are the principal game fish in this reach. But the river is small, with limited cover, so fish are neither large nor plentiful.

Access: Aurora put-in: From Aurora, drive south 3 miles on County Route 100. **Forbes take-out:** From Forbes, drive east 1 mile on County Route 16 to the dam, with a carry-in canoe access downstream and boat ramp upstream.

Shuttle: 25 miles one way. About one hour.

ADDITIONAL HELP

MA&G: 76, D1; 75, D8–9.
Camping: No river campsites exist on this stretch. Auto camping is possible at Forest Service campgrounds at Cadotte Lake and Whiteface Reservoir.
Food, gas, and lodging: Virginia, Eveleth.
For more information: MDNR Information Center.

20 Forbes to Floodwood

Character: The slow-moving St. Louis flows by farms and forest. With few rapids, it's a good choice for beginners. Camp out to run the whole stretch, or use alternate accesses for day trips.
Length: 51.5 miles.
Average run time: Two to three days.
Class: Mostly quiet with a few class I rapids.
Skill level: Beginner.
Optimal flow: Above 2.1 feet on the gauge on the County Route 7 bridge at Forbes, or above 1.2 feet on the gauge on the County Route 8 bridge at Floodwood.
Average gradient: 1.4 feet per mile.
Hazards: No particular hazards.
Maps: MDNR *St. Louis River Canoe Route.*

The paddling: The St. Louis continues its placid march across the flatlands north of Cloquet. After meandering about 4 miles, the river races through several class I rapids, including a long series near the confluence with the East Two Rivers. After

20 Forbes to Floodwood
21 Floodwood to Cloquet

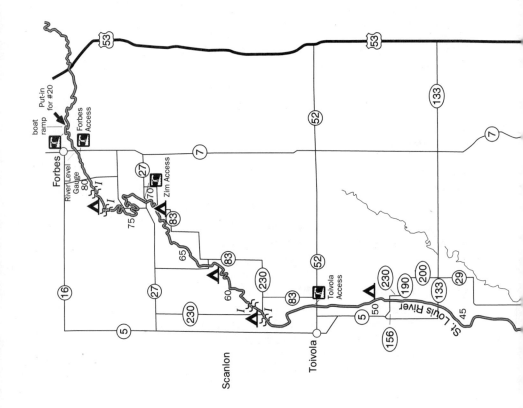

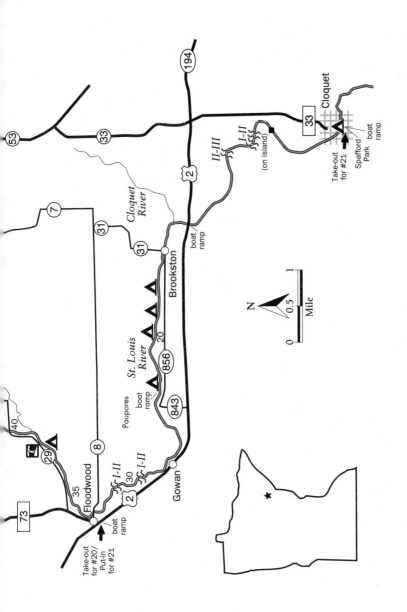

53

194

33

Cloquet

7

33

Cloquet River

2

II-III

I-II

II

(on island)

33

31

31

Brookston

boat ramp

Take-out for #21

Spafford Park boat ramp

N

0.5

0   Mile   1

St. Louis River

Paupores

boat ramp

20

856

843

Gowan

40

29

Floodwood

I-II

30

I-II

8

35

2

boat ramp

73

Take-out for #20/ Put-in for #21

the rapids, the river meanders again, passing several campsites. The surrounding land varies from deciduous forest to farmland. Near the County Route 230 bridge, the St. Louis runs through two more stretches of class I rapids. As the river nears Toivola, the river grows straighter and the landscape becomes more open, with peatlands and farm fields becoming more common. Midway between Toivola and Floodwood, the Whiteface River, the second-largest tributary of the St. Louis, joins from the east. At Floodwood, paddle up the Floodwood River a half mile to the take-out.

Access: **Forbes put-in:** From Forbes, drive east 1 mile on County Route 16 to the dam, with a carry-in canoe access on the downstream and boat ramp on the upstream side. An access is also located a mile south of Forbes. **Floodwood take-out:** The access is located in town on the Floodwood River, about a half mile above the confluence with the St. Louis.

Alternate accesses are located 3 miles west of Zim, 2 miles east of Toivola, and 6 miles northeast of Floodwood.

Shuttle: 50 miles one way. About 1.75 hours.

ADDITIONAL HELP

MA&G: 75, E7–8; 65
Camping: Several river campsites are located on this stretch. See map for locations. Auto camping is possible at Savanna Portage State Park.
Food, gas, and lodging: Cloquet, Floodwood
For more information: MDNR Information Center.

21 Floodwood to Cloquet

Character: The St. Louis runs through short stretches of rapids, but most of the run is quiet.
Length: 33 miles.
Average run time: One to two days.
Class: I–III.
Skill level: Intermediate.
Optimal flow: Above 1.2 feet on the gauge on the County Route 8 bridge at Floodwood, or above 9 feet on the gauge at U.S. Highway 2 just downstream from Brookston.
Average gradient: 1.5 feet per mile.
Hazards: No particular hazards.
Maps: MDNR *St. Louis River Canoe Route*.

See map on page 66

The paddling: Launch your canoe on the Floodwood River and, after a half mile, paddle out onto the broad St. Louis. Within a quarter mile, you'll pass the East Savanna River, a stream whose historical importance is greater than its small size.

It provided fur traders a route from Lake Superior to the upper Mississippi watershed. Voyageurs traveling Lake Superior entered St. Louis Bay (at the present site of Duluth) until they were stymied by the many miles of cataracts now found in Jay Cooke State Park. They portaged their canoes and trade goods around these obstacles via the Grand Portage (not to be confused with the Grand Portage on the Pigeon River). Near the site of Cloquet, they re-embarked upon the river, paddled up the St. Louis, ascended the East Savanna, and crossed (in a 6-mile portage) small creeks, bogs, and other terrain most eminently suited for mosquitoes, to the West Savanna River and the Mississippi River. Today, it is possible to hike this historic portage in Savanna Portage State Park and swat the descendants of mosquitoes that sucked the blood of the voyageurs.

Below the East Savanna, the St. Louis flows quietly for more than a mile but then runs through several rapids that rate class I in low water, class II in high water. The river splits around an island near its confluence with McCarty Creek from the north.

Below the small community of Gowan the river runs through a couple small rapids and then hits a long, quiet stretch. Several riverside campsites lie along the left (north) side of the river. The Cloquet River, the St. Louis's largest tributary, joins from the northeast. A class I rapids occurs just downstream. Four miles below US 2, the St. Louis runs through a steep, bouldery drop that rates class II at medium levels and class III in high water. A mile later, the river runs through a bouldery class I–II drop.

About a half mile below the mouth of the White Pine River, a trout stream, a picnic area sits on an island in the St. Louis.

As the river enters Cloquet, look for the access at Spafford Park. In the 2 miles below the park, the St. Louis flows over three dams, for which there are no developed portages.

The St. Louis watershed is extensively developed for hydropower generation. Dams at Whiteface Reservoir, Boulder Lake Reservoir, Island Lake Reservoir, Fish Lake Reservoir, and Wild Rice Lake Reservoir meter water to supply power-generating dams and turbines in Cloquet, Scanlon, Thomson, and Fond du Lac.

This stretch of the St. Louis, with its large size and occasional rapids, harbors a variety of game fish, including walleye, northern pike, smallmouth bass, and channel catfish.

Access: The **Floodwood put-in** is located in town on the Floodwood River, about a half mile above the confluence with the St. Louis. The **Spafford Park take-out** is located in Cloquet on Dunlap Island, where Minnesota Highway 33 crosses the St. Louis.

Alternate accesses are located at Paupores, Brookston, and US 2 near the confluence with the Cloquet River.

Shuttle: 26 miles one way. About one hour.

ADDITIONAL HELP

MA&G: 65.

Camping: Several river campsites are located on the left (north) bank of the river between Paupores and Brookston. Auto camping is possible at Spafford Park in Cloquet and Jay Cooke State Park.

Food, gas, and lodging: Cloquet, Floodwood.

For more information: MDNR Information Center.

22 Scanlon to Thomson Reservoir

Character: Though short, this section provides a wild and beautiful ride down distinctive rapids and falls. It also provides the only commercial rafting in the state.

Length: 3 miles.

Average run time: Two to three hours, allowing time for scouting and playing in rapids.

Class: II–III below 5,000 cfs; class III–IV at higher levels.

Skill level: Intermediate at lower levels; expert in high water.

Optimal flow: More than 1,000 cfs from Knife Falls Powerhouse in Cloquet. Call Minnesota Power at 800-582-8529 for a recording of water-level information on the St. Louis and other rivers and reservoirs managed by Minnesota Power. Because the river is so large and upstream reservoirs are managed to maintain water flows to hydro dams in the area, this stretch remains runnable much of the summer. Minnesota Power is required to boost the flow to 1,000 cfs twice a day during the summer if water is available.

Average gradient: 10 feet per mile. The first mile and last mile of the run are nearly flat, leaving the middle mile to fall nearly 30 feet.

Hazards: Several rapids are steep and long. Paddle with friends who can retrieve your boat and haul your soggy carcass from the river if you dump.

Maps: PRIM *Duluth*. USGS *7.5-minute MN*.

The paddling: About a half mile into the run, the river runs through a short, wavy drop called **Wave Train** or, simply, the Wave. Nothing to it, you think—an easy class II with no real obstacles. But because of its size, the river is pushier and its waves are bigger than they at first appear. Waves up to 2 feet at higher levels will bounce you around and give you a chance for a bit of surfing to warm up.

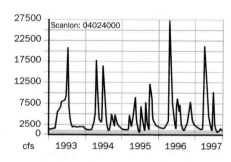

1000 cfs = minimum for good paddling

22 Scanlon to Thomson Reservoir

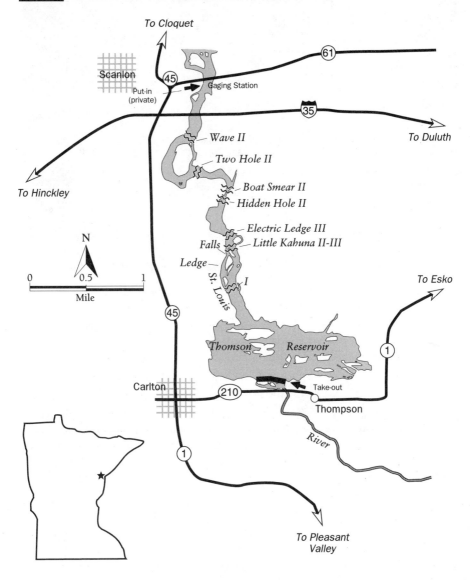

Around the corner, the St. Louis drops through **Two Hole,** a long, bouldery class II drop. Watch out for the pesky holes—one at the top and one near the bottom—that form on the right in medium to high levels. Stay left.

After about a quarter mile, the river necks down and curves to the right as it smashes into a cliff on the outside of the bend. This is **Boat Smear.** The trick in running this class II drop is to avoid the rocky holes on the right while staying away from the cliff on the left.

The short but intense run from Scanlon to Thomson Reservoir is popular with rafters, kayakers, and skilled open boaters. MINNESOTA OFFICE OF TOURISM

Keep your eyes open for **Hidden Hole,** a class II. Run to the right to avoid the hole.

Paddle through another pool and suddenly the river disappears over a 6-foot falls, dubbed **Electric Ledge** for the power line crossing the river. Scout from the right, where the ledge is sheer and little water flows over it except at high levels. Run the drop toward the middle, between two large holes. Because the river is about 100 yards wide at this point, it's tough to identify the runnable chute once you get back into your boat and back onto the river. Rate Electric Ledge class III. The penalty for hitting one of the holes head-on may be a long swim through the rapids that follows.

Right below Electric Ledge, the St. Louis splits around a large island. The right channel drops over a rocky, 8-foot falls. Though the drop has been run in high water, a mishap spells pinning, abrasions, and broken bones. Better to go down the left channel, which sails down a long string of 2- and 3-foot waves that culminate in a 4-foot backroller. This is **Little Kahuna,** and it rates class II in low water and class III at levels over 10,000 cfs. Continue down this channel to the end, or swing into the channel between two islands on the right to see the 8-foot falls. Then you'll find you have a shot at a class II, 3-foot-high ledge in the right channel.

The whitewater ends with a class I riffle. Then paddle into Thomson Reservoir and to the take-out to the left (east) of Thomson Dam. In high water, watch out for current sweeping toward the dam.

Few paddlers will pay much attention to the fishing; their attention will be riveted to the whitewater instead. However, the river and Thomson Reservoir harbor smallmouth bass, northern pike, walleyes, and channel catfish.

Access: The **Scanlon put-in,** a private access for which permission is required, is located next to the County Route 61 bridge, on the west side of the river, about a quarter mile upstream from the I-35 bridge. The **Thomson Reservoir take-out,** owned by the University of Minnesota–Duluth Outdoor Center is located less than a mile west of the town of Thomson, on the east side of the Thomson Dam.

Shuttle: 4 miles one way. About 15 minutes.

ADDITIONAL HELP

MA&G: 65, E9.
Camping: No campsites on this stretch of river. Camp by car at Jay Cooke State Park.
Food, gas, and lodging: Cloquet.
For more information: MDNR Information Center; Superior Whitewater, a private outfitter.

23 Thomson Dam to Swinging Bridge

Character: This wild ride culminates in a falls so unusual it is almost surreal.
Length: 2 miles.
Average run time: Two hours, to allow for scouting and portaging.
Class: IV–5.
Skill level: Expert.
Optimal flow: Up to 3,000 cfs is diverted from Thomson Reservoir at the beginning of this stretch to the Thomson Hydroelectric Station at the bottom. Take a look to make sure the water left behind is sufficient to make the run; 350 cfs is sufficient. Four weekends a summer, Minnesota Power releases up to 1,300 cfs for races. Call The University of Minnesota–Duluth Outdoor Center to learn when releases are planned.
Average gradient: 65 feet per mile.
Hazards: Sloping rocks in the riverbed are jagged and sharp.
Maps: MDNR PRIM, UNITAL.

The paddling: If you carry upstream from the put-in, you can catch a 6-foot drop with a sticky hole and powerful outwash, one of the trickiest spots in the whitewater slalom that is often run at this site. Rate this one class III in low water and class 5 when the hole turns into a stopper.

23 Thomson Dam to Swinging Bridge

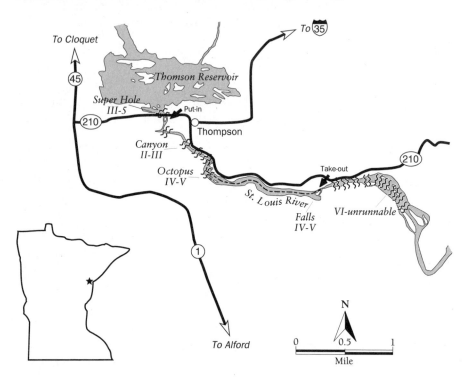

The river soon passes under Minnesota Highway 210 and into Jay Cooke State Park through a canyon of gnarled, metamorphic rock. Most of the water through this stretch rates class II–III. But then comes **Octopus**. Ah, yes, Octopus— straight and wide, with a ledge and a nasty hole. Pick your way through boulders (or in high water, a train of waves) and punch through the hole, if you can. Rate it class IV in low flows; class 5 in high. Many choose to walk.

Finally, the river splits around an island. Most paddlers run the left channel, which plunges over a 10-foot falls within about 200 yards of the take-out. This drop rates class IV in low water; class 5 in high. The dark layers of slate and other metamorphosed bedrock have been tilted almost vertically, so that they appear as jagged walls, guiding the river through a maze.

At the take-out, you'll be able to marvel at the thunderous cascade below the Swinging Bridge, where the bottom falls out of the river. It plunges 200 feet in the next mile in a class VI series of waterfalls and twisting rapids. Though this stretch has been run at very specific water levels, it rates class VI to unrunnable at most flows.

Jay Cooke State Park, which surrounds this portion of the river, has more than 50 miles of trail for hikers, mountain bikers, and horseback riders. The trails wind through woods and along the river, providing vistas of the nearly mountainous valley cradling the St. Louis.

The tilted, rugged bedrock of the St. Louis River between Thomson Dam and the Swinging Bridge, in the background, creates difficult rapids and some waterfalls. It is shown here in very low waters. MINNESOTA OFFICE OF TOURISM

Whitewater slalom races are often staged at the MN 210 bridge below the Thomson Dam; local kayakers organize races which draw international competitors. Even if you don't race, watching the competition and enjoying the hubbub of the race site is a great way to spend an afternoon.

If you're not up for running the river in a canoe or kayak, you can join a commercial raft trip run by Superior Whitewater, an outfitter in Carlton.

Anglers fish the quiet pools in this stretch for smallmouth bass and walleye. Two tributaries in Jay Cooke State Park Otter Creek and Silver Creek hold brown trout.

Access: Thomson Dam put-in: Park at the University of Minnesota–Duluth Outdoor Center site on river left and put in just below the bridge. Or put in on river right just upstream of MN 210 to catch the first big hole in the run. **Swinging Bridge take-out:** From Thomson, follow MN 210 into Jay Cooke State Park 2 miles to park headquarters, located next to Swinging Bridge, a suspension footbridge over the St. Louis. You'll need a vehicle permit to drive into the park.

Shuttle: 2 miles one way. About ten minutes.

ADDITIONAL HELP

MA&G: 65, 9E; 66, 1E.
Camping: None on the river itself. Camp by car in Jay Cooke State Park.
Food, gas, and lodging: Cloquet.
For more information: MDNR Information Center (ask for Jay Cooke State Park map). University of Minnesota–Duluth Outdoor Center.

24 Minnesota Highway 23 to Duluth Harbor

Character: In its final miles, the St. Louis spreads into a broad estuary containing backwaters and islands.
Length: About 16 miles, following the main channel from the access to the harbor.
Average run time: Not applicable. Most paddlers will opt to leave and return from the same access.
Class: Quiet.
Skill level: Beginner.
Optimal flow: Any.
Average gradient: Virtually none.
Hazards: No special hazards.
Maps: MDNR PRIM *Duluth.*

The paddling: Our trip down the St. Louis skips the canyon and reservoir between Swinging Bridge and Fond du Lac Dam, which is nearly unrunnable (class VI) and largely inaccessible. Our description resumes at the MN 23 access on the river. From here downstream, the river spreads out into a broad estuary known initially as Spirit Lake and, farther downstream, as St. Louis Bay. At its mouth, the estuary forms the busy Lake Superior harbor of Duluth, Minnesota, and Superior, Wisconsin. Land surrounding the river rises in distant hills. The mouths of small tributary streams form channels for paddlers to explore.

Just downstream of the put-in is the now-listless burg of Fond du Lac, which stems from an old fur-trade settlement and today ranks as Minnesota's oldest European settlement. In this area, voyageurs heading from Lake Superior to the upper Mississippi River watershed would begin their long portage around the cascades of the lower St. Louis.

As you continue downstream, the Minnesota shore of the estuary becomes more developed as you move into the suburbs and far-flung western neighborhoods of Duluth. Morgan Park was built as a model community to house the workers of the U.S. Steel mill that once operated on the banks of the river. Nonetheless, there are still plenty of wetlands and isolated backwaters. The Wisconsin shore is more undeveloped, a refuge for waterfowl, eagles, and other wildlife.

For a different view of the estuary, put in at the harbor. From your boat you'll get a close look at the ore boats and ocean-going vessels that enter the harbor. Keep a safe distance from the ships, especially if they are underway.

24 Minnesota Highway 23 to Duluth Harbor

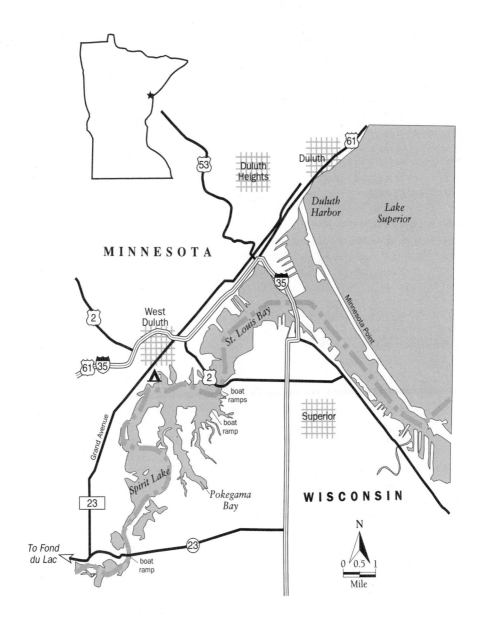

The fishery of this stretch of the St. Louis includes smallmouth bass, walleye, northern pike, and even an occasionally muskie. A popular place to fish is the swift water below the Fond du Lac Dam. Unfortunately, the Duluth-Superior harbor has been an entry point for several harmful exotic species that hitched a ride from Europe and Asia in the ballast tanks of ocean-going freighters. Among the most damaging are the ruff, a perchlike fish now ranked as the most plentiful fish in the harbor, the round goby, zebra mussel, and spiny water flea.

Access: MN 23 put-in: From Fond du Lac drive west 1 mile on MN 23 to the access. Alternate accesses are located at Morgan Park, the Minnesota side of the Interstate 535/U.S. Highway 53 bridge over the St. Louis, and the harbor side of Minnesota Point (commonly called Park Point).

Shuttle: Most paddlers opt to use a single access for an out-and-back trip.

ADDITIONAL HELP

MA&G: 66, E1–2.

Camping: A campground is located on a peninsula on the Minnesota shore at the Lake Superior Zoological Gardens. Camp by car at Jay Cooke State Park.

Food, gas, and lodging: Duluth.

For more information: MDNR Information Center.

STURGEON RIVER

25 Side Lake to County Road 766

Character: This marshy, winding section of stream makes for a pleasant day trip with a good chance of spotting waterfowl and shorebirds.

Length: 8.3 miles.

Average run time: Three to four hours.

Class: Quiet.

Skill level: Beginner.

Optimal flow: No gauge reading available. Medium to high levels are best, usually in late April to early June.

Average gradient: 1.4 feet per mile.

Hazards: No particular hazards.

Maps: PRIM *Vermilion Lake.* USGS *Side Lake, Minnesota; Dewey Lake NW, Minnesota 7.5-minute.*

The paddling: The Sturgeon (not to be confused with the tributary of The Big Fork) is a charming stream that undergoes some surprising changes. Some sections are slow and marshy. Others are filled with difficult whitewater. Yet others meander through dense forest.

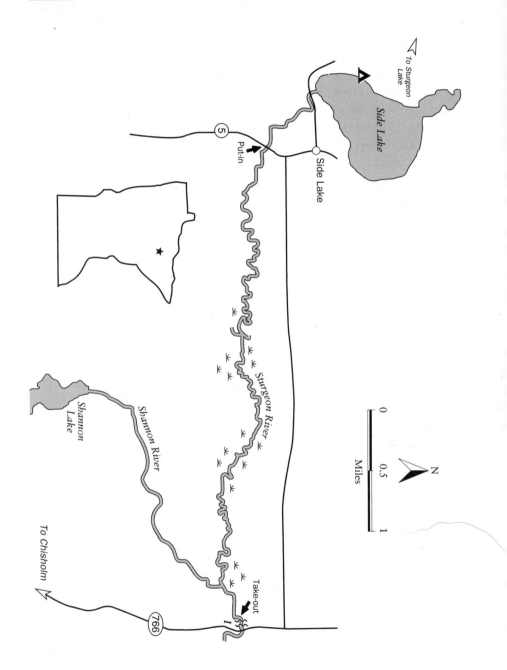

The first section, beginning at Side Lake, is slow and placid, winding by marsh and forest. Its course is exceedingly sinuous. Rarely can you see very far ahead. For this reason, it's a great stream for surprising waterfowl and shorebirds such as great blue herons.

Right before the end of the trip, the Shannon River joins from the south. It's possible to ascend the Shannon as far south as Shannon Lake for more opportunities to watch critters and do some fishing for big northern pike and largemouth bass.

The only swift water in this section of the Sturgeon comes in a small riffle right before the CR 766 bridge. It shouldn't cause anyone any trouble, but don't stray too far beyond the bridge. As you'll see in the following trip description, the Sturgeon undergoes a sudden transformation and becomes a raging whitewater run.

Access: The **Side Lake put-in** is the County Route 5 bridge over the Sturgeon. To reach the **CR 766 take-out** from the put-in, drive east on County Road 739 about 4 miles to CR 766; turn south and drive a half mile to the river.

Shuttle: 4.5 miles one way. About 15 minutes.

ADDITIONAL HELP

MA&G: 74, B4; 75, B5.
Camping: No campsites on the river. Camp by car at McCarthy Beach State Park.
Food, gas, and lodging: Side Lake, Chisholm, Hibbing.
For more information: Superior National Forest, LaCroix Ranger District. The upper reaches of the river lie within the national forest, though the Sturgeon is not promoted as a canoe route.

26 County Road 766 to County Route 65

Character: This short stretch runs through as difficult and concentrated a whitewater run as can be found in the area.
Length: 3.5 miles.
Average run time: Two to four hours, depending on the time spent scouting and portaging.
Class: II–III.
Skill level: Intermediate to expert, depending on whether you paddle a kayak or open canoe.
Optimal flow: At least 3.3 feet on the gauge on the County Route 65 bridge (about 200 cfs on the USGS gauge near Chisholm) (this reading is not available from the MDNR). The river is usually runnable in May, but later in the year you'll have to try to catch it after a heavy rain.
Average gradient: 15.7 feet per mile.
Hazards: The bouldery rapids can pin a boat.
Maps: PRIM *Vermilion Lake*. USGS *Dewey Lake NW, Minn. 97.5-minute*.

The paddling: And you think Clark Kent makes a quick change. Right below the CR 766 bridge, the Sturgeon changes from a mild-mannered stream to a super

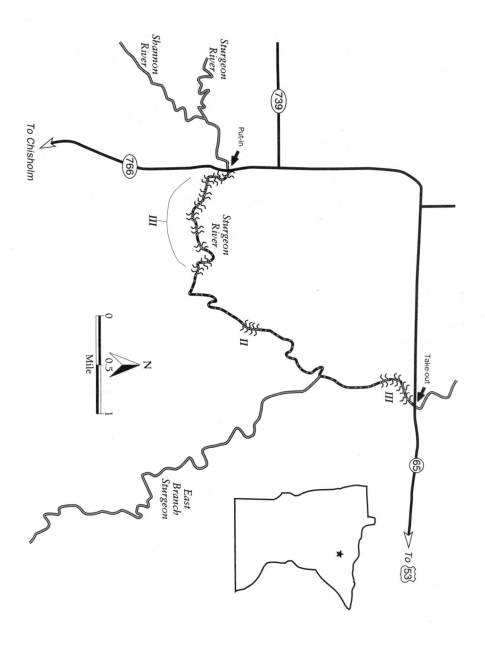

stretch of whitewater. The river races through three class III rapids that drop about 30 feet in 0.75 mile. The narrow, winding channel is clogged with large boulders that throw large standing waves in high water. The waves and tight turns are particularly tough in an open canoe.

Farther along, the Sturgeon runs through a class II rapids but then finishes strong, running through a class III rapids right before the County Route 65 take-out.

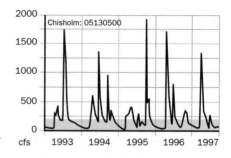

200 cfs (3.3 feet on gauge) = minimum for good paddling

Access: To reach the **CR 766 put-in from Side Lake,** drive east on CR 739 about 4 miles to CR 766; turn south and drive a half mile to the river. To reach the **County Route 65 take-out** from the put-in, drive north about 1.5 miles on CR 766 and 931 to County Route 65, turn east, and drive 1.5 miles to the take-out.

Shuttle: 3 miles one way. About ten minutes.

ADDITIONAL HELP

MA&G: 75, B5.
Camping: No developed campsites along the river. McCarthy Beach State Park has a campground.
Food, gas, and lodging: Side Lake, Chisholm, Hibbing.
For more information: Superior National Forest, LaCroix Ranger District.

27 County Route 65 to County Road 923

Character: The Sturgeon undergoes another change—from hair-raising whitewater run to a lazy stream blocked by frequent logjams.
Length: 25.1 miles. It's advisable to use alternate accesses to make a shorter trip.
Average run time: 10 to 14 hours.
Class: Generally quiet, with three class II rapids.
Skill level: Intermediate. Beginners will want to portage the rapids.
Optimal flow: No information available. If the previous section is runnable, this section will be as well.
Average gradient: 2.4 feet per mile.
Hazards: Don't be lulled to sleep by the long quiet sections and overlook the few notable rapids on this stretch. Be careful around the logjams.
Maps: PRIM *Vermilion Lake.*

27 County Route 65 to County Road 923

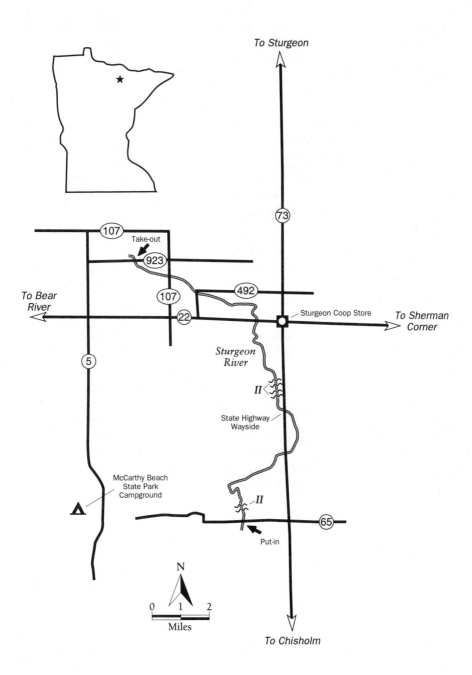

To Sturgeon

73

107   Take-out
923

To Bear
River

107
492
22   Sturgeon Coop Store   To Sherman
Corner

5

*Sturgeon
River*

II

State Highway
Wayside

McCarthy Beach
State Park
Campground

II

65

Put-in

N

0   1   2
Miles

To Chisholm

The paddling: After a whitewater tantrum in the previous stretch, the Sturgeon seems exhausted. It winds past slumping banks of clay. Downed trees cross the channel. In places dozens of logs lodge in a bend or shallow stretch of the river. If you choose to run this section, you'll have to pick your way through perhaps a half dozen jams. Often you'll have no choice but to portage. The locations and sizes of the logjams vary as floods break up the jams and move them elsewhere.

Fishing can be good for walleye, northern pike, smallmouth bass, and even a few muskies.

Access: The **County Route 65 put-in** is located at the bridge 2 miles west of Minnesota Highway 73. **CR 923 take-out:** From Side Lake, drive north 10 miles on County Route 5 to CR 923; turn right (east) and drive 2 miles to the river.

Several alternative accesses are available, including two MN 73 bridges, County Road 491, County Route 22, and County Route 107.

Shuttle: 17 miles one way. About 50 minutes.

ADDITIONAL HELP

MA&G: 75, B5.
Camping: There are no developed campsites along the river but many places to make your own camp on public forest land. Campgrounds are located at McCarthy Beach State Park and George Washington State Forest near Bear River.
Food, gas, and lodging: Hibbing, Side Lake.
For more information: Superior National Forest, LaCroix Ranger District, MDNR Information Center (ask for information about Sturgeon River State Forest).

28 County Road 923 to Little Fork River

Character: The Sturgeon perks up a bit as it flows toward the Little Fork. You'll encounter four tough rapids—and probably no logjams.
Length: 11.3 miles, including a mile on the Little Fork.
Average run time: Four to six hours.
Class: II–III.
Skill level: Intermediate.
Optimal flow: Runnable except in very low water.
Average gradient: 3.1 feet per mile
Hazards: Watch for logjams, though they are much less likely in this stretch than in the previous.
Maps: PRIM *Vermilion Lake*.

The paddling: Though the gradient increases only slightly in this section, the river changes perceptibly. Perhaps because of the combination of soils and gradient, logjams are less likely to block the channel. You'll encounter four rapids. The first three are class II, but the final one, about a mile downstream from the confluence

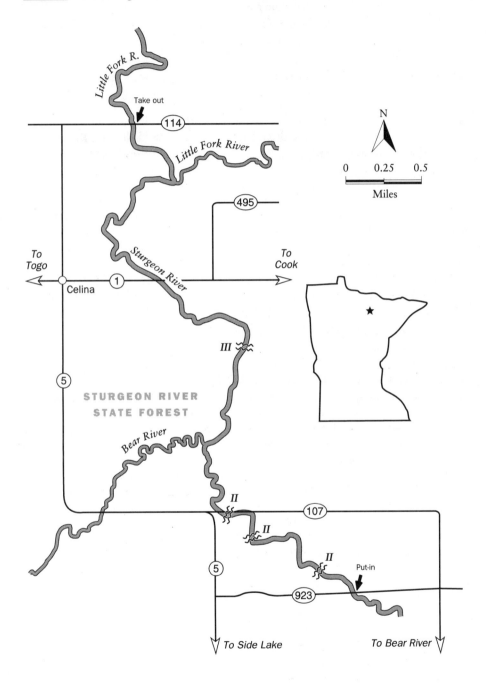

with the Bear River, is a class III. The mouth of the Bear River, by the way, is one of the most beautiful spots along the river.

About 4 miles below this final rapids, the Sturgeon joins the Little Fork. Paddle an additional mile on the Little Fork to the take-out.

This stretch is larger and has deeper holes than the sections upstream. Fishing can be good for walleye, northern pike, smallmouth bass, and even an occasional muskie.

Access: CR 923 put-in: From Side Lake, drive north 10 miles on County Route 5 to CR 923; turn right (east) and drive 2 miles to the river. **Little Fork River take-out:** Drive north on County Route 5 to County Route 114; turn right (east) and drive a mile to the river.

Shuttle: 11 miles one way. About 30 minutes.

ADDITIONAL HELP

MA&G: 74, A4; 86, E4.
Camping: No developed campsites along the river but plenty of sites to set a tent. Campgrounds at McCarthy Beach State Park and George Washington State Forest.
Food, gas, and lodging: Hibbing, Side Lake, Cook.
For more information: MDNR Information Center.

29 Timber-Frear Lakes Loop

Character: This 15-mile loop of backcountry lakes resembles a route in the Boundary Waters Canoe Area Wilderness, but without the regulations or the need to register.
Paddling time: You can easily make the loop in a single day, but there's enough water to keep you occupied for several days.
Hazards: As in the Boundary Waters, take precautions against bears in camp. And watch out for the roads—especially Forest Roads 170, 347, 348, and 1225—which are rocky, muddy, and rutted. A truck or SUV will help you get through.
Maps: Superior National Forest map and *Timber-Frear Loop,* a photocopied hand-out available from the national forest.

The paddling: The Timber-Frear Loop is one of several routes the USDA Forest Service promotes as resembling the Boundary Waters but without the hassle of many of the regulations. Just drive up, launch the canoe, and paddle off.

You can launch at either Whitefish Lake or Finger Lake and take the loop in either direction. The loop joins seven lakes, which are, with the exception of Elbow Lake, less than a square mile in size.

For example, from Whitefish Lake portage 65 rods (770 yards) into Elbow Lake, 140 rods (770 yards) into Lost Lake, 120 rods (660 yards) into Frear Lake,

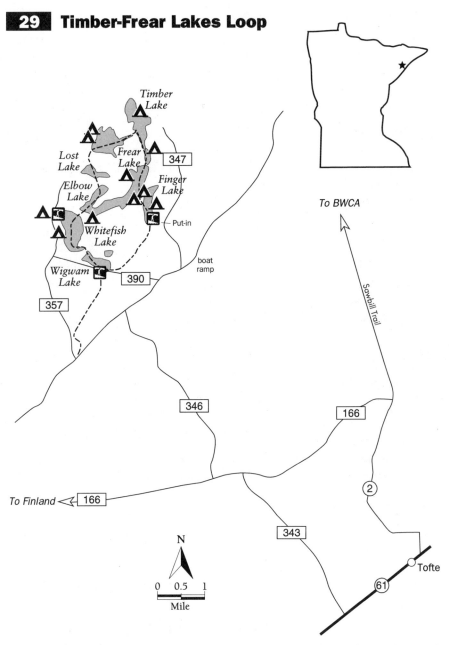

5 rods (28 yards) and then 60 rods (330 yards) into Timber Lake, and 45 rods (248 yards) into Elbow Lake again. From there you can paddle and portage 65 rods (358 yards) back into Whitefish, or portage 30 rods (165 yards) into Finger Lake. From Finger Lake, paddle about 2 miles on the Cross River into Wigwam Lake. Then portage 20 rods (110 yards) into Whitefish and paddle back to the access.

Like lakes in the Boundary Waters, these waterways are a mix of rocky, wooded, and marshy shores. You stand a good chance of spotting a bald eagle, surprising a moose, or even hearing the howl of a wolf.

Fishing is good for walleye and northern pike, especially in the larger lakes along the route.

Access: The **Whitefish Lake put-in** is located 14 miles north and west of Tofte along Forest Roads 343, 166, 346, 170, and 348. You must carry in about 6 rods (33 yards) to water's edge. The **Finger Lake put-in** is 12 miles north and west of Tofte along Forest Roads 343, 166, 346, 347, and 1225. You can drive almost to the edge of the lake.

ADDITIONAL HELP

MA&G: 78, E1.
Camping: Primitive campsites are located at Whitefish, Frear (2), Timber, Elbow (5), and Finger.
Food, gas, and lodging: Tofte.
For more information: Superior National Forest, Tofte Ranger District.

30 Twin Lake Loop

Character: Here's a route between backcountry lakes that offers primitive camping and good fishing for walleye and trout.
Paddling time: You can reach any of these lakes and paddle back out again in an afternoon, but there are several campsites for an overnight trip.
Hazards: Take precautions against bears in camp.
Maps: Map and a photocopied hand-out from Superior National Forest.

The paddling: From the landing, which straddles East Twin Lake and West Twin Lake, you can paddle west to a short portage into tiny Talus Lake. An even shorter portage leads to Kemo Lake. Portage into Pine Lake, paddle almost to the eastern end, and portage back to the access.

The Twin Lakes offer good walleye fishing. Kemo has lake trout and splake (a cross between brook and lake trout). Pine is stocked with rainbow trout.

Access: From Grand Marais, follow the Gunflint Trail (County Route 12) 16.5 miles to Forest Road 325. Follow FR 325 to the west for 6 miles to Forest Road 152. Turn left (south) and drive 4 miles to the landing.

ADDITIONAL HELP

MA&G: 79, C6.

Twin Lake Loop

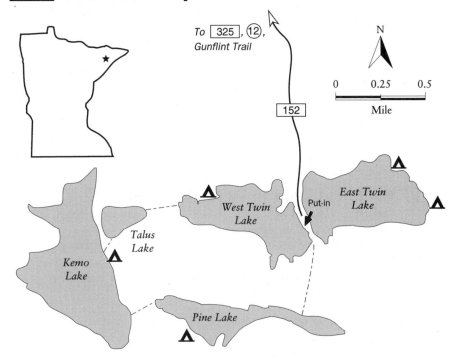

To 325 , 12 ,
Gunflint Trail

N

0   0.25   0.5

Mile

152

East Twin
Lake

West Twin
Lake

Put-in

Talus
Lake

Kemo
Lake

Pine Lake

Camping: Primitive campsites are located on East Twin (2), West Twin, Kemo, and Pine Lakes.

Food, gas, and lodging: Grand Marais.

For more information: Superior National Forest, Gunflint Ranger District.

THE VERMILION RIVER

The Vermilion River, which runs 39 miles from Lake Vermilion to Crane Lake, can't decide whether it wants to be a raging torrent of whitewater or a lake. For several miles it tumbles through difficult and sometimes dangerous rapids. Then for several miles it eases along with no perceptible current at all. The following route descriptions divvy up the river to separate the whitewater from the flat water. You can certainly take a delightful two- or three-day trip down the Vermilion. Approach it as you would a canoe trip in the Boundary Water Canoe Area Wilderness: Plan to portage your gear (and perhaps your canoe as well) around all but the easiest rapids.

Despite logging along the river, the Vermilion River watershed is remote and wild. The river is given to sudden bursts of stunning scenery. Deer and moose are common. So are black bears, so plan to hang your food at night if staying at a heavily used campsite where bears might be snooping for food. You may hear or even see timber wolves, which have become fairly abundant in the region.

Fishing for smallmouth bass, northern pike, and walleye can be excellent. Especially good are pockets of fairly deep water immediately above or below rapids. With the clear water and often slight current, topwater lures such as fly-rod poppers often are good bets for both bass and pike. If you can't find fish near the swift water, search deep holes with jigs and live bait.

Don't misspell the name of this river. There are two others in the state spelled Vermillion—a shorter one in Cass County and another southeast of the Twin Cities.

31 Vermilion Dam to Twomile Creek

Character: The Vermilion starts out with a bang, running through several difficult rapids and short pools. Note that the take-out requires a 1.5-mile paddle up Twomile Creek, a marshy tributary.
Length: 5.5 miles (including the paddle up Twomile Creek).
Average run time: Two to four hours, depending on the time spent scouting and playing in rapids.
Class: II–IV.
Skill level: Intermediate to expert.
Optimal flow: More than 4 feet at the gauge on County Route 24 at Buyck.
Average gradient: 8.7 feet per mile.
Hazards: None, except the rapids themselves. Vermilion Dam Rapids and Shively Falls are steep and bouldery—perfect for pinning and wrapping swamped canoes.
Maps: *Vermilion River Canoe Route.*

The paddling: The Vermilion slides over the dam at the outlet of Lake Vermilion and roars over a steep pile of boulders, forming a difficult pitch of whitewater about 200 yards long. In low water you'll have to pick your way down a complicated route between and over large boulders (class III). In high water, waves kick up, holes form, and your job becomes all the tougher (class IV). Portage either side, about 275 yards.

Take a breather as you paddle a mile of calm water to **Shively Falls,** three distinct pitches that rate class III. The first two pitches are steep, powerful, and wavy in high water. Maneuvering through the clear channel can be difficult as the river washes you downstream. The third pitch is a wide, bouldery obstacle course. Portage left about 400 yards.

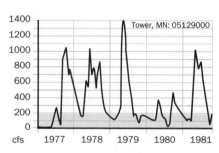

200 cfs = minimum for good paddling

31 Vermilion Dam to Twomile Creek

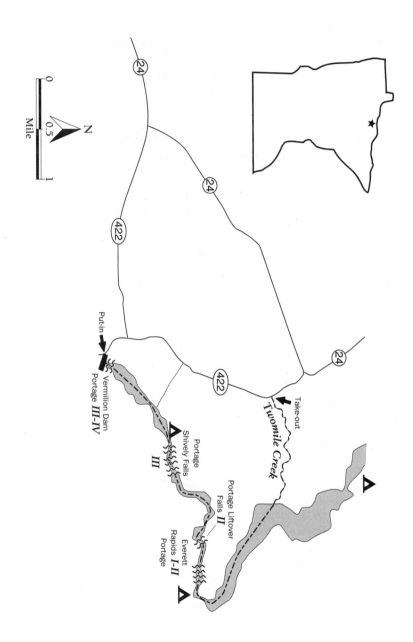

After another mile of calm water the river abruptly turns left and plunges over **Liftover Falls** (class II), a straightforward, three-foot drop with a foamy and generally not troublesome souse hole at the bottom. The portage, over a low rock outcrop on river right, is so easy and the rapids so much fun, you may want to carry back upstream and run it again and again.

Everett Rapids is class I in low water, class II in high water. Just downstream is a nondescript class I pitch. Portage right if you feel the need.

After these rapids, the Vermilion forms a long lake. Paddle about a mile of this flat water and look for the mouth of Twomile Creek on river left. Paddle up this slow, meandering stream about 1.5 miles to the County Road 422 bridge.

Access: The **Vermilion Dam put-in** at the outlet of Lake Vermilion is privately owned. To use it, make arrangements with the lodge on the site. From Cook, drive north and east about 17 miles on County Route 24, and then east 2 miles on CR 422. If you'd prefer to put in at a public site and don't want to run Vermilion Dam Rapids anyway, put in just upstream of Shively Falls. From the dam, drive north about 1 mile on CR 422 and turn right to the put-in. **Twomile Creek take-out:** From Vermilion Dam, drive north about 2 miles on CR 422 to the bridge over Twomile Creek. This is not a developed access.

Shuttle: 4 miles one way. About 15 minutes.

ADDITIONAL HELP

MA&G: 87, E9.

Camping: River camping is possible just above Shively Falls on river left and just below the last rapids on river right.

Food, gas, and lodging: Cook, Tower, Virginia.

For more information: Information Center; Superior National Forest, Gunflint Ranger District.

32 Twomile Creek to Eightmile Creek

Character: The Vermilion forms a long lake, lined with marsh.
Length: 6 miles.
Average run time: Two to three hours.
Class: Quiet.
Skill level: Beginner.
Optimal flow: Runnable at any level.
Average gradient: Less than 1 foot per mile.
Hazards: None.
Maps: MDNR *Vermilion River Canoe Route.*

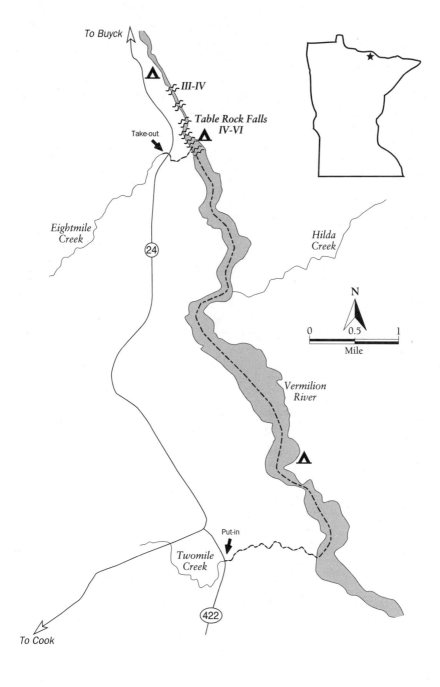

To Buyck

III-IV

Table Rock Falls
IV-VI

Take-out

Eightmile
Creek

24

Hilda
Creek

N

0   0.5   1
Mile

Vermilion
River

Put-in

Twomile
Creek

422

To Cook

The paddling: The Vermilion pools up and forms a narrow, riverine lake with little perceptible current. If you're into whitewater, you'll probably want to avoid this stretch. But if you like wild country and undeveloped shore, give it a try—by itself or as an add-on to the stretch above or below. The lake is shallow, averaging less than 6 feet deep. The shores are predominantly low and boggy; hills rise far in the distance.

Look for Eightmile Creek on your left and paddle up this tributary for about a quarter mile to reach County Route 24 and the take-out. Whatever you do, do not paddle blithely to the lip of **Table Rock Falls.** The experience could be fatal. (See the description for the following stretch, Route 33).

Access: Twomile Creek put-in: From Vermilion Dam, drive north about 2 miles on County Road 422 to the bridge over Twomile Creek. **Eightmile Creek take-out:** From the put-in, drive north on CR 422 (it will join County Route 24) about 5 miles to the bridge over Eightmile Creek. This is not a developed access.

Shuttle: 5 miles one way. About 15 minutes.

ADDITIONAL HELP

MA&G: 87, D9.

Camping: A primitive campsite is located about 1.5 miles downstream from the put-in, on river right. Camping is also possible at the access off County Route 24 a mile downstream (north) of the take-out.

Food, gas, and lodging: Cook, Tower, Virginia.

For more information: MDNR Information Center; Superior National Forest, Gunflint Ranger District.

33 Table Rock Falls Canyon

Character: Yikes! It can only get easier.

Length: 1 mile.

Average run time: 15 minutes if you were to run straight through. But if you're expert enough to run the falls and steepest part of the canyon, you'll probably want to carry back up and run it again and again.

Class: IV–VI, with the difficulty increasing with water level.

Skill level: Expert.

Optimal flow: More than 4 feet at the gauge on County Route 24 at Buyck.

Average gradient: 80 feet per mile.

Hazards: The whole run is a hazard. The falls and first 300 yards of the canyon are especially steep and difficult.

Maps: MDNR *Vermilion River Canoe Route.*

The paddling: As though it sets out to be deceiving, the Vermilion slyly glides around a bend, picks up a bit of speed and suddenly plunges over a cascading

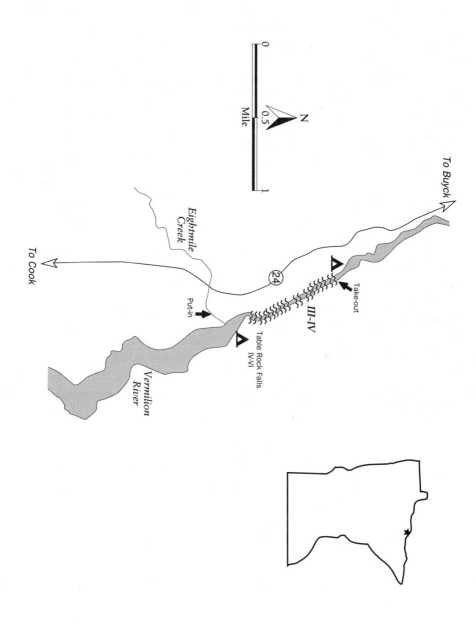

20-foot drop. The sight from the precipice is riveting. It would be beautiful—affording a long, dramatic view of the rapids-filled gorge below—except that you are too occupied with the business of saving your hide to enjoy it. The falls descends in about four closely spaced pitches, with the clearest route toward river right. Class IV in low water, the falls gets harder and harder as the water level increases.

Mere mortals and open-boaters will opt to portage on river right and put in near the base of the falls. You'll have 100 yards of rather nondescript rapids to help you get limbered up before the Vermilion carries you into the depths of the canyon, where the channel narrows to about 30 feet and flows swiftly through a twisting series of pitches. Rate this section class III in low water, class IV in high water.

With the steepest, narrowest part of the canyon behind you, the rapids gradually ease up over the next 0.75 mile. Rate this section about class II.

Access: Eightmile Creek: From the put-in (see previous trip), drive north on County Road 422 (it will join County Route 24) about 5 miles to the bridge over Eightmile Creek. This is not a developed access. **County Route 24 take-out:** From the put-in, drive north on County Route 24 for a mile and take a dirt road east a short distance toward the river.

Shuttle: 1 mile one way. Less than five minutes.

ADDITIONAL HELP

MA&G: 87, D9.
Camping: Camping is allowed at the take-out.
Food, gas, and lodging: Cook, Tower, Virginia.
For more information: MDNR Information Center; Superior National Forest, Gunflint Ranger District.

34 Table Rock Falls to High Falls

Character: The Vermilion resumes a placid character with only a few mild rapids. This most wild and undeveloped stretch of river makes a good overnight trip.
Length: 24.5 miles.
Average run time: One to two days.
Class: II.
Skill level: Beginner to intermediate, with wilderness camping skills.
Optimal flow: More than 4 feet at the gauge on County Route 24 at Buyck.
Average gradient: Less than 1 foot per mile.
Hazards: High falls just before the take-out. Portage left.
Maps: MDNR *Vermilion River Canoe Route.*

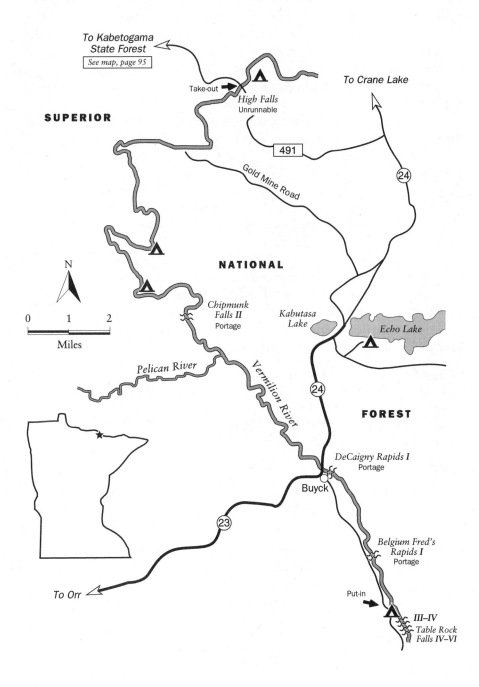

To Kabetogama
State Forest
See map, page 95

To Crane Lake

Take-out

High Falls
Unrunnable

SUPERIOR

491

Gold Mine Road

24

N

0   1   2

Miles

NATIONAL

*Chipmunk
Falls II*
Portage

*Kabutasa
Lake*

Echo Lake

Pelican River

Vermilion River

24

FOREST

DeCaigny Rapids I
Portage

Buyck

23

*Belgium Fred's
Rapids I*
Portage

Put-in

To Orr

III–IV

*Table Rock
Falls IV–VI*

The paddling: The Vermilion finds a groove and quietly flows past a forest of fir, spruce, birch, and aspen. After a couple of miles, the river meets **Belgium Fred's Rapids.** A short, bouldery stretch that rates class I, it is a feeble effort compared to the fury of **Table Rock Falls.** Portage left about 200 yards if you wish to bypass it.

After 2 miles of quiet water, the Vermilion runs through **DeCaigny Rapids,** another bouldery class I pitch. Portage right about 300 yards, if necessary.

Right after the rapids, the river passes the Country Route 24 bridge and the burg of Buyck (pronounced "bike"), where canoes can be rented. At this point, County Route 24 heads for points north, leaving the Vermilion to wind unaccompanied through the north woods. This stretch is the most remote section of the river.

About 5 miles beyond Buyck, the Pelican River, the largest tributary of the Vermilion, joins the larger river. In another 1.5 miles, the Vermilion roars through **Chipmunk Falls.** Okay, "roar" is a bit strong; the rapids rates class II.

For the next 14 miles, the river flows slowly and quietly past banks that alternate between forest and wild rice and other wetland plants. Two campsites in this stretch accommodate overnight travelers.

Beware when you pass an island: just downstream, the river runs through a short stretch of rapids and then plunges down a 25-foot-high, narrow, twisting cleft in a cliff known variously as **High Falls, Vermilion Falls,** or **Upper Gorge.** Take the left channel around the island and portage left, about 300 yards. The USDA Forest Service maintains a picnic area near the portage with picnic tables, fire grates, privies, and an observation railing along the falls.

Access: County Route 24: From Buyck, drive south on County Route 24 for 5 miles and take a dirt road east a short distance toward the river. **High Falls take-out:** From Buyck, drive northeast on County Route 24 about 10 miles; turn west on Forest Road 491 and drive about 5 miles to the river.

Alternate access is possible where Gold Mine Road crosses Holmes Creek.

Shuttle: 20 miles one way. About one hour.

ADDITIONAL HELP

MA&G: 87, C8.

Camping: River campsites are located about 2.5 miles and 6 miles downstream of Chipmunk Falls, both on river right. Auto camping is possible at a Superior National Forest campground at Echo Lake and a private campground at Crane Lake.

Food, gas, and lodging: Crane Lake, Orr, Cook.

For more information: MDNR Information Center; Superior National Forest, Gunflint Ranger District.

35 High Falls to Crane Lake

Character: The final stretch of the Vermilion is predominantly quiet, but it includes two of the river's most distinctive rapids.
Length: 5 miles, including the paddle on Crane Lake.
Average run time: Three hours.
Class: III–5, depending on water level.
Skill level: Intermediate to expert. Less skilled paddlers can enjoy this stretch if they portage the two difficult rapids.
Optimal flow: More than 4 feet at the gauge on County Route 24 at Buyck, or at least 300 cfs on gauge near Crane Lake—check the USGS website.
Average gradient: 13.2 feet per mile.
Hazards: Watch for undercut cliffs on both sides of the Chute.
Maps: MDNR *Vermilion River Canoe Route.*

The paddling: Once again the Vermilion starts out with a bang. Not yet out of sight of the Forest Road 491 bridge, it gathers, glides swiftly, and plunges over **The Chute,** a twisting 10-foot drop over a ledge and large boulders. Don't get pushed into the undercut cliff on either side of this rapids. The Chute rates class III in low water; up to class 5 at very high levels, when the waves become explosive and the current exceedingly pushy.

Again, the Vermilion shows its dual nature, flowing slowly and quietly eastward past a boreal forest of spruce, fir, birch, and aspen for about 2.5 miles.

Finally, the river shows its furious side one last time. It warms up by running through about 0.4 mile of class II–III boulder-bed rapids. Pick your way through the rocky course. Scoot to the left and, as the river turns sharply and ominously to the left, exit stage left and scout **The Gorge,** certainly one of the river's most beautiful rapids. After bending, the river drops over two ledges and disappears down a dark cleft in the rock, where gradually diminishing rapids run between vertical walls about 50 feet high. The Gorge rates class III in low water and up to class 5 in high. The two ledges and turbulent entry to the canyon provide most of the difficulty. Once you enter the cleft, you're home free. If you choose not to run The Gorge or the boulder rapids leading up to it, portage left about 0.75 mile.

Shortly downstream from The Gorge, is a rest area. Frenchman René Bourassa built a fur trade post in this area in 1736. Continue into Crane Lake and turn south into the first large bay to the take-out.

Access: High Falls put-in: From Buyck, drive northeast on County Route 24 about 10 miles; turn west on FR 491 and drive about 5 miles to the river. Put in on the downstream side of the bridge. **Crane**

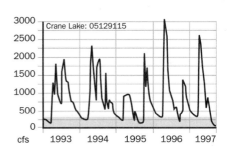

300 cfs = minimum for good paddling

35 High Falls to Crane Lake

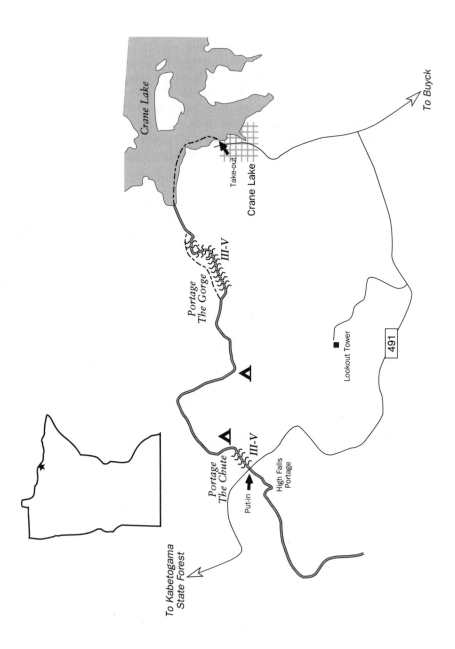

Lake take-out: From Buyck, drive northeast on County Route 24 about 11.5 miles to the public access in the town of Crane Lake on the shore of Crane Lake.

Shuttle: About 6.5 miles one way. About 20 minutes.

ADDITIONAL HELP

MA&G: 87, B8–9.
Camping: A river campsite is located midway between the Chute and the Gorge on river right. Auto camping is possible at a Superior National Forest campground at Echo Lake and a private campground at Crane Lake.
Food, gas, and lodging: Crane Lake, Orr, Cook.
For more information: MDNR Information Center; Superior National Forest, Gunflint Ranger District.

36 Voyageurs National Park

Character: With all their islands and campsites, the large, interconnected lakes of Voyageurs National Park provide fascinating exploration for boaters, especially sea kayakers. Unlike wide-open Lake Superior, the lakes of Voyageurs have plenty of protected coves and shorelines to paddle when weather is windy.
Paddling time: Day trips to trips of several days.
Hazards: Stormy weather on the big lakes can make paddling difficult or even hazardous. Paddlers must keep an eye out for motorboat traffic. Black bears are campsite pests, even on some islands; hang food or use bear lockers.
Maps: Small maps with information about the park are available from Voyageurs National Park. Larger-scale navigational charts and other publications are available from Lake States Interpretive Association. Both addresses and phone numbers are in the appendix.

The paddling: Voyageurs National Park, stretching 40 miles along the Minnesota-Ontario border, is a varied country, where the interplay of rock, water, and forest is almost continual. In fact, a third of the park's area is water, most of it contained in four large lakes: Kabetogama, Namakan, Sand Point, and the giant Rainy, which extends more than 20 miles into Canada. The lakes are rock-ribbed and windy, bound by cliffs and outcrops. Their hilly shorelines are covered with a dense forest of birch, aspen, spruce, pine, and other conifers. They are often too windy and wavy for pleasant or safe canoeing. But with miles of water available without a portage, they are perfectly suited to sea kayaking. Channels and islands provide shelter and points of interest. Plenty of campsites front the water.

36 Voyageurs National Park

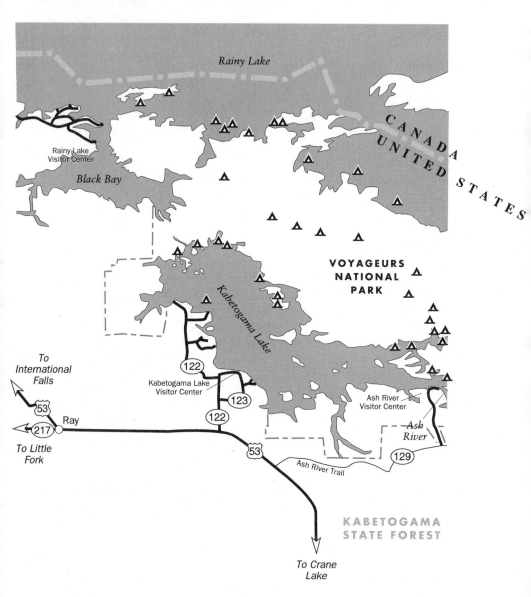

American
Channel

Oakpoint
Island

Canadian
Channel

ONTARIO

Kettle
Falls

Squirrel
Island

Namakan Lake

Blackstone
Island

Namakan
Island

Grassy
Portage

Grassy Bay

*Sand
Point
Lake*

Ash
River

Moose River

*Sullivan
Bay*

*Mukooda
Lake*

*Sand
Point
Lake*

N

0   2.5   5
        Mile

*Crane
Lake*

*Vermilion
River*

Launching from Ash River, for example, you can paddle west directly into Kabetogama or slip eastward through a maze of protected channels and islands into Namakan, which has dozens of primitive campsites on isolated peninsulas and islands. Paddle into the end of Hoist Bay to see pilings that mark the one-time location of a hoist that loaded logs onto the rail cars bound for the Virginia and Rainy Lake Company's mammoth sawmill. Turning northward and following the international boundary takes you to the Kettle Falls Hotel, built in 1913 to serve the lumberjacks and rising tide of bootleggers, prostitutes, prospectors, and sportsmen. Accessible only by boat or plane, the hotel still serves the public with rooms, a restaurant, and bar. By making a short portage you gain access to Rainy Lake, with hundreds of channels and islands on the Minnesota and Ontario shores. By paddling west toward the Rainy Lake Visitor Center, you pass the played-out gold mine on Bushyhead Island. A little farther west, interpretive exhibits among the old shafts of a mine on Little American Island describe the short-lived gold rush during the 1890s that brought a flood of prospectors and speculators to the area.

From a small boat you are likely to see beavers, black bears, moose, deer, and eagles. At night you may hear wolves, which live in the wild, remote forestland and marshes of the Kabetogama Peninsula at the center of the park.

With a canoe and light pack, it's possible to follow the shoreline of the peninsula and portage inland to the lightly traveled interior lakes. For example, from Rainy Lake Visitor Center, follow the north shore of the peninsula to Rainy Lake and Cranberry Bay. Paddle deep into the bay and ascend Cranberry Creek to a portage that leads to the upper reaches of the creek and Locator Lake. A series of short channels and portages leads through War Club, Quill, Loiten, and Shoepack Lakes. You can make reservations with the National Park Service to use boats and canoes that are stashed at some of the interior lakes.

The 10-mile-long Cruiser Lake Hiking Trail crosses the peninsula. A round-trip provides a pleasant all-day break from paddling.

Voyageurs's large lakes provide often-exceptional fishing for walleye, northern pike, and smallmouth bass. Look for these fish, pike and smallmouth bass especially, in shallow water in late spring. As the water warms, expect to fish deeper, along weedlines, drop-offs, and reefs. Inland lakes generally hold walleyes and pike. Shoepack and Little Shoepack harbor muskies, while Cruiser, Mukooda, and Little Trout hold lake trout.

Combining a houseboat with canoes or kayaks provides a great way to see these lakes. Round up a bunch of friends or family and rent a fully-equipped boat near International Falls. Throw a couple of canoes or kayaks on board and follow the navigation buoys in Rainy Lake to any number of shoreline campsites. Use the small boats to fish and explore. Cook and take shelter from bad weather in the big boat.

Access: Points include **Rainy Lake Visitor Center,** located 12 miles east of International Falls on Minnesota Highway 11; **Kabetogama Lake Visitor Center,** located

Islands and large expanses of water characterize Voyageurs National Park.
MINNESOTA OFFICE OF TOURISM

in the community of Kabetogama, on the southwest shore of Kabetogama Lake; **Woodenfrog State Forest Campground,** located about 5 miles north of Kabetogama on County Route 122; **Ash River Visitor Center,** located on the south shore of the channel between Kabetogama and Namakan lakes, off County Route 129; **Ash River access,** located at the end of County Route 129 on Sullivan Bay; **Crane Lake access,** located in the town of Crane Lake, on the southwest shore of its namesake.

ADDITIONAL HELP

MA&G: 86–87, 94–95.
Camping: About 130 primitive campsites are scattered along the shorelines and islands of the park. Campgrounds are located at Woodenfrog State Forest Campground and about 2 miles west of Ash River access.
Food, gas, and lodging: International Falls, Virginia, Cook, Orr, Crane Lake.
For more information: Voyageurs National Park.

WHITEFACE RIVER

37 Whiteface Reservoir to Cotton

Character: The Whiteface is a little-traveled wilderness stream with many bouldery rapids in its upper reaches.
Length: 20 miles.
Average run time: Seven to ten hours.
Class: Class I–II.
Skill level: Intermediate, with some whitewater experience and wilderness camping skills.
Optimal flow: Call Minnesota Power at 800-582-8529 to find out how much water is being released from Whiteface Reservoir. Not much of a record is available to correlate discharge with canoeability, though 100 cfs will probably be sufficient.
Average gradient: 4.75 feet per mile.
Hazards: Watch for downed trees that might block the channel.
Maps: PRIM *Hibbing.*

The paddling: The Whiteface is a narrow, winding stream that races past banks forested with aspen, birch, spruce, fir, and occasional pine. The upper reaches are particularly intimate, only about 50 feet wide and often disappearing around a bend just a few hundred feet downstream. Frequent beaver dams can be annoying, depending on water level and size of the local beaver population. The rapids are bouldery but are not technically difficult. The main challenge lies in dodging boulders through a stretch of 100 yards or more. Through the pools, the bottom is often sandy.

The river is undeveloped for most of its length, even though County Road 52 parallels much of the run. The last mile of this stretch passes several farms and fields.

Because much of the river corridor is undeveloped, you may see moose, black bears, and even timber wolves.

Access: Whiteface Reservoir put-in: County Route 4 at the southwest end of the reservoir. **Cotton take-out:** located at the County Route 52 bridge about a mile east of U.S. Highway 53.

An alternate access is possible at the County Route 52 bridge about 6.5 miles east of Cotton.

Shuttle: 24 miles one way. About 1.25 hours.

ADDITIONAL HELP

MA&G: 76, E2; 66, A1; 65, A9.
Camping: No campsites have been developed along the river. Camp by car at the campground at the northeast end of Whiteface Reservoir at the end of Forest Road 417.
Food, gas, and lodging: Cotton, Virginia, Duluth.
For more information: MDNR Information Center (ask for information about Cloquet Valley State Forest.)

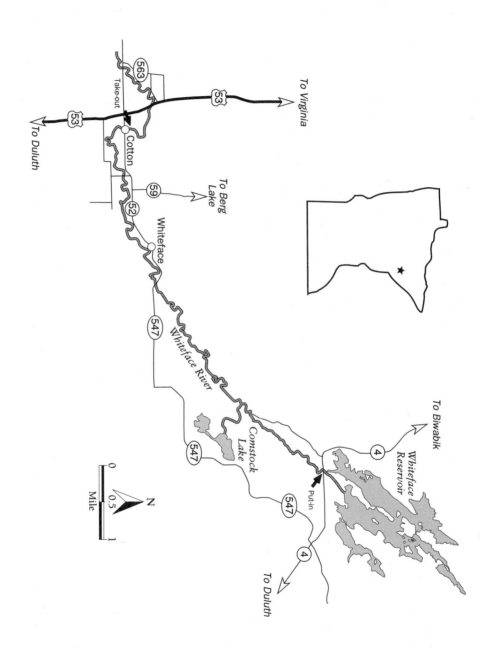

38 Cotton to St. Louis River

Character: Below Cotton, the Whiteface is a swift but gentle stream that passes a mix of woods, pasture, and hay fields.
Length: 33 miles.
Average run time: Two days. Use an alternate access to break this stretch up and make a day trip.
Class: I.
Skill level: Beginner.
Optimal flow: Not available. Below Cotton, the Whiteface is runnable much of the summer.
Average gradient: 2 feet per mile.
Hazards: No particular hazards.
Maps: PRIM *Hibbing, Duluth.*

The paddling: Below Cotton, the Whiteface flows across the flat and often boggy terrain that characterizes much of the larger St. Louis River watershed. At times the river runs swiftly. About a mile downstream from the County Route 7 bridge, the river drops about 5 feet over a quarter mile to form a notable rapids just above the confluence with Joki Creek. Otherwise there are few rapids. In places, the banks slump and drop trees into the river. You may have to work through or portage an occasional logjam. Near Meadowlands, the steep banks and forests of the upper stretch give way to a more open countryside of aspen forests and pastureland.

Fishing for walleye, northern pike, smallmouth bass, and channel catfish can be good, especially near the St. Louis River, where deep water is found.

Access: Cotton put-in: County Route 52 bridge about a mile east of U.S. Highway 53, or the County Route 52 bridge about 2 miles west of US 53. The **St. Louis River take-out** is located on the west side of the St. Louis River about 1 mile below the confluence with the Whiteface, off County Route 29.

Additional access is available at several county roads, including County Route 7, County Route 29, and County Route 133.

Shuttle: 30 miles one way. About 1.25 hours.

ADDITIONAL HELP

MA&G: 65.
Camping: No developed campsites lie along the river.
Food, gas, and lodging: Cotton, Cloquet.
For more information: MDNR, Information Center (ask for information on Cloquet Valley State Forest).

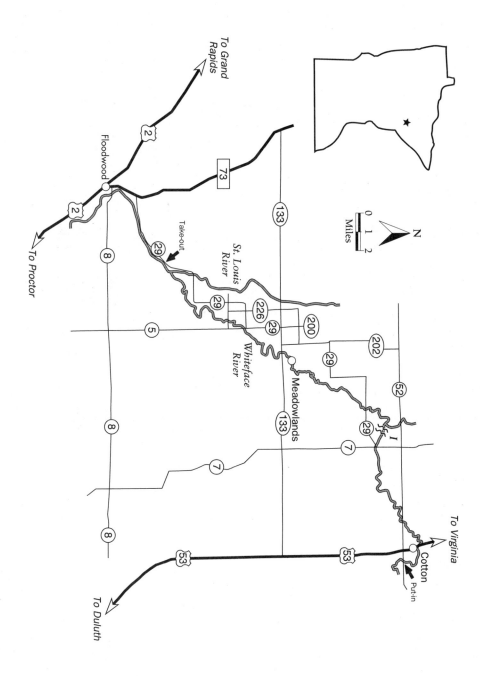

Lake Superior and the North Shore

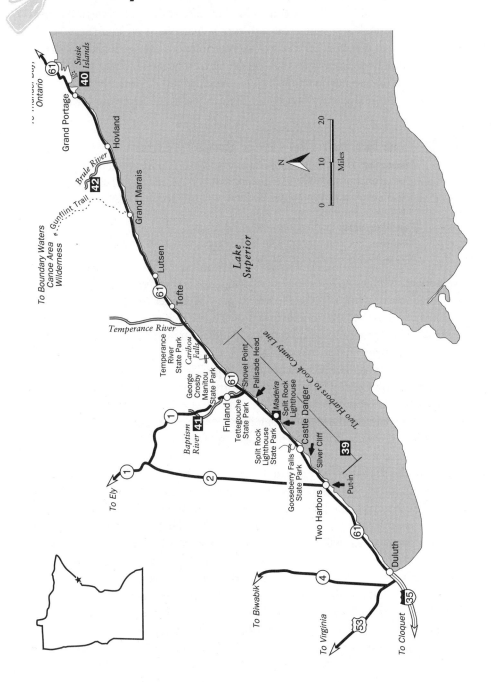

LAKE SUPERIOR

Paddling a sea kayak unlocks the beauty and mystery of the Lake Superior shoreline. A kayak is small and agile enough to explore narrow river estuaries and land on small, isolated beaches. Yet it is seaworthy enough to use on the lake perhaps four days out of five. (Even with a sea kayak, plan on being windbound occasionally.) The cliffs and points that appear so beautiful from the North Shore highway are absolutely stunning when they tower hundreds of feet above your kayak.

39 Two Harbors to Cook County Line

Character: The North Shore of Lake Superior is a rocky shoreline, often treacherous, but also beautiful. It can be traveled by canoe, but a sea kayak is better suited to these unprotected and often windswept waters.
Paddling time: One to three days.
Hazards: Sudden storms with high waves, very cold water.
Maps: MDNR *Lake Superior Water Trail.*

The paddling: Minnesota's portion of Lake Superior is sheer, unforgiving shoreline with comparatively few islands or coves to provide shelter from sudden onshore winds. Many sites that are suitable for landing and camping are privately owned. To give kayakers more sites to take shelter, paddlers are working with resorts and various government agencies to establish a "water trail" along the shore. The trail, still in its infancy, presently stretches only from Two Harbors up the shore 43 miles to the Cook County Line. Still, this short stretch includes spectacular views of Split Rock Lighthouse, Palisade Head, and Shovel Point towering far overhead. Of course, you can paddle anywhere along the Minnesota shore, carefully noting places to take shelter and finding your own campsites on public land or by asking landowners to camp, or staying at shore-side resorts.

Logistically, the easiest way to paddle a portion of Minnesota's shore is to return to where you put in. But because the shore is linear with no way to take a different route on the return, many paddlers will opt to run a shuttle, as though they were running a river. That's the advantage of having U.S. Highway 61 run along the shore. The disadvantage will be clear after a few minutes on the lake in calm weather during the summer or fall tourist season—the steady drone of traffic is annoying.

Putting in at Two Harbors, you can paddle close to the iron ore docks for a closer view of giant ore boats—some up to 1,000 feet long—as they are loaded for their trip to steel mills on the lower lakes. Keep your distance, especially when boats are underway. Watch out, too, for boats entering the harbor.

As you head northeastward, you'll paddle beneath the brow of cliffs and forested outcrops. For the next 6 miles, you'll pass several public landing sites, but between Halcyon Harbor Cabins and Gooseberry Falls State Park, there are no public sites. Land only in an emergency.

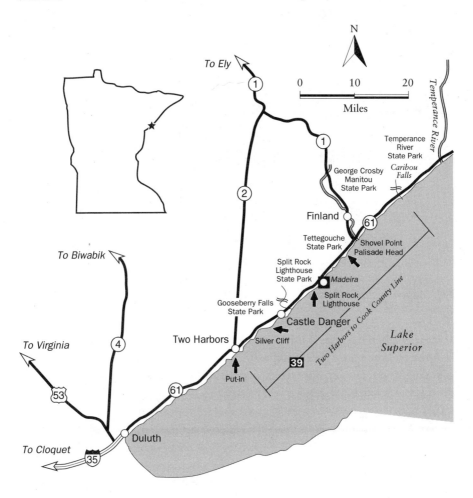

The mouth of the Gooseberry River, most likely named for French explorer Sieur des Groseilliers (whose name means "gooseberries"), is nearly blocked by a gravel bar, but you can sneak through a narrow channel into the broad, slow estuary of the river. A kayaker campsite sits next to the estuary. Follow the trails to the new interpretive center near the US 61 bridge, a new building of glass, native stone, and recycled warehouse lumber with expansive views of the lower Gooseberry River. Hike along the waterfalls on the lower river, or head farther inland on the many miles of hiking trails in the hills overlooking Lake Superior.

Northeast of Gooseberry lie two small public-use sites at Thomson Beach and Twin Points. A bit farther on, near the Split Rock River, shoreline cliffs become more prominent. Here, several bays are publicly owned and open to paddlers. After Corundum Point, you'll catch sight of Split Rock Lighthouse, perched high

Lake Superior's waves lick the cliffs below Split Rock Lighthouse. MINNESOTA
DEPARTMENT OF NATURAL RESOURCES

above the lake on a sheer cliff. The lighthouse is one of the most imposing and
beautiful on the entire lake. A Minnesota historic site, it is open for tours. Surrounding land makes up Split Rock Lighthouse State Park. Several miles of hiking
trails wind through the park.

At the north end of the park, Gold Rock Point juts into the lake. The ship
Madeira, driven ashore by a storm in 1905, lies scattered at the base of the cliff in
10 to 100 feet of water. Some wreckage is visible in calm water. A small rest area
lies just west of the point.

For the next several miles, there are few public sites for kayakers. Bayside Park
lies in the shelter of the Pellet Island breakwater. Beyond lies the mammoth
Northshore Mining Company, the site where the former owner, Reserve Mining
Company, for years discharged millions of tons of taconite tailings, building up a
broad peninsula in the lake.

Three miles beyond this industrial eyesore, you come to Palisade Head, one of
the most dramatic cliffs along the Minnesota shore. Look for sea caves and arches
at the base of the sheer cliff, which rises more than 200 feet above the lake. Palisade Head has been home to peregrine falcons, which nest on a small ledge on the
rock face. These large, fast raptors disappeared from the region because pesticides
caused their eggshells to thin. They have reappeared in recent years, after DDT
and similar chemicals were banned in the United States. A half mile beyond Palisade is a small campsite and picnic area.

In another half mile, you'll come to the mouth of the Baptism River and Tettegouche State Park, the largest and perhaps most varied of Minnesota's state parks along the shore. You can land and walk to the cart-in campground—as well as gain access to the extensive network of hiking trails that lace the park. At the very least, paddle into the estuary of the Baptism—you may have to drag up a small, gravelly rapids—for an impressive view of the rugged cliffs that flank the lower river.

Paddling northeastward again, you'll pass a small sea arch, an arch of stone eroded by the force of waves, on your way to Shovel Point, which, like Palisade Head, is part of a rhyolite lava flow 60 meters thick, laid down during a continental rift 1.1 billion years ago that formed the basin that much later would become Lake Superior.

Very few public shoreline sites are found beyond Tettegouche. Nonetheless, the mouth of the Manitou River is worth a visit. But look only! The shore is private property. With high water, the Manitou thunders into a plunge pool separated from Superior only by a gravel bar. The river slides along a cliff and out into the lake beneath the protective embrace of a sea arch. It is one of the most idyllic scenes along the shore.

Lake Superior is difficult to fish from a kayak. Lake trout, the most prevalent game fish, retreat to very deep water during the summer, when most paddlers are on the lake. Your best chance for success comes in spring and fall, when lake trout occupy shallower water near shore. Troll a spoon or deep-diving plug as you paddle. You might also hook steelhead (migratory rainbow trout), which ascend tributary streams in the spring, or pink and chinook salmon, which appear at stream mouths in fall. A few brown trout inhabit the lake and may lurk at river mouths throughout the year. You may catch trout—usually small rainbows with a few brook trout—by fly-fishing the lower reaches of small tributaries to the lake.

Access: Access to this stretch of shore is possible at several public sites. All are located just off US 61. Moving northeastward up the shore, they are Agate Bay and Burlington Bay, both in Two Harbors; Flood Bay, Stewart River, Gooseberry Falls State Park, Split Rock River, Little Two Harbors, Bayside Park, and Tettegouche State Park.

ADDITIONAL HELP

MA&G: 67, 77.
Camping: Kayak campsites are located at Gooseberry Falls State Park, Thompson Beach, Crazy Bay, and Split Rock Creek (near Corundum Point). Campgrounds are located at Burlington Bay, Gooseberry Falls State Park, Split Rock Lighthouse State Park, and Tettegouche State Park.
Food, gas, and lodging: Two Harbors, Beaver Bay. Resorts are located along much of the shore.
For more information: MDNR Information Center or Cascade Kayaks.

NORTH SHORE

The small streams that free fall off the rocky northern brow of Lake Superior are special streams for special paddlers. The streams themselves are small and rocky. In fact, they are hardly anything except rock. Most of all, they are steep, falling 100 to 200 feet per mile, and in short bursts, even more than that. From the perspective of a boat, they are simply a maelstrom of white, rushing downhill and around a bend. The most difficult rapids are simply runnable chains of waterfalls.

North Shore streams lose their water quickly. Runoff hits the rocky ground and rushes away toward the lake. The steep, small river channels have little storage capacity, and there is little groundwater to keep the rivers running. Generally speaking, streams farther up the shore (nearer to Canada), have more lakes and marshes in their headwaters and tend to hold their level better. But even these streams tend to be runnable only in late April and May and right after heavy rains. If you're planning to make a run, cultivate a local source to tell you about water levels and be ready to paddle at a moment's notice.

If you're going to paddle the North Shore, you must be able to keep your head in class IV water. Your Eskimo roll should be virtually fail-safe. Because of the difficult and continuous nature of the whitewater, rescuing swimming paddlers is difficult. Often it's impossible to fish an overturned kayak or decked canoe out of the river before it sails over a falls. Because of the difficulty of rescue, open canoes are not advised.

If you'd like to paddle the North Shore, join a whitewater club. Hook up with boaters who have paddled these streams before. At the very least, start off with a group of strong boaters. Dress warmly if it's early in the year. Be prepared to portage long and often. Don't paddle around a corner blindly, unless you see an eddy where you can pull out of the river.

We have included a couple of the easier and more familiar North Shore runs. Many others are steeper, more difficult, and more treacherous. Because of the difficulty and danger of these streams, we've deliberately been a bit sketchy in the how-to descriptions of the rapids. Rely on your own ability to read rapids and the judgment of your companions. If you have to ask, don't do it.

40 Susie Islands

Character: This cluster of islands provides protected water for a day trip—the only such spot on Minnesota's North Shore. Unfortunately, the islands themselves are not open for public use.
Paddling time: Half day.
Distance: 8 to 12 miles round trip, depending on the distance paddled among the islands.
Hazards: Sudden storms with high waves, very cold water.
Maps: NOAA navigational charts (U.S. 14968) and USGS *Grand Portage, Minn.; Pigeon Point, Minn.* (7.5-minute).

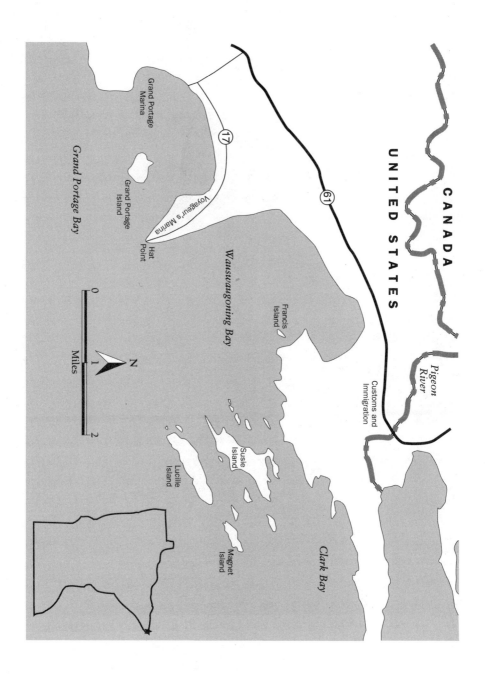

The Witch Tree, or Spirit Little Cedar, on Hat Point on the shore of Lake Superior near the Susie Islands.

The paddling: The North Shore of Minnesota is the hard edge of a stone knife, running northeastward along the lake from Duluth. Then suddenly, as Minnesota turns to Ontario, the character of this coast abruptly changes. The transition begins with the Susie Islands, the first islands in a long archipelago that stretches from the international border to the very top of Lake Superior.

The Susie Islands are named for the largest island in a cluster of 13 islands lying near to the shore at the border. Susie Island, 140 acres, makes up the Francis Lee Jaques Memorial Preserve, owned and managed by the Minnesota chapter of The Nature Conservancy. The other islands are owned by the Grand Portage Band of Ojibwa.

Landing on any of the islands is not allowed without permission of The Nature Conservancy, in the case of Susie Island, or the Grand Portage Band of Ojibwa for the others. But to paddle among them makes a pleasant trip of several hours.

Begin your trip in Grand Portage Bay. The bay was the site of one of the most important fur-trade posts on the Great Lakes, the Grand Portage fur-trade post of the North West Company, a vital relay point in the trade to the interior of Canada. A reconstructed post, Grand Portage National Monument, sits on the site today and is worth a visit.

On your way to the islands, paddle around the back side of Hat Point, which protects the west side of the bay. About a third of the way down the point, a gnarled, northern white cedar grows from the rocky shore. Known to Lake Superior travelers for hundreds of years, it is known as the Witch Tree, or Spirit Little Cedar. It is revered by some members of the Ojibwa tribe as sacred.

If the weather is calm, cut across Wauswauconing Bay to the cluster of islands. The islands nearest to shore, including Susie, lie only about a quarter mile from the mainland. The most distant islands, such as Lucille and Magnet, are less than 2 miles from shore.

The Susies are rocky and rugged, covered only by a thin veneer of spruce, fir, and bog birch and a variety of ground-hugging plants. Surrounded by Lake Superior, the islands are bathed by cool, moist air, creating a micro-climate quite different from the conditions found on the mainland. Among the plants living in this shoreline environment are purple crowberry, northern eyebright, pearlwort, arctic lupine, alpine bistort, and slender hairgrass, which are more commonly found hundreds of miles to the north. On the interior of the islands, thick layers of moss form a carpet up to 3 feet thick. This "bog blanket" of sphagnum moves gradually to the cliffy shorelines and "calves" into the lake. Carnivorous sundew and butterwort capture insects on their sticky leaves. Paddling within arm's reach of the cliffs, you'll see plants that cling to craggy perches and the colorful lichen that finds sustenance on the rock.

For centuries, Indians of the area have netted whitefish and lake trout. Many Ojibwa band members continue the tradition, tending nets strung in the shallow waters between the islands. The most prominent wildlife among the islands are mergansers and loons. Herring gulls form rookeries on the outer islands.

Access: The nearest boat access is the Voyageur Marina. From Grand Portage, drive about 2 miles on County Route 17 along the western edge of Grand Portage Bay to the marina.

ADDITIONAL HELP

MA&G: 79 (inset).
Camping: No camping is allowed on the islands. Auto camping is possible at Voyageur Marina or the tribal marina on the east side of the bay.
Food, gas, and lodging: Grand Portage, Grand Marais.
For more information: The Nature Conservancy, Grand Portage Band of Ojibwa, Cascade Kayaks.

41 Baptism River

Character: Typical of North Shore streams, the Baptism is steep, twisting, and potentially lethal.
Length: 3.3 miles.
Average run time: Three to five hours.
Class: III–VI.
Skill level: Expert. Like all North Shore rivers, the Baptism should not be attempted except by accomplished whitewater boaters who have bomb-proof rolls and are comfortable in class IV water.
Optimal flow: Medium to high water is necessary: At least 2 feet on the gauge below the U.S. Highway 61 bridge. Check the weekly stream flow report on the MDNR website: http://solum,soils,umn,edu/researach/climatology/doc/streams—flow—weekly.html
Average gradient: 136 feet per mile.
Hazards: Several unrunnable falls give little warning. Stay on your toes and be ready to grab an eddy.
Maps: USGS topo *Doyle Lake, MN; Finland, MN; Illgen City, MN* (all 7.5-minute); MDNR *Tettegouche State Park* map shows foot trails and some river features.

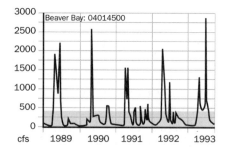

400 cfs = minimum for good paddling

41 Baptism River

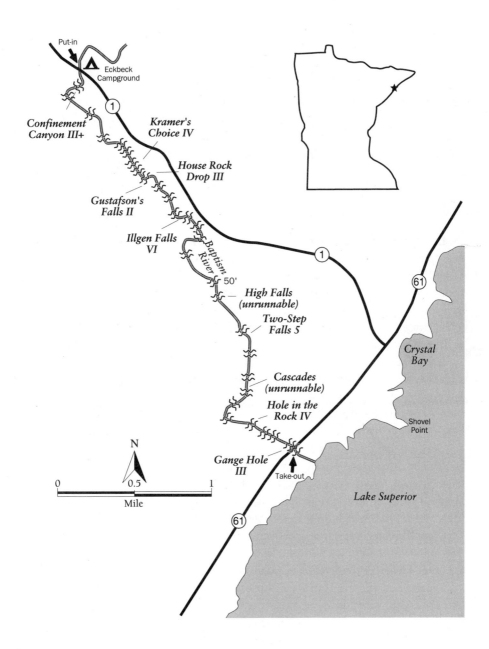

Put-in
Eckbeck Campground
Confinement Canyon III+
Kramer's Choice IV
House Rock Drop III
Gustafson's Falls II
Illgen Falls VI
Baptism River
50'
High Falls (unrunnable)
Two-Step Falls 5
Cascades (unrunnable)
Hole in the Rock IV
Gange Hole III
Take-out
Crystal Bay
Shovel Point
Lake Superior

N
0   0.5   1
Mile

The paddling: The Baptism is as good an introduction as any to the North Shore streams. It's easier than most (albeit, only slightly). It's also accessible by road and foot trail, so you can walk out if you tire of portaging and being scared to death.

Put in at the Eckbeck Campground. The river takes a sharp right bend and tumbles through a long stretch of bouldery class III rapids known as **Confinement Canyon.**

Below the canyon, the river opens up and lets up slightly. Soon large boulders appear in the river, signaling the beginning of **Kramer's Choice,** class IV. Scout this first, then aim left of the big boulder that blocks the middle of the channel.

Soon the river drops over **Gustafson's Falls,** a difficult class II drop of about 7 feet that pillows off the right cliff as the river bends left. After a short straightaway, the river bends hard right at **House Rock Drop,** a class III drop with a hole on the far left.

After about 0.3 mile, the Baptism takes a sharp, left bend and plunges 30 feet over **Illgen Falls.** This sheer, class VI drop has been run at certain levels, but to do so is a form of whitewater roulette that sane paddlers will pass by. Portage left.

Put in below the falls, but you'll be able to run less than a half mile before you must pull out for **High Falls,** the second-highest falls in the state (after the like-named falls on the Pigeon river). The footbridge for the Superior Hiking Trail, about 100 feet above the falls, marks the beginning of the portage to the left. Put in below the falls. When the water is high, great pillows of foam pile below the falling water (which creates a significant wind), and it's fun to paddle through it, as though navigating a bubble bath.

In another quarter mile, the Baptism roars over **Two Step Falls,** one of the most difficult and trickiest of the river's runnable rapids. This class 5 drop consists of two 10-foot waterfalls in quick succession. There's enough rock in the first falls to catch the bow of a boat and pile-drive an unlucky paddler onto the foot pegs. The second falls has a large hydraulic at its base. Most paddlers will want to portage left.

Get back on the river, but you can't relax for long. In about a quarter mile, you'll start the portage (on the left) for the **Cascades,** a long, sloping, unrunnable falls. Put back into the river in the large plunge pool below the Cascades. In a few hundred yards, after the river splits around an island and rejoins, the river narrows and drops through **Hole in the Rock,** class IV.

Class III water follows on down to just above the US 61 bridge. Most of the flow funnels right and drops over a low drop that forms a sticky hydraulic known as **Gauge Hole** (for the river-level gauge nearby).

Beyond this, the river flows into the estuary at Lake Superior. Take out on the left, about 200 yards downstream of the US 61 bridge. Carry your boat back up the hiking path to the parking lot next to the old highway bridge. If you're up for a side trip and Lake Superior isn't rough, paddle to the river's mouth and then southwest about a mile to the 200-foot Palisades. Or paddle northeast a half mile to see the massive lava headland called Shovel Point.

Tettegouche State Park, at more than 9,000 acres, is the crown jewel of Minnesota state parks. It encompasses, in addition to much of the Baptism River, nearly 20 miles of hiking trails, with views of the Baptism, a self-guided interpretive trail along Shovel Point, and several overlooks from the high granite knobs in the park.

Steelhead run up the Baptism in spring as far as the Cascades. In the fall various species of salmon make the trip. They require some specialized tackle and techniques to catch, but the fight of these big fish is exciting. Four small inland lakes provide fishing for northern pike and walleye.

Access: The **Eckbeck Campground put-in** is located where Minnesota Highway 1 crosses the Baptism about 2.7 miles northwest of US 61.

Shuttle: 4 miles one way. About 15 minutes.

ADDITIONAL HELP

MA&G: 77, E10.
Camping: Eckbeck Campground, Tettegouche State Park.
Food, gas, and lodging: Beaver Bay, Silver Bay, Finland.
For more information: MDNR Information Center can provide information on Tettegouche State Park and Finland State Forest (including Eckbeck Campground). The MDNR will be able to provide little information about the river itself. For general conditions, call Cascade Kayaks.

42 Brule River

Character: The Brule roars through one big, distinctive rapids after another as it races toward the big lake.
Length: 5.8 miles.
Average run time: Four to eight hours.
Class: III–5.
Skill level: Expert.
Optimal flow: Medium to high. At least 1 foot on the hand-painted gauge on the cliff at the footbridge near the campground in Judge C.R. Magney State Park. The MDNR does not report on this gauge. The Brule holds its level better than most North Shore streams because it is larger and has more lakes in its headwaters.
Average gradient: 129 feet per mile.
Hazards: Big drops don't give you much notice. The take-out to portage Devil's Kettle is really tricky, and the penalty for screwing up is severe—maybe fatal.
Maps: USGS *Tom Lake, MN, Marr Island, MN* (7.5 minute); MDNR *Judge C.R. Magney State Park* map shows foot trails and some river features.

42 Brule River

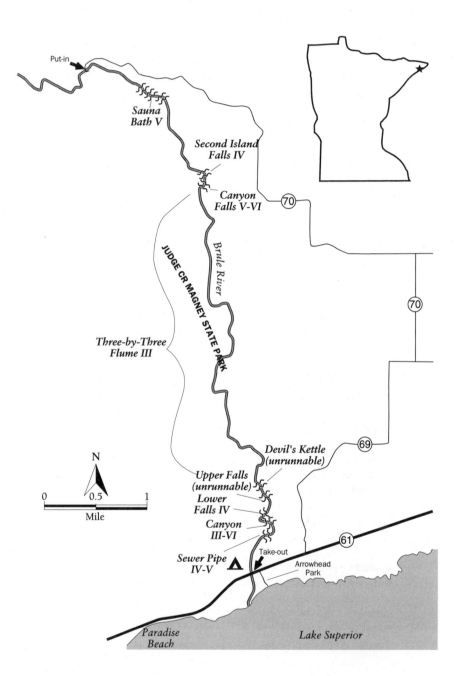

Put-in

*Sauna
Bath V*

*Second Island
Falls IV*

*Canyon
Falls V-VI*

70

Brule River

JUDGE CR MAGNEY STATE PARK

*Three-by-Three
Flume III*

N

0   0.5   1
Mile

*Devil's Kettle
(unrunnable)*

69

*Upper Falls
(unrunnable)*

*Lower
Falls IV*

*Canyon
III-VI*

*Sewer Pipe
IV-V*   ▲   Take-out

Arrowhead
Park

61

*Paradise
Beach*   *Lake Superior*

The paddling: The run begins with a little class II, warm-up water. But after about 0.5 mile, the river kicks into high gear with a class 5 screamer called **Sauna Bath,** for the old sauna house sitting by the riverside. It's a long, steep, bouldery drop that requires deft moves in fast, heavy current.

The river eases up after Sauna Bath, but not much, running through class III to class IV water. About a mile below Sauna Bath, the river comes to **Second Island Falls,** a two-step drop with a powerful hole on the left. It rates class IV. Scout and portage on the right. Immediately downstream, the Brule necks down to a slot and drops 30 to 40 feet over Canyon Falls. Once always portaged, this class 5–VI drop has been run in recent years. Portage right.

Now you can relax (sort of) as the Brule runs through a long roller coaster, nearly 3 miles of class III water called **Three-by-Three Flume.** No particular problems here, provided you're comfortable in long strings of dancing waves and boulders. The problem is that the ride will lull you into a trance, and that would be a real shame, because the river takes a sudden right bend, splits around a tiny spit of rock and plunges over **Devil's Kettle,** one of the most distinctive falls along the shore. Half the river drops about 50 feet to the river below; the other half sails over the ledge and suddenly disappears into a huge hole in the bedrock. Where this underground cavern rejoins the river, or even if it does, is an enduring mystery. Of more immediate concern to boaters is the portage, which is on river left. Don't bet on your chances if you miss the take-out.

While you're portaging Devil's Kettle, keep on going around **Upper Falls,** another sheer drop, for a portage of about 0.3 mile on the left bluff, high above the water. Find your way back down to the river and put back in right below Upper Falls. Run downstream about 0.25 mile to **Lower Falls,** a big, straight-ahead, class IV drop with a churning hole at the bottom.

The river runs through a deep, picturesque canyon for about 0.3 mile. But don't get lost in the scenery, because several large, sticky hydraulics block your path. Rate this section class III in medium water, difficult class IV in high.

The canyon ends with **Sewer Pipe,** class IV in medium water, class 5 in high. It is one of the strangest rapids on the river. As the canyon narrows to about 20 feet, the river slams into the right wall and spirals into a vortex as it drops over a 6-foot falls. It is a tough rapids to read, giving some paddlers a smooth ride and trashing others.

About 0.25 mile below Sewer Pipe, the Brule drops over **Footbridge Falls,** a class III drop named for the nearby footbridge near the park campground. Just downstream is the take-out at the US 61 bridge.

Judge C.R. Magney State Park takes in about 4,500 acres, including the final 7 miles of the Brule. Scenic hiking trails flank both sides of the river. You can fish for brook and rainbow trout in the Brule and a tributary, Gauthier Creek. In spring, steelhead ascend the Brule. In fall, the river receives runs of various salmon.

Access: Mons Creek put-in: From the US 61 bridge at the mouth of the river, head east 0.5 mile; turn left on County Road 69 and drive generally north about 2 miles to the junction with County Road 70. Turn left (north) on CR 70, cross the Flute Reed River twice and then cross Mons Creek. Continue about 0.75 mile past Mons Creek and carry your boat left (south) to the river. Watch out for posted land. The **Lake Superior take-out** is located at the US 61 bridge about 0.4 mile above the river's mouth.

Shuttle: 8 miles one way. About 30 minutes.

ADDITIONAL HELP

MA&G: 79, D9.
Camping: Judge C.R. Magney State Park.
Food, gas, and lodging: Grand Marais.
For more information: MDNR Information Center can provide information about Judge C.R. Magney State Park, but not about the kayaking itself. For general information, call Cascade Kayaks.

Northwest

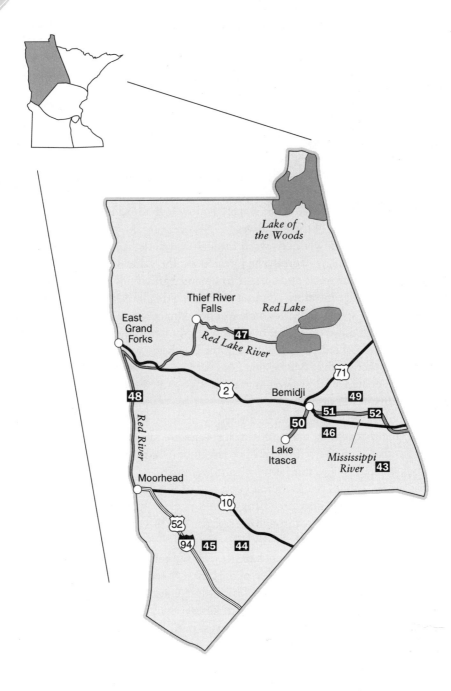

Lake of
the Woods

Thief River
Falls

Red Lake

East
Grand
Forks

Red Lake River 47

Red River

48

2

Bemidji

71

49

51 52

50 46

Lake
Itasca

Mississippi
River 43

Moorhead

10

52

94 45 44

43 Boy River

Character: The Boy River is a quiet, slow stream that wends past unsettled forest and marsh.
Length: 17 miles.
Average run time: Six to eight hours.
Class: Quiet.
Skill level: Beginner.
Optimal flow: No gauge. With no rapids, the river is runnable in all but the lowest water.
Average gradient: Less than 1 foot per mile.
Hazards: No particular hazards.
Maps: Chippewa National Forest *Boy River Canoe Route.*

The paddling: Begin your trip where County Road 129 crosses Laura Brook (also known as Trelipe Creek) just upstream from where it empties into Inguadona Lake. The name of this long, narrow lake name comes from the Ojibwa word equademog, meaning "edge of the slope." Follow Inguadona northward about 2 miles to the beginning of the Boy River.

The river flows slowly northward through a well-defined channel with low banks and often marshy shores. The forest along the water varies from lowland conifers such as tamarack and spruce, to upland hardwoods such as aspen and birch, to open sedge meadow. About a mile downstream of Inguadona is the remains of an old "splash dam," a simple wooden dam used to build a head of water to carry saw logs down on a surge of water when the gates were opened. The once-expansive stands of red and white pine in the Boy River watershed attracted loggers from farther south in Minnesota. Logs cut from the Boy River country in the 1870s were floated far downstream to the mills of T.B. Walker's Red River Lumber Company in Minneapolis.

The Boy River is clear, slow, and weedy—in many ways more lake-like than riverine. For that reason, many of its fish species are more commonly associated with lakes than with rivers. These include largemouth bass, crappies, yellow perch, and rock bass, as well as northern pike and walleye.

For nearly 2 miles the route follows a bay of Boy Lake. Downstream of the lake, the river spreads into large beds of wild rice, which provide an important crop every fall. Ricers move through the ripe rice two to a canoe. The person in the stern poles the canoe through the thick vegetation while a person sitting amidships uses two sticks to first draw a bunch of rice over the gunwale and second to knock the ripe heads of rice into the bottom of the canoe. In fact, wild rice grows so thick on the Boy that a canoe trip can be difficult in August when the rice is thickest. Within the boundaries of the Leech Lake Reservation, only licensed residents of the reservation and tribe members can harvest rice.

Most paddlers will want to end their trip at County Route 8, before reaching the windy expanses of Leech Lake. If you wish to continue downstream to the

43 Boy River

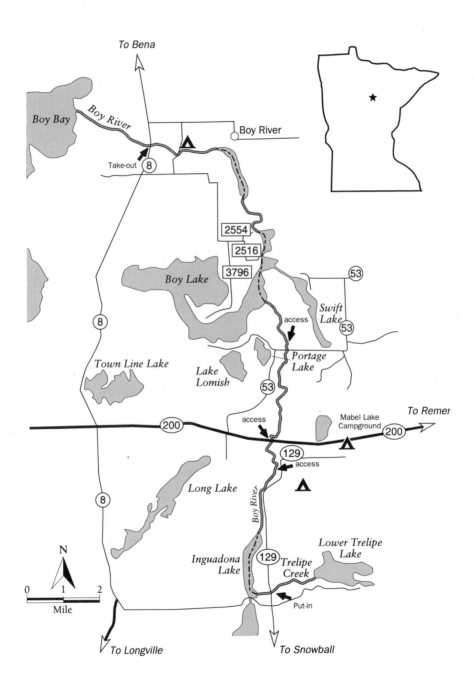

lake, take out at Blackduck Point or Sugar Point. Watch out for winds and high waves on Leech.

Access: The **Lower Trelipe Lake put-in** is located at the east end of the lake, off an unnamed road. From Longville, drive east 10 miles on County Route 7, turn north (left) on Forest Road 2103 for about 1.5 miles to the turn off toward Lower Trelipe Lake. To reach the **County Route 8 take-out** from Longville, drive north about 14 miles on County Route 8 to the Boy River.

An alternate access is located at Minnesota Highway 200, about 8.5 miles into the trip.

Shuttle: 22 miles one way. About one hour.

ADDITIONAL HELP

MA&G: 63, C–B6; 62, A5.
Camping: River campsites are located on the east (right) side of the river, about a mile upstream of MN 200, and on the south (left) side of the stream at the County Road 51 bridge about a mile upstream of the take-out.
Food, gas, and lodging: Longville.
For more information: Chippewa National Forest, Forest Supervisor's Office.

44 Glendalough State Park

Character: Two clear lakes in west-central Minnesota provide a pleasant paddling trip and an interesting contrast in fishing opportunities.
Paddling time: Two hours.
Hazards: No particular hazards.
Maps: MDNR *Glendalough State Park.*

The paddling: Rimmed by bulrushes and hardwoods, Molly Stark and Annie Battle Lakes are two clear, sparkling gems set in the rolling hills of west-central Minnesota. They are among the major features of Glendalough State Park, a new park that once was a corporate retreat of Cowles Media, one-time owner of the Star Tribune. As corporate retreat, it was visited by Daytons and Pillsburys, various governors, and even a couple of noteworthies named Eisenhower and Nixon. In 1990, Cowles donated the 1,924 acres to The Nature Conservancy, which in turn gave the property to the state. Glendalough is a mix of prairie and wooded hills. The property surrounds or touches six lakes with more than 9 miles of undeveloped shoreline, one of the last large tracts of natural lakeshore in the area. More than 600 acres of old fields are being reseeded in prairie. Some tracts of native prairie are routinely burned or mowed to beat back sumac and oak.

Molly Stark and Annie Battle Lakes both offer good fishing for largemouth bass, northern pike, and sunfish. What sets Annie Battle apart from other lakes in

44 Glendalough State Park

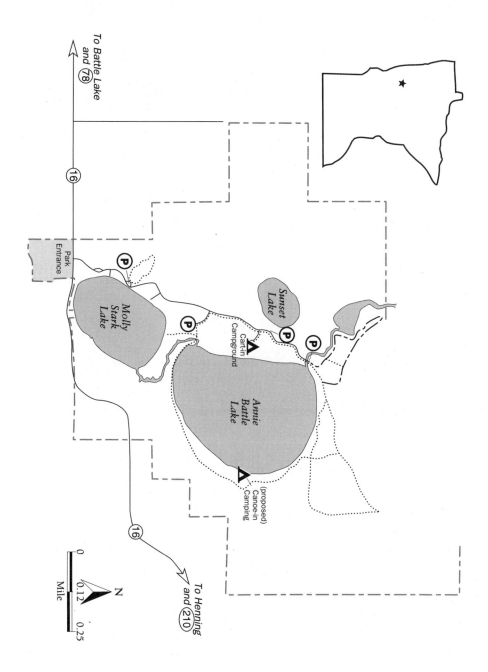

A canoe on Annie Battle Lake in Glendalough State Park. MINNESOTA OFFICE OF TOURISM

the state are the "heritage fishery" regulations in effect on the lake. On Annie Battle Lake, anglers must release all largemouth bass and northern pike. Each angler may keep only five sunfish, compared with 30 in most other lakes. Fishermen may not use gas or electric motors, electronic fish finders, depth finders, GPS units, or electronic temperature and pH meters. The catch-and-release is intended to improve the average size of fish—to replicate, if you will, fishing in the "good old days." Restrictions on gear are also designed to recreate the atmosphere of the past. Molly Stark, by contrast, has no special regulations. A small stream about 0.3 mile long connects the two lakes.

Access: Put in at the boat ramp on the west shore of Molly Stark Lake or the northwest corner of Annie Battle Lake.

ADDITIONAL HELP

MA&G: 52, C2.
Camping: Glendalough has a cart-in campground. Park your car and cart your gear a short distance to the site. It's quieter and more peaceful than the usual drive-up campground.
Food, gas, and lodging: Fergus Falls.
For more information: Glendalough State Park, MDNR Information Center.

45 Otter Tail River

Character: The Otter Tail races through several rapids, some rather challenging, as it passes woods, marsh, and some open country.
Length: 12.8 miles.
Average run time: Four to six hours.
Class: I–II, approaching class III in very high water.
Skill level: Intermediate.
Optimal flow: At least 110 cfs spilling over **Diversion Dam** at the start of the run. Otter Tail Power Company is required to release at least that amount during April and May.
Average gradient: 5.9 feet per mile.
Hazards: Wall Lake Bridge, located about halfway through the run, is extremely dangerous in high water, when there is no clearance for a canoe. The bridge is slated to be removed soon. Till then, watch out!
Maps: No good maps are now available. The MDNR plans to publish canoe route maps after the hazardous Wall Lake Bridge is removed.

The paddling: For many years, very little water ran through the natural channel of the river. Instead, it was diverted for use in a power plant and returned to the channel near the take-out for this run. Under a recent agreement negotiated between Otter Tail Power Company and the MDNR and federal officials, the power producer will maintain minimum flows through the channel for the benefit of fish and canoeists.

45 Otter Tail River

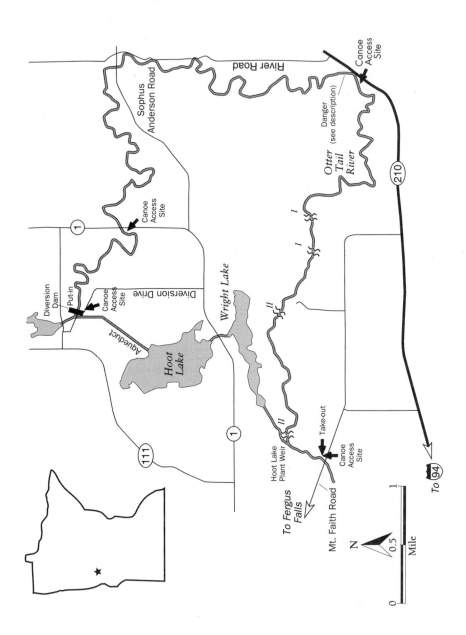

For the first half of the run, the Otter Tail is placid. Its clear water flows past farms and woodlands. Downed trees block part of the channel, but since the current is moderate, they aren't much of a hazard unless the water is very high.

About 8 miles into the run, the river squeezes through the Wall Lake Bridge and its abutments. In appearance and effect, the underpass resembles a square hole cut in a dam. At most water levels, there's no problem. But in high water, the river flushes through the opening, leaving no room for a canoe. Then, portage either side. The MDNR hopes to soon remove this hazard.

Downstream from the bridge, the river's gradient increases, passing through riffles and then through two class I rapids. In Broken-Down Dam Park, the river tumbles through the remains of two old dams, creating a long stretch of class II rapids, which end as the river squeezes between the remnants of the second dam. This stretch borders on class III in high flows. Portage left if you wish.

About a mile downstream, the Otter Tail plunges over the **Hoot Lake Plant Weir**, a low dam that has been modified to allow the relatively safe passage of canoes over a drop of about 3 feet. Do scout the dam before running it to make sure that a dangerous hydraulic has not formed at the particular level at which you are seeing the river. Under medium levels, the drop rates class II.

About a half mile downstream the run ends at the Mount Faith Road take-out.

Access: The **Diversion Dam put-in** is located about 3 miles northeast of Fergus Falls via County Road 111. The **Mount Faith Road take-out** is less than a mile east of town at the Mount Faith Road bridge.

Shuttle: 3.7 miles one way. About 15 minutes.

ADDITIONAL HELP

MA&G: 51, C9.
Camping: No riverside camps are available. Camp by car at Glendalough State Park or Maplewood State Park.
Food, gas, and lodging: Fergus Falls.
For more information: MDNR Information Center.

46 Pike Bay Connection

Character: This trail of waterways and portages through woods, streams, and lakes makes a tough but pleasant day trip with historical overtones.
Paddling time: Three to six hours.
Hazards: Poison ivy, mosquitoes, wading.
Maps: Chippewa National Forest *Pike Bay Connection*.

46 Pike Bay Connection

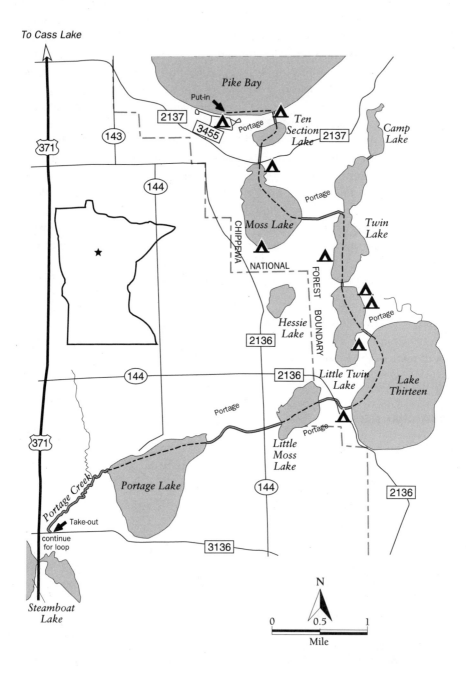

To Cass Lake

Pike Bay

Put-in

2137

3455

Portage

Ten Section Lake

2137

Camp Lake

143

144

371

CHIPPEWA

Moss Lake

NATIONAL

FOREST BOUNDARY

Twin Lake

Portage

Hessie Lake

2136

Little Twin Lake

Lake Thirteen

Portage

144

2136

Portage

Little Moss Lake

2136

371

Portage Creek

Portage

Portage Lake

144

3136

Take-out

continue for loop

Steamboat Lake

N

0   0.5   1

Mile

The paddling: In traveling the Pike Bay Connection you will trace the footprints of Woodland Indians who have used this short route between Cass Lake and Leech Lake for hundreds, perhaps thousands, of years. A large village, dating to A.D. 600 to 800, was located at the present site of Pike Bay Campground. Undoubtedly, these people were intimately familiar with this canoe route. Explorers Zebulon Pike, Joseph Nicollet, and Henry Schoolcraft paddled these waters nearly 200 years ago.

The following route can be run in either direction. The directions are for a trip from north to south.

From the boat ramp at Pike Bay Campground, paddle east several hundred yards to the stream at the south end of Pike Bay. Portage right about 30 yards around a small dam. Continue along the channel to Ten Section Lake, a shallow, wild-rice lake where you are likely to see waterfowl and ospreys. In late summer, when the rice is ripe, you may have to force your way through thick beds of vegetation.

Paddle to the south shore of Ten Section Lake and a small creek to Moss Lake. Depending on the water level, you may have to push and drag your canoe. In low water, you can portage along the left bank. Carry over Forest Road 2137 into Moss Lake.

Proceed along the east shore, where a turquoise blaze marks the portage into Twin Lake. The trail follows a small road and then jogs right to follow a trail. The portage, which totals about 850 yards, has two canoe rests.

Paddle to the south end of Twin Lake and through the channel into Little Twin Lake. Pass along the east shore of Little Twin to the 165-yard portage into Lake Thirteen. Along the shore of this clear-water lake are stands of old-growth pine. Paddle to the southwest shore to the 75-yard carry into Little Moss Lake. The portage begins at the boat ramp, turns right on Forest Road 2136 for about 285 yards to a trail just north of a swamp, and turns left on a trail to Little Moss Lake.

Head southwest across Little Moss Lake to the take-out just south of an old stand of jack pine and aspen. Fight your way through marsh grass and floating bog to reach shore. Portage 1,300 yards along a flat trail with two canoe rests. It follows a trail to County Route 144, jogs right about 20 yards, and then left down a sandy road to another trail and Portage Lake.

Paddle along the north shore of Portage Lake to a small stream at the northwest corner. You'll have to duck and push your way through two large culverts at normal water levels. The second culvert is the take-out at Forest Road 3136.

The Pike Bay Connection is a small part of a 120-mile loop called the Chippewa Headwaters Loop. Chippewa National Forest provides a map to help you navigate the route, which continues south down Steamboat Bay Lake and the Steamboat River into Leech Lake, east along the Leech Lake River, up the Mississippi River to Lake Winnibigoshish, and west on "Winni" and the Mississippi back to Cass Lake and Pike Bay.

Access: The **Pike Bay put-in** is located on the south shore at the Forest Service campground and boat ramp along the south shore. From Cass Lake drive south 3 miles on Minnesota Highway 371; turn east on FR 2137 and drive about 2 miles; follow Forest Road 3455 north to the access. To reach the **FR 3136 take-out**, drive south 7.5 miles from Cass Lake on MN 371; turn left (east) on FR 3136 and drive a few hundred yards to Portage Creek.

ADDITIONAL HELP

MA&G: 72, E2.

Camping: Shoreline campsites are located at the south shore of Pike Bay near the first portage, at the north and south ends of Moss Lake, on the west shore of Twin Lake, along the east shore of Little Twin Lake (three sites), and at the southwest shore of Lake Thirteen.

Food, gas, and lodging: Cass Lake, Walker.

For more information: Chippewa National Forest, Cass Lake Ranger District.

47 Red Lake River

Character: With swift water and several easy rapids, this section of the Red Lake River is the best bet for paddlers in the Red River Valley.

Length: 36 miles.

Average run time: Two days.

Class: I.

Skill level: Beginner to intermediate.

Optimal flow: Above 1,101 feet at the U.S. Army Corps of Engineers gauge just downstream of the Thief River Falls Municipal Power Plant. For the reading, call the MDNR or the power plant, listed in appendix.

Average gradient: 5.2 feet per mile.

Hazards: No particular hazards.

Maps: MDNR *Red Lake River Canoe Route*.

The paddling: The Red Lake River heads up in giant Lower Red Lake and flows slowly through the bog country of north-central Minnesota, a land where soils are perpetually waterlogged and plant communities are dominated by runty black spruce, sphagnum moss, and various sedges.

In its lower reaches, the Red Lake River meanders slowly across the Red

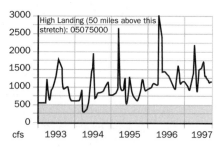

500 cfs = estimated minimum for good paddling

47 Red Lake River

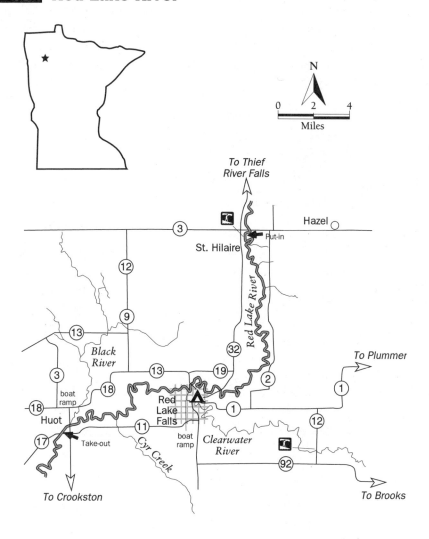

River Valley, the one-time bed of Glacial Lake Agassiz, a land where the eye can see for dozens of miles in all directions.

It is in between these two griddle-flat landscapes—essentially from St. Hilaire to Huot—that the Red Lake River is most interesting to canoeists. Here, the river drops from the higher ground that once surrounded Glacial Lake Agassiz down through the old beach lines of the ancient lake. In the process, it flows quickly through sand and gravel riffles and even flows through bouldery class I rapids.

Start your trip at the St. Hilaire access. Throughout much of this stretch the banks are steep, high, and wooded. In places, the bluffs have eroded and slumped, leaving impressive cliffs of clay and sand. After several miles, the gradient increases and the frequency and difficulty of the rapids increases a bit. At lower water levels you'll have to maneuver between boulders and shoals.

At Red Lake Falls is a popular campground that paddlers often use before continuing on down to Huot the next day.

Just downstream from Huot is the Old Crossing Treaty State Historical Wayside Park, where in 1863 Ojibwa Indians ceded several million acres of land for white settlement of the Red River Valley. This was an important crossing of the Red River Oxcart Trail, which ran from Fort Garry, where Winnipeg now stands, to St. Paul.

With its moderate gradient and numerous riffles and rapids, the St. Hilaire–Huot stretch has good fishing for walleye, smallmouth bass, northern pike, and channel catfish.

While the St. Hilaire–Huot stretch is probably the most popular stretch to paddle, it is by no means the only one. You can put in at Lower Red Lake, though you will need a permit (for a small fee) from the Red Lake Reservation to cross tribal property. Much of the stretch within the reservation boundaries has been channelized. Two dams must be portaged.

You can also put in at one of several landings downstream from the reservation and paddle to Thief River Falls or St. Hilaire. Farmland flanks the river for much of this stretch; near Thief River Falls you'll see many homes. In Thief River Falls, portage the power dam on river left (east) about 100 yards.

You can also paddle downstream from Huot. By now, the river is losing its gradient and beginning its meandering path across the bed of Glacial Lake Agassiz. Beware of the remains of a dam about 5 miles downstream from County Route 11. You'll also have to avoid a dam at Crookston and two in East Grand Forks. This lower stretch of river is known for good walleye and channel catfish fishing.

Throughout its length, the river corridor provides good habitat for wildlife, including white-tailed deer, beavers, mink, raccoons, and various species of waterfowl, shorebirds, and songbirds.

Access: The **St. Hilaire put-in** is located in town, just east of Minnesota Highway 32. The **Huot take-out** is located in town, such as it is.

Shuttle: 20 miles one way. About one hour.

ADDITIONAL HELP

MA&G: 81, D–E8; 69, A6.
Camping: River camping is possible at Red Lake Falls and Huot. (Although it lies outside the featured trip, a river campsite is also located about 3 miles downstream from Thief River Falls.
Food, gas, and lodging: Red Lake Falls, Thief River Falls, Crookston.
For more information: MDNR Information Center.

48 Red River of the North

Character: Besides weaving a strip of natural green through country that is intensively farmed, the Red River offers incredible catfish fishing.

Length: 394 miles. Many shorter trips are possible.

Average run time: The entire stretch would keep you going for about three weeks.

Class: Quiet.

Skill level: Beginner.

Optimal flow: Rarely too low to paddle. The Red River often floods in spring. Stay off in extremely high water.

Average gradient: 0.5 foot per mile.

Hazards: Watch out for downed trees, especially in the narrow upper reaches. Avoid dams at Breckenridge, Christine, Fargo-Moorhead (4), and Grand Forks.

Maps: MDNR PRIM *Fergus Falls, Moorhead, Ada, Crookston, Thief River Falls, Hallock.*

The paddling: The Red River is predominantly muddy and thoroughly flat but is interesting because it is such an unusual river. For starters, it runs nearly 400 miles along the Minnesota-North Dakota border over a straight-line distance of less than 200 miles. The length is taken up by the river's wormlike meanders. The river's indecision is a result of the second notable fact of the Red, the incredible flatness of its valley. Indeed, "valley" is an exaggeration, for the watershed within many miles of the river is as level as a griddle, the ancient lacustrine sediments of Glacial Lake Agassiz. There are no real rapids along its course. Do watch out for low-head dams, though.

Despite its sinuosity, the Red was an important avenue of transportation. Hudson's Bay Company maintained a post in the Red River Valley. In 1871 railroad magnate James J. Hill began shipping freight on the Red River by steamboat. Goods traveled downstream from Manitoba to Moorhead, where they were loaded on cars of the Northern Pacific. There was no further use for steamboats on the Red after 1879, when trains spanned the distance between Winnipeg and St. Paul.

Nowadays, the Red River Valley is one of the most intensively farmed landscapes in existence. The verdant bottomlands and thin fringe of woods on the riverbanks screen out the surrounding farmland and enable canoeists to imagine a time when the valley was undeveloped and bison still roamed the plains. Drifting along,

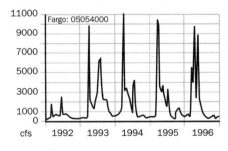

No minimum determined

48 Red River of the North

Emerson, Manitoba

CANADA

Hallock

Drayton

Warren

Alvarado

East Grand Forks

Grand Forks

Crookston

NORTH DAKOTA

MINNESOTA

Climax

Hillsboro

Halstad

Gardner

Fargo-Moorhead: Four dams.

Fargo

Moorhead

Moorhead: Two accesses.

Christine

Breckenridge: Dam with boat ramps above and below.

Breckenridge

Wahpeton, ND

N

0   20   40
Miles

you're likely to see beaver, white-tailed deer, and raccoons. River banks rise higher as you move northward.

Another unusual trait of the Red is its robust channel catfish population, one of the northernmost occurrences of this species. The Red is probably the best place in the state to catch a channel catfish weighing more than 20 pounds. Fishing for them is a bit different from catching them in other rivers because the channel, especially in the lower reaches where the fish are largest, is scoured clean of most debris and features. What is left is an undulating trough of clay. Simply anchor right above a hole, where the streambed slopes into somewhat deeper water. Cast out cut fish threaded on a large hook, weighted with a 1-ounce sinker. Wait for 5 minutes. If there's no bite, reel in and cast again. After a half dozen casts, move to a new hole.

Access: Many accesses are available along the river's length. Even so, they are widely spaced. Use county roads as well to make short trips. Consult *DeLorme's Minnesota Atlas & Gazetteer* for details.

ADDITIONAL HELP

MA&G: 50, 58, 68, 80, 90.

Camping: There are no developed campsites along the river. With mud everywhere and little public land, there aren't many natural campsites open to canoeists. Campgrounds in the area include Buffalo River State Park, Old Mill State Park, and Lake Bronson State Park.

Food, gas, and lodging: Breckenridge; Wahpeton, ND; Fargo, ND; Moorhead, Crookston, Grand Forks, ND; East Grand Forks, Hallock.

For more information: U.S. Army Corps of Engineers web page.

49 Turtle River

Character: The Turtle River provides an intimate and generally placid route through thick northern forest.
Length: 15 miles.
Average run time: Five to seven hours.
Class: I.
Skill level: Beginner.
Optimal flow: No gauge readings available. The river is runnable in all but very low conditions.
Average gradient: Less than 1 foot per mile.
Hazards: No particular hazards.
Maps: Chippewa National Forest.

The paddling: The Turtle River winds gently through the marshes and sparsely settled woods north of Cass Lake. Keep an eye out for bald eagles, many of which nest in the area.

49 Turtle River

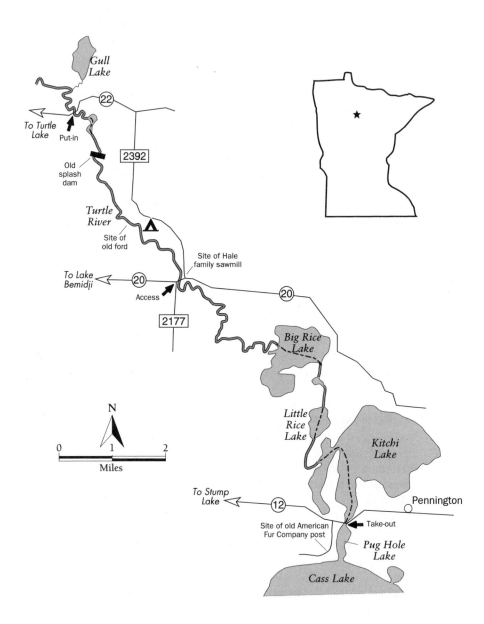

Gull
Lake

22

To Turtle
Lake
Put-in

2392

Old
splash
dam

*Turtle
River*

Site of
old ford

Site of Hale
family sawmill

To Lake
Bemidji

20

Access

2177

20

*Big Rice
Lake*

N

0   1   2

Miles

*Little
Rice
Lake*

*Kitchi
Lake*

To Stump
Lake

12

Pennington

Site of old American
Fur Company post

Take-out

*Pug Hole
Lake*

Cass Lake

Launch your boat at County Route 22, just south of Gull Lake. You'll soon be paddling through large beds of wild rice, a staple of Woodland Indians for thousands of years, including the Ojibwa, the tribe to control the area most recently. The plant appears at the surface of the water in early summer. When ripe in late summer, the plant stands tall above the surface. The heads turn purple and the rice springs easily from the plant.

About 2 miles below the put-in, the river runs by the site of a "splash dam" operated by the J. Nells Lumber Company between 1908 and 1924. Many companies used splash dams on small streams. After a large number of logs piled up behind the dam, the gates were opened, and a surge of water carried the saw logs through the shallows and riffles. Often, several splash dams were constructed to move logs to a deep channel. The remains of several splash dams are located along the river.

About 3.5 miles into the trip, you'll pass a ford that was used to cross the river by horse and wagon a century ago. Just downstream is the site of the old Hale family sawmill. Extensive stands of red and white pine in the Turtle River region were logged early in the twentieth century. The mill site later became a small farm.

After about 10 miles, the Turtle enters Big Rice Lake, an important source of wild rice and a good fishing lake for walleye, northern pike, crappies, and yellow perch. Paddle straight across the lake and pick up the river channel again. After about a mile, you'll enter Little Rice Lake and then Kitchi Lake. Paddle to the south end of Kitchi to the take-out at County Route 12.

The take-out lies at the upstream end of Pug Hole Lake. You can paddle to the south end of the lake to the site of an American Fur Company post that operated in 1820. Pug Hole opens directly into Cass Lake.

Access: The **County Route 22 put-in** is located 6.5 miles east of the town of Turtle River. The **County Route 12 take-out** is located at the north end of Cass Lake, about 16.5 miles east of Bemidji.

Alternate access is possible at the County Route 20 bridge, about 5 miles into the trip.

Shuttle: 13 miles one way. About 30 minutes.

ADDITIONAL HELP

MA&G: 72, C2.

Camping: There are no developed campsites along the river, though you can camp on state or federal forest land along the route.

Food, gas, and lodging: Bemidji, Cass Lake.

For more information: Chippewa National Forest, Cass Lake Ranger District.

Mississippi River

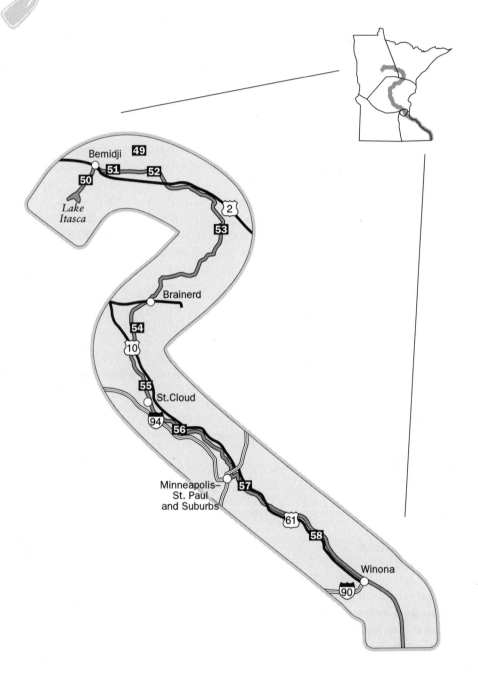

MISSISSIPPI RIVER

Mississippi, Father of Waters, Old Man River, Great River—by any name, the greatest of American rivers presents many different faces to canoeists along its nearly 700 miles in Minnesota. The great river begins its life in Minnesota as an intimate, wooded stream. By the time it last touches the state's borders, it is a sprawling panoply of channels, islands, and riverine lakes, bounded by lofty bluffs. The river offers so much to canoeists—wilderness tripping and camping, great fishing, innumerable day trips—that this chapter can't begin to be comprehensive on the subject. That is especially true on the river below the Twin Cities, where you'll want detailed maps to navigate the intricate backwaters flooded by the navigation dams along the river. Use this book to narrow your search and then order more detailed maps from the MDNR.

50 Lake Itasca to Bemidji

Character: The uppermost stretch of the Mississippi is narrow, winding, and wooded with a few easy rapids to negotiate and beaver dams to pull over.

Length: 62 miles. Many shorter trips are possible.

Average run time: Two to four days for the whole stretch.

Class: I, mostly quiet.

Skill level: Beginner to intermediate, with wilderness camping skills.

Optimal flow: Above 1.9 feet on the gauge next to the trail bridge at Coffee Pot Landing; above 6 feet on the gauge on the County Route 5 bridge; or above 4.2 feet on the gauge on the township bridge south of County Route 7 (north of Fern Lake).

Average gradient: 2.1 feet per mile.

Hazards: You may have to pull over deadfalls and beaver dams.

Maps: *Mississippi Headwaters River Trail 1: Lake Itasca to Cass Lake* published by Mississippi Headwaters Board and the MDNR.

The paddling: Few tasks captured the imagination of early white explorers like that of finding the headwaters of the Mississippi. A steady parade of European explorers moved up the river. By the late 1700s, the search for the river's source had reached northern Minnesota. In 1798 English surveyor David Thompson proposed Turtle Lake north of Bemidji as the source. Zebulon Pike, who led an expedition up the river in 1805,

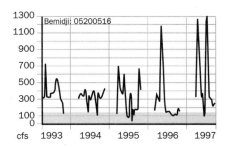

150 cfs = estimated minimum
for good paddling

50 Lake Itasca to Bemidji

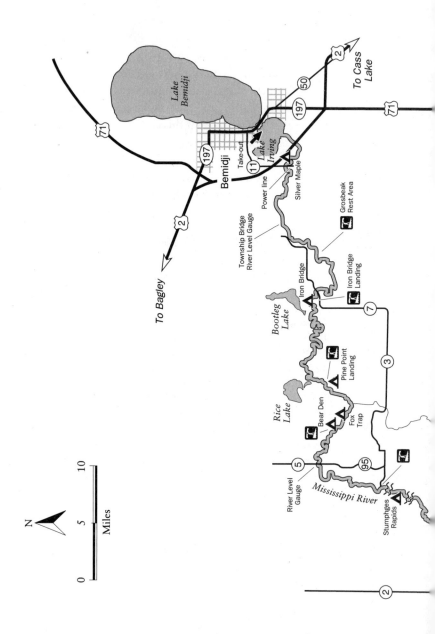

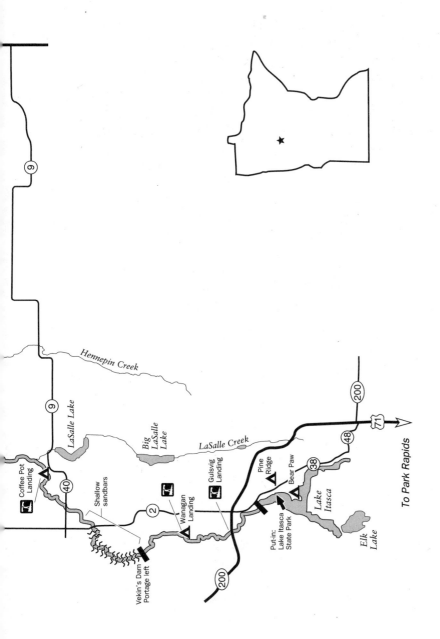

Hennepin Creek

LaSalle Lake

Big LaSalle Lake

LaSalle Creek

Coffee Pot Landing

Shallow sandbars

Wanagan Landing

Gulsvig Landing

Pine Ridge

Bear Paw

Put-in: Lake Itasca State Park

Lake Itasca

Elk Lake

Vekin's Dam Portage left

To Park Rapids

149

identified both Leech Lake and Cass Lake (then known as Red Cedar Lake) as sources. Lewis Cass, who ascended the Mississippi in 1820, agreed with Pike that the source was Upper Red Cedar Lake.

These pronouncements of "discovery" must have seemed rather odd to to the various Indian tribes that had occupied the headwaters of the river for millennia. An archaeological site in Itasca State Park show that Paleo-Indians butchered bison at the headwaters 8,000 years ago. Explorers' journals make it clear that the local Indians knew that the lake they called *Omushkos* (Elk Lake) ultimately fed the Mississippi. At most, white explorers could only claim to be documenting by notes and maps the location of the river's headwaters.

One of these explorers was Henry Rowe Schoolcraft, geologist for the Cass expedition. Schoolcraft, notes historian William E. Lass, "dutifully reported that Cass had found the Mississippi's 'true source'; but he obviously did not believe it, for later on in the same report he noted that two rivers entered the lake."

In 1832 Schoolcraft was ordered to return to the headwaters region. He mounted an expedition out of proportion to the rather simple task of joining local Indians on a long canoe trip. As Mississippi River historian Timothy Severin observed, "It was a sledgehammer to crack a rather insignificant nut." In fact, by 1805 trader William Morrison had already accompanied Indians on a trip to Itasca, then known as Elk Lake.

Schoolcraft apparently thought the Ojibwa word for Elk Lake too prosaic for the birthplace of the Mississippi. By combining portions of the Latin *veritas caput* for "true head," Schoolcraft fabricated Itasca. As Lass wryly notes, "Once he had the name he had only to reach the lake."

Schoolcraft hired the Ojibwa Ozawindib as his guide. Ozawindib, in fact, knew the country well enough that he took a shortcut. From Lake Bemidji, he ascended the Schoolcraft River. Then, leading the way and carrying one of the canoes, Ozawindib portaged west to the fledgling Mississippi. In his diary, dated July 13, 1832, Schoolcraft wrote, "On turning out of a thicket, into the small weedy opening, the cheering sight of a transparent body of water burst upon our view. It was Itasca Lake—the source of the Mississippi."

Itasca is an attractive (albeit small) lake to canoe, not only for its geographical and historical appeal, but also because the surrounding park is undeniably one of the state's finest. Be sure to drive the Wilderness Loop and visit Douglas Lodge, a stately log building.

From Itasca, you'll have to carry around or drag over the line of boulders that forms a crude dam at the outlet of the lake. Downstream, the Mississippi is wild and intimate as it meanders slowly past birch and spruce forest and, at times, open marsh. Be prepared to pull over beaver dams. The river is managed by the Mississippi Headwaters Board, an eight-county, joint-powers board organized to help protect the wild character of the river.

The Mississippi spills from Elk Lake over a line of hand-laid boulders. MINNESOTA OFFICE OF TOURISM

About 8 miles below the lake, the stream flows over Vekin's Dam, a logging dam built to store water and logs and then to flush them through the several miles of sandy shoals downstream. Portage left, about 50 yards.

About 20 miles below Itasca, the Mississippi enters a large wetland, where the channel can be difficult to find and follow. In fall, when wild rice grows thick and tall, you may have difficulty in pushing through the vegetation.

After about 4 miles of marshy shores, the stream enters a narrow wooded valley and for the next 2 miles runs through riffles and class I rapids known as **Stumphges Rapids.**

The river continues a meandering path past woods and marsh. About 60 miles into the trip, between Pine Point and Iron Bridge Landing, the river flows by floating bog.

Nearing Bemidji, the Mississippi is joined by the Schoolcraft River from the south. Though usually runnable only in the spring, the Schoolcraft is recommended by its wild, densely forested valley. The river has no difficult rapids.

End your trip at Lake Irving, or continue into Lake Bemidji.

Access: The Lake Itasca put-in is located in Itasca State Park, about 20 miles southwest of Bemidji as the crow flies. **The Bemidji take-out** is located on the south edge of town, on the north shore of Lake Irving.

Alternate accesses are Gulsvig Landing, Wanagan (sic) Landing, Coffee Pot Landing, County Route 3, Bear Den Landing, Pine Point, Iron Bridge Landing, and Grosbeak Rest Area.

Shuttle: 40 miles one way. About 1.75 hours.

ADDITIONAL HELP

MA&G: 61, A6; 71.
Camping: Several riverside campsites are available, including Wanagan Landing, Coffee Pot Landing, Stumphges Rapids, Bear Den Landing, Fox Trap, Pine Point, Iron Bridge Campsite, and Silver Maple Campsite. Camp by car at Itasca State Park and Lake Bemidji State Park.
Food, gas, and lodging: Bemidji.
For more information: MDNR Information Center.

51 Bemidji to Lake Winnibigoshish

Character: Short stretches of the Mississippi join large lakes. The river segments make pleasant day trips, especially for watching wildlife.

Length: 48 miles, including the distance across lakes, which are big, windy, and not much fun or safe to cross by canoe.

Average run time: Unestimated, since few will choose to run the whole stretch.

Class: Quiet.

Skill level: Beginner.

Optimal flow: Above 3 feet on the gauge on the County Route 8 bridge. Check gauge near Bemidji on USGS website for at least 150 cfs.

Average gradient: Mostly lake. See gradients for individual segments.

Hazards: The lakes get wavy and windy in a hurry.

Maps: *Mississippi Headwaters River Trail 1: Lake Itasca to Cass Lake,* and *Mississippi Headwaters River Trail 2: Cass Lake to Vermillion River* published by Mississippi Headwaters Board and the MDNR; MDNR.

The paddling: This section is more lake than river. The fledgling Mississippi strings together several large lakes, including Bemidji, Cass, and Winnibigoshish. The lakes are pretty and provide excellent fishing for walleyes, northern pike, muskies, and crappies. But they are tedious to cross by canoe and can be dangerous when the wind comes up. Most canoeists will prefer to stick to the following river segments, which run between the lakes.

51A. Ottertail Power Company Dam to Cass Lake: Bald eagles and great blue herons are common along this 11.5-mile stretch. Average gradient: 1.7 feet per mile. About 2.5 miles below the put-in, you'll run down a short section of class I rapids in medium to low water. The High Banks campsite and landing on the left about a half mile above Wolf Lake provides an impressive view of the lake and river. You'll have a half-mile paddle across a bay of Wolf Lake and, after a bit more river paddling, a similarly short paddle across a bay of Lake Andrusia to the take-out. The **put-in** is located below the dam, where County Route 12 crosses the river, about 5 miles east of Lake Bemidji. The **take-out** is located on the south shore of Lake Andrusia off County Route 33. The **shuttle** is about 7 miles one way and will take about 25 minutes.

51B. Knutson Dam Recreation Area to Lake Winnibigoshish: This 10.5-mile trip begins as a wooded corridor. Average gradient: 0.1 feet per mile. About half-way through the route, the river widens to form the Mississippi Meadows. Bald eagles are common. You're also likely to spot ospreys, herons, and various waterfowl. **Put in** below Knutson Dam on the northeast shore of Cass Lake off County Route 39. **Take out** at either Reese Landing, south of the river mouth off West

51 Bemidji to Lake Winnibigoshish

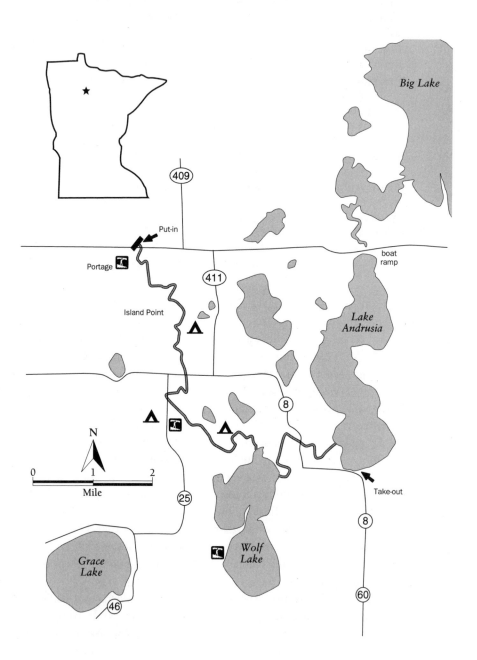

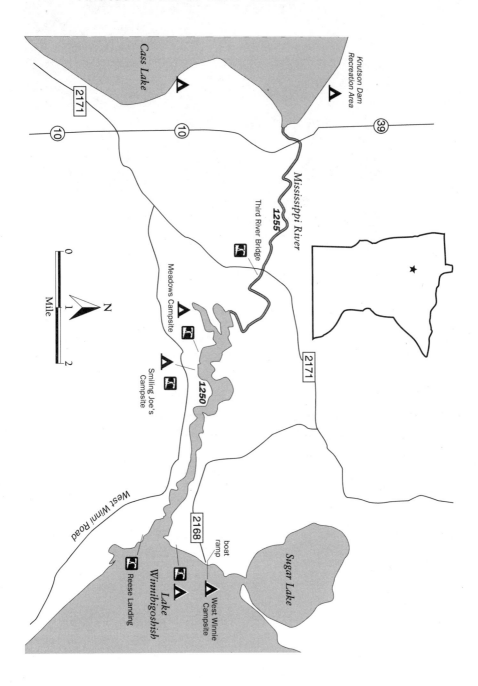

In its upper reaches, the Mississippi is not the big, wide river most people know it as. MINNESOTA OFFICE OF TOURISM

Winnie Road, or Governor's Point Campsite, on the north side of the river at the end of Forest Road 2168. Both are on the western shore of Winnibigoshish. The **shuttle** is about 12 miles one way and will take about 40 minutes.

ADDITIONAL HELP

MA&G: 72, D1–3.
Camping: Canoe camping along the first stretch is possible at Island Point Campsite, County Route 25 landing, and High Banks. On the second route, camp at Knutson Dam Recreation Area, Meadows Campsite, Smiling Joe's Campsite, or Governor's Point Campsite.
Food, gas, and lodging: Bemidji, Cass Lake.
For more information: MDNR Information Center.

52 Lake Winnibigoshish Dam to Pokegama Dam

Character: The Mississippi, still a small river, follows an extremely tortuous path over flat woodlands.

Length: 46 miles.

Average run time: Two to three days.

Class: Quiet.

Skill level: Beginner to intermediate, with wilderness camping skills.

Optimal flow: Over 2 feet on the gauge on the U.S. Highway 2 bridge near Ball Club.

Average gradient: 0.3 feet per mile.

Hazards: No particular hazards.

Maps: *Mississippi Headwaters River Trail 2: Cass Lake to Vermillion River,* and *Mississippi Headwaters River Trail 3: Vermillion River to Palisade* published by Mississippi Headwaters Board and the MDNR.

The paddling: Start your trip below the U.S. Army Corps of Engineers dam at the east end of Lake Winnibigoshish. The dam was authorized in 1881 to control the level of the upper Mississippi and supply a more dependable flow of water far downstream. Opposed by many Ojibwa of the area, the dam raised the level of the natural lake about 8 feet and covered cemeteries and village sites.

Downstream from the dam, the Mississippi flows through wild woodlands. After several miles, the river flows over white sand, a remnant of sand dunes that formed on Lake Winnie's southeast shore 6,000 years ago when the land was hotter and drier.

Flowing across table-flat land near Ball Club, the Mississippi meanders more and more wildly. The present river channel is flanked by abandoned meander loops known as oxbows. Many of the meanders were dredged during logging days to open a straighter route for logs to follow downstream.

Below Little White Oak Lake, the river channel gradually straightens. The Vermillion River joins from the south at Schoolcraft State Park, a small park created to protect an old stand of red pine. Near Grand Rapids, the river enters Blackwater Lake, the reservoir created by the Pokegama Dam, operated by the U.S. Corps of Army of Engineers. Take out at the dam, or portage left 44 yards into the reservoir formed by the Blandin Paper Company Dam 3 miles downstream. The reservoirs are known for muskie fishing.

Access: The Lake Winnibigoshish Dam put-in is located at the dam, where County Route 9 crosses the Mississippi. The **Pokegama Dam take-out** is located on U.S. 2 about 4 miles northwest of Grand Rapids.

Shuttle: 30 miles one way. About 1.25 hours.

ADDITIONAL HELP

MA&G: 73, 63, A8–9.

52 Lake Winnibigoshish Dam to Pokegama Dam

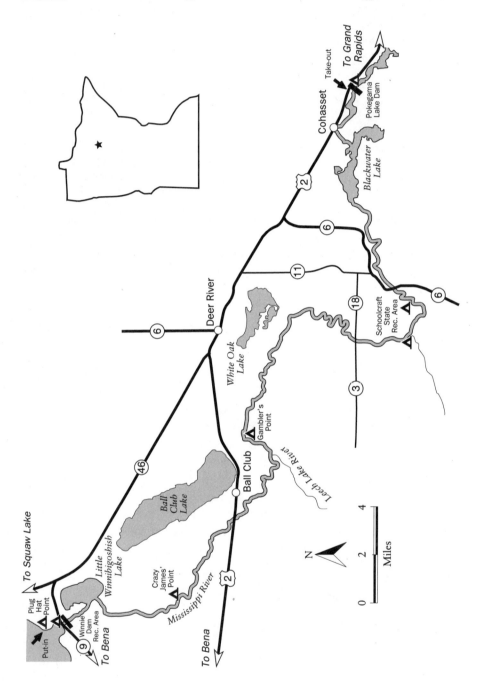

To Grand Rapids

Take-out

Cohasset

Pokegama Lake Dam

Blackwater Lake

2

6

11

18

Schoolcraft State Rec. Area

6

Deer River

6

White Oak Lake

3

Gambler's Point

Ball Club

Leech Lake River

46

Ball Club Lake

N

4

Miles

2

0

To Squaw Lake

Little Winnibigoshish Lake

Crazy James' Point

Mississippi River

2

Plug Hat Point

Put-in

Winnie Dam Rec. Area

9

To Bena

To Bena

A party departs for another day on the Mississippi, this one near Lake Winnibigoshish. MINNESOTA OFFICE OF TOURISM

Camping: Canoe campsites are located at Crazy James' Point, Leech Lake River Access, Gambler's Point Campsite, and Leaning Willow Campsite. Campgrounds are at Winnie Dam Recreation Area, Schoolcraft State Park, and Pokegama Lake Recreation Area.

Food, gas, and lodging: Deer River, Cohasset, Grand Rapids.

For more information: MDNR Information Center.

53 Grand Rapids to Brainerd

Character: This winding woodland stream offers plenty of opportunities for long-distance paddling and overnight camping.
Length: 163.5 miles. Many shorter trips are possible.
Average run time: A week or more to run the whole stretch.
Class: Quiet.
Skill level: Beginner to intermediate, with wilderness camping skills.
Optimal flow: Above 1.8 feet on the gauge on the County Road 441 bridge; or above 5 feet on the gauge on the Minnesota Highway 6 bridge north of Crosby. Check USGS website for at least 400 cfs on gauge at Grand Rapids or at least 1,000 cfs on gauge at Aitkin.
Average gradient: 0.5 foot per mile.
Hazards: Watch out for the low-head dam on river right that separates the main channel from the flood diversion channel that flows to the west. When the gauge at the U.S. 169 bridge (9 miles upstream) reads 6 feet or more, water is spilling over the dam, forming a backroller hazard. Stay left, to the inside of the bend.
Maps: *Mississippi Headwaters River Trail 3: Vermillion River to Palisade,* and *Mississippi Headwaters River Trail 4: Palisade to Brainerd* published by Mississippi Headwaters Board.

The paddling: Below Grand Rapids, the Mississippi continues a winding course through woods, marsh, and some pastureland. Within a few miles, the Prairie River joins from the north, about doubling the flow of water.

This stretch of river is unspectacular, but it is undeveloped and pretty and makes an excellent route for a camping trip of several days. You'll encounter a few stretches of fast water and rocks, but for the most part, this stretch is placid. There are no dams to block the route until the city of Brainerd. Above Split Hand Creek, steep banks flank much of the river. The Ojibwa called the hills west of the river *Piquadinaw,* "it is hilly." The highest hill in the group, about 20 miles south of Grand Rapids, was called Poquodenaw Mountain by lumbermen. The name has since been shortened to Quadna. South of Split Hand, the landscape flattens as the river winds across the former beds of Glacial Lakes Upham and Aitkin. The oxbows in this section of river provide habitat for a variety of species—spawning areas for northern pike and slack water for muskrats to build their mound-shaped homes.

Big Sandy Lake lies just to the east of the Mississippi and drains into the river though the Sandy River. The lake was the site of a pivotal battle between Ojibwa and Dakota Indians in the 1760s, in which the Ojibwa pushed

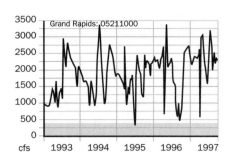

400 cfs = estimated minimum
for good paddling

53 Grand Rapids to Brainerd

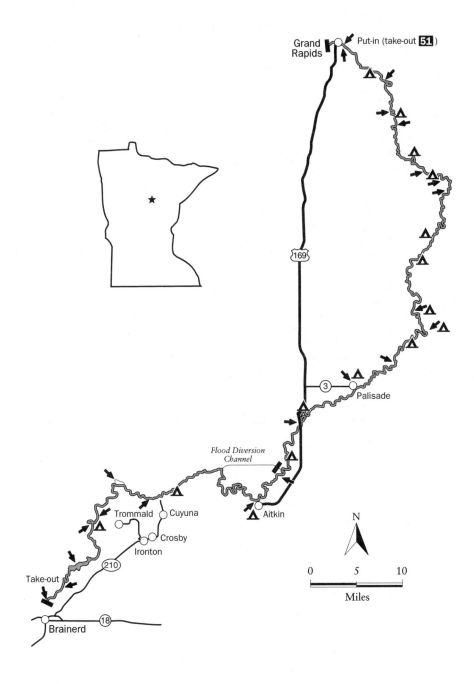

Grand Rapids

Put-in (take-out **51**)

169

3

Palisade

Flood Diversion Channel

Trommald

Cuyuna

Crosby

Ironton

210

Aitkin

Take-out

Brainerd

18

N

0   5   10

Miles

their enemies from north-central Minnesota.

A century ago steamboats plied this section of the Mississippi, hauling passengers and freight between Grand Rapids and Aitkin. Boats here were much smaller than those on the larger lower river. Even so, the stern-wheeler *Andy Gibson*, at 140 feet, was so long she sometimes clipped the bank on sharp bends. In 1894 the steamer *Fawn Lake* sank at

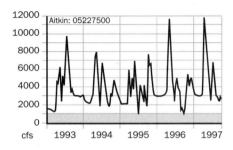

1000 cfs (3.0 feet on gauge) = estimated minimum for good paddling

Jacobson, a once-busy lumbering town where many boats would dock. Remains of other wrecks lie near the confluence with the Sandy River. The wreckage of the *Gibson* is visible in low water near the Aitkin Campground.

Below Aitkin, the river banks grow higher and steeper. The confluence with the Pine River was a long-time village site for various Woodland Indians. Episcopalians built a mission there in the early 1800s.

Near Pine River, the Mississippi flows by the old towns of the Cuyuna Iron Range, including Cuyuna, Trommald, Crosby, and Ironton. The ore body was discovered in the 1890s by surveyor Cuyler Adams, who named the region with the combination of his first name and that of his dog, Una. The Milford Mine, which operated south of the river, east of MN 6, was the site of Minnesota's worst mine disaster when, in 1924, Foley Lake collapsed into an underground mine shaft, entombing 41 miners in water and mud.

Near Half-Moon Landing the river melds with the reservoir impounded by the Potlatch Dam in Brainerd. Pull out here or at any of several sites on the impoundment.

This stretch of the river offers good fishing for northern pike, walleye, and some smallmouth bass.

Access: The **Grand Rapids put-in** is located just downstream from the Blandin Paper Company Dam at Steamboat Access, on the south side of the river in the center of town. The **Brainerd take-out** is located at Half-Moon Landing; from Merrifield, drive northeast 3 miles on County Route 3 and then 2 miles east on County Route 19, and then another mile east on an unnumbered road to the access.

Many alternate accesses are possible. Consult the map in this book and the *Mississippi Headwaters River Trail* maps published by Mississippi Headwaters Board and the MDNR.

Shuttle: 75 miles one way. About three hours.

ADDITIONAL HELP

MA&G: 64; 63, E9; 55, A6–9.

Camping: Riverside camping is possible at several sites: Sucher's Campsite, Blackberry Campsite, Swimming Bear Campsite, Jacobson Campground, Willow Wood Campsite, Ms. Keto Campsite, Libby Township Campsite, Scott's Rapids Campsite, Berglund County Park in Palisade, Willow River Campsite, Hassman Campsite, Aitkin Campgrounds, Lone Pine Creek Campsite, and Half-Moon Campsite. Auto camping is possible at the Sandy Lake Recreation Area and Lum Park, on the northeast edge of Brainerd.

Food, gas, and lodging: Grand Rapids, Aitkin, Brainerd.

For more information: MDNR Information Center.

54 Brainerd to Little Falls

Character: No longer a small stream, the broad Mississippi flows swiftly through the mixed forest and fields of central Minnesota. Fishing can be great on this section.

Length: 36.4 miles. Shorter trips are possible.

Average run time: Two days.

Class: I.

Skill level: Beginner.

Optimal flow: Check the USGS website for at least 1,800 cfs on gauge near Fort Ripley. The stream is big enough that it is usually passable in a canoe.

Average gradient: 1.2 feet per mile.

Hazards: Swift current in high water.

Maps: *Mississippi Headwaters River Trail 5: Brainerd to Little Falls* published by Mississippi Headwaters Board and the MDNR.

The paddling: The Mississippi River leaves Brainerd as a sizable stream with a sometimes swift current. Dozens of islands in this stretch were created when saw logs, floated to mills a century ago, jammed on shoals or in bends. Sediment swirled into the eddies created by the obstructions and eventually buried the logs, forming islands.

After 3 miles, Buffalo Creek joins from the east. The journals of early nineteenth-century explorers such as Zebulon Pike, Lewis Cass, and Henry School-craft, all remark on the prairie bounding the creek, where bison often grazed. From this area south, the Mississippi passed many areas where wildfire, often set by Indians, opened the forest to spreading prairies and oak savannas.

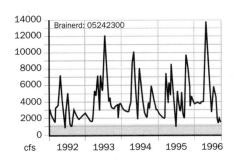

1800 cfs (4.0 feet on gauge) = estimated minimum for good paddling

54 Brainerd to Little Falls

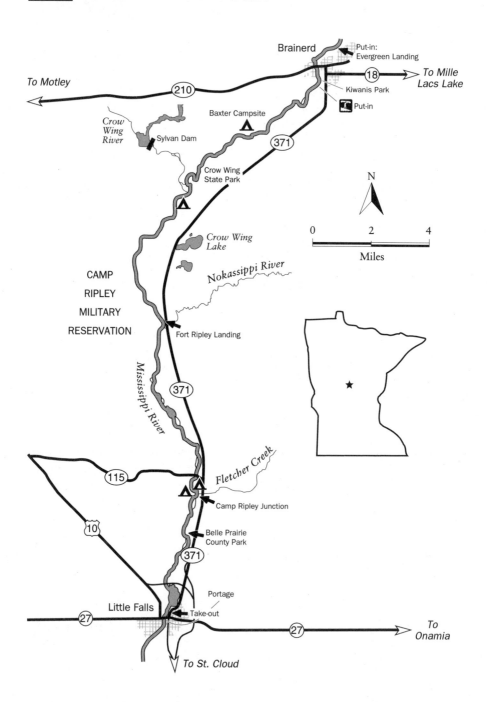

Ten miles into the trip, the Crow Wing River joins the Mississippi from the west. The confluence was the site of one of several important battles between Ojibwa and Dakota in the mid-1700s that eventually resulted in the expulsion of the Dakotas from north-central Minnesota. The confluence was also the site of the town of Crow Wing, an important trading location that quickly with-

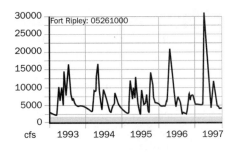

1200 cfs = estimated minimum for good paddling

ered once the Northern Pacific bypassed the town and crossed the Mississippi farther upstream. Today Crow Wing State Park lies at the confluence of the two rivers.

For nearly 20 river miles, from Crow Wing State Park downstream to Camp Ripley Junction, the Camp Ripley Military Reservation flanks the western bank of the Mississippi. Despite the explosions of artillery and roar of tanks used in ma-neuvers, the 53,000-acre area with its scattered wetlands, oak woodlands, and grasslands serves as an important refuge for wildlife.

In the last few miles of this stretch, the Mississippi enters the reservoir created by the Minnesota Power Dam at Little Falls. Pull out at one of the boat ramps in town (one on either side of the river) or portage left 325 yards around the dam and continue downstream.

With deep holes, rocky riffles, and woody cover in deep bends, this section of river provides great fishing for smallmouth bass, walleye, northern pike, and even muskies.

Access: Brainerd put-in: A good access is the Kiwanis Park on the east side of the river, just downstream from the College Drive bridge. You can also put in at Evergreen Landing, on the east side of the river, about 2 miles upstream. **Little Falls take-out:** Use either of two accesses located less than a mile above the dam. One is at North End Park, on the east side of the river. The other is located off West River Road.

Alternate accesses to shorten the trip are available at Crow Wing State Park, the mouth of the Nokassippi River, Fletcher Creek Landing, and Belle Prairie County Park.

Shuttle: 32 miles one way. About 1.2 hours.

ADDITIONAL HELP

MA&G: 54; 46, A4.
Camping: Camp by canoe at Crow Wing State Park (group camp) and Fletcher Creek Landing. Camp by car at Crow Wing and Charles A. Lindbergh State Parks.
Food, gas, and lodging: Brainerd, Little Falls.
For more information: MDNR Information Center.

55 Little Falls to St. Cloud

Character: The trip begins on a reservoir, but after 9 miles of paddling and a portage, you're back again on a wide, often swift river with good fishing.

Length: 38 miles. Several shorter trips are possible.

Average run time: Two days. A good 12-mile day trip begins about 2 miles below the Blanchard Dam and ends at Stearns County Park north of Sartell.

Class: I.

Skill level: Beginner.

Optimal flow: More than 2,000 cfs from the dam at Little Falls and Blanchard Dam. Call the MDNR or Minnesota Power at 800-582-8529 for recorded readings.

Average gradient: Not applicable. Most gradient is taken up by dams.

Hazards: Watch out for two big dams, the Blanchard Dam and Champion Dam—and Sauk Rapids, the most difficult rapids on the river.

Maps: *Mississippi Headwaters River Trail 6: Little Falls to St. Cloud* published by Mississippi Headwaters Board and the MDNR.

The paddling: The first 9 miles of this trip is spent on the reservoir created by the Blanchard Dam. So, the paddling may not be exciting, but there are a few consolation prizes. First, the fishing can be good, especially for muskies. Second, there are a couple historical sites of note. A half mile below the put-in are the Weyerhauser, Musser, and Rosenmeier mansions, which overlook the river. The first two owe their existence to the area's timber industry. The third, built in 1903 in a classical revival style, was the home of Gordon Rosenmeier, who served in the Minnesota senate from 1941 to 1971.

Another mile downstream is Charles A. Lindbergh State Park and Historic Site, which preserves the boyhood home of the first aviator to cross the Atlantic. The site is actually named for the aviator's father, a Republican Congressman who represented central Minnesota from 1907 to 1917. The Blanchard Dam had not yet been built when Charles Jr. was a lad. "The river," he wrote later, "was so swift and usually so full of shallow rapids that my use of the boat was confined to two or three hundred yards up and downstream."

About 2.5 miles downstream, at the confluence of the Swan River, the site of a wintering post built by Zebulon Pike in 1805–6, now lies near the west bank, covered by the reservoir. Fur trader William Aitkin is buried on the river's east bank.

Portage right 125 yards to bypass the Blanchard Dam, the largest hydroelectric dam on the upper

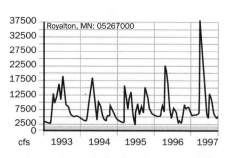

2000 cfs = minimum for good paddling

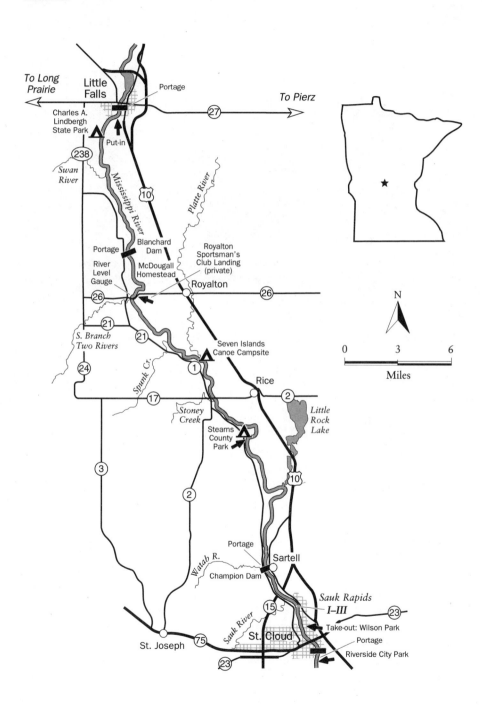

To Long Prairie

Little Falls

Portage

To Pierz

27

Charles A. Lindbergh State Park

Put-in

238

Swan River

Mississippi River

10

Platte River

Portage

Blanchard Dam

Royalton Sportsman's Club Landing (private)

River Level Gauge

McDougall Homestead

26

Royalton

26

21

S. Branch Two Rivers

21

24

Spunk Cr.

Seven Islands Canoe Campsite

1

Rice

2

17

Stoney Creek

Little Rock Lake

Stearns County Park

3

2

10

Portage

Watab R.

Champion Dam

Sartell

Sauk Rapids I–III

15

23

Take-out: Wilson Park

Portage

Riverside City Park

St. Joseph

75

Sauk River

St. Cloud

23

N

0   3   6

Miles

The boyhood home of the aviator Charles Lindbergh, along the Mississippi River in the state park named for his father, Charles A. Lindbergh. MINNESOTA DEPARTMENT OF NATURAL RESOURCES

Mississippi. Once through the dam, the river races through shallow riffles, easy rapids, and quick-moving pools. The McDougall Homestead sits on the left bank about a mile below the dam. The site has been purchased and protected by The Nature Conservancy for the heron rookery on the 60-foot bluff. The McDougalls were Scots who immigrated from Nova Scotia and built the homestead's buildings in the late 1860s and early 1870s. The barn, its frame built of hand-hewn logs, is typical of those in Nova Scotia and the eastern United States.

If you choose to bypass the dam and reservoir, begin your trip at the Royalton Sportsman's Club Landing a few hundred yards upstream from the County Route 26 bridge. The river passes several clusters of wooded islands and runs through frequent stretches of fast, riffly water. The outside of bends are often deep and filled with woody debris—perfect habitat for large muskies. This stretch also holds smallmouth bass, walleye, and northern pike.

By the time you reach Stearns County Park, the river is already starting to assume the lake-like slowness and weediness of the reservoir formed by the Champion Dam in Sartell. Pull out here or continue downstream 9 miles to the Champion Dam in Sartell. Portage right 300 yards. You'll be paddling in quick water again, including the Sauk Rapids just below the mouth of the Sauk River. This stretch of whitewater rates class I in low water and up to class III in high water, with 4-foot waves forming at a large ledge. Use caution and scout from the bridge just downstream. Portage if necessary on the left through the city park. Pull out (before yet another dam in St. Cloud) at Wilson Park on the left (east). If you wish to continue downstream, portage the dam on the left, 300 yards.

Access: To run the whole stretch, **put in** at LeBourget Park in Little Falls (renamed recently for the French city where Charles Lindbergh landed in 1927). The park is located in Little Falls on the east bank, about a quarter mile downstream of the Little Falls Dam. **Take out** at Wilson Park on the left (east), about a mile upstream of the Minnesota Highway 23 bridge and 2 miles above the St. Cloud Dam.

For a trip that skips the reservoirs and sticks to the free-flowing portion of this segment, put in at the Royalton Sportsman's Club Landing on the east side of the river, off County Route 26, about a quarter mile above the County Route 26 bridge. Take out at Stearns County Park, located off County Route 1 about 7 miles north of Sartell.

Shuttle: 32 miles one way. About 1.2 hours.

ADDITIONAL HELP

MA&G: 46.
Camping: Canoe camping is possible at Seven Islands Canoe Campsite, at a private outfitter at the mouth of the Platte River, and at Stearns County Park. A campground is located at Charles A. Lindbergh State Park.
Food, gas, and lodging: Little Falls, St. Cloud.
For more information: MDNR Information Center.

56 St. Cloud to Anoka

Character: A broad, swift river with wooded banks and islands, this section of the Mississippi is a favorite among anglers.
Length: 55 miles.
Average run time: Two to three days. The current is fast; by paddling steadily, you can easily make 4 to 5 miles an hour if the water is fairly high.
Class: I.
Skill level: Beginner.
Optimal flow: Above 2,000 cfs from the St. Cloud Dam; above 2 feet on the gauge on the Minnesota Highway 24 bridge. Or check the USGS website for the gauge at St. Cloud. This section is big enough to be always runnable by canoe.
Average gradient: 2.2 feet per mile.
Hazards: No particular hazards.
Maps: MDNR *Mississippi River: St. Cloud to Anoka.*

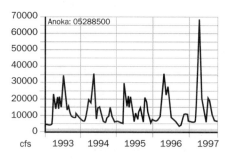

2000 cfs (4.2 feet on gauge) =
minimum for good paddling

The paddling: This stretch starts with one of the most pleasant places on the Mississippi, the Beaver Islands, just downstream from St. Cloud. Savor the narrow, winding, shaded channels before you head downstream. If you're fishing and the water is low, step out of your canoe and pepper the deeper runs and holes with a crankbait, jig, or fly.

The entire section of river to Anoka is known for its fishing. With its deep holes and extensive riffles and easy rapids, it's excellent for smallmouth bass. In fact, it's probably the best big-bass stream in the state, producing a lot of smallmouths over 3 pounds. It's also good for walleye, northern pike, and even a few muskies. In recent years, channel catfish have been stocked in this stretch and are now common and large. Previously, they lived only below St. Anthony Falls.

Below the Beaver Islands, the many channels join into a single broad stream and flow swiftly by wooded hills, eroded banks, and pockets of residential development. Periodically, the channel splits again around one or several islands. Most fast water in this section amounts to no more than riffles. Some drops, however, do require a sharp eye for rocks and bit of maneuvering to avoid them. Even so, none rate more than class I. The greatest danger is running the river in the high, cold water of spring. On such a wide river, an upset may leave you a long way from shore.

At Anoka the river begins to enter the slack water impounded by the Coon Rapids Dam. Take out at the mouth of the Rum River (paddle about 100 yards up the Rum) or continue downstream 5 miles to the access at the dam.

Access: St. Cloud put-in: You have your choice of two put-ins below the St. Cloud Dam, both on the west side of the river. The first is a fishing pier and carry-in area just off Third Avenue, just downstream from the dam, near the 10th Avenue bridge. The second is a boat ramp about 500 yards downstream at 1503 3rd Avenue.

The **Anoka take-out** is located on the east side of the Rum River about a quarter mile below the Main Street bridge. You'll have to paddle about 100 yards up the Rum River to reach the access.

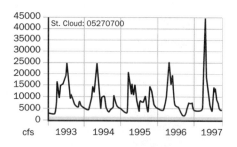

2000 cfs (about 1.4 feet on gauge) =
minimum for good paddling

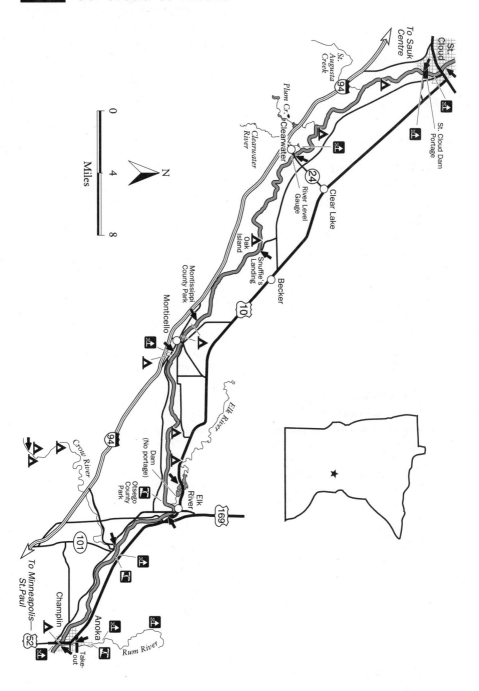

St. Cloud

To Sauk Centre

St. Augusta Creek

94

St. Cloud Dam Portage

Plum Cr.

Clearwater

Clearwater River

24

River Level Gauge

Clear Lake

0

4

Miles

8

N

Oak Island

Snuffie's Landing

Becker

10

Montissippi County Park

Monticello

Elk River

94

Crow River

Dam (No portage)

Otsego County Park

Elk River

169

101

To Minneapolis— St. Paul

Champlin

Anoka

Take-out

Rum River

52

There are several alternate accesses on this stretch: MN 24 bridge northeast of the river, Snuffie's Landing, Montissippi County Park upstream from Monticello, Ellison Park in Monticello, Otsego County Park upstream from Elk River, Babcock Highway Rest Area just upstream from the Minnesota Highway 101 bridge, a boat ramp in Dayton; Daytonport across the river from Dayton, Point Park in Champlin, and an access on each side of the Coon Rapids dam.

Shuttle: 50 miles one way. About 1.8 hours.

ADDITIONAL HELP

MA&G: 47, E6–7; 40–41.
Camping: River campsites are located at Putnam's Pasture, Boy Scout Point, Oak Island, and Dimmick Island. Camp by car in Montissippi County Park or Lake Maria State Park.
Food, gas, and lodging: St. Cloud, Monticello, Elk River, Anoka.
For more information: MDNR Information Center.

57 Coon Rapids Dam to Hastings

Character: The metro Mississippi, at times gritty and industrial, nonetheless offers an oasis of nature in the heart of the city.
Length: 47 miles. Many short trips are possible.
Average run time: Few people paddle the whole stretch in one take.
Class: I, mostly quiet.
Skill level: Beginner.
Optimal flow: Always runnable.
Average gradient: Not applicable, since most of the gradient in the stretch is taken up by Upper and Lower St. Anthony Falls and the Ford Dam.
Hazards: Watch out for barges, towboats, and recreational boat traffic.
Maps: MDNR *Mississippi River Canoe Routes 8* and *9* and the *Metro Area Rivers Guide* published by MDNR.

The paddling: The metro stretch of the Mississippi varies dramatically. The 6-mile stretch from Coon Rapids Dam to Interstate 694 resembles the river farther upstream, with several easy rapids, deep rocky holes, a fringe of woods along the bank, and good fishing. Homes line the banks in places, but the river appears largely natural.

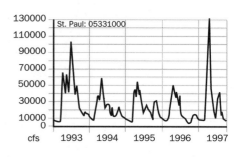

Always runnable

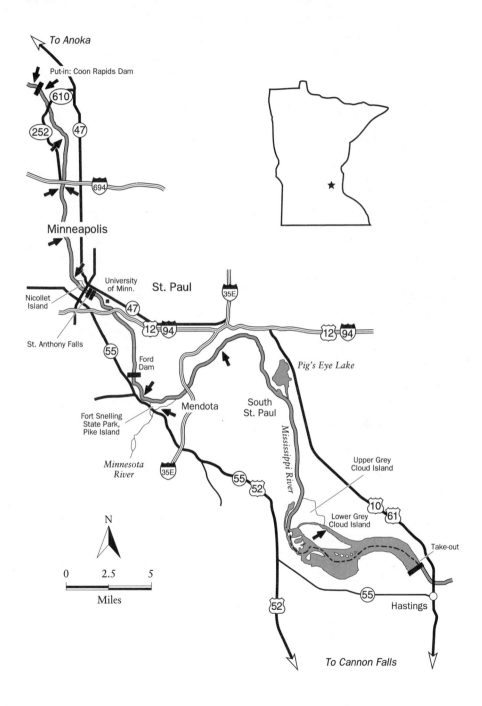

The 6 miles from I-694 to Nicollet Island are deeper and slower. As the river moves toward downtown Minneapolis, it appears more and more industrial. From Nicollet Island, the view of the Minneapolis skyline at night is stunning. Keep an eye open for barges and tow boats.

The locks and dams at Upper and Lower St. Anthony Falls sit at the site of a natural falls about 40 feet high that was well-known to explorers and called by the Dakota *Kakabikah* (the severed rock) or *Minirara* (curling water). Some cartographers, such as Joseph Nicollet, recognized the beauty and accuracy in many aboriginal names and preserved them, either in their original language or in their translation to English. Father Louis Hennepin apparently recognized no such thing and named the falls for his favorite saint.

When Hennepin visited the falls in 1680, it was located about 1,000 feet downstream of its present site. When Jonathan Carver visited in 1766, the falls had moved 400 feet closer to its present site by undercutting the soft sandstone that underlies the hard limestone lip. The engraving of the scene from Carver's *Travels* shows the the whole Mississippi falling as a broad curtain into rapids below. On both banks and far into the distance hardly any trees grow at all—only the grassy savanna groomed by Indian fires. On the west bank of the great river, above the falls, where the Whitney Hotel now stands, sit several Dakota tepees. Indian canoes rest lightly on the slick water above the falls.

The water power of the falls built the city of Minneapolis. Sawmills and then flour mills crowded the bluffs to take advantage of the water power. The falls continued to collapse, dragging mills into the river. Had nature run its course, the falls would have reached the end of the limestone cap and disintegrated into a pile of rubble—and a terrific stretch of whitewater. By building the dam, early engineers at the very least preserved the illusion of a waterfall. For years Minneapolis has explored the possibility of using the gradient of the falls to build a whitewater course for canoes and kayaks.

It's possible, even in a canoe or kayak—to pass through the locks around the falls and continue downstream. Otherwise, put in at the University of Minnesota flats on the east side of the river. The 4-mile stretch that follows is one of the most stunning natural features in the Twin Cities. The river passes through a dramatic gorge of limestone. In fall, the bluffs come alive with red and yellow leaves. Paddle back upstream to the put-in or lock around the Ford Dam. As at St. Anthony Falls, there is no reasonable portage.

About 1.5 miles below the Ford Dam, the Mississippi joins the Minnesota River. The confluence of these two major streams was a sacred site to the Dakota. In many ways the confluence is the cradle of Minnesota history. Fort Snelling stands atop the tall cliffs, overlooking the two rivers and Pike Island as it has since 1821, an outpost of European-American civilization in Dakota territory. Surrounding the historic fort is Fort Snelling State Park, 3,300 acres encompassing wooded uplands, savanna, bottomland forest, backwaters, and spring-fed lakes. The tangle

The Mississippi River, near St. Anthony Falls, with downtown Minneapolis within easy walking distance. MINNESOTA OFFICE OF TOURISM

of trails and waterways provides canoeing, boating, fishing, biking, hiking, picnicking, and cross-country skiing. Fort Snelling is a major wildlife area in the metro area, with white-tailed deer, red and gray foxes, woodchucks, badgers, and various herons, egrets, American bittern, waterfowl, and songbirds.

The river glides downstream past bottomland forest and the tall bluffs carved by ancient Glacial River Warren. On the right bluff sits the small town of Mendota, the first permanent non-Indian settlement in Minnesota. There you'll find the house of Henry H. Sibley, fur trader and first governor of the state. The house was built of native limestone in 1835. The spires of St. Peter's Church, built in 1853, are visible nearby.

The river soon arrives in St. Paul, founded at a cleft in the bluffs. The site was as far upstream as a large boat could reliably navigate and unload. Downstream of downtown, the river makes a big right bend. Up on the bluff is Indian Mounds Park, which contains a half dozen prehistoric Indian burial mounds. They are all that remain of 18 that existed when the city was settled in 1856.

The Mississippi slides by the railroad yards south of St. Paul and Pig's Eye Lake, a backwater named for St. Paul's founding tavern keeper and ruffian, Pierre "Pig's Eye" Parrant. The lake is a haven for egrets, herons, eagles, and other wildlife.

The river passes several other backwaters and riverine lakes before wrapping around Upper and Lower Grey Cloud Island. The channels around and between the islands provide a fascinating route for a day trip. Animals such as shorebirds, waterfowl, eagles, and beavers are common. Downstream, the Mississippi spreads out in the broad pool formed by Lock and Dam 2, the navigational dam at Hastings. Good take-outs for this section are the boat ramp on the back side of Lower Grey Cloud Island or the ramp at Spring Lake Park.

Access: Plenty of accesses exist along the metro Mississippi. Consult the map in this book and the MDNR canoe route maps for the metro area.

Shuttle: The possibilities are too numerous to mention. We leave this to you.

ADDITIONAL HELP

MA&G: 41; 42, E1.
Camping: There are no canoe campsites or campgrounds along this stretch.
Food, gas, and lodging: Minneapolis, St. Paul.
For more information: MDNR Information Center, U.S. Army Corps of Engineers web page.

58 Hastings to Iowa

Character: Below Hastings, the Mississippi spreads wide into innumerable backwaters, side channels, and riverine lakes. These features provide great opportunities to watch birds and other wildlife.

Paddling time: Day trips and overnights are possible.

Hazards: Watch for barges and other large watercraft. Wind can kick up big waves on wide-open lakes and stretches of river. Don't approach too close to either the upstream or downstream sides of the big navigation dams.

Maps: MDNR *Mississippi River Canoe Routes 10* and *12* and the MDNR *Mississippi River Guide,* which shows the river in greater detail.

The paddling: From the Twin Cities to the Iowa border, the Mississippi flows over several locks and dams, built earlier this century to create a chain of navigable pools along the river. The backwaters created by these dams form a fascinating labyrinth for paddlers.

58 Hastings to Iowa

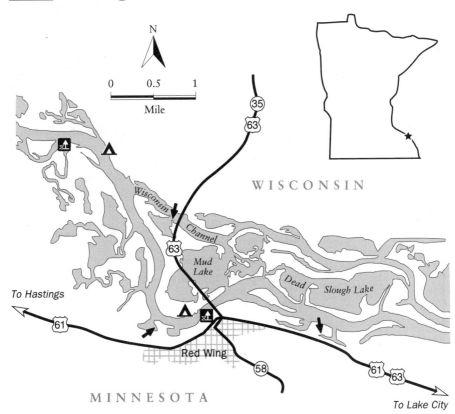

58 Hastings to Iowa

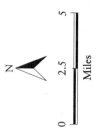

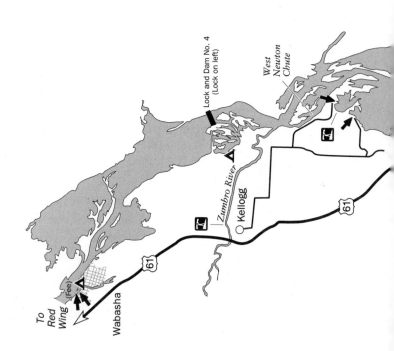

To Winona,
La Crescent

61

Lock and Dam No. 5
(Lock on right)

(Fee)

Weaver
Bottoms

Minneiska

Weaver

M I N N E S O T A

179

Some paddlers will want to start at one point and paddle downstream for many miles, as if they were traveling a run-of-the-mill river, but the Mississippi ain't no run-of-the-mill stream. It's big and sprawling and varied with bluffs on each side, like a spine of mountains winding down each shore. Many stretches are lakelike. Tow boats maneuver mammoth strings of barges up and downriver.

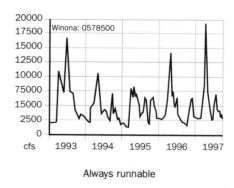

Always runnable

A good way to paddle the river is to explore the backwaters and lakes and return to your point of departure. Places to explore include the sloughs around Colville Park downstream from Red Wing, the islands and sand spits between Wabasha and Weaver Bottoms, and the islands and back channels just upstream from Fountain City. Most paddlers will want to pass on Lake Pepin, which can be windy and dangerous for small craft.

Many parks and rest areas lie along the river. Moreover, most of the islands and dredge spoil sites (beachlike accumulations of dredged sands) are open to public use, including camping.

The river and its backwaters provide an incredible variety of fishing. Species such as smallmouth bass, walleye, sauger, white bass, flathead catfish, and channel

Lake Pepin is a natural widening of the Mississippi River below Red Wing.
MINNESOTA OFFICE OF TROUISM

catfish are found along the edge of the main channel, often congregating around wing dams and riprap. Largemouth bass, crappies, sunfish, and northern pike are often found in backwaters, depending on the season and water level.

The backwater lakes and channels also support a great variety of shorebirds, waterfowl, and raptors. Look for herons and egrets wading the shallows, kingfishers perching on low limbs overhanging the water, and bald eagles, turkey vultures, and white pelicans soaring in the thermals. Migrating waterfowl are common in spring and fall. In late fall, thousands of tundra swans flock to Weaver Bottoms, a backwater lake between Wabasha and Winona.

Access: Consult MDNR canoe route maps and the *Mississippi River Guide* for accesses.

ADDITIONAL HELP

MA&G: 27; 34–35.

Camping: Check maps for campsites. Most islands and dredge spoil sites are open to camping. State parks in the area with camping include Frontenac and O.L. Kipp.

Food, gas, and lodging: Hastings, Red Wing, Wabasha, Winona.

For more information: MDNR Information Center and U.S. Army Corps of Engineers web page.

Central

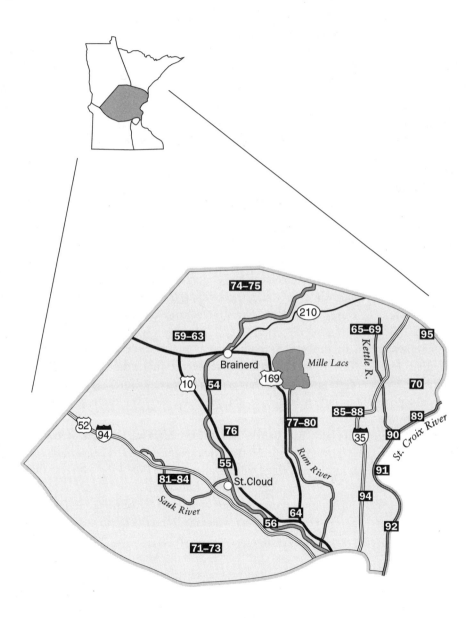

CROW WING RIVER

`59` Seventh Crow Wing Lake to First Crow Wing Lake

Character: The upper Crow Wing scarcely resembles a river at all, but runs through a series of lakes. The lakes and short connecting streams provide good fishing.
Length: 20 miles.
Average run time: Ten hours.
Class: Quiet.
Skill level: Beginner.
Optimal flow: The river in this stretch is rarely too low to run.
Average gradient: 1 foot per mile.
Hazards: Watch out for the dam at the outlet of Fifth Crow Wing Lake.
Maps: MDNR *Crow Wing River Canoe Route.*

The paddling: Eleven lakes, joined by short sections of stream, form the upper Crow Wing River. The lakes are named in reverse order, from Eleventh Crow Wing Lake near the head of the drainage to First Crow Wing Lake, where the Crow Wing takes on its riverine character. The stream segments connecting the first four lakes are short and very small, providing little of interest to canoeists looking to paddle a moving stream. The stretch from Eleventh to Tenth is not passable.

But downstream, beginning at Seventh Crow Wing Lake, the waterway is popular with canoeists. The river in this stretch takes on the characteristics of the lakes it joins; the water is clear and the fish that occupy the river are more typical of lake environments, such as largemouth bass and panfish. The river and lakes provide excellent fishing.

The 11 headwaters lakes are "kettle" lakes, formed as huge blocks of ice, left behind by retreating glaciers about 10,000 years ago, melted. The ground collapsed and the resulting basins filled with water. In all, they total about 5,000 acres. Most are ringed by cottages and homes, but First Crow Wing Lake, surrounded by state wildlife land, remains quite wild. Because of the abundance of lakes and groundwater in the Crow Wing watershed, the river's flow is stable.

The Crow Wing was called *Kagiwegwon* ("raven feather" or "raven's wing") by the Ojibwa for an island near its confluence with the Mississippi that is shaped like the wing of a bird. The watershed was touched by the events so typical of much of Minnesota. During the 1700s and early 1800s, Ojibwa battled the Dakota and eventually pushed them from the region. French, British, and then American fur traders traveled the basin's waterways. In 1792 the North West Company established the Wadena Trading Post on the west bluff of the Crow Wing at its confluence with the Partridge River. Well-known trader Jean Baptiste Cadotte

59 Seventh Crow Wing Lake to First Crow Wing Lake

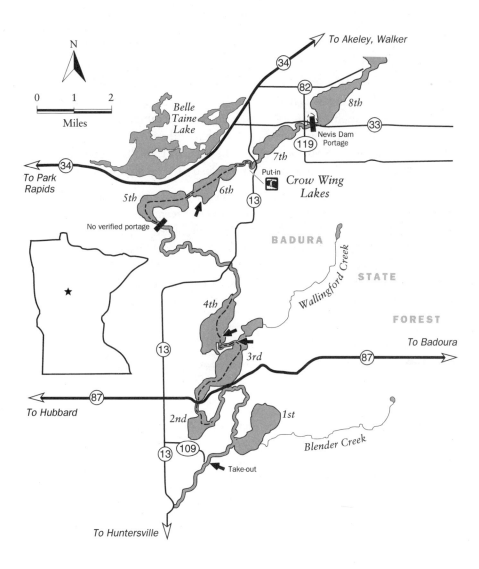

N

0   1   2
Miles

To Akeley, Walker

34

82

8th

33

Belle
Taine
Lake

Nevis Dam
Portage

119

34

To Park
Rapids

7th

Put-in

Crow Wing
Lakes

5th

6th

13

No verified portage

BADURA

Wallingford Creek

STATE

4th

FOREST

To Badoura

3rd

87

13

87

To Hubbard

2nd

1st

Blender Creek

13   109

Take-out

To Huntersville

operated a post at the mouth of the Leaf River. Several posts of less importance were located throughout the area. A site along the Mississippi across from the mouth of the Crow Wing, the location of English and then American trading posts, became the village of Old Crow Wing. The town became a stop on one branch of the network of trails from the Red River to St. Paul, followed by two-wheeled ox carts carrying furs, bison hides, powder, shot, sugar, tea, apples, and flour. The carts' ungreased wooden wheels and axles let loose frightful screams that carried across the countryside for miles.

Logging was the chief industry of the area during the late 1800s and early 1900s. Each spring, dams were built on the Crow Wing, Redeye, and Shell Rivers to store water for log drives to mills on the Mississippi River at Little Falls and St. Cloud. Nimrod, established in 1879 as a railroad tie camp, was an important logging town when timber was being cut throughout the Crow Wing basin. Lumbering grew and railroads spread through the area. By the 1900s, however, most virgin timber had been cut and the logging industry fell off sharply.

Access: **Seventh Crow Wing Lake put-in:** From Nevis, drive south 2 miles on County Route 13 to the bridge and access between Seventh and Sixth Crow Wing Lakes. **First Crow Wing Lake take-out:** From Hubbard, drive east 7 miles on County Route 109 to the bridge and access at the outlet of First Crow Wing Lake.

Alternate accesses are available at the southern tip of Sixth Crow Wing Lake off an unmarked county road, the east shore of Fourth Crow Wing Lake, and the northeast shore of Third Crow Wing Lake off an unmarked county road along those shores.

Shuttle: 11 miles one way. About 30 minutes.

ADDITIONAL HELP

MA&G: 61, D9–D8; 62, B1.
Camping: Camping is possible at the Eleventh Crow Wing Lake access north of Akeley. Camping is also possible at several sites farther downstream along the Crow Wing. See the following trip descriptions for details.
Food, gas, and lodging: Akeley, Park Rapids, Walker.
For more information: MDNR Information Center.

60 First Crow Wing Lake to Mary Brown Landing

Character: Leaving First Crow Wing Lake, the Crow Wing River takes on the character of a free-flowing stream. Clear and placid, it's perfect for the first-time river runner. Wooded and largely undeveloped, this stretch has many campsites and is a good choice for an overnight trip.
Length: 11.5 miles.
Average run time: Four to six hours.
Class: Quiet.
Skill level: Beginner.
Optimal flow: Above 1.5 feet on the gauge at the County Road 12 bridge in Nimrod or more than 250 cfs on the gauge at Nimrod (check USGS website). The lakes and permeable soils of the watershed soak up and hold runoff, moderating the river's response to heavy rains. The river is rarely too low to run.
Average gradient: 1 foot per mile.
Hazards: No special hazards.
Maps: MDNR *Crow Wing River Canoe Route*

The paddling: The current is lively, but there are no rapids along this section of the Crow Wing River. Because of its beginnings in a series of lakes, the river flows exceedingly clear. The riverside is wooded.

About 2 miles below the put-in, the Shell River joins from the west. At this point, the Shell is considerably larger than the Crow Wing. It, too, is clear with a sandy bottom. Its name springs from the abundance of freshwater mussels in the river. The lower 15 miles of the Shell make fine canoeing for beginners. Put in at the boat ramp on Lower Twin Lake about 5 miles northeast of Menahga, or at the Shell City Landing at the County Route 24 bridge about 3 miles above the river's confluence with the Crow Wing.

In another 3 miles, the Crow Wing passes Tree Farm Landing, an access and campsite. It is one of more than a dozen riverside campsites, most owned and maintained by Wadena County. See the map for locations of others.

Access: The **First Crow Wing Lake put-in** is located at the County Road 109 bridge over the Crow Wing at the outlet of First Crow Wing Lake. From Menahga, drive northeast about 8 miles to Hubbard; then drive east about 8 miles to the bridge and put-in. **Mary Brown take-out:** from Menahga, drive east 4.5 miles on County Route 17 to County route 23; turn south and drive 3 miles to County Route 15; drive east 4 miles to access.

Shorten the route by using alternative accesses, listed in route description above.

Shuttle: 12 miles one way. About 30 minutes.

60 First Crow Wing Lake to Mary Brown Landing

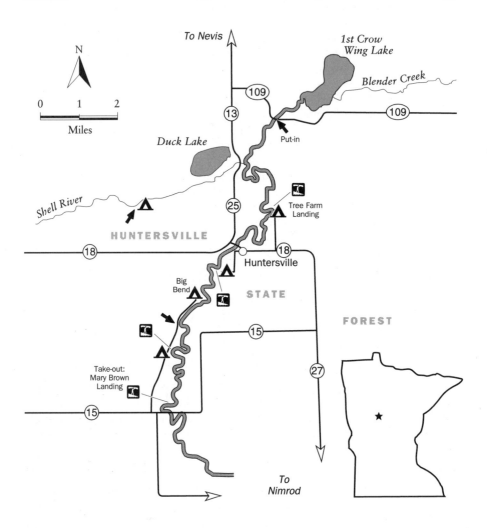

ADDITIONAL HELP

MA&G: 61, D9–E8.

Camping: Camping is possible at several sites along the Crow Wing. See map description for locations.

Food, gas, and lodging: Menahga, Park Rapids.

For more information: MDNR Information Center.

61 Mary Brown Landing to Nimrod

Character: The current speeds up and the Crow Wing races through several easy rapids—not exactly whitewater, but a fun ride, especially for novice paddlers.
Length: 10 miles.
Average run time: Three to five hours.
Class: I.
Skill level: Beginner.
Optimal flow: Above 1.5 feet on the gauge at the County Road 12 bridge in Nimrod or check the USGS website for at least 250 cfs on the Nimrod gauge. The river is rarely too low to run.
Average gradient: 3.5 feet per mile.
Hazards: No special hazards, but several easy rapids.
Maps: MDNR *Crow Wing River Canoe Route.*

The paddling: Hold on to your paddle — the Crow Wing picks up the pace! Actually, the river flirts with the wild side only briefly as it runs through several swift, bouldery stretches that rate class I. The first, about 3 miles into the run, is **Butterfield Rapids.** Then, at intervals of a mile or more, are **Walkins Rapids, Burrows Rapids,** and **Westra Rapids.**

Despite the presence of these few rapids, the river remains more placid than wild and continues to flow with its characteristic clarity. The bed is mostly sandy and loaded with freshwater mussels.

Fishing on the Crow Wing River near Nimrod. MINNESOTA OFFICE OF TOURISM

61 Mary Brown Landing to Nimrod

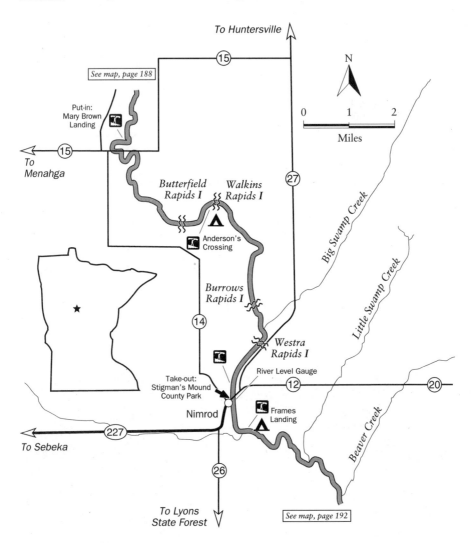

To Huntersville

N

See map, page 188

Put-in:
Mary Brown
Landing

15

15
To
Menahga

0   1   2
Miles

27

Butterfield
Rapids I

Walkins
Rapids I

Anderson's
Crossing

Burrows
Rapids I

14

Westra
Rapids I

River Level Gauge

Take-out:
Stigman's Mound
County Park

12

20

Nimrod

Frames
Landing

227

To Sebeka

26

To Lyons
State Forest

See map, page 192

Big Swamp Creek

Little Swamp Creek

Beaver Creek

Access: **Mary Brown put-in:** From Menahga, drive 4.5 miles east on County Route 17 to County Route 23; turn south and drive 3 miles to County Route 15; drive east 4 miles to the access. **Nimrod take-out:** drive to Stigman's Mound County Park at the County Route 12 bridge on the north edge of town.

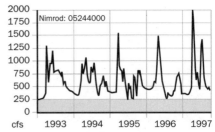

250 cfs = estimated minimum
for good paddling

Other access is possible at Anderson's Crossing 4 miles north of Nimrod off County Route 14, and Frames Landing a mile south of Nimrod on County Road 139.

Shuttle: 8 miles one way. About 20 minutes.

Pillager, MN: 05247500

400 cfs = minimum for good paddling

ADDITIONAL HELP

MA&G: 61, E8.

Camping: Camping is possible at Anderson's Crossing, river right, about 4 miles below the put-in. Other sites are available, both upstream and down. See the previous trip map for locations.

Food, gas, and lodging: Menahga, Park Rapids, Wadena, Brainerd.

For more information: MDNR Information Center.

62 Nimrod to Motley

Character: The Crow Wing resumes its placid character, winding past woodlands and settling into lazy oxbows. Many public campsites make for good overnight trips.

Length: 43 miles.

Average run time: Two to three days. Many shorter trips are possible.

Class: Quiet.

Skill level: Beginner.

Optimal flow: Above 1.5 feet on the gauge at the County Road 12 bridge in Nimrod, or above 1.5 feet on the gauge on the Minnesota Highway 210 bridge in Motley. Or check the USGS website for at least 250 cfs on the Nimrod gauge. The river is rarely too low to run.

Average gradient: 2.4 feet per mile.

Hazards: No special hazards.

Maps: MDNR.

The paddling: Once past Nimrod, you've seen the last of the Crow Wing's rapids. Nonetheless, it's a popular canoe route, with easy current, clear water, and largely wooded shores. It also has many accesses, campsites, and picnic areas.

Compared to the upper river, the view is more open, the vistas longer. Below Knob Hill, the river meanders frequently. The river channel has created many oxbows. Gradually the riverside becomes marshier. As you approach Staples, you'll notice more farmland and houses.

62 Nimrod to Motley

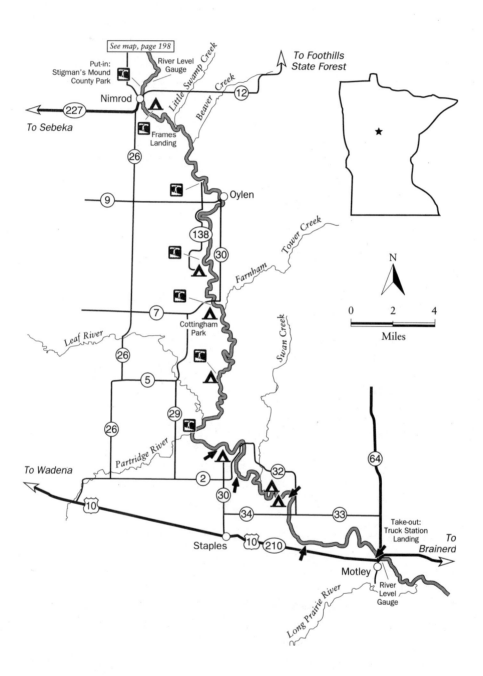

See map, page 198

Put-in:
Stigman's Mound
County Park

River Level
Gauge

To Foothills
State Forest

Little Swamp Creek

Beaver Creek

227

Nimrod

To Sebeka

Frames
Landing

26

9

Oylen

138

30

Tower Creek

Farnham

7

Cottingham
Park

Leaf River

26

5

Swan Creek

29

26

Partridge River

2

32

30

34

33

64

To Wadena

10

Staples

10

210

Take-out:
Truck Station
Landing

To
Brainerd

Motley

River
Level
Gauge

Long Prairie River

N

0   2   4
Miles

12

Many small county parks appear along the river, providing convenient access and camping. See the map for locations.

With its sandy bottom and lack of deep pools, the Crow Wing provides rather marginal fish habitat. The most common fish are white suckers and shorthead redhorse. Still, anglers can find northern pike, rock bass, and a few walleye scattered throughout the river.

Access: **Nimrod put-in:** Drive to Stigman's Mound County Park at the County Route 12 bridge on the north edge of town. **Motley take-out:** On the north edge of Motley, at the MN 210 bridge over the Crow Wing.

This stretch of the river is peppered with other public accesses that can be used for shorter trips. See the map for locations.

Shuttle: 37 miles one way. About 1.5 hours.

ADDITIONAL HELP

MA&G: 61, E8; 53, A9–B9; 54, B1.
Camping: Camping is possible at several sites along the Crow Wing, both upstream and down. See the map for details.
Food, gas, and lodging: Wadena, Motley.
For more information: MDNR Information Center.

63 Motley to Mississippi River

Character: The final stretch of the Crow Wing is influenced by two long reservoirs formed by the Pillager and Sylvan Dams. This stretch will be of little interest to most canoeists, though it is possible to paddle the reservoirs, portage the dams, and continue downstream on the Mississippi.
Length: 20.5 miles.
Average run time: Eight to ten hours.
Class: Quiet.
Skill level: Beginner.
Optimal flow: Always runnable.
Average gradient: Virtually none, except for the two dams.
Hazards: Do not paddle too close to the dams.
Maps: MDNR *Crow Wing River Canoe Route.*

The paddling: About 3 miles downstream from Motley, the Crow Wing River reaches the still waters of Lake Placid, the reservoir formed by the Pillager Dam. Several more miles of perfectly flat water greet the intrepid paddler, who can portage the power dam on river right, 125 yards. Within just a couple miles more, you will reach the still waters of Sylvan Reservoir. Portage river right, 125 yards. Below the Sylvan Dam, the Crow Wing flows as a free river once again for 4 miles to its confluence with the Mississippi River.

63 Motley to Mississippi River

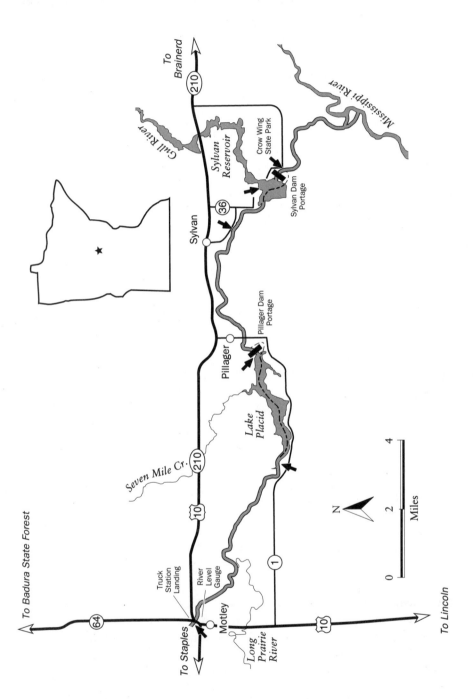

Largemouth bass, typical of lake environments, are found in Sylvan Reservoir. Below the Sylvan Dam, anglers fish for species that travel upstream from the Mississippi, including walleyes and smallmouth bass.

Access: **Motley put-in:** On the north edge of town at the Minnesota Highway 210 bridge over the Crow Wing. The **Mississippi take-out** is located on the east bank of the Mississippi River about a mile upstream from its confluence with the Crow Wing in Crow Wing State Park.

Alternative accesses are available at the upstream end of Lake Placid off County Route 28; at the Pillager Dam on the south edge of the town of Pillager; at the upstream end of the Sylvan Reservoir just south of the town of Sylvan; on the north shore of Sylvan Reservoir off County Route 36; and below the Sylvan Dam off County Route 36.

Shuttle: 35 miles one way. About 1.5 hours. Note that the Mississippi River take-out is inconvenient because you have to travel all the way into Brainerd to cross the Mississippi. Consider one of the alternative take-outs.

ADDITIONAL HELP

MA&G: 54, C1–4.
Camping: Crow Wing State Park.
Food, gas, and lodging: Motley, Brainerd.
For more information: MDNR Information Center.

64 Elk River

Character: The Elk is a quiet woodland river, tailor-made for a day's paddle or fishing trip.
Length: 6 miles.
Average run time: Three to five hours.
Class: I.
Skill level: Beginner.
Optimal flow: At least 200 cfs on the gauge near Big Lake—check the USGS website.
Average gradient: 4.7 feet per mile.
Hazards: Watch for snags, especially if you start your trip upstream from Big Lake.
Maps: PRIM.

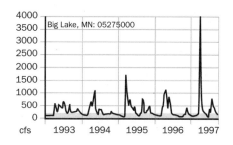

200 cfs = estimated minimum
for good paddling

195

64 Elk River

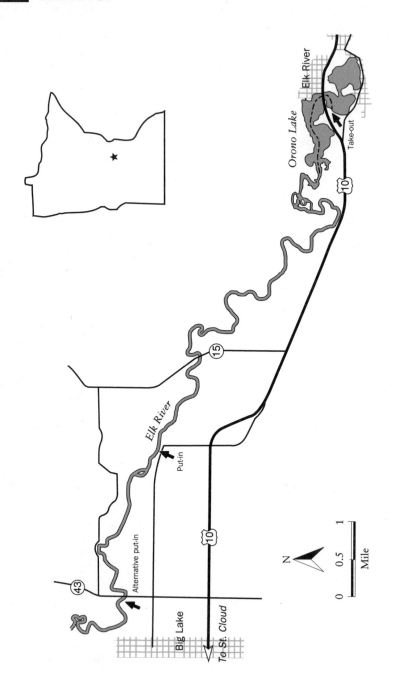

The upper Elk River is a good stream for northern pike fishing. GREG BREINING

The paddling: The Elk, a tributary of the Mississippi, glides through shallow, rocky rapids and sandy swifts as it passes marshes, rolling hills, forested bluffs, and farmland. Although the rapids are short and easy, windfalls may block the river. In fact, the upper reaches, near Becker, can be impassable. Fishing can be good for smallmouth bass, walleye, and especially northern pike.

Finish your trip by paddling east across Orono Lake and under the U.S. Highway 10 causeway to the boat landing.

Access: Big Lake put-in: Launch at the canoe landing 2.5 miles east of Big Lake on an unnumbered county road. Otherwise, put in on County Road 43 a mile northeast of town for a trip 4 miles longer. The **Elk River take-out** is located on the south shore of Orono Lake, just south and west of the US 10 causeway over the lake. Take US 10 to the road that loops around the south shore of the lake.

Shuttle: 6 miles one way. About 15 minutes.

ADDITIONAL HELP

MA&G: 40, A5.
Camping: River campsites are not available.
Food, gas, and lodging: Elk River, Big Lake.
For more information: Not much information is available.

KETTLE RIVER

65 County Road 131 to County Route 52

Character: When this small headwaters stream is high or very high, canoeists will enjoy a swift run through long, wavy rapids.
Length: 16 miles.
Average run time: Four to six hours.
Class: I (medium flow), II (high flow).
Skill level: Intermediate.
Optimal flow: At least 2.5 feet on the gauge on the County Route 12 bridge near the town of Kettle River or 2.5 feet on gauge at State Route 23 bridge in Banning State Park. As the County Route 12 gauge reading creeps above 4.5 or more, many rapids turn to class II. Or check the USGS website for at least 1,200 cfs on the gauge below Sandstone.
Average gradient: 10 feet per mile.
Hazards: Water is usually cold when this stretch is high.
Maps: MDNR *Kettle River Canoe Route* (starts at Minnesota Highway 27 near Moose Lake).

The paddling: Because the river is small, steep, and drains quickly, it's too low and rocky to run most of the year. But when heavy snowmelt or spring rains funnel

65 County Road 131 to County Route 52

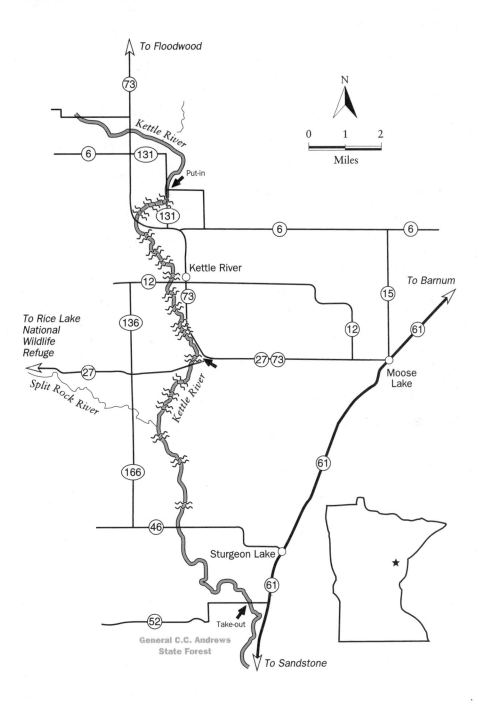

To Floodwood

73

N

Kettle River

6 131

0 1 2
Miles

Put-in

131

6 6

Kettle River

12

73 15 To Barnum

136

12

To Rice Lake
National
Wildlife
Refuge

27 27 73

Moose
Lake

Split Rock River

61

Kettle River

166

61

46

Sturgeon Lake

61

52

Take-out

General C.C. Andrews
State Forest

To Sandstone

down the watershed, hop aboard for a roller coaster ride on a series of long, wavy rapids. Rapids are steepest and most numerous in the first half of the run. They're great for beginning whitewater paddlers to develop their skills. To stay dry in an open canoe, you'll need to pick your way past the largest waves. At lower levels, the river will keep you busy dodging boulders. Otherwise, the rapids don't pose many technical difficulties, just a fun ride.

The Kettle River was designated the state's first wild and scenic river in 1975; on the basis of beauty alone, it deserves the distinction. Even though most of the valley's white pine was logged during the late 1800s, much of the valley and riverside today is heavily forested with hardwoods and scattered conifers.

Access: **CR 131 put-in:** From the town of Kettle River, drive north on Minnesota Highway 73 about 2 miles to CR 131; turn right and drive about a mile to the bridge. **County Route 52 take-out:** From town of Sturgeon Lake, drive south 2 miles on County Route 61 to County Route 52; turn right and drive 0.5 mile to bridge.

To shorten the run and shuttle time, use these alternate access points: MN 27 bridge 5.5 miles west of Moose Lake, or County Route 46 3 miles west of Sturgeon Lake. In planning a trip, remember that this stretch gets easier as you go.

All accesses are undeveloped, with roadside parking.

Shuttle: 18 miles one way. About one hour.

ADDITIONAL HELP

MA&G: 57, B5.
Camping: A canoe-only campsite is located about a mile downstream from County Route 46. Camp by car at Moose Lake State Park and Willow River Campground in General C.C. Andrews State Forest.
Food, gas, and lodging: Moose Lake, Cloquet.
For more information: MDNR Information Center.

66 County Route 52 to Minnesota Highway 23

Character: Here's a stretch of river for those looking for a peaceful, wooded route that is runnable even when the water is low.
Length: 16 miles.
Average run time: Six to eight hours.
Class: Quiet (one class I rapids).
Skill level: Beginner.
Optimal flow: More than 1 foot at the gauge on the Minnesota Highway 23 bridge in Banning State Park, or check the USGS website for at least 500 cfs on the gauge below Sandstone.
Average gradient: 1.9 feet per mile.
Hazards: Watch for fallen trees and driftwood on outside river bends.
Maps: MDNR.

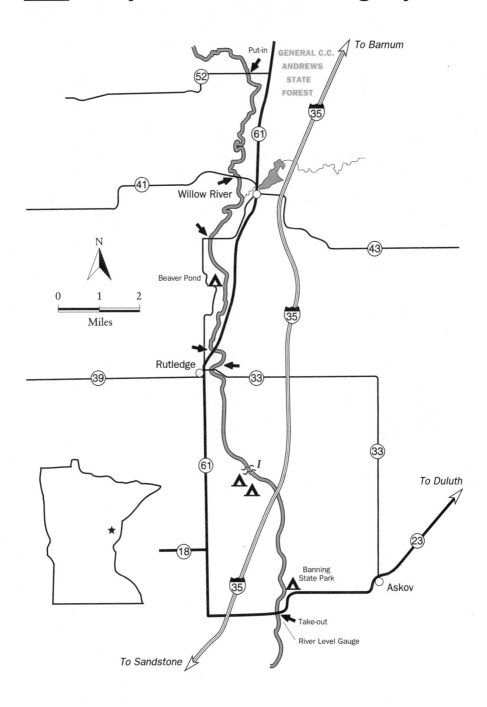

To Barnum

Put-in

GENERAL C.C.
ANDREWS
STATE
FOREST

52

61

35

41

Willow River

N

43

Beaver Pond

35

0   1   2

Miles

Rutledge

39

33

33

To Duluth

61

I

23

18

Askov

35

Banning
State Park

Take-out

River Level Gauge

To Sandstone

The paddling: Plan on a slow, lackadaisical meander through wooded bottomlands. The only rapids of note is a bouldery class I pitch about a mile above Interstate 35. With several campsites available and little chance of dumping your gear, this is a good stretch for an overnight trip. Keep an eye out for songbirds, waterfowl, kingfishers, herons, beavers, and even river otters. With its long build, powerful tail, and webbed feet, the otter is supremely adapted to catching fish underwater. When they encounter a paddler, they often bob and dive near the boat, as if out of curiosity.

Access: County Route 52 put-in: From town of Sturgeon Lake, drive south 2 miles on County Route 61 to County Route 52; turn right and drive 0.5 mile to bridge. **MN 23 take-out:** Exit I-35 on MN 23 east, drive 1.5 miles across Kettle River bridge and turn left to the access.

Alternate access is available at County Route 41 northwest of Willow River; unmarked county road southwest of Willow River; and County Route 61 and County Route 33, both in Rutledge. All access is undeveloped, without parking lots.

Shuttle: 15 miles one way. About 45 minutes.

ADDITIONAL HELP

MA&G: 57, 6C.
Camping: Canoe campsites between Willow River and Rutledge, a mile above I-35, and above MN 23. Auto camping at Willow River Campground in General C.C. Andrews State Forest and Banning State Park.
Food, gas, and lodging: Hinckley, Sandstone, Cloquet.
For more information: MDNR Information Center.

67 Banning State Park to Old Dam Site

Character: With medium to high water, this stretch fills with waves, souse holes and many play spots; it is suitable only for experienced paddlers. If you paddle an open canoe, stuff it with plenty of flotation to make it easier to fish from the river.

Length: 4.5 miles.

Average run time: Four to six hours. You could paddle straight through in much less time, but you'll want to scout rapids and explore play spots.

Class: II–III (low to medium flow), II–IV (high flow).

Skill level: Intermediate to expert.

Optimal flow: 2 to 5 feet on the gauge on the Minnesota Highway 23 bridge in Banning State Park. It is runnable (but very rocky) down to about 1 foot (about 500 cfs on the USGS gauge below Sandstone— check the USGS website). Above 5 feet, the explosive waves get downright spooky.

Average gradient: 11 feet per mile. The first 1.5 miles is much steeper.

Hazards: Sandstone cliffs have been severely undercut by the river. Several inexperienced paddlers, not realizing the dangers, have died on this stretch.

Maps: MDNR.

The paddling: Whoever designed the Kettle River never heard of saving the best for last. No sooner do you push off from the state park landing than you plunge into the toughest, most complex rapids the river offers, **Blueberry Slide** (class II in low water; class IV in very high water, when large waves form). Scout on river right before you launch, or, for a better view, paddle across to the island at the head of the rapids and scout from river left. The river slides over a long, gnarly slab of sandstone, sending up a dandy surfing wave. Run this rapids toward the left, where you find the deepest water and then follow the dancing waves, moving to the right to drop over a couple more ledges about 100 yards downstream. A sandstone ramp on far river right may tempt you, but don't give in. The shallow water will slow you down and the hole at the bottom will suck you back and spit you out (though at low to medium levels, it's a fun place to play). If the water is over 3 feet, you can run the small channel on the backside of the island and drop over a 4-foot falls. But don't do it if logs have jammed in the drop. Portage Blueberry Slide on the left.

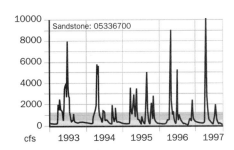

500 cfs = minimum for good paddling on No. 1
1200 cfs = minimum for good paddling on No. 2

67 Banning State Park to Old Dam Site

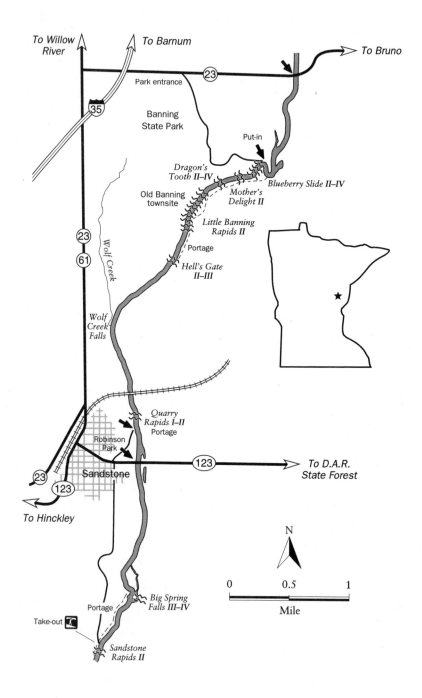

To Willow River

To Barnum

To Bruno

23

Park entrance

35

Banning State Park

Put-in

Dragon's Tooth II–IV

Blueberry Slide II–IV

Old Banning townsite

Mother's Delight II

Little Banning Rapids II

23

Portage

61

Hell's Gate II–III

Wolf Creek

Wolf Creek Falls

Quarry Rapids I–II

Portage

Robinson Park

23

Sandstone

123

To D.A.R. State Forest

123

To Hinckley

Big Spring Falls III–IV

Portage

Take-out

N

Sandstone Rapids II

0   0.5   1

Mile

A solo paddler negotiates Little Banning Rapids. GREG BREINING

Next is **Mother's Delight,** a bouldery, wavy class II pitch run down the middle. Then comes **Dragon's Tooth** (class II–IV), where cliffs pinch the river down to about 50 feet wide. Portage and scout on river left. The **Tooth,** a large boulder near the bottom of this short, powerful rapids, forms a souse hole at most levels and an explosive wave at high levels. Start your run on river left and then move decisively toward the middle, threading your way between the jutting cliff on the left and the tooth on the right. Yes, at low and medium levels you can run the skinny channel to the right of the tooth, but it's a tight fit and the cliffs are badly undercut.

Take a deep breath and relax. The **Little Banning Rapids** (class II) are pure enjoyment, a swift, bouncy chain of waves. Get out on river right to explore the remains of the old town site of Banning. Built on the riverside in the late 1800s, Banning once had a population of about 300. Twenty million tons of sandstone were quarried from the nearby cliffs. But the industry collapsed in the early 1900s. By 1918 Banning stood deserted. Today the remnants of an old road follow the river. The walls of two old quarry buildings stand next to the rapids. Trees grow inside the roofless powerhouse, forming a decrepit and joyless kind of Japanese garden.

For several hundred yards, the river runs dark and quiet through a picturesque gorge. On river right, note the potholes, formed when glacial meltwater spun stones and boulders in the soft sandstone. It was for these features that the Kettle

The dismantling of an old dam just downstream lowered the water level, revealing this runnable drop, called Big Spring Falls. MINNESOTA DEPARTMENT OF NATURAL RESOURCES

was named. (Misnamed, actually. In geological parlance, a "kettle" is something altogether different, a lake formed by a huge ice block buried and left behind by a glacier.)

Suddenly, the slick water gathers speed. Soon it erupts into a 100-yard-long chain of 2- to 3-foot waves that lead to a passageway of tall sandstone bluffs on either side of the river. This is **Hell's Gate** (class II–III). Portage left. Despite its name and formidable first impression, it's a clear shot down the middle. Get ready for the peaking waves and turbulence at the bottom.

Flat water follows Hell's Gate. On river right at the next bend, Wolf Creek enters the Kettle. Hike back into the woods 100 feet to find a pretty 10-foot waterfall.

About 0.3 miles downstream from Wolf Creek, a cave lies in the sandstone bluffs on the right. The remains of several quarries are found along the bluff downstream to Robinson Park.

Just before Robinson Park the river drops over **Quarry Rapids** (class I–II). Portage right. Despite its benign appearance, a tricky crosscurrent has flipped many a canoe and kayak. Large waves form in high water. In low water, watch out for jagged boulders and spikes from an old log dam.

Many paddlers end their trip at Robinson Park. Otherwise, continue downstream 1 mile to **Big Spring Falls,** an 8-foot falls that splits around a pine-crowned island. Big Spring Falls had remained hidden beneath the placid waters of a small reservoir for nearly a century, revealed only when the Sandstone Dam was dismantled in 1995. Scout from the island at the top of the drop. Portage on the right. The right side (class III–IV) plunges over a steep drop with a big sucky hole at the bottom. The left side (class III–IV) slides down a slope of sandstone and scours an undercut cliff; work from eddy to eddy and avoid the deceptively strong hole at the bottom of the drop. At extremely high water, a runnable chute (class III) begins to flow on the extreme far right.

On the series of low ledges where the dam once stood is **Sandstone Rapids** (class II), which kicks up good surfing waves at medium to high water levels. The take-out lies next to the rapids on the right. Portage right.

Access: Banning State Park put-in: Exit Interstate 35 at MN 23 east, drive 0.5 mile to the park entrance. Follow park road to river. A state park vehicle permit is required. A parking lot is available nearby. **Old Dam Site take-out:** From the city of Sandstone, drive east on Minnesota Highway 123. Right before the Kettle River bridge, turn south and follow Pine Avenue (which turns to dirt) about 2 miles to dead end. Park on the edge of dirt road.

Alternate MN 23 put-in: Exit I-35 on MN 23 east, drive 1.5 miles across Kettle River bridge and turn left to access. **Alternate Robinson Park access:** From Sandstone, drive east on MN 123. Right before the Kettle River bridge, turn north into park. Good parking is available at both sites.

Shuttle: 8 miles one way. About 30 minutes.

ADDITIONAL HELP

MA&G: 57, D6.
Camping: Auto camping at Banning State Park.
Food, gas, and lodging: Hinckley, Sandstone, Banning Junction.
For more information: MDNR Information Center.

68   Old Dam Site to Minnesota Highway 48

Character: Having spent most of its gradient and energy in its wild ride through Banning State Park, the Kettle now slows and settles, winding past wooded banks, with only a few minor outbursts.
Length: 14 miles.
Average run time: Five to seven hours.
Class: Quiet (two rapids rate class I–II, depending on level).
Skill level: Beginner.
Optimal flow: Over 5 feet on the gauge on the MN 48 bridge. At lower levels, you'll probably have to wade and drag through rapids.
Average gradient: 2.5 feet per mile.
Hazards: Watch for fallen trees and driftwood on outside river bends.
Maps: MDNR *Kettle River Canoe Route.*

The paddling: For the most part, this stretch provides a placid route through a shallow, wooded valley. Look for songbirds, waterfowl, great blue herons, beavers, and river otters, especially in the backwaters that lie off the main channel.

The only navigational problems come early in the trip. The put-in lies beside class II **Sandstone Rapids** (see previous trip). If the prospect of running the final 100 yards of the rapids intimidates you, carry down the right side to the end of the rapids. A bouldery class I–II rapids less than a mile downstream can also cause problems for beginners, especially when high water kicks up waves. An additional 3 miles downstream lies another class I–II rapids. From there on, it's clear sailing.

As you drive the shuttle on this section, about a mile east of Hinckley on MN 48, you'll pass a dark rock obelisk that rises about 40 feet above a country cemetery. Erected by the state, it is dedicated to the 418 known victims in the region of the Hinckley fire of September 1, 1894. Buried in four trenches next to the monument are the remains of 248 residents of Hinckley who died in the forest fire, which ignited the slash left from white-pine logging in the area and swept northwest through Hinckley and across the Kettle River. Many townsfolk caught the last two trains traveling out of town through dense smoke. Others took shelter in the Kettle River and a shallow depression known as Skunk Lake. In an old train station on the west side of town, the Hinckley Fire Museum, open 10 A.M. to 5 P.M. May through October, tells the story of this notorious disaster.

Access: Old Dam Site put-in: From the city of Sandstone, drive east on Minnesota Highway 123. Right before the Kettle River bridge, turn south and follow the

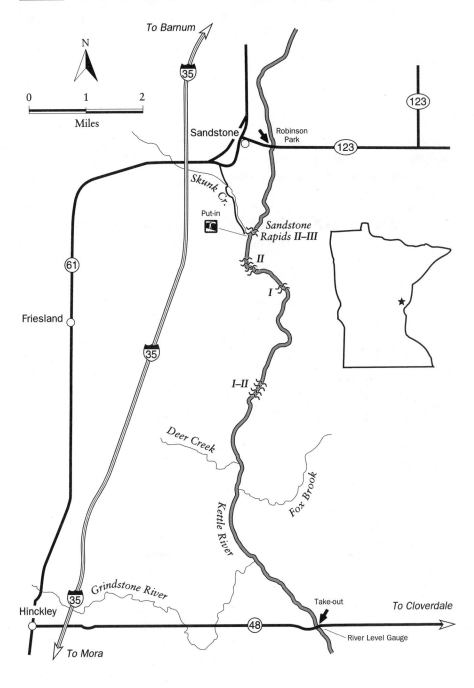

To Barnum

N

0 1 2
Miles

35

123

Sandstone

Robinson
Park

123

Skunk Cr.

Put-in

Sandstone
Rapids II–III

II

I

61

I–II

Friesland

35

Deer Creek

Fox Brook

Kettle River

Grindstone River

Take-out

35

Hinckley

48

To Cloverdale

River Level Gauge

To Mora

road (which turns to dirt) about 2 miles to a dead end. **MN 48 bridge take-out:** From Hinckley exit off Interstate 35, drive east 4.5 miles on MN 48; cross the bridge and turn left. There is a developed access for canoes and small boats with parking.

Shuttle: 15 miles one way. About 45 minutes.

ADDITIONAL HELP

MA&G: 57, E6.
Camping: Auto camping at Banning State Park, St. Croix State Park.
Food, gas, and lodging: Hinckley, Sandstone.
For more information: MDNR Information Center.

69 Minnesota Highway 48 to St. Croix River

Character: With mile after mile of long, easy rapids, wooded bluffs, and good fishing, the final section of the Kettle River is one of the finest day-long canoe runs in Minnesota.
Length: 18.5 miles.
Average run time: Six to nine hours.
Class: I (medium flow), II (high flow).
Skill level: Intermediate.
Optimal flow: At least 5 feet on MN 48 bridge gauge or 500 cfs on USGS gauge below Sandstone.
Average gradient: 4.6 feet per mile.
Hazards: The river is more than 200 feet wide in its final few miles, and swamping in the rapids can lead to a long swim. Be especially careful in cold water.
Maps: MDNR *Kettle River Canoe Route.*

The paddling: Whether you're paddling to enjoy scenery, to watch wildlife, to fish, or to get a dose of light-duty whitewater, this stretch of the Kettle makes for one of the best canoe trips going. The first 7 miles of this stretch wind through bottom-land forest, where you're likely to spot songbirds, waterfowl, kingfishers, and perhaps beavers and otters.

At Maple Island (in St. Croix State Park) the river picks up speed. For the next 7 miles, to its confluence with the St. Croix, the Kettle races through long, bouldery rapids—not much to worry about at medium water levels except dodging a few exposed rocks. In high water, however, a ledge just below **Big Eddy** forms large backrollers that easily can swamp or flip a canoe. In high water it rates class II. Keep right to miss the heaviest water. A couple areas of high banks and cliffs in this stretch are particularly picturesque.

The Kettle joins a channel of the St. Croix known as the Kettle River Slough. This mile-long stretch contains several rapids. All rate class I except a ledge where

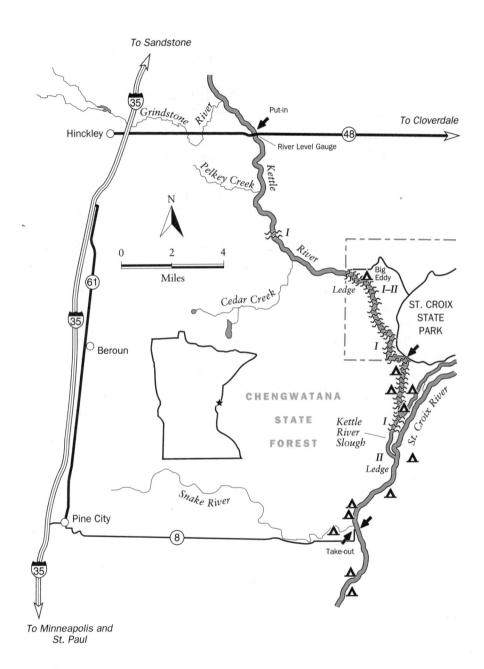

To Sandstone

To Cloverdale

Grindstone River

Hinckley

Put-in

River Level Gauge

Pelkey Creek

Kettle

N

0   2   4
Miles

River

I

Big Eddy

Ledge   I–II

ST. CROIX STATE PARK

Cedar Creek

Beroun

I

CHENGWATANA

STATE

Kettle River Slough

I

FOREST

St. Croix River

II
Ledge

Snake River

Pine City

8

Take-out

To Minneapolis and St. Paul

the slough joins the main channel. The ledge forms a large, wide backroller in high water and rates class II. Stay right to avoid the worst of it.

While most of the Kettle provides good fishing, the rapids and pools in the last few miles provide the most and biggest fish. Smallmouth bass provide supreme sport; fish for them with small jigs, spinners, crankbaits, and minnow lures pitched into deep eddies or the deep water immediately below riffles. Fly-rodders can do well with small poppers, divers, and streamers. Also common in the river are walleye, northern pike, and channel catfish. The state-record lake sturgeon, more than 94 pounds, was caught in the Kettle River. Want to break the record? Fish a worm on the bottom of a deep pool.

Access: **MN 48 bridge put-in:** From Hinckley exit off Interstate 35, drive east 4.5 miles on MN 48; cross the bridge and turn left. The **St. Croix take-out** is located at the confluence of the St. Croix and Snake Rivers. From Pine City, drive 10.5 miles east on County Route 8 to boat ramp. Alternate accesses are available in St. Croix State Park at Maple Island and Kennedy Brook. A vehicle permit is required in the park. Good parking is available at these accesses, as well as the alternate accesses mentioned below.

Shuttle: 29 miles one way. About 1.5 hours. The long shuttle is the drawback of this trip. Using the Maple Island access as a put-in cuts out the long stretch of flat water at the beginning of the trip, but makes the shuttle down to the Snake River take-out even longer. It's possible to make a short run (all whitewater!) from Maple Island to the Kennedy Brook access with a shuttle of only 6 miles one way. But then you miss several miles of fun rapids. Life is full of tough choices.

ADDITIONAL HELP

MA&G: 57, E6; 49, A6.
Camping: Canoe campsites at Big Eddy and several spots near the Kettle's mouth. Auto camping at St. Croix State Park.
Food, gas, and lodging: Pine City, Hinckley.
For more information: MDNR Information Center.

70 Lower Tamarack River

Character: The Lower Tamarack River is an intimate tributary of the St. Croix River with a lively current. Unfortunately, it is runnable only in spring or after heavy rains.

Length: 17 miles.

Average run time: Six to eight hours.

Class: I.

Skill level: Beginner to intermediate.

Optimal flow: No gauge reading available. The river, especially in upper reaches, should be bankfull to get you through the rapids and shallows.

Average gradient: 10 feet per mile. The first 3 miles or so are relatively flat. Gradient picks up after that.

Hazards: Watch for downed trees blocking the narrow channel. If you launch at the County Route 30 bridge near Duxbury, you'll have to paddle through a culvert. Be sure to check for obstructions, such as logjams, before you commit to entering.

Maps: MDNR *St. Croix State Forest.*

The paddling: Without a gauge reading, you'll have to rely on your intuition about the Lower Tamarack's water level before you set out on the river. Generally, the river is runnable only during a full flush of runoff during the spring or after heavy local rains. That is especially true if you intend to put in at one of the two bridges at Duxbury. If water appears a bit on the low side, try putting in at one of the bridges farther downstream where the river channel is larger and is capable of floating a canoe in lower water.

The first 3 miles or so are relatively flat as the river winds through a mix of marsh and low forest. After it passes under the first of three County Route 25 bridges, the river picks up gradient and speed, racing down its narrow channel and winding through woodlands of pine, birch, and other hardwoods. The river is steepest and quickest from the third County Route 25 bridge downstream 9 miles to the river's mouth, about 14 feet per mile. Even so, the rapids rate class I.

The run lies entirely within St. Croix State Forest; much of the land is publicly owned and is open to camping. A horse camp and trails are located along the last several miles of river. Several primitive campsites developed along the horse trails are also suitable for use by paddlers.

The river runs around a prominent round knob about a half mile above the river mouth. Paddle onto the St. Croix River and downstream for 2 miles. Cross to the Wisconsin side of the river to reach the take-out.

Because it's small and steep, the Lower Tamarack has limited habitat for fish. Game fish such as northern pike, walleye, and smallmouth bass swim up the lower river from the St. Croix.

Access: Duxbury put-in: From town, drive west 0.2 miles on County Route 30 (see note in **Hazards** about culvert) or south 0.2 miles on County Route 24.

70 Lower Tamarack River

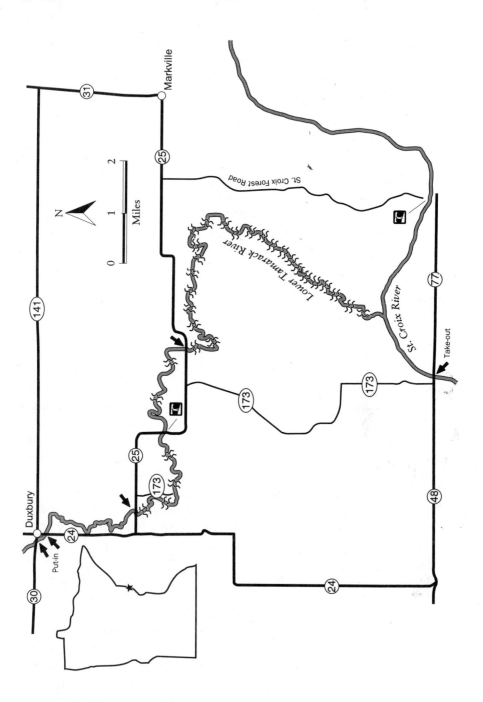

St. Croix River take-out: From the Hinckley exit off Interstate 35, drive east 23 miles on Minnesota Highway 48 to the bridge over the St. Croix; take-out is south of the highway on the Wisconsin side of the river.

Three bridges along County Route 25 provide put-ins when water is too low to run the uppermost stretch. A developed access exists only at the second bridge. See map for details.

Shuttle: 13.5 miles one way. About 40 minutes.

ADDITIONAL HELP

MA&G: 57, E9.
Camping: St. Croix State Forest, St. Croix State Park.
Food, gas, and lodging: Hinckley.
For more information: MDNR Information Center. For additional information call the MDNR area forestry office in Hinckley.

NORTH FORK OF THE CROW RIVER

71 Lake Koronis to Minnesota Highway 22

Character: This small river with a lively current provides an oasis of woodland in an area otherwise devoted to agriculture. It is passable only in medium to high water levels.
Length: 13 miles.
Average run time: Four to six hours.
Class: I.
Skill level: Beginner to intermediate.
Optimal flow: High water is needed to get down this small channel. There's a gauge on the County Route 2 bridge at Forest City, but the readings are rarely called into the MDNR.
Average gradient: 3.1 feet per mile.
Hazards: Impassable shallows in low water. Snags and farm fences may block the channel and pose a hazard in high, swift water.
Maps: MDNR *North Fork Crow River Canoe Route.*

The paddling: The North Fork of the Crow River spills from Lake Koronis near Paynesville and runs more than 100 miles to its confluence with the Mississippi at Dayton, providing an oasis of bottomland forest in the midst of rolling farmland. The river forms several easy rapids in its upper reaches. For the rest of its length, however, the river is undeniably placid. It is a river that writer and conservationist John Madson may have had in mind when he praised "small farmland rivers. Modest places, rarely spectacular, but lending a measure of freedom and wildness to landscapes that are thoroughly plowed, cowed and put to cash grain, such

71 Lake Koronis to Minnesota Highway 22

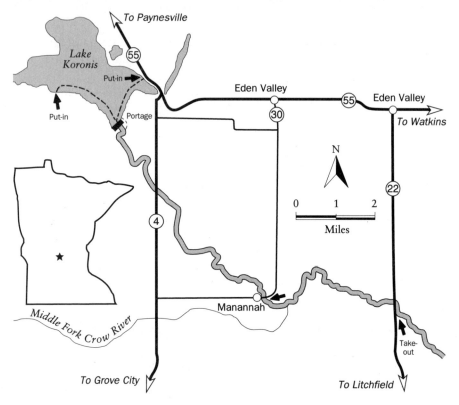

streams are some of the best escape routes from the soul-bruising press of modern living."

The North Fork from Lake Koronis to the Meeker–Wright county line (near Kingston) is a recreational component of the state wild and scenic rivers system, a designation that helps to protect the thin strip of natural land flanking the river in this heavily farmed watershed.

This initial 13-mile section, frankly, is not the best the North Fork has to offer. It is small—impassable in low water, and often riddled with snags, which pose a hazard when the water is high and swift. About 2 miles of river a bit downstream from Lake Koronis have been channelized. On the plus side, high bluffs occasionally rise from the streamside and the channel provides a haven for wildlife such as herons and beavers.

In the town of Manannah lies the site of an old mill; the rubble of a rock dam is still visible.

The Crow River Valley was the scene of several skirmishes between Dakota Indians and settlers in 1862. (See Minnesota River for details.) Dakota warriors attacked the village of Manannah, killing four farmers.

Access: Lake Koronis put in: Choose either of two boat ramps on Lake Koronis and portage the spillway at the lake's outlet (see map for details). You can put in at several county roads, including County Route 20 at the spillway, and a boat ramp at County Route 30. **MN 22 take-out:** From the Lake Koronis put in, drive east 6 miles to Eden Valley; drive south 5 miles on Minnesota Highway 22.

Shuttle: About 12 miles one way. About 30 minutes.

ADDITIONAL HELP

MA&G: 39, A6–7.

Camping: There are no campsites along river. Auto camping is available at Sibley State Park and Monson Lake State Park north of Willmar and Lake Maria State Park near Monticello.

Food, gas, and lodging: Willmar, Litchfield.

For more information: MDNR Information Center.

▇72▇ Minnesota Highway 22 to Kingston

Character: The North Fork runs through several easy rapids as it passes several high bluffs and woodlands. The channel is now deep enough to be canoeable much of the year and wide enough to allow room to maneuver around snags.

Length: 20 miles.

Average run time: Six to ten hours.

Class: I.

Skill level: Beginner to intermediate.

Optimal flow: Little information is available. There's a gauge on the County Route 2 bridge at Forest City, but the readings are rarely called into the MDNR. Medium to high water levels are best to get through the rocky shallows.

Average gradient: 3.2 feet per mile.

Hazards: Watch for farm fences stretched across the river. Watch out, too, for low bridges. The County Road 112 bridge about 4 miles downstream from the put-in and the County Road 133 bridge downstream from Forest City allow little clearance during high water.

Maps: MDNR.

The paddling: The North Fork of the Crow, now larger and deeper, continues its path through central Minnesota's rolling fields of corn and soybeans. This stretch of the North Fork, which includes most of the portion designated in the state wild and scenic rivers system, is perhaps the most attractive part of the river for canoeists because of the river's intimacy and varied speed. Thin belts of woodlands line the river. Banks more than 50 feet high occasionally flank the river. Several class I rapids break the river's course. Neither steep nor long, they wash out in high water.

72 Minnesota Highway 22 to Kingston

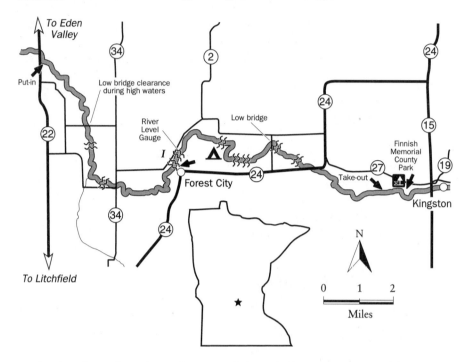

During the mid-1800s, settlers spread through the Crow River Valley, coming into direct conflict with Dakota Indians. At Shaw Memorial Park, located near the old Forest City dam site, stands a replica of a frontier log cabin. In low water, you may have to pull though the rock dam or portage. A half mile south of town stands a replica of the Forest City stockade, frantically erected by settlers during the U.S.–Dakota War of 1862. There, farmers withstood an attack by about 20 Dakota horsemen. The stockade has been restored and furnished with artifacts of the past.

Access: Put in at the MN 22 bridge 9 miles north of Litchfield. **Take out** at Finnish Memorial County Park, located between the north side of the river and County Route 27, about 2 miles west of Kingston.

Shuttle: About 14 miles one way. About 45 minutes.

ADDITIONAL HELP

MA&G: 39, B7–9.
Camping: A river campsite is located on river right about 2 miles downstream from Forest City. Camp by car at Sibley State Park north of Willmar or Lake Maria State Park near Monticello.
Food, gas, and lodging: Willmar, Buffalo.
For more information: MDNR Information Center.

73　Kingston to Dayton

Character: A slow, winding river bordered by a fringe of woods, the North Fork is a good bet for beginning paddlers and families out for a day or even overnight.

Length: 93 miles; many shorter trips are possible.

Average run time: Three to five days if you were to run the whole stretch.

Class: Quiet.

Skill level: Beginner.

Optimal flow: 3 feet to 7.5 feet on the gauge on the Minnesota Highway 55 bridge at Rockford and check the USGS website for at least 500 cfs on the Rockford gauge.

Average gradient: 1.9 feet per mile.

Hazards: Low bridge at County Route 14 crossing above Rockford—watch out in high water.

Maps: MDNR *North Fork Crow River Canoe Route.*

The paddling: By the time it flows through Rockford, the North Fork has burned up the steepest of its gradient. It settles into a slower pace, meandering across a floodplain sometimes several miles wide. High, wooded bluffs often line the channel. Commonly seen wildlife include waterfowl, shorebirds such as herons, and white-tailed deer.

Several riverside parks provide access and camping along the river for paddlers who wish to take a trip of more than one day.

Below Rockford, where the North Fork and South Fork join, the river widens and straightens. Unfortunately, County Route 19 swings close to the west bank of the river. Forest cover becomes spotty. Downstream, however, the east bank is protected within the borders of Crow-Hassan Park Reserve, a 2,600-acre Hennepin County Park. The park is one of the best places to see the tallgrass prairie of big bluestem and Indian grass as it once existed on the western fringes of the Twin Cities. Each spring, the park burns part of its prairie to invigorate the native grasses.

The North Fork usually runs muddy, caused by a combination of fine soils in the basin and agricultural activity in the watershed. Because of the turbidity, the fishery is dominated by species such as carp, white suckers, and black bullheads. The best fishing on the river is for channel catfish, many of more than 5 pounds. Once existing in the Mississippi drainage only below the barrier of St. Anthony Falls in Minneapolis, channel

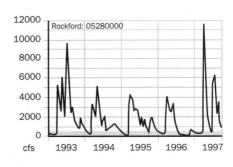

500 cfs = estimated minimum
for good paddling

73 Kingston to Dayton

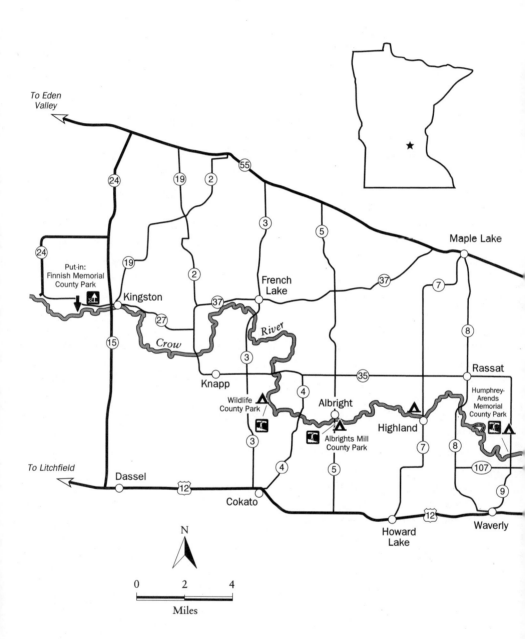

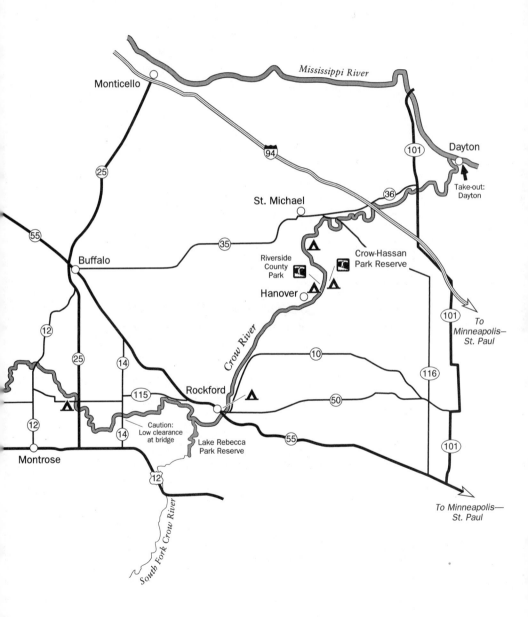

Monticello

Mississippi River

94

101

Dayton

Take-out:
Dayton

25

36

55

St. Michael

35

Riverside
County
Park

Crow-Hassan
Park Reserve

Buffalo

Hanover

Crow River

101

*To
Minneapolis—
St. Paul*

12

25

14

10

116

115

Rockford

50

12

14

Caution:
Low clearance
at bridge

Lake Rebecca
Park Reserve

55

101

Montrose

12

South Fork Crow River

*To Minneapolis—
St. Paul*

cats have been stocked in recent years above the falls and have migrated into the Crow River system.

Access: The **Kingston put-in** is located at Finnish Memorial County Park, located between the north side of the river and County Route 27, about 2 miles west of Kingston. The **Dayton take-out** is located at the confluence of the Crow and Mississippi rivers.

A developed access occurs about every 10 miles or so to the river's mouth. Bridges provide many undeveloped accesses for a trip of just about any length. See map for details.

Shuttle: 50 miles one way. About two hours.

ADDITIONAL HELP

MA&G: 39–41.

Camping: Canoe and auto camping is possible at several parks along the river. The largest and most varied is Crow-Hassan, where group camping is available (accessible by canoe and car) with a reservation.

Food, gas, and lodging: Buffalo, Dayton.

For more information: MDNR Information Center.

PINE RIVER

74 Lake Hattie to Upper Whitefish Lake

Character: The Pine River is a hidden gem, unheralded, largely unappreciated. Yet it is a joy to paddle—gentle, with clear water, a sandy bottom and wooded banks. This upper stretch is small and intimate.

Length: 14.5 miles.

Average run time: Five to seven hours.

Class: I.

Skill level: Beginner.

Optimal flow: More than 100 cfs by the gauge at the Pine River Dam.

Average gradient: 5.2 feet per mile. The gradient upstream from Pine River Dam is less than the average, and the gradient between the Pine River Dam and Upper Whitefish Lake is greater, about 7 feet per mile.

Hazards: Low dams at Pine Mountain, Bowen, and Hattie lakes (located upstream from the area covered by this trip description), and at the town of Pine River. Watch out for low clearance at the County Route 43 bridge 2 miles above Norway Lake, and Hopper's Bridge near the Cass–Crow Wing county line.

Maps: MDNR *Pine River Canoe Route.*

The paddling: The Pine heads up in the bogs, woodlands, and small lakes near Backus. It flows through several small lakes and tumbles over a couple of small

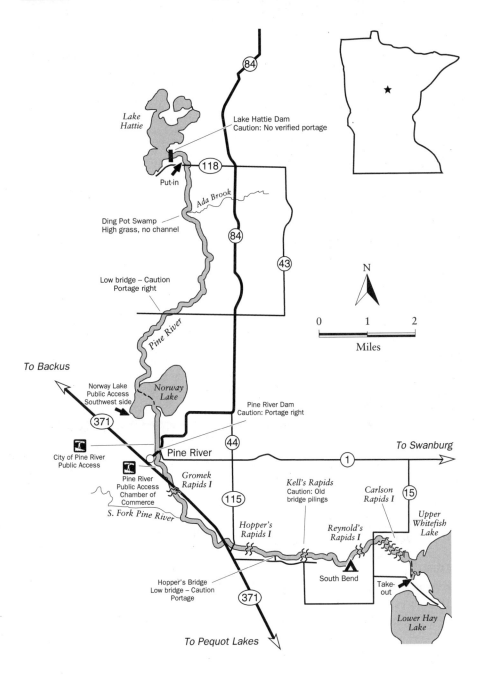

Lake Hattie

Lake Hattie Dam
Caution: No verified portage

84

118

Put-in

Ada Brook

Ding Pot Swamp
High grass, no channel

84

43

N

0   1   2
Miles

Low bridge – Caution
Portage right

Pine River

To Backus

Norway Lake
Public Access
Southwest side

Norway
Lake

Pine River Dam
Caution: Portage right

371

City of Pine River
Public Access

Pine River

44

To Swanburg

1

Pine River
Public Access
Chamber of
Commerce

Gromek
Rapids I

115

Kell's Rapids
Caution: Old
bridge pilings

Carlson
Rapids I

15

S. Fork Pine River

Hopper's
Rapids I

Reynold's
Rapids I

Upper
Whitefish
Lake

South Bend

Take-
out

Hopper's Bridge
Low bridge – Caution
Portage

371

Lower Hay
Lake

To Pequot Lakes

dams before sliding over a third dam at the outlet of Lake Hattie, finally of a size and depth of interest to most canoeists. It winds with gentle current and emerges into Ding Pot Swamp, an expanse of high grass where the channel may be tough to follow. Soon, the river returns to woodlands of aspen, birch, and conifers and then flows into Norway Lake. You'll have to paddle a half mile across the lake and then

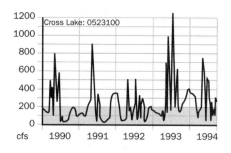

200 cfs = minimum for good paddling

portage (river right, 125 yards) the small dam at the town of Pine River. The Pine slips under Minnesota Highway 371 and runs though Gromek Rapids. It ducks back east of the highway, joins a major tributary, the South Fork of the Pine, and runs through several more class I rapids—**Hopper's Rapids, Kell's Rapids, Reynold's Rapids,** and **Carlson Rapids**—before emptying into Upper Whitefish Lake.

If you wish, you can continue to paddle the 10 miles through Upper Whitefish and Lower Whitefish Lakes. But the so-called Whitefish chain is ringed by cabins and traveled heavily by motorboats, so most canoeists will opt to bypass the experience and take out at the boat ramp at the far western end of Upper Whitefish Lake.

Access: **Lake Hattie put-in:** From Pine River, drive north 7.5 miles on Minnesota Highway 84; turn west on County Road 118 to the bridge over the Pine River, about a half mile downstream from the dam. There is no developed access at the bridge. **Upper Whitefish Lake take-out:** From Pine River, drive east on County Route 2 (which turns into County Route 1 at the Cass–Crow Wing county line) about 5 miles to County Route 15; turn south and follow the road about 3 miles and turn east on the unnumbered road that leads to the take-out.

Alternative access is possible at the southwest corner of Norway Lake, the town of Pine River just downstream of the dam, and at several bridge crossings.

Shuttle: 15 miles one way. About 45 minutes.

ADDITIONAL HELP

MA&G: 62, D3–E4.

Camping: Riverside camping is available at South Bend Canoe Campsite about 2 miles upstream from Upper Whitefish Lake. Auto camping is possible at the Cross Lake Recreation Area Campground in Cross Lake.

Food, gas, and lodging: Cross Lake, Pine River.

For more information: MDNR Information Center.

75 Cross Lake Dam to Mississippi River

Character: A clear stream with sandy bottom and a few easy rapids, the Pine provides an enjoyable trip for beginning and experienced canoeists.

Length: 18.8 miles.

Average run time: Six to nine hours.

Class: I.

Skill level: Beginner.

Optimal flow: More than 200 cfs at the gauge at the Pine River Dam, or more than 2 feet on the gauge on the County Route 11 bridge (Harvey Drake Landing).

Average gradient: 2 feet per mile.

Hazards: Low rock dam just downstream from Pine Lake.

Maps: MDNR *Pine River Canoe Route.*

The paddling: The Pine emerges from Lower Whitefish Lake a much larger river than the stream near Pine River. Put in just downstream from the U.S. Army Corps of Engineers dam at the outlet of Cross Lake in the resort community of Cross Lake. About 1.5 miles downstream, the Pine speeds through **Gould Rapids** and **Anton Rapids,** both class I. The river enters Pine Lake and emerges a mile later. The river then winds quietly through woods of pine and hardwoods. A mile before the confluence with the Mississippi, the Pine again speeds through easy rapids. Unfortunately, paddlers will have to pass most of them by if they plan to take out at the Harvey Drake Landing. An alternative is to continue to the Mississippi and then downstream 8 miles to Half Moon Landing (see Mississippi River).

The Pine isn't renowned as a fishing stream, though it is likely to hold any number of species that might swim up from the Mississippi. It does have some of the largest and most willing rock bass you are likely to find anywhere, great quarry for a beginner with a fly rod. Other species include northern pike, walleye, smallmouth bass.

Access: Cross Lake Dam put-in: From Cross Lake, follow County Route 3 to the south edge of town. The carry-in access is on river right, below the dam. **Mississippi River take-out** at Harvey Drake Landing: From Cross Lake, take County Route 3 south 4 miles to County Route 11; turn east and drive for 7 miles to the bridge over the Pine and the landing.

For a shorter trip, choose one of the other accesses, Staircase Landing southeast of Cross Lake off County Route 36 or the boat ramp at the west end of Pine Lake off County Route 3.

Shuttle: 11 miles one way. About 30 minutes.

75 Cross Lake Dam to Mississippi River

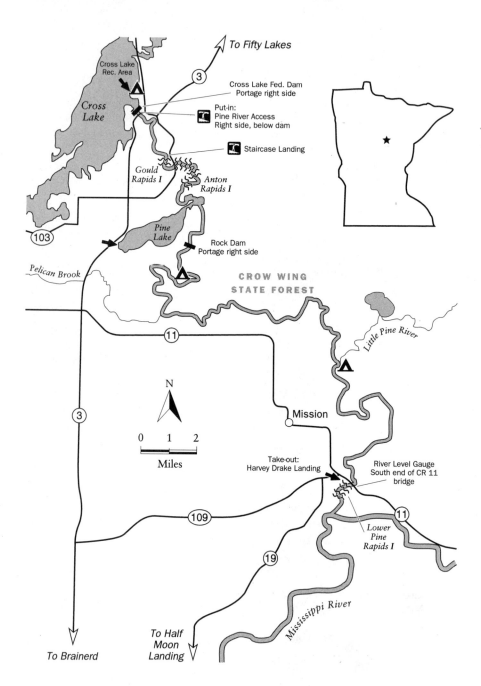

To Fifty Lakes

Cross Lake Rec. Area

Cross Lake

(3)

Cross Lake Fed. Dam
Portage right side

Put-in:
Pine River Access
Right side, below dam

Staircase Landing

Gould Rapids I

Anton Rapids I

(103)

Pine Lake

Rock Dam
Portage right side

Pelican Brook

CROW WING
STATE FOREST

Little Pine River

(11)

N

(3)

0   1   2

Miles

Mission

Take-out:
Harvey Drake Landing

River Level Gauge
South end of CR 11
bridge

(109)

(11)

Lower Pine Rapids I

(19)

Mississippi River

To Half Moon Landing

To Brainerd

A misty moment on the Pine River. MINNESOTA DEPARTMENT OF NATURAL RESOURCES

ADDITIONAL HELP

MA&G: 63, E6; 55, A6.

Camping: Riverside camping is available at Little Pine Canoe Campsite at the confluence with the Little Pine River, about 6 miles upstream from the Pine's confluence with the Mississippi. Auto camping is possible at the Cross Lake Recreation Area Campground in Cross Lake.

Food, gas, and lodging: Cross Lake, Crosby, Brainerd.

For more information: MDNR Information Center.

76 **Platte River**

Character: The Platte, for much of its length a meandering farmland stream, cuts through hills and woods in its last few miles. Paddling and fishing are best from Royalton to the Mississippi River.
Length: 15 miles.
Average run time: Five to eight hours.
Class: I.
Skill level: Beginner.
Optimal flow: No gauge reading available. Medium to high levels (river at or above terrestrial vegetation on bank) are needed to run the river.
Average gradient: 5 feet per mile. The Royalton-to-Mississippi stretch is steepest, about 9 feet per mile.
Hazards: Watch out for wire farm fences across the river.
Maps: PRIM *St. Cloud*

The paddling: Put in at the boat launch and portage the low dam at the outlet of Rice Lake. The Platte meanders slowly through the marshes of the Crane Meadows National Wildlife Refuge. In spring and early fall, look for sandhill cranes. More than 30 pairs have been nesting in the area of Rice, Skunk, and Mud Lakes. In autumn, up to 400 cranes may gather. Many other birds are common to the area, including bald eagles, northern harriers, short-eared owls, American bitterns, great blue herons, various waterfowl, and many species of songbirds.

After about 4 miles, the river leaves the boundaries of the wildlife refuge. It continues to wind through marsh and farmland toward Royalton. A city park provides good access to the river.

Below Royalton, the river changes character. The countryside becomes hillier and more wooded. The banks rise along the river. The current quickens, and the river tumbles through a few class I rapids. This is no wilderness—farm fields and the occasional gravel pit lie near the river—but the stretch is quite pretty in places.

One of the selling points of the lower Platte is the fishing. Stretches of the lower 5 miles are rocky and deep and provide good fishing for game fish that swim up from the Mississippi, including smallmouth bass, walleye, northern pike, and channel catfish.

Access: Rice Lake put-in: From Royalton, drive 7 miles north on U.S. Highway 10 to County Route 35; drive east 4 miles to the boat launch. **Mississippi River take-out:** Two Rivers Park, a private campground at the confluence of the Platte and Mississippi, allows canoeists to take out for a small fee. From Royalton, drive southeast 3 miles on US 10; drop due south 1 mile on County Road 73; turn west at park entrance.

To take advantage of the best paddling on the river, put in at the Royalton city park on the east edge of town near the County Route 26 bridge. Access is also possible at several bridge crossings (from Rice Lake downstream): County Route 35, County Route 34, County Route 27, and County Road 40.

76 Platte River

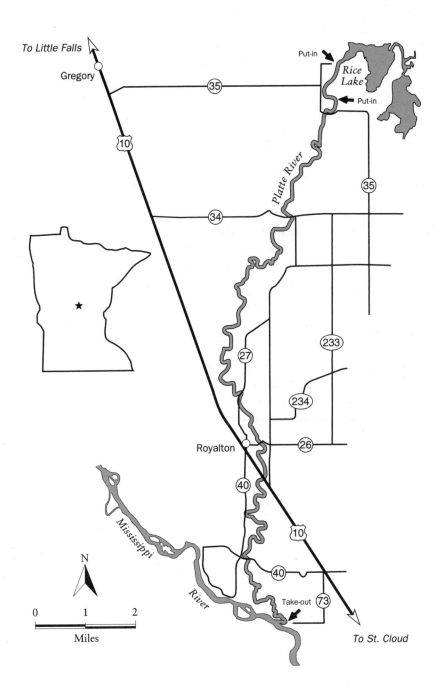

To Little Falls

Gregory

35

10

Platte River

Put-in
Put-in
Rice Lake

35

34

27

233

234

Royalton

26

40

10

Mississippi

River

N

0   1   2
Miles

40

Take-out   73

To St. Cloud

Shuttle: 17 miles. About 45 minutes.

ADDITIONAL HELP

MA&G: 46, A4–B4.

Camping: Two River Park and several sites along the Mississippi River (see Mississippi description). Auto camping is possible at Charles A. Lindbergh State Park in Little Falls.

Food, gas, and lodging: St. Cloud, Little Falls.

For more information: For more information, call Two Rivers Park.

RUM RIVER

77 Mille Lacs Lake to Onamia

Character: Flowing from its source, Mille Lacs Lake, the Rum River slowly winds through a series of shallow lakes.

Length: 9 miles.

Average run time: Three to four hours.

Class: Quiet.

Skill level: Beginner.

Optimal flow: Over 0.5 feet on the gauge on the County Route 25 bridge south of Onamia. Mille Lacs acts as a huge reservoir, slowly metering water into the Rum. As a result, the river remains runnable much of the year and rarely floods. The upper section, with no rapids, is nearly always passable.

Average gradient: 0.4 foot per mile

Hazards: Three small dams must be portaged.

Maps: MDNR *Rum River Canoe Route.* Also check the MDNR map for *Mille Lacs Kathio State Park.*

The paddling: The Rum River has nothing to do with rum; nor respect, apparently. The Dakota Indians lived for centuries along the shore of Mille Lacs, known to them as *Mde Wakan*, "Spirit Lake." And so the river that issued from it was known similarly as Spirit River. The settlers who came after dubbed the river Rum, after that other common spirit of the frontier. A mistake of translation? A pun? Maybe so. But like a lot of other naming of the last century, translating every Indian reference to spirit as a reference instead to the devil, the name seems designed to diminish.

But the name need not diminish the river itself. It is lovely. Gliding quick and clear from the big lake, it courses through innumerable riffles in its 135-mile path through central Minnesota to the Mississippi River at Anoka. Much of the riverbank is wooded, though the massive pines of the watershed disappeared in the

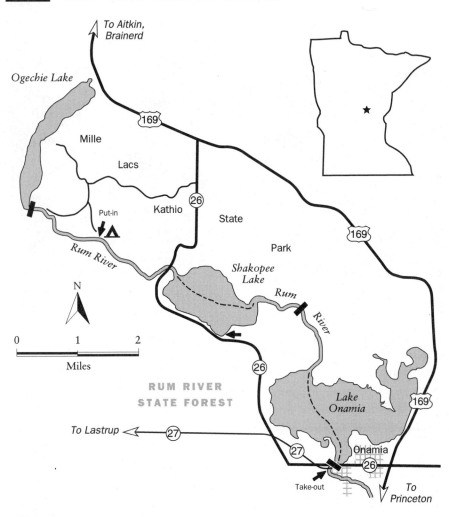

To Aitkin, Brainerd

Ogechie Lake

169

Mille

Lacs

Put-in

Kathio

26

State

Park

169

Shakopee Lake

Rum River

Rum

River

N

0   1   2

Miles

RUM RIVER STATE FOREST

26

Lake Onamia

169

To Lastrup   27

27

Onamia

26

Take-out

To Princeton

logging heyday of the nineteenth century. Along the way, the Rum provides good fishing for walleye and northern pike, and often spectacular angling for small-mouth bass, which thrive in the crayfish-filled riffles and rocky pools.

Ah, but all that comes later. The first 9 miles are flat, quiet, and flow as the clear river flows between lakes Ogechie, Shakopee, and Onamia. Most of this stretch lies within the rolling hills of Mille Lacs Kathio State Park. The name "Kathio" is the result of a botched translation. In this case, French explorer Daniel Greysolon, Sieur du Luth, who visited Mille Lacs in 1679, called the area *Izatys*, a phonetic representation of the Dakota name for the several settlements in the area. Later, however, the first two letters were mistaken for a "K" and several other

The Rum River runs through large, shallow lakes in Mille Lacs Kathio State Park.
MINNESOTA OFFICE OF TOURISM

letters were apparently misread as well. And so the name became *Kathio*, which means nothing at all, in Dakota, French, or English.

Humans have occupied the headwaters of the Rum for at least 4,000 years. Extensive archaeological digs in Mille Lacs Kathio have produced copper tools and weapons from Minnesota's Old Copper Culture and pottery from later Woodland groups. Burial mounds are common.

During the 1700s, Ojibwa Indians, moving westward from Lake Superior, drove the Dakota from Mille Lacs. Raid followed upon raid, retribution upon retribution, until the Ojibwa drove the Dakota from central and northern Minnesota's woodlands. "In these days, the hunter moved through the dense forests in fear and trembling," wrote historian William W. Warren, himself Ojibwa. "He paddled his light canoe over the calm bosom of a lake or down the rapid current of a river, in search of game to clothe and feed his children, expecting each moment that from behind a tree, an embankment of sand along the lake shore, or a clump of bushes on the river bank, would speed the bullet or arrow which would lay him low in death."

Southeastern Mille Lacs Lake and the first few miles of the Rum lie within the borders of the Mille Lacs Indian Reservation. The Mille Lacs Indian Museum, located on US 169 10 miles north of Onamia, describes the seasonal cycles of the Ojibwa and other Woodland Indians in their long tenure at the headwaters of the Rum River.

Access: Mille Lacs Lake put-in: While it's possible to put in on the lake or at the U.S. 169 bridge, the safer and more practical put-in is located in Mille Lacs Kathio State Park. The **Onamia take-out** lies on the west side of town on Minnesota Highway 27.

An alternate access is located on the southwest shore of Shakopee Lake on County Route 26.

Shuttle: About 9 miles one way. About 30 minutes.

ADDITIONAL HELP

MA&G: 55, E8.

Camping: A canoe campsite is located in Mille Lacs Kathio State Park. Auto camping is also available in the park.

Food, gas, and lodging: Onamia, Garrison, Brainerd. Resorts and lodges are available along the shores of Mille Lacs Lake.

For more information: MDNR Information Center.

78 Onamia to Vandell Brook

Character: Soon after leaving its headwater lakes, the Rum begins its run through many easy rapids. This stretch makes for fun canoeing at most water levels and provides terrific fishing, especially for smallmouth bass.

Length: 38 miles. Access is possible at many established accesses and bridges. Most paddlers will opt for day trips, but a few campsites make overnight trips possible.

Average run time: Two days to run the whole stretch.

Class: I.

Skill level: Beginner.

Optimal flow: 0.5 feet or higher on the gauge on the County Route 25 bridge south of Onamia. Mille Lacs acts as a huge reservoir, maintaining water levels through much of the summer.

Average gradient: 6.7 feet per mile.

Hazards: Portage the dam at Milaca.

Maps: MDNR *Rum River Canoe Route.*

The paddling: Emerging from the broad headwaters lakes, the nascent Rum takes on its full riverine character. It flows quietly for several miles past shores of bulrush and cattails, but soon gains speed. Below Onamia, near its confluence with Bradbury Brook, the Rum races through **Bradbury Rapids** (a borderline class II in medium water levels), the trickiest rapids on the river. From then on the river runs through many class I rapids. Portage the dam in Milaca on river left, about 70 yards.

The riverbanks vary from hardwood-covered uplands to farmland and pasture. Even the river's brief foray through Milaca is peaceful and bucolic as it flows

78 Onamia to Vandell Brook

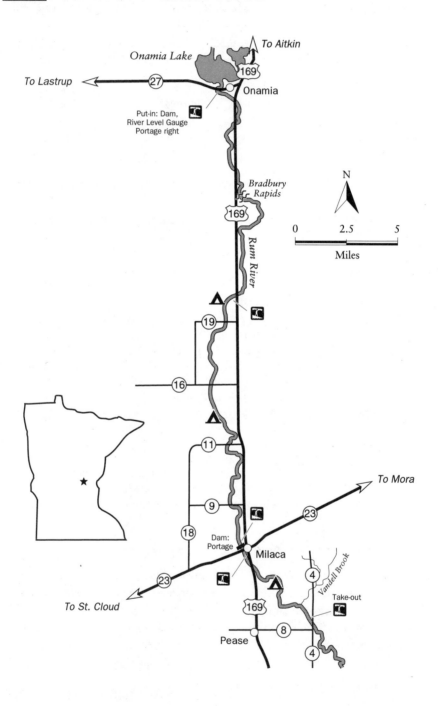

through a city park. Unlike rivers to the east, which are stained the color of tea from bog drainage, the Rum flows nearly clear and colorless because of its source at Mille Lacs.

The alternating easy rapids and pools provide exceptional habitat for small-mouth bass. Look for them in all the usual spots: deep areas in riffles, deep runs where rapids tail out into a pool, deep eddies along the banks. Deep, still shore-lines hold northern pike up to several pounds.

Access: The **Onamia put-in** is located on the west edge of town on Minnesota Highway 27. To reach the **Vandell Brook take-out,** drive south from Milaca on U.S. Highway 169 about 3.5 miles to Pease; turn east on County Route 8 and drive about 3 miles to County Route 4; turn north about 0.25 mile to the bridge.

Access is also possible at the highway wayside rest at US 169, the Milaca dam, the Milaca city park in town on County Route 36, and at the many county road bridges between Onamia and Milaca.

Shuttle: About 30 miles one way. About 1.25 hours.

ADDITIONAL HELP

MA&G: 55, E9; 47, 9A-C.
Camping: Canoe campsites are located near the US 169 wayside rest area, about 1.5 miles downstream from County Route 16, and about 3 miles downstream from Milaca. Auto camping is possible at Mille Lacs Kathio State Park and Sand Dunes State Forest near Zimmerman.
Food, gas, and lodging: Onamia, Milaca, Princeton.
For more information: MDNR Information Center.

79 Vandell Brook to St. Francis

Character: The Rum loses speed and meanders slowly through wooded lowlands. It passes two towns, Princeton and Cambridge, but overall presents a wild character.
Length: 78 miles. Many shorter trips are possible.
Average run time: Three to four days to paddle the whole stretch.
Class: I, but mostly quiet.
Skill level: Beginner.
Optimal flow: Above 2.5 feet on the gauge on the Minnesota Highway 95 bridge at Cambridge. With few rocky shallows, this stretch is usually passable.
Average gradient: 1.4 feet per mile.
Hazards: Remnants of rock dams at Princeton and Cambridge form short stretches of swift water. Watch for downed trees.
Maps: MDNR *Rum River Canoe Route.*

79 Vandell Brook to St. Francis

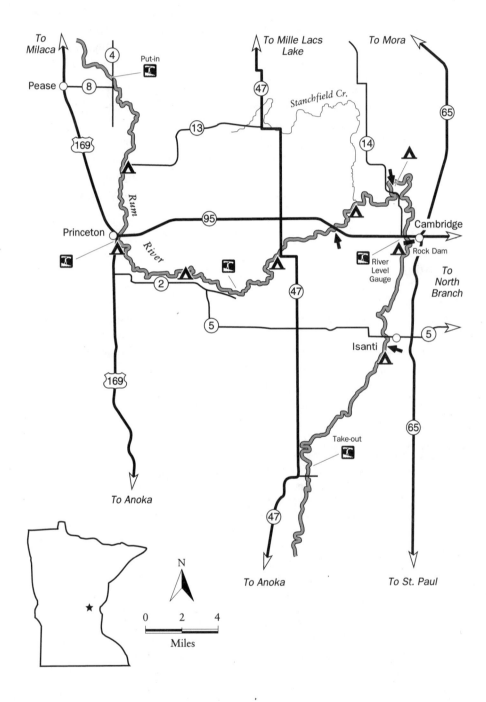

The paddling: At Vandell Brook, the Rum changes quickly from a riffly, racing stream to a slow, tightly winding ribbon of meanders, backwaters, and oxbows. The banks and river bottoms are heavily wooded, giving the impression that the river is wild and isolated. The pace of the stream does not pick up again until the river races over the remnants of old rock dams at Princeton and Cambridge, and again at a few small rapids just above the St. Francis take-out.

Despite a few bridges, little development is visible along the stream. This stretch is good for watching wildlife, with mink, beavers, and plenty of shorebirds and songbirds. Two common denizens that paddlers are likely to see are the great blue heron and belted kingfisher. These two piscivores take radically different approaches to spearing dinner. The heron quietly and patiently stalks the shallows, sneaking up on small fish and other small animals, and striking with a lightning thrust of its bill. The kingfisher perches on a prominent branch overlooking the river. On sighting a fish, it dives toward its target and plunges headlong into the water to snatch its prey.

With no rough water, no portages, and an abundance of riverside campsites, this section of the Rum is a good choice for a multi-day canoe trip.

Some folks fish for northern pike in this stretch. This stretch holds some small-mouth bass and walleyes, but without rocky rapids and pools, it is not as good for these species as the sections above and below.

Access: Vandell Brook put-in: Drive south from Milaca on U.S. Highway 169 about 3.5 miles to Pease; turn east on County Route 8 and drive about 3 miles to County Route 4; turn north about 0.25 mile to the bridge. The **St. Francis take-out** is located in town in Rum River North County Park east of the river and just north of County Route 24.

Shuttle: About 38 miles one way. About 1.5 hours.

ADDITIONAL HELP

MA&G: 47–48.

Camping: Canoe camping is possible at several sites along the river (see map). Auto camping is possible at several of these sites, as well as at Sand Dunes State Forest near Zimmerman.

Food, gas, and lodging: Princeton, Cambridge.

For more information: MDNR Information Center.

80 St. Francis to Anoka

Character: The Rum picks up its pace, running through class I rapids for several miles. It then settles down and flows quietly for its last few miles to the Mississippi. This section provides excellent fishing.
Length: 21 miles.
Average run time: Seven to ten hours.
Class: I.
Skill level: Beginner.
Optimal flow: Above 3 feet on the gauge on the Minnesota Highway 95 bridge at Cambridge, or at least 500 cfs on the gauge near St. Francis—check the USGS website.
Average gradient: 1.7 feet per mile.
Hazards: A broken-out dam at St. Francis, long rocky rapids just above County Route 22, and the 10-foot-high dam at Anoka.
Maps: MDNR *Rum River Canoe Route.*

The paddling: Just downstream from the put-in, the river slides over the broken-down remains of a dam at the bridge in St. Francis. There's no particular problem here; just stay to the center where the river is deepest. For the next several miles, the river alternates between swift, easy rapids and quiet pools. In the last mile above County Route 22, the river flows through several long pitches—probably the toughest water on the trip, but still class I. Below the bridge (often used as an access, even though the carry down to the river is steep and eroded), the river continues its rocky run. After Rum River Central Regional Park, however, the river runs quietly to Anoka. There the river enters the small reservoir created by the Northern State Power Company Dam in town (portage right, 30 yards). Below the dam, the river runs through one last burst of swift water and then quietly joins the Mississippi.

Houses and strip malls are springing up throughout the southern end of the Rum River Valley, but the river still manages to look wild along much of its length. This final section of the Rum in some ways resembles the fast water near Milaca, but the river by now has achieved some real size, spanning more than 100 feet and collecting in several deep pools, which provide year-around cover for large fish, including smallmouth bass, walleye, and northern pike. For smallmouth, fish the deep, rocky shorelines. Look for pike in deep, still eddies. For walleye, fish the deep pools.

Access: The St. Francis put-in is located in town in Rum River North County Park east of the river and just north of County Route 24. **Anoka take-out:** An access is located near the

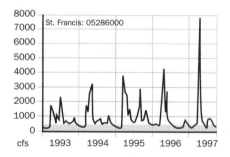

500 cfs (3.0 feet on gauge) = minimum for good paddling

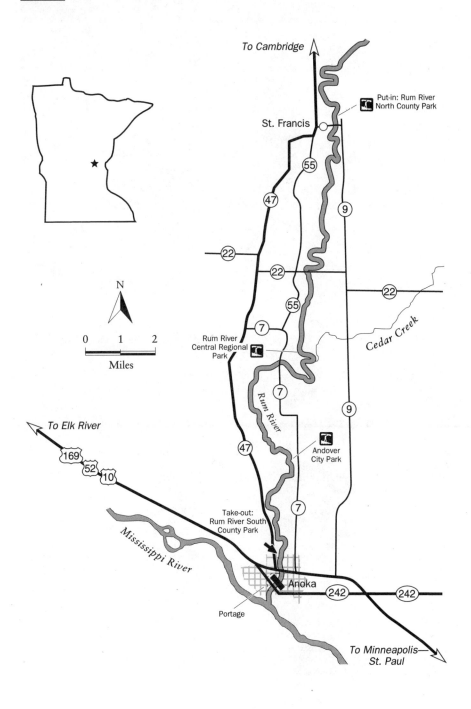

To Cambridge

Put-in: Rum River
North County Park

St. Francis

55

47

9

22

22

22

Cedar Creek

N

55

0   1   2
Miles

7

Rum River
Central Regional
Park

7

9

Rum River

To Elk River

169

52

10

47

Andover
City Park

7

Take-out:
Rum River South
County Park

Mississippi River

Anoka

242

242

Portage

To Minneapolis—
St. Paul

A young girl lands a smallmouth bass upstream of Anoka on the Rum. MINNESOTA DEPARTMENT OF NATURAL RESOURCES

mouth of the river (see map), but to avoid having to portage the NSP Dam, take out at Rum River South County Park, located on the west side of the Rum, about a mile above the dam. Follow Minnesota Highway 47 (also called Ferry Street) to the Anoka County Fairgrounds, where the access is located.

Alternate accesses are located at Rum River Central Regional Park on the west side of the river off County Route 7 immediately north of the Rum River bridge and Andover City Park, located on the east side of the river off County Route 7 and south of the intersection with County Route 20. By running from St. Francis to Rum River Central Regional Park, you can enjoy the rapids and skip the flat water.

Shuttle: About 16 miles one way. About 40 minutes.

ADDITIONAL HELP

MA&G: 48, E2; 41, A6.
Camping: Canoe and auto camping are possible at Rum River North County Park in St. Francis. Auto camping is possible at Sand Dunes State Forest near Zimmerman.
Food, gas, and lodging: Anoka.
For more information: MDNR Information Center.

SAUK RIVER

81 Sauk Centre to Richmond

Character: The upper Sauk, a meandering farmland river, has several public accesses and campsites, making possible overnight trips or several different day trips.
Length: 59.8 miles.
Average run time: Two to four days for the entire stretch.
Class: Quiet.
Skill level: Beginner.
Optimal flow: The MDNR provides weekly gauge readings from a USGS gauge near St. Cloud, but since no interpretation of the numbers is given, they are of limited use. With no rapids in the upper stretches, the river is navigable at all but very low levels.
Average gradient: 2.2 feet per mile.
Hazards: Watch for wire farm fences strung across the river.
Maps: MDNR *Sauk River Canoe Route.*

The paddling: Put in at the Sauk Centre Campground on Sauk Lake and almost immediately portage the dam at US 71. Otherwise put in at the boat launch immediately downstream from the dam.

81 **Sauk Centre to Richmond**

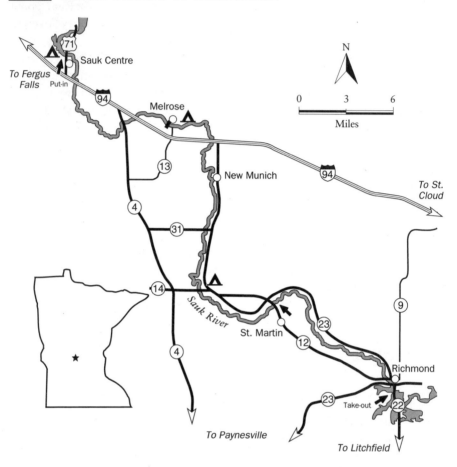

For its first 25 miles, the river winds through marsh and lowlands, which provide habitat for many kinds of waterfowl. Many of these areas are protected in state wildlife management areas.

At Melrose, the river forms a reservoir and passes over a large dam at County Route 13 that must be portaged. Below Melrose, the river enters a long series of tight meanders. Below the third Interstate 94 bridge, as the river approaches New Munich, the Sauk begins to flow past higher ground. Throughout the river's length the valley is heavily farmed, with only a thin screen of hardwoods flanking the river. Approaching Richmond, the Sauk passes an elevated tamarack bog on the north bank. The bog is an unusual feature in this part of the state, where hardwoods, grassland, and farmland predominate. In late fall, the tamaracks turn deep gold. Unique among Minnesota's conifers, the tamaracks drop their needles in winter.

The Sauk is named for the Sauk Indians, a Siouan group that once occupied the area, but that gave way to the Dakota and, later, the Ojibwa. These two groups battled in central Minnesota for much of the 1700s and early 1800s. The Sauk lay in the rather fluid borderland between the two warring tribes.

Wooden ox carts, which shuttled goods between Red River settlements and St. Paul during the early 1800s, followed three routes through western Minnesota, one of which ran through the Sauk River valley and crossed the river at the site of Waite's Crossing in St. Cloud. The location is marked today with a commemorative stone.

Sauk Centre, by the way, is the boyhood home and final resting place of Nobel Prize–winning novelist Sinclair Lewis. Sauk Centre was the inspiration for the thinly disguised Gopher Prairie, which Lewis savaged in *Main Street* for its narrow-mindedness and smugness. Lewis's ashes are buried in Greenwood Cemetery, a mile east of town. Exhibits on Lewis's life are contained in the Sinclair Lewis Interpretive Center, next to I-94.

Access: Sauk Centre put-in: Boat landings, one above and one below the Sauk Lake dam, lie just off U.S. Highway 71 in the middle of town. The **Richmond take-out** is located on the peninsula between Horseshoe Lake and East Lake 1 mile south of Richmond on Minnesota Highway 22.

Alternative developed accesses are located 1 mile northeast of Melrose at Melrose Lions Park, at the Spring Hill Park 3 miles east of Spring Hill on the west side of the river on County Route 14, and 2 miles north of St. Martin at the County Route 12 bridge.

Shuttle: 37 miles one way. About 1.5 hours.

ADDITIONAL HELP

MA&G: 45, C8–D9; 46, D1–E2.

Camping: Camping by canoe or auto is possible at Sauk Centre Campground on Sauk Lake, just above the dam; Melrose Lions Park just east of Melrose; Spring Hill Campsite just east of town. Nearby state parks include Lake Maria, Sibley, and Charles A. Lindbergh. Camping is also available on Birch Lake at Birch Lake State Forest, about 10 miles east-northeast of Sauk Centre.

Food, gas, and lodging: Sauk Centre, St. Cloud.

For more information: MDNR Information Center, Stearns County Park Department.

82 Richmond to Cold Spring (Chain of Lakes)

Character: This isn't river paddling at all. Rather, the route follows a chain of lakes to the dam at Cold Spring, where the Sauk resumes its free-flowing life as a river. It's a good route for an afternoon or day of paddling, and you can paddle back to the put-in rather than run a shuttle.

Length: About 6 miles, depending on route.

Average run time: Two to three hours—more if you care to explore.

Class: Quiet.

Skill level: Beginner.

Optimal flow: Not applicable. Always runnable.

Average gradient: None.

Hazards: Don't approach too close to the dam at Cold Spring. Portage the dam on river right.

Maps: MDNR *Sauk River Canoe Route.*

The paddling: A chain of lakes provides a crooked path between Richmond and Cold Spring. The lakes exist at their present level and size by the existence of the dam at Cold Spring. For the most direct route, from the access on Horseshoe Lake paddle east around the peninsula into East Lake, south and then east into Koetter Lake. Continue eastward through Zumwaldes, Great Northern, Krays, and Knaus

82 Richmond to Cold Spring (Chain of Lakes)

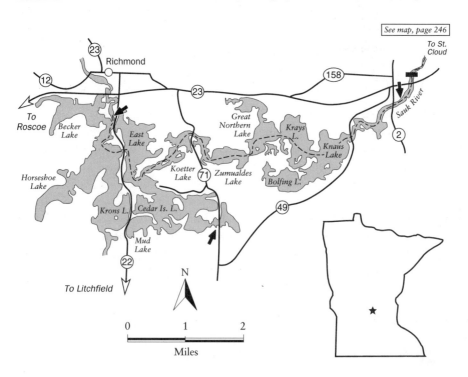

Lakes and down the flooded channel of the Sauk River to the take-out just above the dam. Or portage the dam to river right and continue downstream on the Sauk.

Unfortunately, you won't mistake the shoreline for the Boundary Waters. The lakes are lined with homes. The lakes do provide probably the best fishing in the Sauk River system. Most common are sunfish, crappies, walleye, and northern pike. Channel cats have been introduced to the lakes and reach large size.

Access: The **Richmond put-in** is located on the peninsula between Horseshoe Lake and East Lake 1 mile south of Richmond on Minnesota Highway 22. The **Cold Spring take-out** is located at the Minnesota Highway 23 bridge on the west side of the channel. Because no current is involved, you may want to simply paddle back to your put-in instead of running a shuttle.

Shuttle: 6 miles one way. About 20 minutes.

ADDITIONAL HELP

MA&G: 46, E2–3.
Camping: Several private resorts and campgrounds are located on the lakes in the chain.
Food, gas, and lodging: Richmond, Cold Spring, St. Cloud.
For more information: Stearns County Park Department.

83 Cold Spring to Pine View Park

Character: The Sauk resumes its riverine nature, meandering calmly toward St. Cloud.
Length: 15.3 miles.
Average run time: Five to seven hours.
Class: I.
Skill level: Beginner.
Optimal flow: At least 300 cfs.
Average gradient: 2 feet per mile.
Hazards: No particular hazards.
Maps: *Sauk River Canoe Route,* available through MDNR Information Center or Stearns County Park Department.

The paddling: Put in below the dam at Cold Spring. The Sauk winds through woods and some pasture. There are no real rapids, but there may be fast water and some maneuvering around snags when the water is high. Granite outcrops are occasionally visible along the river. One drawback in late summer is the thick weed growth in the slower stretches of the river.

Fishing can be good in this section, especially for channel cats and, in spring, walleye.

83 Cold Spring to Pine View Park

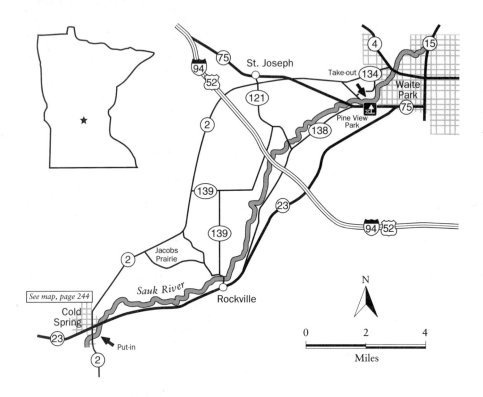

Access: The **Cold Spring put-in** is located just downstream from the dam and Minnesota Highway 23 bridge. The **Pine View Park take-out** is located on river left (north), downstream from the County Route 75 bridge. You can also take out at Miller Landing, about a mile upstream of County Route 75, on the south side of the Sauk, off County Road 138.

Shuttle: 12 miles one way. About 40 minutes.

ADDITIONAL HELP

MA&G: 46, E3–4.
Camping: No river campsites are available. Camp by car at Lake Maria State Park.
Food, gas, and lodging: St. Cloud.
For more information: MDNR Information Center, Stearns County Park Department.

84 Pine View Park to Mississippi River

Character: In its final miles, the Sauk River runs through long stretches of fast water and rapids.

Length: 5.8 miles.

Average run time: Two to three hours.

Class: II in high water; I in low water.

Skill level: Intermediate.

Optimal flow: At least 300 cfs on the St. Cloud gauge—check the USGS website.

Average gradient: 8.6 feet per mile.

Hazards: Rapids and long stretches of fast current can be difficult when the water is high. Watch out for snags where the channel narrows.

Maps: *Sauk River Canoe Route,* available through MDNR Information Center or Stearns County Park Department.

84 Pine View Park to Mississippi River

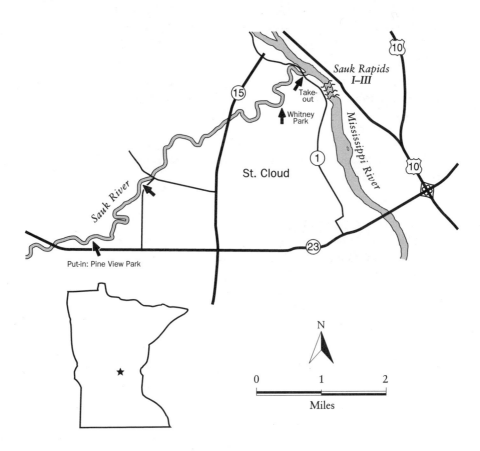

The paddling: In its final 5.8 miles, the Sauk makes a mad dash to meet the Mississippi River, ripping through boulder-filled rapids and sliding swiftly through a winding and often narrow channel. Individual rapids are not terribly difficult, but the long, continuous nature of the fast water makes it difficult for inexperienced canoeists to stop—whether they're in their canoe or swimming after a mis-

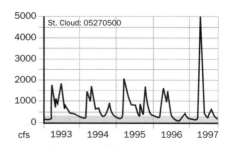

300 cfs = estimated minimum for good paddling

hap. You'll have to negotiate scattered, large boulders and chains of waves up to 2 feet high. The most difficult rapids occur in the final mile before the confluence with the Mississippi.

Look for the take-out on the left, just downstream from the County Route 1 bridge. If you continue down the Mississippi River, you'll flush through the class I–III **Sauk Rapids** (see Mississippi description).

Access: The **Pine View Park put-in** is located north of the Sauk River at the County Route 75 bridge, on the west edge of the town of Waite Park. The **Mississippi River take-out** is the Hiem Mill access at the County Route 1 bridge river left (north) and just upstream from the mouth of the Sauk River. Alternate accesses are Knights of Columbus Park and Whitney Park, both St. Cloud city parks on the south side of the river.

Shuttle: 6 miles one way. About 20 minutes.

ADDITIONAL HELP

MA&G: 46, D5.
Camping: No river campsites are available. Camp by car at Lake Maria State Park.
Food, gas, and lodging: St. Cloud.
For more information: MDNR Information Center, Stearns County Park Department.

SNAKE RIVER

▌85▐ McGrath to County Route 3

Character: The narrow upper Snake tumbles over several rapids. Most are easy, but watch out for Upper and Lower Snake River Falls, especially in high water.
Length: 26.5 miles.
Average run time: About ten hours. As a practical matter, most paddlers will opt for a shorter run through the Upper and Lower Falls. That run takes two to three hours.
Class: I–II in medium water; up to class IV in high water.
Skill level: Intermediate to expert.
Optimal flow: Above 1.2 feet on the gauge on the Ford Township bridge. Call 320-679-0127 for an automated gauge reading.
Average gradient: 7.9 feet per mile.
Hazards: Lower Snake River Falls.
Maps: MDNR *Snake River Canoe Route.*

The paddling: Be sure to get a recent water-level report before heading out on the upper Snake, which drains quickly and can leave you with an abysmal hike instead of an enjoyable paddle.

From McGrath, the river winds through dense wood with low banks. Despite the general flatness through this region, several short, bouldery rapids punctuate the river. In high water, they form quick and lively chains of small waves. These rapids rate class I in medium water, up to class II in high.

The challenge begins with **Upper Snake River Falls,** a pretty run through pines and outcrops. Though not a falls as such, the rapids bends sharply left and forms large waves in high water. Swift current tends to slam your canoe into a cliff on the outside of the bend, unless you keep your boat angled toward the inside of the bend. Rate Upper Falls class II in medium water, class III in high. A 300-yard portage lies on river left.

Relax in easy rapids for another mile. Then scout **Lower Snake River Falls,** which, despite its name, is not a waterfall, but a long, steep stretch of large boulders and ledges in a narrow canyon, dropping about 20 feet in three-quarters of a mile. In extremely high water, big peaked waves form near the top of the rapids. This rapids rates class III-IV in medium water, up to class IV at exceptionally high levels. Portage river left, 900 yards.

In comparison, the rest of the river's obstacles are easy, a smattering of class I–II boulder-bed drops. Many paddlers will opt to clamber out of the river at the Ford Township bridge, despite the lack of a good access. Those who continue downstream will encounter the remains of the Old Bean Logging Company Dam and, about 2 miles later, a second low rock dam. Both rate class I–II.

85 McGrath to County Route 3

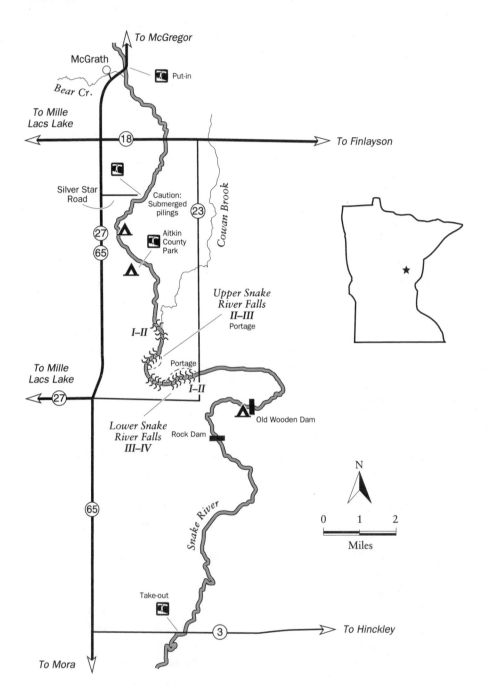

Fishing for smallmouth bass, walleye, northern pike, and rock bass can be quite good in this stretch. The bass are not numerous but tend to be quite large, over a pound. Flies and mosquitoes, on the other hand, are quite numerous. Fishing is best in summer, when insects and water levels are worst, so bring repellent and be prepared to walk your canoe through the shallows. Don't try to cover more than a few miles in low water.

Access: To reach the **McGrath put-in,** drive east from town on County Road 79, cross Minnesota Highway 65, to County Road 61 and the short spur that leads to the access. **County Route 3 take-out:** From McGrath, drive south on MN 65 about 15 miles to County Route 3; turn east and drive 2 miles to the river.

Most paddlers will opt for a shorter trip, putting in at Silver Star Road or Aitkin County Park. If you want to paddle only the best whitewater, including the Upper and Lower Falls, pull out at the Ford Township bridge.

Shuttle: The shuttle for the full stretch, from McGrath to County Route 3, runs about 17 miles one-way and will take about 45 minutes to complete.

ADDITIONAL HELP

MA&G: 56, D2–E3.
Camping: Canoe campsites are located a mile upstream of Aitkin County Park, near Lower Falls, and near the Old Bean Logging Company Dam. Camp by car at Aitkin County Park.
Food, gas, and lodging: Mora.
For more information: MDNR Information Center.

86 County Route 3 to Mora

Character: The Snake loses speed and gradient, but still runs through several easy rapids.
Length: 15 miles.
Average run time: Five to seven hours.
Class: I.
Skill level: Beginner.
Optimal flow: Above 1.2 feet on the gauge on the County Route 3 bridge.
Average gradient: 4 feet per mile.
Hazards: In summer, ravenous mosquitoes and deer flies.
Maps: MDNR *Snake River Canoe Route.*

The paddling: Plenty of water? Plenty of bug repellent? Okay, off you go down one of the least-traveled streams within easy reach of the Twin Cities. The river varies between occasional rapids, slow meanders, upland forest, and shady river bottom. There are enough rapids and shallows to make this stretch a miserable hike in low water.

86 County Route 3 to Mora

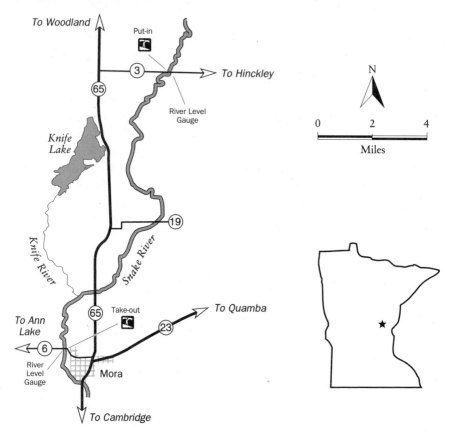

This is no wilderness—the area was thoroughly logged for its white pine during the late 1800s—but the second-growth forest gives the illusion of wild country. Keep an eye out for kingfishers, great blue herons, various forest songbirds, and mammals such as mink, deer, and even black bears and river otters.

Like the previous section, this stretch of the Snake provides good fishing for northern pike, walleye, and smallmouth bass. Best luck usually comes where the river flows over a hard rock bottom, especially near riffles.

Access: To reach the **County Route 3 put-in** from McGrath, drive south on Minnesota Highway 65 about 15 miles to County Route 3; turn east and drive 2 miles to the river. The **Mora take-out** is located on the northwest edge of town on County Route 6.

Shuttle: 13 miles one way. About 40 minutes.

ADDITIONAL HELP

MA&G: 56, E3; 48, A2.

Camping: Auto camping at Aitkin County Park north of Mora. No canoe campsites on this stretch.

Food, gas, and lodging: Mora.

For more information: MDNR Information Center.

87 Mora to Pine City

Character: The Snake flows slowly with few riffles. The forested banks give way to farm fields in much of this stretch.

Length: 28 miles. Most paddlers will opt to use alternate accesses for a shorter trip.

Average run time: 9 to 13 hours for the entire stretch.

Class: Quiet.

Skill level: Beginner.

Optimal flow: 3 to 6.5 feet on gauge on County Route 6 bridge at put-in. Because there are few shallows and riffles, this stretch can be run at all water levels.

Average gradient: 0.6 foot per mile.

Hazards: Watch for fishing boats in the last few miles of river, between Pokegama Lake and Cross Lake at Pine City.

Maps: MDNR *Snake River Canoe Route.*

The paddling: The slow pace of this stretch allows time for quiet reflection and an opportunity to watch wildlife, including waterfowl, shorebirds, forest songbirds, and various forest mammals. The river, if you follow it nearly to Interstate 35 (see map) delivers you to the doorstep of another era. There on the right bank sits a replica of a Northwest Company fur post, restored and operated by the Minnesota Historical Society. With its simple log buildings encircled by a palisade, it resembles the many posts built by fur traders during the late 1700s and early 1800s throughout the St. Croix Valley. Trader John Sayer built a post at this very location in the fall of 1804 and wintered there with his Indian wife (Obemau-Onoqua) and crew of voyageurs. Sayer, the dominant trader in the area from about 1784 to about 1805, left a journal of his time in this country, an important record of the fur trade in the region. Sayer traded with the Ojibwa through the winter for wild rice and furs. In April he packed the furs to company headquarters at Fort William, Ontario, on Lake Superior. The post may have been used only the single winter. By the 1960s, when the Minnesota Historical Society began work on the site, the buildings and stockade had long ago rotted. Their location, however, was clearly evident by compacted soil, charred outlines, wood and food residue, and hundreds of artifacts. The post has been re-created in its original location and stocked with furs, trade goods, and reproductions of furnishings. Guides play the roles of traders, voyageurs, and Indians.

87 Mora to Pine City

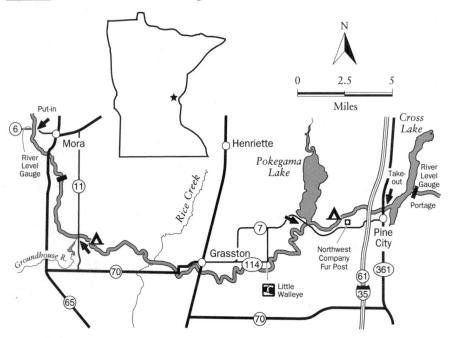

Access: The **Mora put-in** is located on the northwest edge of town on County Route 6. The **Pine City take-out** is located on the north side of the river in Pine City, next to County Route 61. Paddlers will probably opt to use accesses at County Route 11, County Road 114 (Little Walleye), or Pokegama Lake to make for a shorter trip.

Shuttle: About 18 miles one way. About 45 minutes.

ADDITIONAL HELP

MA&G: 48, B2–4.

Camping: Canoe campsites are located near the mouth of the Groundhouse River (Chipmunk Hollow) and across the river and upstream from the fur post. Camp by car at Aitkin County Park north of Mora and St. Croix and Wild River State Parks.

Food, gas, and lodging: Mora, Pine City.

For more information: MDNR Information Center.

88 Pine City to St. Croix River

Character: The Snake picks up the pace again, rushing though long but mostly easy rapids. Fishing is good for a variety of species, especially smallmouth bass.
Length: 12 miles.
Average run time: three to five hours.
Class: I (I–II in high water).
Skill level: Intermediate.
Optimal flow: Above 2 feet on gauge at County Route 9 bridge at put-in, or above 300 cfs on gauge near Pine City—check the USGS website.
Average gradient: 10.8 feet per mile.
Hazards: Hitting rocks and dumping the canoe in low to medium water.
Maps: MDNR *Snake River Canoe Route.*

The paddling: The Snake River has grown from the tiny woodland stream it once was. As a consequence, the rocky rapids present paddlers with a sometimes puzzling number of possible routes. The problem is solved in medium to high water, which covers the rocks but also throws up long chains of standing waves. The rapids-filled first couple of miles give way to a quieter middle stretch before the pace picks up again in the last few miles to the confluence with the St. Croix. The rapids are fun, even thrilling in high water, but they're not difficult. They rate class I at most levels. Some stretches are easy class II in high water.

Canoeing isn't much fun in low water, though that's when the fishing is often best, so anglers may chose to drag a canoe through the riffles to get a shot at northern pike, walleye, channel catfish, and smallmouth bass. Look for pike in quiet, fairly deep water near banks, for walleyes in deep, rocky pools, and smallmouth bass in stretches with rocky streambed, moderate current, and depth of at least a couple of feet.

The river, unfortunately, isn't wild. Cabins appear in bunches, where a road has provided access. The last couple of miles, however, gain protection from Chengwatana State Forest.

Access: The **Pine City put-in** is located on the north side of the river below the Cross Lake dam. From Interstate 35, exit at Pine City. Drive east to the T in the road, turn left on Minnesota Highway 361 into town, turn right on County Route 9 and follow it around the south end of Cross Lake and north to the bridge over the Snake. Turn left to the put-in. To reach the **St. Croix take-out**

300 cfs = minimum for good paddling
(2.0 feet on gauge)

255

88 Pine City to St. Croix River

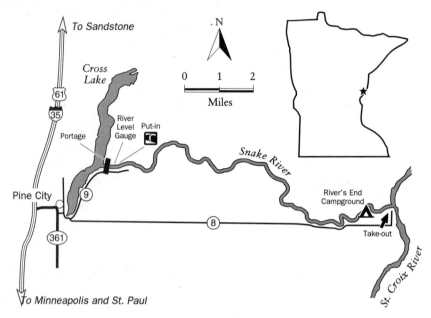

drive south from the put-in on County Route 9 to its intersection with County Route 8 at the south end of Cross Lake. Follow County Route 8 east 9 miles to the end of the road. A carry-in access is available at the River's End Campground, operated by the MDNR Division of Forestry, but that is located a mere mile from the end of the run and is of limited use. See map for details.

Shuttle: 11 miles one way. About 30 minutes.

ADDITIONAL HELP

MA&G: 49, B5–6.
Camping: No canoe campsites are located on this stretch. Camp by car at River's End Campground, operated by the MDNR Division of Forestry, and St. Croix and Wild River State Parks.
Food, gas, and lodging: Pine City.
For more information: MDNR Information Center.

ST. CROIX RIVER

89   Gordon Dam to Wisconsin Highway 35

Character: Lively, clear, and full of fish, the infant St. Croix races through the sand hills of northern Wisconsin. Yes, Wisconsin! It's such a beautiful stretch we include it in a Minnesota guide.

Length: 22 miles.

Average run time: 7 to 11 hours. Allow yourself more time if the water is low because you'll have to drag your canoe in spots. And if you're going to fish every good-looking spot, plan to spend the night.

Class: I–II.

Skill level: Beginner.

Optimal flow: No gauge reading available for this stretch. Call the National Park Service at 715-483-3284, for general information. A reading of 1,500 cfs or more on the USGS gauge near Danbury should ensure good paddling here. Check the USGS website for Wisconsin stations: http://wi.water.usgs.gov

Average gradient: 5.5 feet per mile.

Hazards: Coppermine Dam and a couple of rapids will get your attention. Also, watch out for deer ticks, tiny, reddish, egg-shaped ticks that can transmit Lyme disease, which is common in eastern Minnesota and western Wisconsin.

Maps: National Park Service *St. Croix Riverway.*

The paddling: The St. Croix from Gordon Dam to St. Croix Falls was designated a national scenic river in 1968. The rest of the river was designated in 1972.

Right after the put-in below Gordon Dam, the river runs through class I rapids, past a dense second-growth forest of jack pines, silver maple, and various hardwoods. Among these are **Scotts Rapids,** near the Scotts Bridge. With enough water you'll have no problem. Low water is another matter. Lieutenant James Allen, who ascended the St. Croix in 1832 with troops who were "totally unaccustomed to canoes," had "to wade over all the rapids, which seem to be interminable. Many of them ... were over shelving sandstone rock; the fragments of which, broken and strewed in the channel, have cut up my men's feet, and the bottoms of the canoes, horribly." Allen's men paddled birch bark canoes and probably didn't have good sports sandals. Equipped with modern materials you'll do fine, grinding down the rapids in low water, wading and pushing when you must.

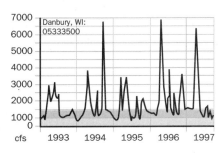

1500 cfs = minimum for good paddling on No. 1

1000 cfs = minimum for good paddling on No. 2

89 Gordon Dam to Wisconsin Highway 35

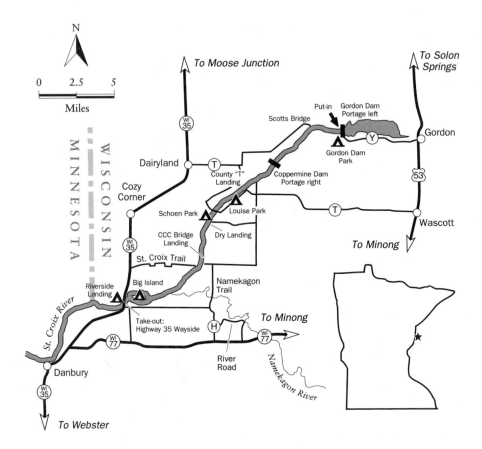

Coppermine Dam, a rock-and-timber relic of the lumberjacks, forms a 2-foot drop. Run it or portage right a few yards. Along this stretch, you'll see many signs of the logging era, when the entire St. Croix Valley was logged for tall, straight, white pine, the most valuable saw log in the northern woods. Low stone levees along the bank cinched in the river channel, providing deeper water to float logs to mill. Logging dams, such as the Coppermine, stored water and logs, which were released in a burst to flush downstream through the rapids and shoals.

The most difficult drop is **Big Fish Trap Rapids** (class II), a long boulder garden which requires plenty of maneuvering in moderate water to reach clear chutes of water. In high water, dodge the largest waves. In low water, drag the canoe and echo Lieutenant Allen's curses.

Near the end of this stretch, the St. Croix joins the Namekagon River, also part of the national scenic riverway and an excellent canoe stream in its own right. Contact the St. Croix National Scenic Riverway for information.

The St. Croix has long provided a link between the Mississippi River Valley and Lake Superior. It was traveled by French-Canadian traders, French explorers, and, long before them, by countless generations of Indians. To travel southward from Superior, for example, a Dakota Indian might paddle from the big lake southward upstream on Wisconsin's Brule River, portage a short distance through the boggy land that forms the divide, launch on the St. Croix and head downstream to the St. Croix's confluence with the Mississippi River at Prescott, Wisconsin.

This shallow upper reach of the river can provide great fishing for smallmouth bass. Because of the lack of deep holes and shortage of cover for large bass, the fish are rather small.

Access: Gordon Dam Park put-in: From the town of Gordon, Wisconsin, drive west about 6 miles on County Route Y and turn right to the park. **WI 35 take-out:** Drive northeast about 9 miles from Danbury, Wisconsin, on WI 35. Take your choice of the wayside on the east side of the bridge or the campsite or landing at Riverside Landing on the west.

See the map for the whereabouts of several alternate access sites to shorten this trip: County Route T Landing, access only; Louise Park, camping and access; Schoen Park, access and camping (no water); Dry Landing, access only; CCC Bridge Landing, access and picnic area.

Shuttle: 30 to 50 miles one way, depending whether you follow the shortcut down zig-zaggy county roads or the longer main highway. Either way, plan to spend 1.5 hours.

ADDITIONAL HELP

Wisconsin A&G: 92–93.
Camping: Gordon Dam Park, Louise Park, Schoen Park. Big Island Campsite accessible only by boat.
Food, gas, and lodging: Hinckley, Danbury, Wisconsin.
For more information: MDNR Information Center or Superintendent, St. Croix National Scenic Riverway.

90 Wisconsin Highway 35 to Minnesota Highway 70

Character: Flowing through some of the wildest country in central Minnesota, the middle reaches of the St. Croix make for excellent overnight camping. Class I and class II rapids quicken the pace. This section also provides good fishing.

Length: 42 miles.

Average run time: Two days.

Class: Mostly quiet with some class I (low water) and class II (high water) rapids.

Skill level: Beginner to intermediate.

Optimal flow: Above 1 foot on the gauge at the boat ramp at St. Croix State Park.

Average gradient: 1.9 feet per mile. The river falls fastest, about 8 feet per mile, in the 5 miles from Nelson Landing to the confluence with the Kettle River.

Hazards: Beginners will want to be careful to avoid spills in the long stretch of rapids near the confluence with the Kettle River. Lyme disease, a tick-borne disease, is relatively common in east-central Minnesota, including the St. Croix Valley. Learn to recognize the deer tick (smaller, redder, and more almond shaped than the wood tick), and don't let them get a hold.

Maps: National Park Service *St. Croix Riverway* or MDNR *St. Croix River Canoe Route, 2.*

The paddling: With the addition of waters from the Namekagon River, the St. Croix is a large stream by the time it touches the Minnesota border near Danbury, Wisconsin. Much of the land along the river is protected not only by the federal scenic river designation, but also by numerous state parks, forests, and wildlife areas in both Minnesota and Wisconsin.

After passing beneath the Minnesota Highway 48 bridge, the placid St. Croix touches the borders of St. Croix State Park, at 34,000 acres, the largest state park in Minnesota. It is also one of the state's wildest parks, with a pack of timber wolves in residence to prey on the plentiful white-tailed deer. The park was once site of logging camps, logging railroads, and log drives. A century ago, Ed St. John's camp stood at St. John's Landing. The old Fleming Railroad hauled logs to the Yellow Banks and dumped them in the river. The logs were floated to mills downstream. If you have a chance, tour the park. It has 127 miles of hiking trails, more than any other state park in Minnesota. St. Croix State Park was also the site of a Civilian Conservation Corps camp in the 1930s. More than 150 park structures date to CCC days. None is more impressive than St. Croix Lodge, built of sandstone blocks and pine timbers.

Across the river (and a few miles from the river) is the 30,000-acre Crex Meadows Wildlife Area, managed by the Wisconsin DNR. Crex, a sprawling complex of wetlands and savanna, attracts more than 100,000 visitors a year to view more than 260 species of birds, including sandhill cranes, trumpeter swans, sharp-tailed grouse, bald eagles, ospreys, and ducks.

After Nelson's Landing, the St. Croix splits into two channels. Both the main channel and the right channel, known as the Kettle River Slough, tumble through a 5-mile stretch of class I rapids (class II in high water). This rocky stretch provides good fishing for smallmouth bass, muskies, northern pike and walleye.

As the St. Croix takes in the waters of the Kettle and the two channels rejoin, the St. Croix spreads out, more than 200 yards wide, and gives the impression of suddenly having become a much larger river. Several islands mark the channel. This location is one of the loveliest spots on the river.

A couple miles below the mouth of the Snake River, dodge behind the island on the east side of the river and check out Sandrock Cliffs. This sheer, 60-foot-high sandstone bluff, one of the most dramatic cliffs on the upper river, is completely invisible to boaters in the main channel.

Woodland Indians and French voyageurs knew the St. Croix was an excellent route for long-distance travel then, and it still is. From this section downstream, it is passable at virtually all water levels (though you may scrape and pull in the rapids). With the abundance of campsites, it's perfect for a trip of several days. Plan to travel about 20 miles a day.

Access: WI 35 put-in: Drive north about 9 miles from Danbury, Wisconsin, on WI 35. Take your choice of the wayside on the east side of the bridge or the campsite and landing at Riverside Landing on the left. **MN 70 take-out:** From Interstate 35, drive east 11 miles to the bridge. The Marshland Visitor Center sits on the Minnesota side of the river; a boat ramp occupies the Wisconsin bank.

Alternate access is possible at several places, including Pansy Landing, MN 48, several sites in St. Croix State Park, Norway Point, Nelson's Landing, Fox Landing, Snake River Landing, and Soderbeck Landing.

Shuttle: 44 miles one way on good road. About 1.75 hours.

90 Wisconsin Highway 35 to Minnesota Highway 70

N

0   2   4
Miles

To Hinckley ←

22

22

Kettle River

Bear Creek

Sand Creek

Sand Creek Landing

MINNESOTA

GOVERNOR

Nelson's Landing

F

II

CHENGWATANA
STATE
FOREST

Redhorse Creek

KNOWLES

STATE

II

II

Fox Landing

II

I–II
Ledge

Snake River

FOREST

F

To Pine City ←   8

Soderbeck Landing

Snake River Landing

Sandrock Cliffs

Take-out

To West Rock and 35

Grantsburg

MN 70

WI 70

River Level Gauge

See map, page 265

To Trade Lake

262

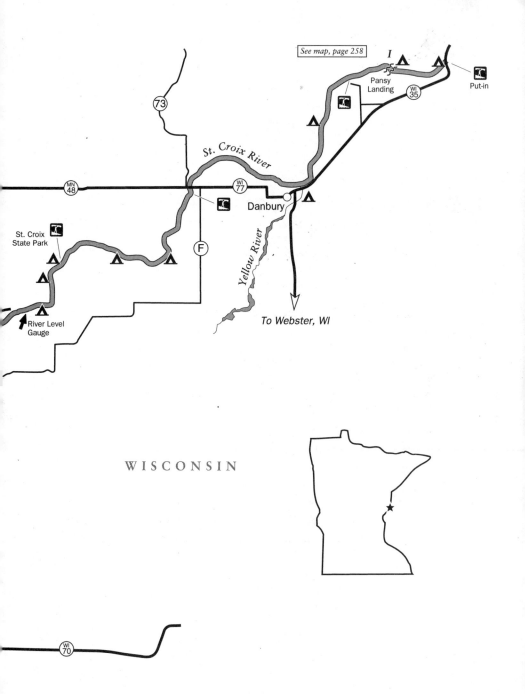

See map, page 258

I

Pansy Landing

Put-in

WI 35

73

St. Croix River

MN 48

WI 77

Danbury

St. Croix State Park

Yellow River

F

River Level Gauge

To Webster, WI

WISCONSIN

WI 70

ADDITIONAL HELP

MA&G: *58, E1; 57, E9; 49.*

Camping: Camp by auto in St. Croix State Park. Canoe campsites are located at several spots along the river, including Norway Point, Nelson's Landing, and several sites in St. Croix State Park. Campsites at Sandrock Cliffs lie on top of the bluff, a tough hike from the river.

Food, gas, and lodging: Pine City, Hinckley.

For more information: MDNR Information Center or Superintendent, St. Croix National Scenic Riverway.

91 Minnesota Highway 70 to Taylors Falls

Character: The St. Croix broadens below MN 70. Though often swift, the river rarely breaks into riffles. The watershed is not as wild as in the upper reaches; nonetheless, state parks and forests protect much of the riverside.

Length: 36 miles.

Average run time: Two days.

Class: Quiet, with some swift water.

Skill level: Beginner.

Optimal flow: Above 6.5 feet on the gauge on the MN 70 bridge.

Average gradient: 1.25 feet per mile.

Hazards: Lyme disease (see above).

Maps: National Park Service *St. Croix Riverway* or MDNR *St. Croix River Canoe Route 3.*

The paddling: Below MN 70, the St. Croix continues its placid but often swift character. It's a fine stretch of river to paddle for a day trip, overnight camping, or fishing for smallmouth bass, walleye, and the occasional northern pike and muskie.

Much of the riverbank is protected in public land holdings, including Governor Knowles State Forest in Wisconsin, and in Minnesota, Chengwatana State Forest and Wild River State Park. Wild River, one of Minnesota's newest state parks, fronts nearly 20 miles of the St. Croix. The park is worth a trip in itself: Its 6,800 acres have 35 miles of hiking and ski trails, 20 miles of horse trails, several backpack and canoe campsites, and a large auto campground. The terrain is a combination of riverbottom forest, upland hardwoods, and native prairie. The river quickens at the site of the old Nevers Dam, a log-piling dam built in 1889 to control the flow of both water and saw logs downstream in an attempt to prevent mammoth log jams common during the height of logging in the St. Croix valley. Damaged by floods in 1950 and 1954, the dam was dismantled in 1955. All that remains today are large sandbars formed when the dam existed and long earthen berms that anchored each end of the dam and provided an approach for a road over the top of the structure.

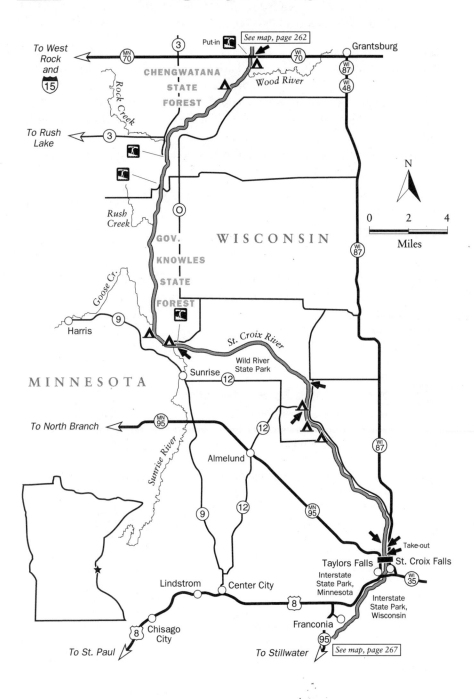

To West Rock and 15

MN 70

Put-in

See map, page 262

WI 87

Grantsburg

WI 48

CHENGWATANA STATE FOREST

Wood River

Rock Creek

To Rush Lake

3

Rush Creek

GOV.

KNOWLES

STATE

FOREST

WISCONSIN

N

0   2   4
Miles

WI 87

Goose Cr.

Harris

9

St. Croix River

Wild River State Park

Sunrise

12

MINNESOTA

To North Branch

MN 95

Sunrise River

12

WI 87

Almelund

9

12

MN 95

Lindstrom

Center City

Taylors Falls

Take-out

St. Croix Falls

Interstate State Park, Minnesota

WI 35

Interstate State Park, Wisconsin

8

8

Chisago City

Franconia

95

To St. Paul

To Stillwater

See map, page 267

Below Wild River State Park the river slackens for several miles as it enters the reservoir formed by the hydroelectric dam at Taylors Falls. Portage right for 1.25 miles or pull out at the National Park Service visitor headquarters on river left.

Access: MN 70 put-in: From Interstate 35, drive east 11 miles to the bridge. **Taylors Falls take-out** at the National Park Service Riverway headquarters and visitor center on river left: From I-35, drive east about 22 miles on U.S. Highway 8 to St. Croix Falls, Wisconsin, and then north through town on Wisconsin Highway 87. The headquarters is on the river side of the highway, on the north edge of town.

Alternate access is possible at several places, to make a shorter trip. See map for details.

Shuttle: About 30 miles one way via WI 70 and WI 87. About 1.2 hours.

ADDITIONAL HELP

MA&G: 49.

Camping: Auto camping is available at Wild River State Park. Canoe campsites are found at several sites, including several in the state park. See map for details.

Food, gas, and lodging: Taylors Falls, and St. Croix Falls, Wisconsin.

For more information: MDNR Information Center or Superintendent, St. Croix National Scenic Riverway.

92 Taylors Falls to Stillwater

Character: The St. Croix enters a valley of dramatic outcrops and soaring bluffs. Overnight camping is limited, but the river is popular for day trips—too popular, in fact, judging by canoe and boat traffic on summer weekends.

Length: 27 miles. Few paddlers will opt to run the whole section but will use alternate accesses for a shorter trip.

Average run time: 9 to 14 hours.

Class: Quiet, except for the class II–III rapids just upstream of the put-in.

Skill level: Beginner.

Optimal flow: 5.5 to 10 feet on the gauge on Minnesota Highway 243 bridge near Osceola, Wisconsin. Water level fluctuates because of releases from power dam at St. Croix Falls, Wis.

Average gradient: 0.5 foot per mile.

Hazards: On busy weekends, watch out for other boat traffic.

Maps: National Park Service *St. Croix Riverway,* MDNR *St. Croix River Canoe Route 4,* or MDNR *Metro River Guide.*

N

0   2   4
Miles

To Almelund

See map, page 265

To Grantsburg, WI

Put-in:
St. Croix
Nat'l Scenic
Riverway Hdqtrs.

Lindstrom   Center City

Taylors Falls   St. Croix Falls

Interstate State Park, Minnesota

Franconia

Interstate State Park, Wisconsin

8

To Chisago City

Dresser

WI 35

MINNESOTA

Osceola

MN 95

River Level Gauge

To Forest Lake

Scandia

WI 35

MN 97

William O'Brien State Park

3

Marine on St. Croix

WISCONSIN

15

7

Canoe Channel

Boat Channel

7

MN 95

11

St. Croix Boomsite Park

Somerset

WI 35

Take-out

WI 64

MN 96

Take-out

Stillwater   Houlton

Take-out

MN 36   MN 212

MN 95

WI 35

To Lake Elmo

See map, page 272

To Hudson, WI

The paddling: A long section of easy rapids follows the hydroelectric dam at St. Croix Falls, Wisconsin, but there's no easy way to get to them. Then, directly beneath the U.S. Highway 8 bridge, the river flows through a deep, powerful rapids, about 50 yards long, that kicks waves up to 3 feet high. In the summer, when smaller stretches of rapids are too low and scratchy to run, whitewater paddlers

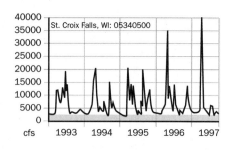

3000 cfs = shoals and sandbars exposed below this level

flock to this single rapids on the St. Croix to practice eddy turns and surfing. Unfortunately, there's no good way of gaining access to these rapids, either. Most boaters park in the upper parking lot in Interstate State Park (in Minnesota) and portage 200 yards up the river.

Flatwater paddlers taking a longer, more placid trip will want to skip the rapids altogether. Instead, put in at the boat landing in Interstate State Park about 1.5 miles below the bridge and rapids. (Access is also possible in Interstate State Park on the Wisconsin side of the river.) Having done this, however, you very well may want to paddle back upstream to view the St. Croix Dalles, a cliff-lined gorge that girds the river for a half mile. "The stream enters a wild, narrow gorge, so deep and dark, that the declining sun is quite shut out. Perpendicular walls of traprock, scarlet and chocolate colored, and gray with the moss of centuries, rising from the water, are piled in savage grandeur on either side." The words were written by Elizabeth F. Ellet in 1852. She perhaps can be forgiven her florid prose, for the view remains impressive even today and encourages strings of adjectives that stretch on like the river itself.

If you decide you don't want the work of paddling upstream, take a look from the cliffs, which are accessible from the upper parking lot in Minnesota's Interstate State Park. Also on display are many large potholes, formed at the close of the last ice age, when glacial meltwater roared down the valley, drowning the cliffs that today tower far above the river. Rocks, caught in the turbulence, swirled and rotated in pockets of basalt, drilling holes in the bedrock until retreating waters filled many of the potholes with silt and eventually stranded them far above river level. The biggest has been dubbed Bottomless Pit, 67 feet deep.

The Dalles was the site of one of many bloody battles between Ojibwa and their traditional enemies, the Fox and Dakota. According to historian James Taylor Dunn, the victorious Ojibwa killed so many of their foes amid the rocks and clefts of the Dalles it became known as the Valley of Bones.

In the following century, the Dalles was known for spectacular logjams that formed between the river's craggy walls at the hard bend known as Angle Rock. In

1886 logs backed up through the entire gorge, forming the most stupendous jam ever known, containing an estimated 150 million board feet of timber. Crews totaling 200 needed six weeks to clear it.

Even as the region's old-growth forests floated down the St. Croix in ever-increasing volume during the mid- to late 1800s, the writing of Ellet and others brought tourists and summer residents to the valley. Steamboats carried visitors as far upstream as the Dalles, where the towering walls of basalt seemed at once enchanting and foreboding.

Escaping the confines of the gorge, the St. Croix enters a broad valley. Despite its proximity to the Twin Cities, the valley retains much of its wild flavor. The wide river has formed many islands, secluded backwaters, and sandbars, which are exposed in low water.

Just upstream from Marine on St. Croix, 1,400-acre William O'Brien State Park provides drive-in camping, and trails for hiking and skiing. Low sandstone cliffs flank the river.

Small towns along the river, tucked into the gentle folds of the hardwood-covered valley, decorate the strand of the St. Croix like pearls. Among the most picturesque is Stillwater. Founded in 1843, it is Minnesota's self-proclaimed birth-place. Many fine old buildings line its downtown streets. In summer, it bustles with tourists.

Just upstream of Stillwater on the Minnesota bank lies Boomsite Park, the site more than a century ago of a logging "boom," a barrier of floating logs stretched

An autumn day of canoeing on the St. Croix, downstream from Interstate State Park. MINNESOTA OFFICE OF TOURISM

across the river to catch floating logs for sorting. Up to 600 men worked the boom to sort the logs by brand and raft them to mills in Stillwater and Winona (on the Mississippi). By 1888, 300 million board feet of logs moved through the boom yearly. Old photographs show the river to be a corduroy of logs. Pioneer newspaper editor James Goodhue wrote that "centuries will hardly exhaust the pineries above us." But exhaust them we did. The boom ended operations in 1914. The following year, with the exhaustion of the northern pineries, the last raft of lumber left town behind the *Ottumwa Belle.*

As is true of many big rivers in the Mississippi drainage, the St. Croix provides fishing for an astounding variety of fish. Walleye, northern pike, smallmouth bass, and muskies continue to be present. But so are white bass, channel and flathead catfish, and freshwater drum. If you fish a jig and nightcrawler through a deep hole, you'll have no idea what you might catch.

To reduce the conflict between river users and erosion to riverbanks, the National Park Service enforces several no-wake and slow-speed zones on this and the downstream segment of the St. Croix.

Access: **Taylors Falls put-in** at Minnesota Interstate State Park. From Interstate 35, drive east about 22 miles on US 8 to the park entrance. **Stillwater take-out:** Three sites are available, all located on Minnesota Highway 95. One access is located just north of the Stillwater bridge over the St. Croix. The second lies just south of the intersection with Minnesota Highway 96. The third is located at St. Croix Boomsite Park about 2 miles north of town.

Cut the length of the trip by using alternate accesses: boat ramp across the river from Osceola, Wisconsin, boat ramp in William O'Brien State Park, Somerset Landing across the river from Marine on St. Croix.

Shuttle: 23 miles one way along US 8 and MN 95 to Stillwater. About one hour.

ADDITIONAL HELP

MA&G: 49, E7; 42.
Camping: Minnesota Interstate State Park, Wisconsin Interstate State Park, William O'Brien State Park. Canoe campsite at Eagle's Nest, near Franconia.
Food, gas, and lodging: Taylors Falls, Stillwater; St. Croix Falls, Wisconsin.

For more information: MDNR Information Center or Superintendent, St. Croix National Scenic Riverway.

93 Stillwater to Prescott

Character: A natural sandbar causes the St. Croix to form a riverine lake, more than a mile across in places. The valley is beautiful, bounded by high bluffs, but you'd feel more at home in a runabout, fishing boat, or sailboat than a canoe.
Length: 25 miles.
Average run time: Not applicable. Few paddlers will opt to run the whole section but will use alternate accesses for a shorter trip.
Class: Quiet with little current for much of the segment.
Skill level: Beginner.
Optimal flow: Any level.
Average gradient: Virtually none.
Hazards: On busy weekends, watch out for other boat traffic.
Maps: National Park Service *St. Croix Riverway,* MDNR *St. Croix River Canoe Route 5,* or MDNR *Metro Rivers Guide.*

The paddling: The sandbar at the river's mouth forms a natural lake that makes this stretch of river far less attractive to canoeists than the upstream sections. Nonetheless, the river is fine for short trips and fishing. Avoid it on summer weekends, when the channel is clogged with big boats of all kinds.

Public land holdings at Kinnickinnic State Park in Wisconsin and Afton State Park in Minnesota are helping to plug the dike against a flood of development in the area. All the parks are worth exploring on foot.

Stillwater and Hudson are bustling tourist traps in summer, but are worth a look for their old downtown buildings, restaurants, and shops. Afton is a quiet and historic backwater with several white clapboard buildings dating to the 1800s. Started by New Englanders in 1855, the town was named from Robert Burn's poem *Flow Gently, Sweet Afton.*

As is true of the previous segment, the final section of the St. Croix provides fishing for many species, including walley, northern pike, smallmouth bass, white bass, channel and flathead catfish, freshwater drum, and a few muskies. You might even catch an American eel.

Several no-wake zones are enforced.

Access: Few canoeists will want to paddle this stretch beginning to end. Instead, put in at accesses at Boomsite Park in Stillwater or St. Croix Bluffs Regional Park about 4 miles from the river's mouth. Other access is available at fee ramps at Stillwater, Bayport, Hudson, Lakeland, and Afton.

Shuttle: Not applicable.

93 Stillwater to Prescott

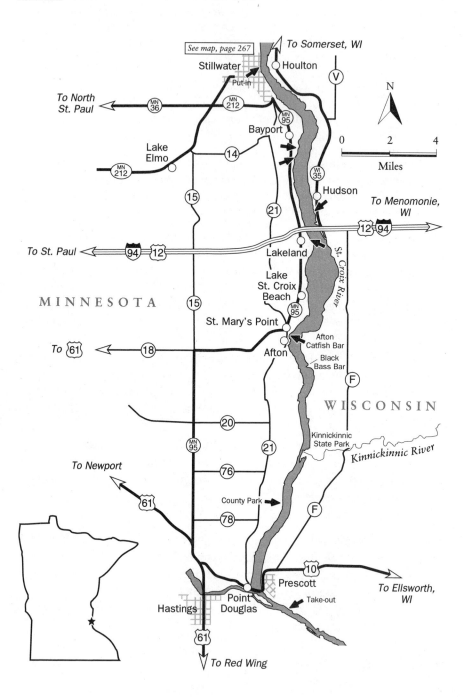

ADDITIONAL HELP

MA&G: 42.

Camping: Canoe campsites are available at Kinnickinnic State Park. Auto camping available at Afton State Park.

Food, gas, and lodging: Stillwater; Hudson and Prescott, Wisconsin.

For more information: MDNR Information Center or Superintendent, St. Croix National Scenic Riverway and St. Croix Bluffs Regional Park.

94 Sunrise River

Character: A small woodland stream with lively current and several easy rapids, the Sunrise is a good bet in the spring or after rain, when the water is high.

Length: 9.5 miles.

Average run time: Three hours.

Class: I–II.

Skill level: Beginner.

Optimal flow: Gauge readings not available. For an indication, check out the rapids below the town of Sunrise to see if there is enough water to get over the rocks.

Average gradient: 8.4 feet per mile.

Hazards: Watch for downed trees blocking the river's narrow channel. On such a narrow stream, you may not have much room to maneuver.

Maps: PRIM *Metro North* and *Mora*.

The paddling: The Sunrise, a tributary of the St. Croix River, is a swift, intimate river. The stream is often less than 50 feet wide. From Kost Dam County Park, the Sunrise winds through mostly open land. But below the town of Kost, the stream slips into bottomland and low-lying forest, passing some houses but running primarily through undeveloped land. About halfway through the run, the Sunrise joins the North Branch of the Sunrise, gaining considerably in size. Tall pines grow along the uplands. The river picks up gradient and speed below the town of Sunrise. Most of the river's rapids are class I, but one drop, where the river narrows about a mile above the river's mouth, rates an easy class II.

Near its mouth, the Sunrise passes through Wild River State Park, a varied and beautiful retreat along the St. Croix River with more than 120 miles of hiking trails.

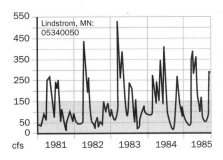

150 cfs = estimated minimum for good paddling

273

94 Sunrise River

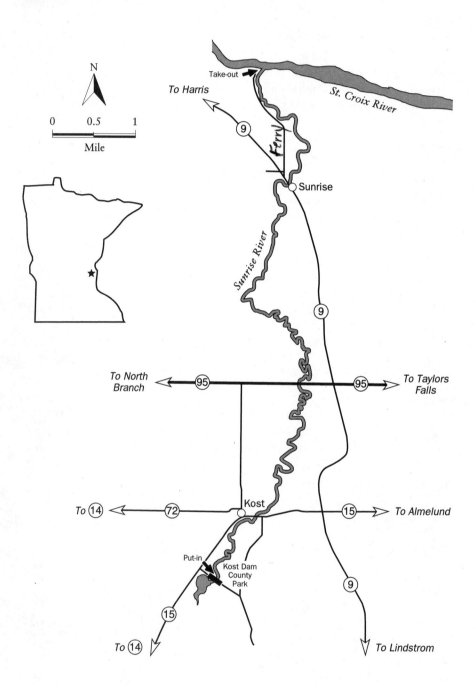

The best fishing in the Sunrise is found in the few miles above the river's mouth, where walleye, northern pike, smallmouth bass, channel catfish, and other species swim up from the St. Croix.

Access: Kost Dam put-in: From North Branch, drive east about 7 miles on Minnesota Highway 95. Turn south on County Route 15 and travel 3 miles to Kost Dam County Park. The put-in is below the dam. **Sunrise take-out:** From the town of Sunrise, drive north on the unnumbered road that runs along the west side of the river 2 miles to the boat ramp at the confluence of the Sunrise and St. Croix Rivers.

Shuttle: 8 miles one way. About 25 minutes.

ADDITIONAL HELP

MA&G: 49, D6.
Camping: None along river. Auto camping at Wild River State Park.
Food, gas, and lodging: North Branch.
For more information: Call the MDNR area forestry office in Hinckley.

`95` Upper Tamarack River

Character: Spanning the Wisconsin-Minnesota border, the Upper Tamarack is a swift, narrow woodland stream. Unfortunately, it is runnable only in high water.
Length: 11.5 miles.
Average run time: Four to five hours.
Class: I–II.
Skill level: Intermediate.
Optimal flow: No gauge readings are available. High water is needed to make this run. If rapids and shallows near Markville are too shallow to run, pack it in and go somewhere else.
Average gradient: 16.5 feet per mile. The steepest gradient—more than 30 feet per mile—occurs in the 2 miles of river upstream from County Route 25 near Markville.
Hazards: Aside from the rapids, look for downed trees blocking the channel.
Maps: USGS *Cloverton MN-WI, Danbury East MN-WN.*

The paddling: For the first several miles from the Swedish Highway put-in, the Upper Tamarack flows through woodland and marsh, dropping through class I rapids at an average of about 10 feet per mile. Approaching Markville, the river enters a steep-banked gorge and falls much faster. The bouldery rapids through this stretch rate class II. The swift current and narrow channel force you to maneuver to stay out of trouble. Watch for sweepers blocking the narrow channel. The rapids ease up a bit from County Route 25 to the river's mouth but still provide a thrill.

95 Upper Tamarack River

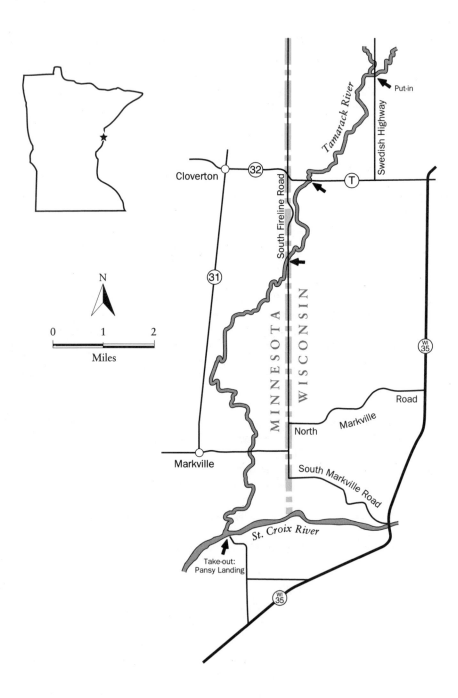

Exciting rapids aside, the Upper Tamarack is a beautiful stream. It runs through deep woods of birch, aspen, and conifers. Little of the river corridor is developed. In the lower reaches, high banks flank the river. Some rise more than 100 feet above the stream.

To reach the take-out, enter the St. Croix River and cross the river to Pansy Landing.

Like most small streams in the region, the Upper Tamarack is infertile and lacks the depth and flow needed to provide good habitat for game fish. Species such as northern pike, smallmouth bass, and walleye will enter the lower few miles of stream and retreat to the deeper sanctuary of the St. Croix River.

Access: Swedish Highway put-in: From Cloverton, drive east 3 miles; turn north on Swedish Highway and drive 2 miles to the bridge. There is no developed access. **St. Croix take-out:** From the Hinckley exit of Interstate 35, drive east about 27 miles on Minnesota Highway 48 across the St. Croix to Danbury, Wisconsin; turn northwest on Wisconsin Highway 35 and drive about 4 miles; turn north and drive 2 miles to Pansy Landing on the Wisconsin side of the St. Croix. From the put-in, drive south about 2 miles on Swedish Highway to County Route T; drive east 1 mile to WI 35; drive south just over 9 miles across the St. Croix to Pansy Landing Road; turn west and drive about 2 miles to the landing.

To shorten the run, use alternate accesses (undeveloped) at County Route T in Wisconsin, South Fireline Road along the state boundary, or County Route 25 in Minnesota.

Shuttle: 14 miles one way. About 40 minutes.

ADDITIONAL HELP

MA&G: 58, D1–E1.
Wisconsin A&G grid: 92, C3–D2
Camping: St. Croix State Forest, St. Croix State Park.
Food, gas, and lodging: Hinckley; Danbury, Wisconsin.
For more information: MDNR area Forester, Hinckley, MN 55037; 320-384-6146.

Minneapolis-St. Paul

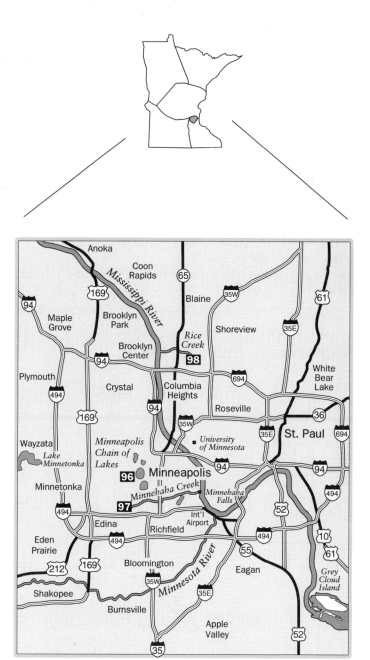

96   Minneapolis Chain of Lakes

Character: With no gas-powered motorboats allowed, the city lakes provide an oasis of calm amid the hubbub of the city.
Paddline time: Day trip.
Hazards: Don't get run over by a windsurfer.
Maps: MDNR *Twin Cities Water Recreation;* Minneapolis Park & Recreation Board *The Grand Rounds Parkway System.*

The paddling: Decades ago, Minneapolis had the foresight to establish an extensive park system. The gems of this system are the lakes. Because outboard motors aren't allowed, the lakes provide an oasis of calm and quiet in the heart of the hectic city.

Four of the lakes in south Minneapolis provide a chain perfectly suited to canoeing. Launch at the access at the northeast shore of Lake Calhoun. Paddle around a bit on Calhoun, dodging the sailboats moored at the north end of the lake. Then head through the channel at the north end of the lake into Lake of the Isles. The two islands on Isles offer a refuge for wildlife, including great blue herons and black-crowned night herons.

Paddle to the east end of Isles and into the long, narrow channel leading to Cedar Lake. Overhung by tree limbs, these channels feel like jungle rivers—except, of course, for the homes, backyards, and joggers. Cedar has a couple of nice

96   Minneapolis Chain of Lakes

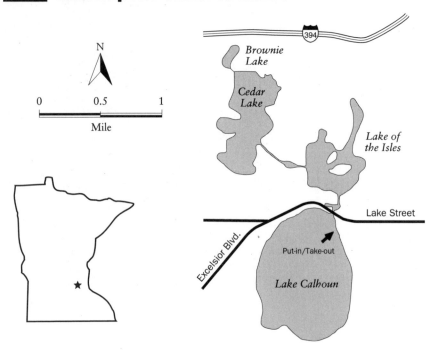

Sailboats and a rowboat at rest at the pavilion on Lake Calhoun. MINNESOTA OFFICE OF TOURISM

beaches, one on the east shore and the other on the peninsula that projects from the west shore. If you paddle to the northwest shore, you'll find the short channel, which leads through a culvert, into tiny Brownie Lake.

The route from Calhoun to Brownie is about 2 miles.

These lakes provide surprisingly good fishing, especially for largemouth bass.

Access: There is a developed access at the northeast shore of Lake Calhoun, south of the intersection of East Calhoun Boulevard and West Lake Street. As a practical matter, however, you can launch a canoe wherever you can park close to the water and cross public parkland.

ADDITIONAL HELP

MA&G: 41, D7.
Camping: None.
Food, gas, and lodging: Minneapolis.
For more information: Minneapolis Park and Recreation Board.

97 Minnehaha Creek

Character: Quick and winding for much of its length, Minnehaha's often natural character belies its urban setting.
Length: 22 miles.
Average run time: Seven to ten hours.
Class: I, with one class II rapids at West 54th Street.
Skill level: Beginner.
Optimal flow: 75 to 150 cfs at the Gray's Bay Dam at Lake Minnetonka. Call the Minnehaha Creek Watershed District for conditions.
Average gradient: 5.5 feet per mile.
Hazards: Watch for downed trees, low culverts, and dams at Browndale Avenue, Lake Nokomis, and Lake Hiawatha. Keep an eye out for tee shots at the Meadowbrook Golf Course near Excelsior Boulevard. And be doubly sure to take out before 50-foot Minnehaha Falls. In high water, the swift turns through narrow sections, especially those with retaining walls and bridges, get tricky.
Maps: Minnehaha Creek Watershed District *Minnehaha Creek Canoe Route.*

The paddling: Minnehaha Creek heads up in Lake Minnetonka, which means "big water" in the Dakota language. To the Indians who lived on its shores, it was an important fishery and village site. It is nothing less today, ringed by multi-million-dollar homes and plied by fishing boats, runabouts, and sailboats.

Put in below the dam at Gray's Bay. For the first couple of miles, the stream flows quietly through marsh. At the Minnetonka Civic Center, however, the current begins to pick up. Occasional easy rapids punctuate the river's course.

Though you occasionally see homes from the creek, much of this stretch appears wooded and wild. The character changes once you pass through the culvert beneath

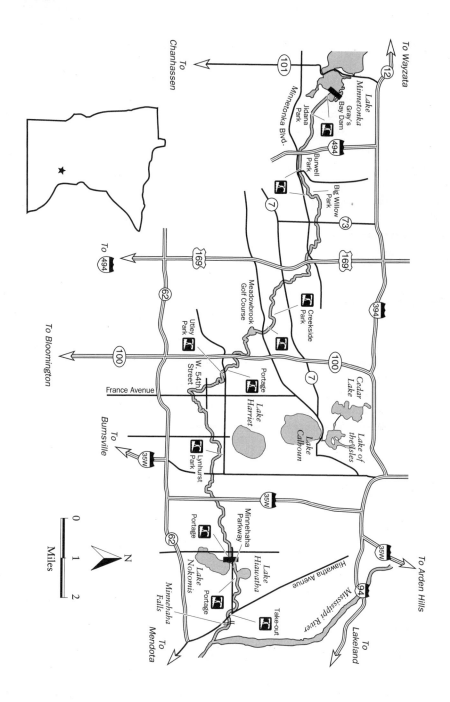

U.S. Highway 169. East of the highway, the creek becomes more urban. Spotting houses and paddling along backyards is the rule rather than the exception. Of course, you can take advantage of this development as well. Just upstream from the Minnesota Highway 7 bridge, you can land and shop at the Knollwood Target. Just downstream from the bridge, beach the canoe and get lunch at the Taco Bell.

At Browndale Avenue, you'll have to portage an old mill dam located beneath the bridge. Just downstream at West 54th Street is rocky class II rapids.

East of France Avenue, Minnehaha is flowing through the old neighborhoods of Minneapolis and for most of its length is flanked by public parkland. At Lake Nokomis, portage the low dam. If you want, you can paddle into Nokomis. At Lake Hiawatha, you'll have to portage a similar low dam.

Take out upstream of Hiawatha Avenue, for just downstream, the creek plunges over 50-foot Minnehaha Falls into a steep-walled gorge. The adventurous and ambitious can portage in below the falls and make a quick, rapids-filled run for one half mile to the Mississippi.

Access: The **Lake Minnetonka put-in** is located at Gray's Bay at the east end of the lake. Take Minnesota Highway 101 (Chanhassen Road) to Gray's Bay Boulevard and then east to the canoe landing. The **Minnehaha Falls take-out** lies south of Minnehaha Parkway and west of Minnesota Highway 55 (Hiawatha Avenue).

Access is possible at many other points. See the map for locations.

Shuttle: 22 miles one way. About one hour.

ADDITIONAL HELP

MA&G: 41, D6–8.
Camping: There are no developed campsites along the river.
Food, gas, and lodging: Minneapolis and suburbs.
For more information: Minnehaha Creek Watershed District.

98 Rice Creek

Character: Rice Creek is a fun run with swift water and easy rapids in the heart of the Twin Cities.
Length: 6.6 miles, plus 1.4 miles on Mississippi.
Average run time: Two to four hours.
Class: I–II. The bends and tight channel get tricky in high water.
Skill level: Beginner to intermediate.
Optimal flow: No gauge readings are available. This stretch is no fun in very low water, which occurs in mid- to late summer.
Average gradient: 9.8 feet per mile (Rice Creek only).
Hazards: Downed trees on sharp bends can upset your canoe.
Maps: PRIM

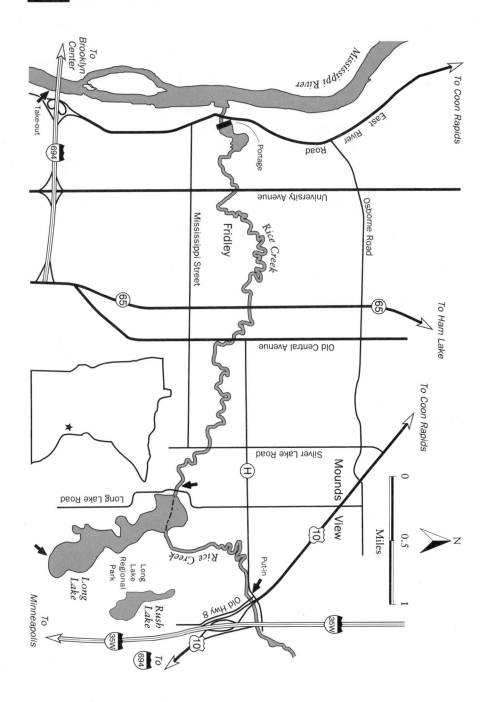

The paddling: From the put-in the river flows about 1.5 miles to Long Lake. A regional park encompasses an attractive natural area on the east shore of the lake. Stop here for a break, or follow the north shore to where Rice Creek exits Long Lake. From here the river runs quickly through a deep, wooded valley that screens the river from the suburban homes over the bluffs. The narrow stream turns this way and that as it races along. The rapids are easy, but tree trunks, especially on sharp bends, can be tough to dodge. Keep on your toes.

After this run though the woods, Rice Creek enters Locke Lake, a small pond with a dam at the downstream (west) end. Portage right of the dam. Reenter the river and paddle about 0.2 mile to the Mississippi River. Continue down the Mississippi 1.4 miles to the take-out on the east side of the river, just south of the Interstate 694 bridge.

Access: **Old Highway 8 put-in:** From U.S. Highway 10, drive west 1 block on County Road H and then south about 0.25 mile on Old Highway 8. Turn east (left) into the parking lot next to Rice Creek. Reach the **Mississippi River take-out** from East River Road (County Route 1), just south of I-694.

Alternate put-ins include Long Lake Regional Park and Long Lake Road, just downstream from Long Lake.

Shuttle: 7 miles one way. About 25 minutes.

ADDITIONAL HELP

MA&G: 41, C8.
Camping: There are no developed campsites along the stream.
Food, gas, and lodging: New Brighton, Fridley.
For more information: Ramsey and Anoka county parks.

Southeast

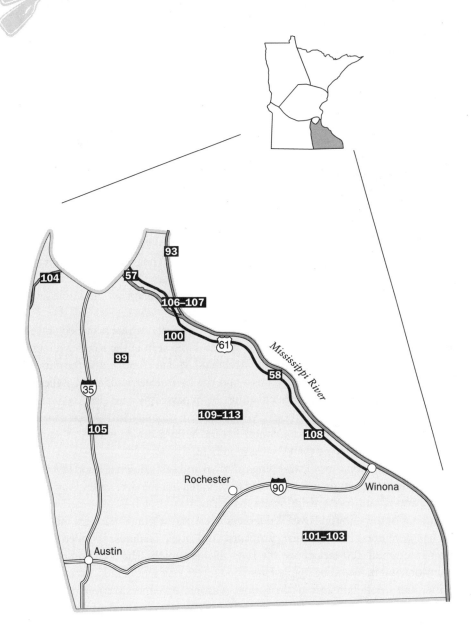

CANNON RIVER

99 Faribault to Northfield

Character: The upper Cannon is an intimate, wooded stream with gentle current.
Length: 16 miles.
Average run time: Five to eight hours.
Class: I.
Skill level: Beginner.
Optimal flow: Above 1 foot on the gauge on the Fifth Street bridge in Northfield.
Average gradient: 3.4 feet per mile.
Hazards: Watch for downed trees, especially in high water on the outside of river bends where current is fast.
Maps: MDNR *Cannon River Canoe Route.*

The paddling: The Cannon is a great route for paddlers. Evidence of that is found in its name, which in reality has nothing at all to do with heavy artillery. Rather, it is a mistranslation of the French *La Rivière aux Canots,* "the river of canoes." Dakota Indians paddled up the Cannon from their settlements on the Mississippi to hunt for bison on the prairies to the west.

During settlement of the mid-1800s, the Cannon's lively current provided power for grain milling and industry. Evidence of that is still seen in the Kings Mill and Woolen Mill Dams in Faribault, the old Archibald Mill in Dundas, and the dam in Northfield. Unfortunately, these dams—and the hydroelectric dam on Byllesby Reservoir downstream of this stretch—must be bypassed by canoeists.

Start this trip below the Woolen Mill Dam in Faribault, at the access at the confluence of the Straight and Cannon Rivers. With a drainage of 443 square miles, the Straight is larger than the Cannon here.

The Cannon soon slips the trappings of town and eases down a wooded valley. Much of the greater landscape is devoted to farming, but the river valley is an oasis of hardwoods and forest wildflowers. Much of this stretch is protected in the boundaries of the Cannon River Wilderness Area. Rice County manages this area and has developed hiking trails, campsites, and other facilities. Wooded bluffs tower more than 200 feet above the river in this stretch. The area comprises a variety of habitat, including maple-basswood forest, oak woodlands, savanna and prairie, and floodplain forests. In spring, seasonal ephemerals cover the forest floor. Woodpeckers of various species search for insects beneath the bark of standing dead elms, killed by Dutch elm disease, and excavate cavities for nests. Eastern bluebirds and wood ducks also nest in cavities found in standing dead trees. The area is a refuge for many other bird species as well, including Cooper's hawks, great-horned and barred owls, wood and hermit thrushes, veeries, and prothonotary and Nashville warblers.

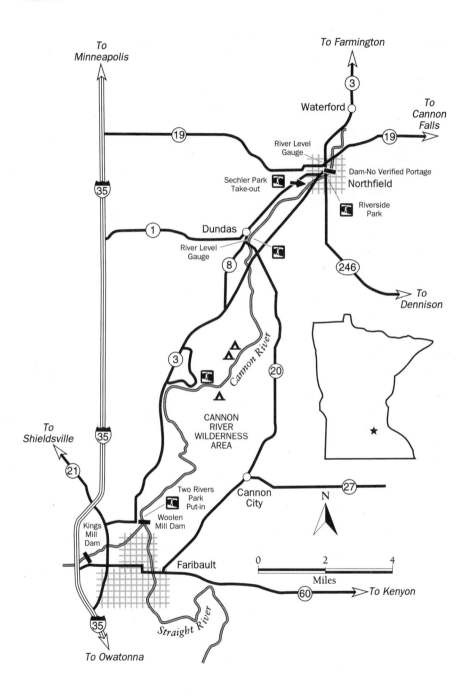

At the town of Dundas, the river passes a city park with picnic area and campground. At the County Route 1 bridge, the river splits around an island and then passes the aging walls of the Archibald Mill on river left. In the mid-1800s, before corn became the major crop of southeastern Minnesota, wheat was grown throughout the region. The grain was processed in mills like the Archibald. In fact, in 1877, there were 15 flour mills along the stretch of the river between Faribault and Northfield alone.

Soon the river slips into the picturesque college town of Northfield, home to Carleton and St. Olaf Colleges. Three city parks line the river banks, providing picnic areas and access. Take out at Sechler Park on river left, about a mile above the dam. A revived historic district flanks the river near the dam. If you have the time, take a stroll through town.

From Northfield, the Cannon flows gently 11 miles to the upper end of Byllesby Reservoir. Although this stretch is wooded and eminently canoeable, access is a problem, since there is no developed portage around the Northfield dam. Nor is there a developed canoe access or boat ramp between Northfield and Byllesby. If you're determined to paddle this stretch, put in at the county road bridge just downstream from Waterford or farther downstream at County Road 59.

At first glance it would appear that habitat for smallmouth bass is excellent. Oddly, very few live in the river. Fishing generally is rather poor. Why? The reasons aren't clear. Perhaps agricultural runoff makes the river unsuitable for some species. Perhaps fish cannot migrate to suitable year-round habitat, such as deep wintering pools, because the river is segmented by dams.

Access: Faribault put-in: Two Rivers Park on the east side of the Cannon, just below its confluence with the Straight River at the north edge of town. **Northfield take-out:** at Sechler Park, a city park on the west side of the river.

Shuttle: About 13 miles one way. About 40 minutes.

ADDITIONAL HELP

MA&G: 33, C–D8.
Camping: Canoe camping is available in the Cannon River Wilderness Area. Auto camping is possible at Dundas City Park and nearby Nerstrand–Big Woods State Park.
Food, gas, and lodging: Faribault, Northfield.
For more information: MDNR Information Center.

100 Cannon Falls to Mississippi River

Character: The Cannon races through a series of easy rapids and passes tall, rocky bluffs on its way to the Mississippi River.

Length: 28 miles, including a 3-mile paddle on the Mississippi to reach a suitable access. Shorter trips are possible.

Average run time: 9 to 13 hours for the whole stretch.

Class: I.

Skill level: Beginner.

Optimal flow: Above 1 foot on the gauge on the Minnesota Highway 20 bridge at Cannon Falls, or above 1.5 feet on the gauge on the County Route 7 bridge at Welch.

Average gradient: 4.5 feet per mile.

Hazards: Watch for downed trees on the outside of river bends, especially in very high water.

Maps: MDNR *Cannon River Canoe Route.*

The paddling: Less than a mile below the put-in, the Cannon runs through the largest rapids on this segment of river, a wavy, class I drop at the railroad trestle just downstream from the confluence with the Little Cannon River. The river scoots out of the town of Cannon Falls, running through quick successions of easy rapids as it burrows ever deeper into its limestone valley.

A railroad once followed the right (south) bank of the river. Today, the rail bed has been converted to the Cannon Valley Trail, a popular route running between Cannon Falls and Red Wing. As you paddle, you'll spot cyclists and skaters zipping past you, far above the river.

A dam once blocked the river at Welch. The aging, useless structure was demolished several years ago; only a mild rapids marks the spot today. A canoe and inner-tube outfitter operates out of the old mill next to the former dam site. During the summer, the outfitter launches dozens to hundreds of tubes between the Trout Brook access and Welch, so avoid this stretch on pleasant summer weekends if you value peace and quiet.

Below Welch, rapids become less frequent, as the river reaches the flood plain of the Mississippi. Near the confluence of the two rivers, the land is so flat that the channel of the Cannon breaks into wormlike segments that follow their own winding, lackadaisical course through open marshland to the big river. When in doubt about the route, follow the channel with the greatest current. At times you may have to use your paddles to pole through the shallow channels. Then, because no road

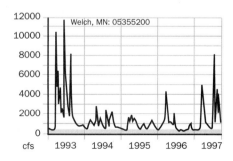

400 cfs = minimum for good paddling

100 Cannon Falls to Mississippi River

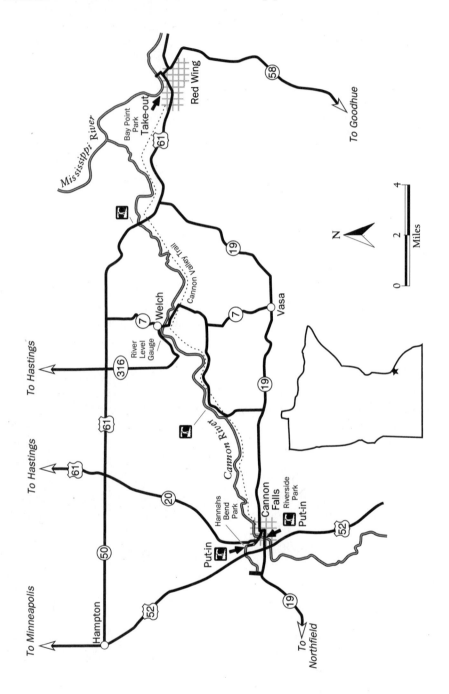

crosses the bottomlands at the mouth of the Cannon, you'll have to enter the channel of the Mississippi and paddle downstream 3 miles to the access on the Mississippi at Bay Point Park in Red Wing. It is also possible to paddle upstream an equal distance to a boat ramp on the Vermillion Slough. While the backwaters are complex and interesting to explore, if you wish to avoid the paddle on the big water of the Mississippi, take out at the U.S. Highway 61 bridge over the Cannon about 7 miles above the mouth.

This section of the Cannon provides good fishing for a variety of species, especially smallmouth bass, walleye, and channel and flathead catfish. With the removal of the dam at Welch, fish from the Mississippi have free access to the river as far upstream as the Byllesby Dam, expanding the range of habitat available to them throughout the year. The result should be more fish, a greater variety of species, and better fishing than the Cannon has seen since the dam was built.

Access: Cannon Falls put-in: Two parks in Cannon Falls allow access for canoes: Riverside Park near the confluence with the Little Cannon and the MN 20 bridge, and Hannah's Bend Park, about a mile upstream, near the U.S. Highway 52 bridge.

Possible take-outs: Mouth of Trout Brook: From Cannon Falls, drive north on MN 20 about 3 miles to 280th Street East; drive east about 4.5 miles to the access. Welch: Make arrangements with the outfitter to take out on private property. US 61: At the highway bridge about 7 miles west of Red Wing. Bay Point Park: Just off US 61 at the west end of Red Wing.

Canoeing the Cannon River between Cannon Falls and the Mississippi River.
MINNESOTA DEPARTMENT OF NATURAL RESOURCES

Shuttle: 20 miles one way from Cannon Falls to Bay Point Park. About one hour. An alternative to a normal two-car shuttle is to spot the car at Welch next to the river and Cannon Valley Trail and travel by bicycle or in-line skates back to River-side Park, which is also located on the trail.

ADDITIONAL HELP

MA&G: 34, B1–4.

Camping: There are no river campsites on this stretch of the Cannon. Camp by car at Lake Byllesby, a private campground in Welch, or Frontenac State Park near Red Wing.

Food, gas, and lodging: Cannon Falls, Red Wing.

For more information: MDNR Information Center.

ROOT RIVER

101 Chatfield to Whalan

Character: Easy rapids, stunning scenery, several campsites, and good fishing make this stretch of the Root an excellent route for a day trip or overnight.

Length: 34.7 miles.

Average run time: Two days. Use alternate access for shorter trips.

Class: I.

Skill level: Beginner.

Optimal flow: Above 1.5 feet on the gauge near the Minnesota Highway 250 bridge.

Average gradient: 4.9 feet per mile.

Hazards: Tread carefully when running the remains of an old dam about 6 miles below the County Route 21 bridge.

Maps: MDNR, *Root River Canoe & Boating Route.*

The paddling: Launch at Chatfield on the North Branch of the Root. The river here is small; paddling is best when water is fairly high. Four miles below the put-in, the North Branch joins the Middle Branch, and a good-sized stream is born.

As the stream moves downhill, it cuts deeper into the ancient limestone topography that makes up this corner of the state. Limestone cliffs flank the river and sprout with greater frequency

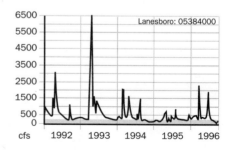

250 cfs = minimum for good paddling

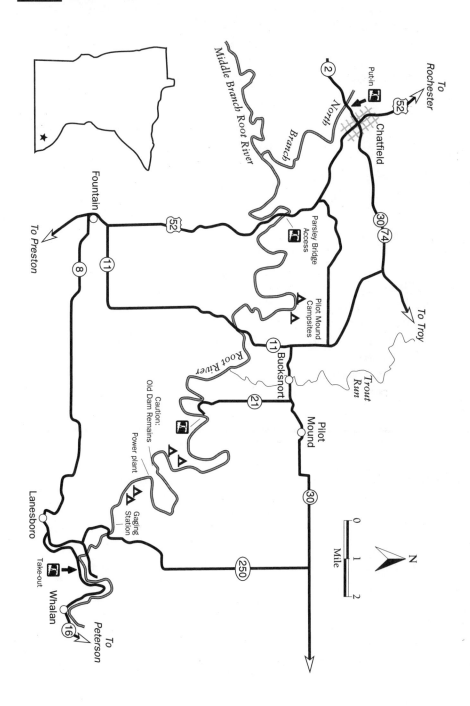

from the hilltops. The far southeastern corner of Minnesota, including the Root River valley, lies in an area largely untouched by glaciers during the most recent ice age. So as glaciers rearranged the rest of Minnesota, forming the low hills and shallow depressions that would become the Land of 10,000 Lakes, streams in the southeast continued to carve the deep wrinkles of old age.

Biologically, too, the Root Valley seems to stand apart from the rest of Minnesota. It is warmer than the forests to the north; wetter than the prairies to the west. For that reason, the forest resembles the woods of the southern Midwest and Ozarks, with a preponderance of oaks and species such as shagbark hickory, black walnut, butternut, witch hazel, and Kentucky coffee tree. The undergrowth is junglelike, filled with grapevines and stinging nettle. The region is also the only part of Minnesota to harbor bobwhite quail, which can't survive harsh winters. Driving the back roads at night, you stand a good chance of seeing (or flattening) an opossum.

The Root is a great route for bird watching. Turkey vultures and hawks often soar on the thermals rising from the bluffs and cliffs. Herons and kingfishers search the shallow shorelines for fish. Songbirds flit through the riverside forest.

The Root flows through many class I rapids. Most are simply swift-flowing shallow water. There's not even much need to maneuver. There is one notable exception, the concrete remnants of an old dam about 6 miles below the County Route 21 bridge. The drop is runnable, but is tougher and more abrupt than other drops on this stretch. The reservoir that formed behind the dam provided water that was piped through the bluff to a power plant about 3.5 miles downstream. The 1,000-foot-long tunnel was blasted and drilled by men working around the clock for two years. By shortcutting the long bend in the river (see map), the power plant designers were able to gain gradient and thus more power for their turbines. The power plant, completed in 1914, was one of the first hydroelectric projects in the valley. Its concrete walls still stand in plain sight next to the river. The structure is inaccessible by road. Its builders used teams of horses, cables, and pulleys to lower building materials and machinery, some pieces weighing several tons, from the bluff top.

About 3.5 miles downstream from the powerhouse, the Root joins the South Branch of the Root. A half mile downstream is the access, on river right.

Throughout this stretch, the Root is joined by several trout streams, including Trout Run, one of the state's finest. While some trout will drift downstream into the bigger river, the Root is in its soul a smallmouth stream. Other game species include walleye and channel catfish.

Access: The **Chatfield put-in** is located a mile southwest of town on County Route 2. **Whalan take-out** is located midway between Lanesboro and Whalan on Minnesota Highway 16.

Shuttle: 25 miles. About 1.25 hours.

ADDITIONAL HELP

MA&G: 26, C1–4.

Camping: Canoe campsites are located about 5 miles downstream of the U.S. Highway 52 bridge on river left, at the County Route 21 bridge river right, about 5 miles downstream from the County Route 21 bridge on river right, and a half mile downstream from the old powerhouse on river left.

Food, gas, and lodging: Chatfield, Lanesboro.

For more information: MDNR Information Center.

102 South Branch from Preston to Whalan

Character: A swift trout stream with easy rapids, the South Branch makes a good one-day canoe trip when the water is fairly high.

Length: 18 miles.

Average run time: Six to nine hours.

Class: I.

Skill level: Beginner to intermediate.

Optimal flow: Above 28.5 feet on the gauge on the County Route 17 bridge in Preston.

Average gradient: 7.8 feet per mile.

Hazards: Watch for deadfalls blocking the channel.

Maps: MDNR *Root River Canoe & Boating Route.*

The paddling: In its uppermost reaches, where it flows from Mystery Cave, the South Branch is one of the state's best trout streams. Clear and riffling, it cuts through a deep, wooded valley. At times the view is intimate and cloistered, hemmed in by a dense forest of hardwoods. Occasionally the trees give way to open fields and views of lowering hills and limestone cliffs.

Only as the South Branch approaches Preston does it get large enough for canoeing. Still, you'll need fairly high water levels to get through the riffles without dragging. The river flows swiftly through a quick succession of riffles and pools.

The railroad track that once paralleled much of the South Branch was recently converted to a state trail, used in summer by hikers, cyclists, and in-line skaters. As you paddle from Preston, you'll cross the trail several times. The Root River State Trail has contributed to an explosion of tourist traffic in Lanesboro in recent years. Businesses that cater to travelers have been able to maintain or restore many of the town's original buildings, which date to the mid- and late 1800s. The result is an attractive, historical town with a vibrant local economy. Plan to spend a couple hours in town after your canoe trip.

102 South Branch from Preston to Whalan

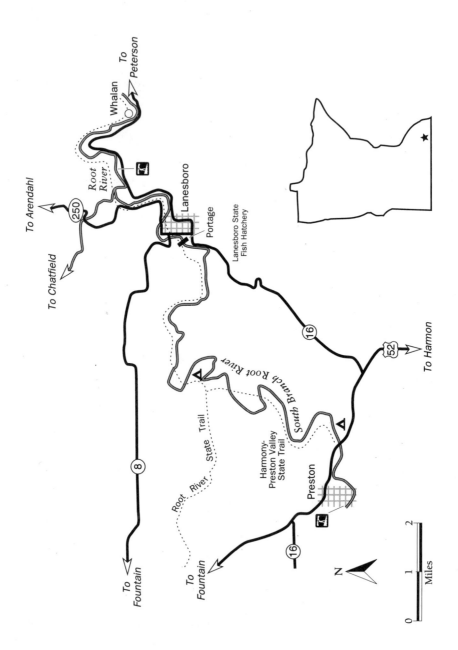

If you plan to fish for trout on your trip, beach your canoe at the heads of riffles and then walk downstream to fish the run and pool below the riffle. The South Branch is small enough and clear enough that you'll have trouble fishing from the canoe without scaring the fish. As you travel downstream, you'll probably encounter wading anglers. Give them as wide a berth as possible and move through the water they are fishing with a minimum of disturbance.

In Lanesboro you'll encounter a small hydroelectric dam. Portage on river right, 800 feet. Many paddlers choose to end their trip here, in the city park on the right. Built in 1868, the dam provided water power to three local gristmills. The reservoir it created was used for boating and fishing until erosion from logged and plowed hillsides filled the pool with sand and mud. The area now makes up the Lost Lake State Game Refuge. A century ago, the dam was converted to a hydroelectric plant, which still operates today.

Downstream from town, the South Branch races through bouldery class I rapids to its confluence with the main stem of the Root. This section of the river provides fishing for both trout and smallmouth bass.

Access: The **Preston put-in** is located on the southwest edge of town at the County Route 12 bridge. **Whalan take-out** is located midway between Lanesboro and Whalan on Minnesota Highway 16.

Shuttle: 10 miles one way. About 30 minutes.

ADDITIONAL HELP

MA&G: 26, D3–4.
Camping: A private campground is located near the river, 2 miles below the put-in. Five miles farther downstream is another private campground. A public campground is located at Forestville–Mystery Cave State Park.
Food, gas, and lodging: Preston, Lanesboro.
For more information: MDNR Information Center.

103 Whalan to the Mississippi

Character: Quick current and towering bluffs reward canoeists on this stretch.
Length: 54.5 miles, plus several miles to an access on the Mississippi.
Average run time: Two to four days.
Class: I.
Skill level: Beginner.
Optimal flow: Above 3 feet on the USGS gauge at Houston. Check the USGS website for at least 400 cfs on the gauge near Houston.
Average gradient: 2.7 feet per mile.
Hazards: Watch for snags in high water, when the current is fast.
Maps: MDNR *Root River Canoe & Boating Route.*

103 Whalan to the Mississippi

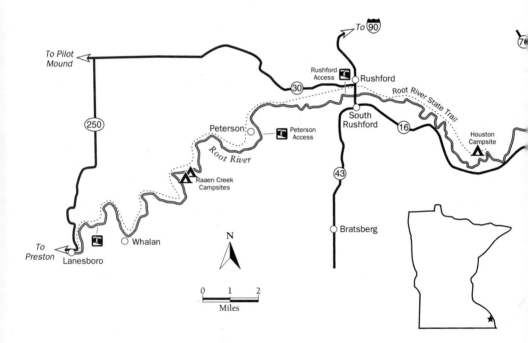

To Pilot Mound

(250)

To Preston

Lanesboro

○ Whalan

Raaen Creek Campsites

Root River

Peterson ○

Peterson Access

(30)

Rushford Access

Rushford ○

Root River State Trail

South Rushford

(16)

(43)

Houston Campsite

Bratsberg ○

To (90)

(7

N

0   1   2
Miles

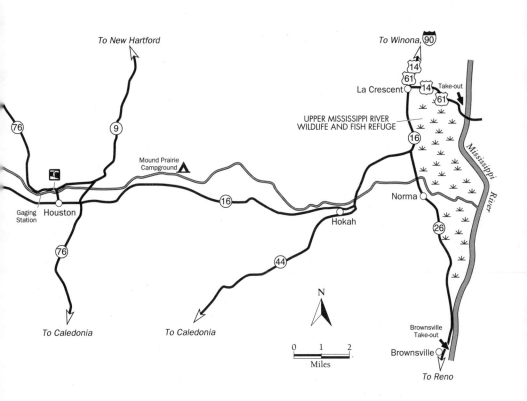

To New Hartford

To Winona, 90

14
61

14 Take-out
La Crescent

61

UPPER MISSISSIPPI RIVER
WILDLIFE AND FISH REFUGE

76

9

16

Mound Prairie
Campground

16

Norma

Gaging
Station

Houston

Hokah

26

Mississippi River

76

44

N

Brownsville
Take-out

To Caledonia

To Caledonia

0   1   2

Miles

Brownsville

To Reno

The paddling: The Root continues its path to the Mississippi, alternating through pools and sections of light rapids. Unfortunately for the paddler, Minnesota Highway 16 hugs the river all the way down to Peterson. With traffic speeding by, it's tough to lose yourself in solitude. On the other hand, the valley is becoming deeper and more spectacular with every mile, as high bluffs and cliffs rise on either side.

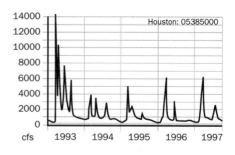

400 cfs = minimum for good paddling

After Peterson, the flood plain grows broader and the highway backs off, giving the river a bit more elbow room. Gradually the river loses gradient. Rapids become less frequent, and the riverbed turns sandier. Below Houston, the river has been channelized and has lost much of its charming sinuosity.

Passing beneath Minnesota Highway 26, the Root enters the tangled maze of backwaters of the Mississippi River. Follow the winding channel to the main channel of the Mississippi and paddle either upstream to the access at La Crescent, downstream to the Brownsville access, or across the Mississippi to one of several accesses in Wisconsin.

With a shifting sand bottom below Peterson, this stretch of the Root doesn't hold many fish. Anglers do catch some walleye, sauger, and catfish in the deep pools, especially those with snags. Big brown trout hang near the mouths of coldwater tributaries of the Root.

Access: The **Whalan put-in** is located midway between Lanesboro and Whalan on MN 16. The **La Crescent take-out** on the Mississippi is located 2 miles east of town on U.S. Highway 14/61. The **Brownsville take-out** is located southeast of town, a half mile east on MN 26.

Many paddlers will make a shorter trip of this by using public accesses at Peterson, Rushford, or Houston.

Shuttle: About 46 miles one way. About 1.75 hours.

ADDITIONAL HELP

MA&G: 26–27.

Camping: River campsites are located at the mouth of Raaen Creek, midway between Rushford and Houston on river left, and on river left a mile upstream of the County Route 25 bridge at Mound Prairie. State park campgrounds are located at O.L. Kipp and Beaver Valley State Parks.

Food, gas, and lodging: Peterson, Rushford, Houston, La Crescent, Winona; La Crosse, Wisconsin.

For more information: MDNR Information Center.

104 Sand Creek

Character: Sand Creek is a swift, thrilling run when the water is high.
Length: 3.5 miles.
Average run time: One to two hours.
Class: II.
Skill level: Intermediate.
Optimal flow: Medium to high with the river into terrestrial vegetation. No specific water-level information is available.
Average gradient: 20 feet per mile.
Hazards: Large trees occasionally lodge in the narrow river channel.
Maps: PRIM *Metro South*, USGS *Jordan West-MN.*

The paddling: Sand Creek is a springtime favorite with whitewater boaters. It's usually runnable in late March and early April. It consists of class I and class II chains of waves, with plenty of maneuvering required down a narrow, twisting river channel. **Railroad Rapids**, a series of small ledges located beneath a railroad trestle near the end of the run, is probably the toughest of Sand Creek's whitewater. Even so, the penalty for messing up isn't great, unless a sweeper has lodged in the current. If so, give it a wide berth. Portage if necessary.

Pull out just downstream from the Minnesota Highway 21 bridge at the Jordan city park and just above a 13-foot-high dam. Kayakers have run the dam in the past, but according to one report, crumbling debris from the dam has made the landing rocky and hazardous.

Access: **County Route 8 put-in:** From the take-out at the city park, drive south 2.4 miles, turn left (east) on County Route 8, and drive about 1 mile to the put-in. There's little room to park at the bridge; you may have to drive along a small county road about 100 yards to the west of the bridge. **The MN 21 take-out** is located in the city park on the south edge of Jordan, just south of the mill pond.

Shuttle: 3.4 miles one way. About ten minutes.

104 Sand Creek

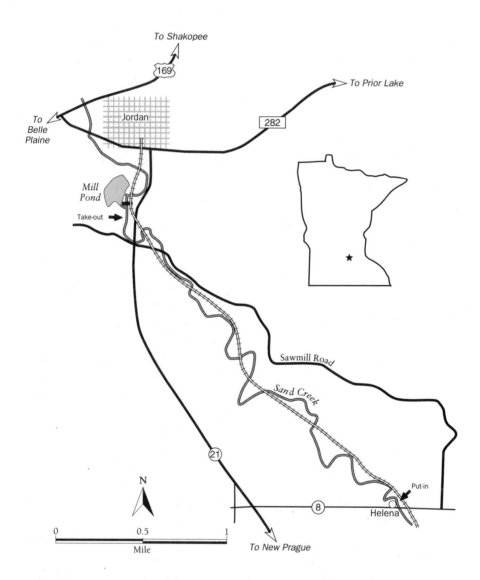

To Shakopee

169

To Prior Lake

To
Belle
Plaine

Jordan

282

Mill
Pond

Take-out

Sawmill Road

Sand Creek

21

N

Put-in

Helena

8

0   0.5   1
Mile

To New Prague

ADDITIONAL HELP

MA&G: 32, A5.

Camping: There are no campsites along the river. State park camping is available at the Minnesota Valley Recreation Area near Belle Plaine.

Food, gas, and lodging: Jordan.

For more information: Not much additional information is available.

105 Straight River

Character: Flowing gently through a wooded corridor, the Straight is a good match for beginning canoeists.

Length: 27.2 miles.

Average run time: 9 to 14 hours.

Class: I (the rapids in Clinton Falls rates as high as class III in high water).

Skill level: Beginner.

Optimal flow: Above 1 foot on the gauge on the Rose Street bridge in Owatonna, or above 1 foot on the gauge on the County Route 45 bridge in Medford. Check the USGS website for at least 200 cfs on the Faribault gauge.

Average gradient: 6.2 feet per mile.

Hazards: The drop at Clinton Falls (see **Class**). Remnants of an old dam 2 miles upstream of the Minnesota Highway 60 bridge are runnable but tricky.

Maps: MDNR *Straight River Canoe Route.*

The paddling: Put in at the Morehouse access in Owatonna, a town known for its many parks and hiking and biking trails. A particularly striking building is the Norwest Bank, a Prairie School–style building built by Louis Sullivan in 1908 as the National Farmer's Bank. It is one story with elaborate arched windows and ornamentation of terra cotta and mosaic. The inside is lavishly decorated with ornamented chandeliers and two large murals depicting the rural countryside. According to a historical guide published by the Smithsonian Institution, "More than any other single Midwestern building, it justifies a journey."

The town and river have the same name, in two different languages. When a Dakota woman named Owatonna (a Dakota word translated as morally "straight," or honest) was healed by waters from the spring, her

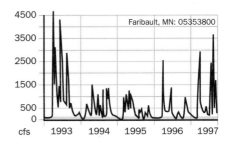

200 cfs = estimated minimum for good paddling

105 Straight River

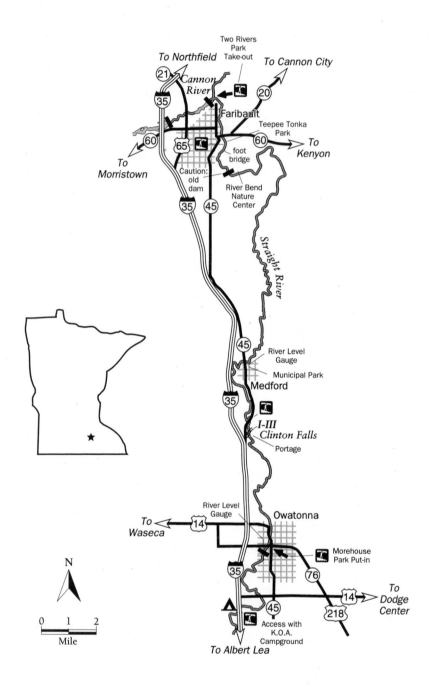

To Northfield

Two Rivers
Park
Take-out

To Cannon City

21

Cannon
River

35

20

Faribault

Teepee Tonka
Park

60

60

To
Kenyon

65

foot
bridge

To
Morristown

Caution:
old
dam

River Bend
Nature
Center

35

45

Straight River

45

River Level
Gauge

Municipal Park

35

Medford

I-III
Clinton Falls

Portage

River Level
Gauge

Owatonna

To
Waseca

14

35

Morehouse
Park Put-in

76

To
Dodge
Center

14

218

N

45

Access with
K.O.A.
Campground

0   1   2

To Albert Lea

Mile

father, Chief Wabena (or Wadena), moved the village to the *minnewakan,* or water spirit. A statue of Owatonna now watches over the spring in Mineral Springs Park.

Outside of town, the Straight forms a shining path of quick water down a narrow corridor of woods in a landscape otherwise thoroughly planted and pastured. In Clinton Falls, the river takes a sharp bend and drops over a steep rapids at the site of an old mill. Scout the rapids from the old bridge in town. The difficulty ranges from class I in low water to class III in high water, when the river pushes hard into the bank. If you decide the rapids is too tough, portage left, 30 yards. Remains of the mill, which was destroyed by fire in 1896, still stand by the river.

The Straight continues toward Medford. The woods in the valley are home to two rare species. The first is the wood turtle, listed as a threatened species in Minnesota. Its name comes from the texture of its shell, which looks like carved wood. The second is the dwarf trout lily, a diminutive, frail flower found only in a few populations in southeastern Minnesota and nowhere else in the world.

North of Medford, the river slows. It curves in tight meanders and gives the feeling of winding through remote country. The curves loosen as the river approaches Faribault. Just south of town, the river ducks under a footbridge. River Bend Nature Center, which comprises more than 600 acres of woods and prairie, flanks the river.

Soon the river runs through the remnants of an old dam. The stream plunges through a well-defined chute. It's runnable (in fact, it rates only class I) but it does form a hole in high water.

In its last several miles, the Straight skirts Faribault, a one-time wool-milling town named for French-Canadian Alexander Faribault, who established a trading post at the confluence of the Straight and Cannon Rivers in 1826 to trade with the Dakota Indians. Faribault's home, built in 1873, is open for tours.

According to local lore, President Calvin Coolidge found terrific fishing for smallmouth bass on the Straight River. The stream looks much as it did then, but recent electro-fishing surveys have turned up no bass whatsoever. What happened? According to state fisheries managers, the fish may have been killed by chemical and organic runoff from the intensively farmed land in the upland portions of the watershed. Moreover, dams farther downstream on the Cannon River limit the distance fish can migrate to find deep water.

Access: The **Owatonna put-in** is located in the center of town at Morehouse Park, just south of Bridge Street on the east bank. The **Faribault take-out** is located at Two Rivers Park on the east side of the Cannon River, just below its confluence with the Straight River at the north edge of town.

Shuttle: 18 miles one way. About one hour.

ADDITIONAL HELP

MA&G: 24, A3; 33, D–E7.

Camping: No river campsites are located on this stretch. Camp by car at Rice Lake State Park or Nerstrand–Big Woods State Park.

Food, gas, and lodging: Owatonna, Faribault.

For more information: MDNR Information Center.

VERMILLION RIVER

106 Vermillion Falls Park

Character: The Vermillion gorge is a short but challenging whitewater run, but only in the high water of early spring.

Length: 0.6 mile.

Average run time: Less than an hour.

Class: III–IV.

Skill level: Intermediate to expert.

Optimal flow: Readings unavailable. The river must be medium to high, with water into the terrestrial vegetation.

Average gradient: About 60 feet per mile, not counting the unrunnable falls at the head of the gorge.

Hazards: In high water, holes that form below ledges get grabby.

Maps: PRIM *Metro South.*

The paddling: The Vermillion River riffles and glides through the rolling hills of farmland and outer suburbs south of the Twin Cities. It pulls into Hastings, slides under U.S. Highway 61 and leaps into the abyss—literally. This gentle farmland stream steps completely out of character, plunging over a falls of about 20 feet and running through a third of a mile of ledges and rapids. High cliffs of dolomite press in on the river. The river is narrow and steep, and maneuvering is tight. As the river passes under the old Hastings and Dakota railroad trestle (now a pedestrian bridge) it narrows in a steep drop and then eases up. Rate this stretch class III in medium water and class IV in high water.

The falls at the head of the gorge was created as Glacial River Warren, an ice age torrent that drained Glacial Lake Agassiz, carved the deep valley of the Minnesota River and the Mississippi River below Fort Snelling in Minneapolis, leaving less erosive streams such as the Vermillion hanging far above the floodplain. The falls and fast water provided power to three mills in Hastings's early days. Harrison Graham built the first mill at the site in 1854. The Con Agra Mill next to the waterfall at the head of the gorge has incorporated the stone walls of earlier mills.

A couple hundred yards below the end of the whitewater in Old Mill Park stand the stone walls of the mill built in 1857 by Alexander Ramsey and Thomas Foster. The mill burned in 1894 and today is a Minnesota historic site.

106 Vermillion Falls Park

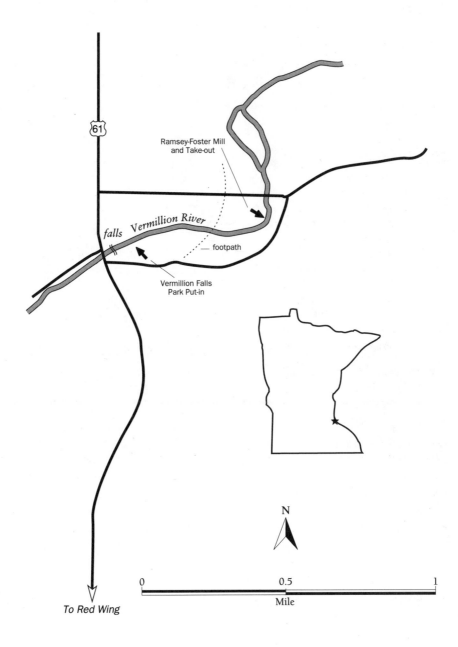

61

Ramsey-Foster Mill
and Take-out

falls *Vermillion River*

footpath

Vermillion Falls
Park Put-in

N

0   0.5   1
Mile

To Red Wing

The falls which once powered a grain mill tumbles into the gorge at Vermillion Falls Park. MINNESOTA OFFICE OF TOURISM

Hiking trails lace both Vermillion Falls and Old Mill Parks.

Access: The **Vermillion Falls Park put-in** is located on the south side of the river, off 21st Street, across from the Con Agra mill at the head of the gorge. Carry down to the river along the footpath. The **Old Mill Park take-out** is located next to the 18th Street Bridge. Carry out along the footpath.

Shuttle: 0.8 mile one way. About 10 minutes.

ADDITIONAL HELP

MA&G: 34, A1.
Camping: Auto camping at Afton State Park.
Food, gas, and lodging: Hastings.
For more information: Hastings Parks and Recreation.

107 Old Mill Park to Vermillion Slough

Character: The final miles of the Vermillion River wind slowly over the flood plain of the Mississippi. The backwaters are interesting to explore, but you may have to pull around several logjams.
Length: 19 miles.
Average run time: Six to ten hours.
Class: Quiet.
Skill level: Beginner.
Optimal flow: Since there are no rapids, water level isn't important.
Average gradient: Less than 1 foot per mile.
Hazards: If water is high, don't let the current push you into log jams.
Maps: MDNR *Mississippi River Guide; Mississippi River Canoe Route 10.* PRIM *47.*

The paddling: And now for something completely different. The Vermillion as farmland river and difficult whitewater run are history. The river wanders over the floodplain of the Mississippi. A bottomland forest of silver maple, elm, and ash overhang the river. Herons and egrets wade the shallows. Kingfishers are poised on branches overhanging the water. Woodpeckers find nesting cavities in dead trees. Common mammals in this environment include white-tailed deer, raccoons, and red fox. In the spring and fall, look for a variety of migrating waterfowl in the backwaters.

After about 7 miles, the Vermillion joins Truedale Slough, which connects the river to the Mississippi (though the channel is blocked by a closing dam). Downstream, the river channel joins several backwater lakes, such as Clear Lake and Lower Rattling Springs Lake, which allow for further exploration. A major logjam forms at the County Route 18 bridge near the community of Eggleston. You may have to carry around it.

311

107 Old Mill Park to Vermillion Slough

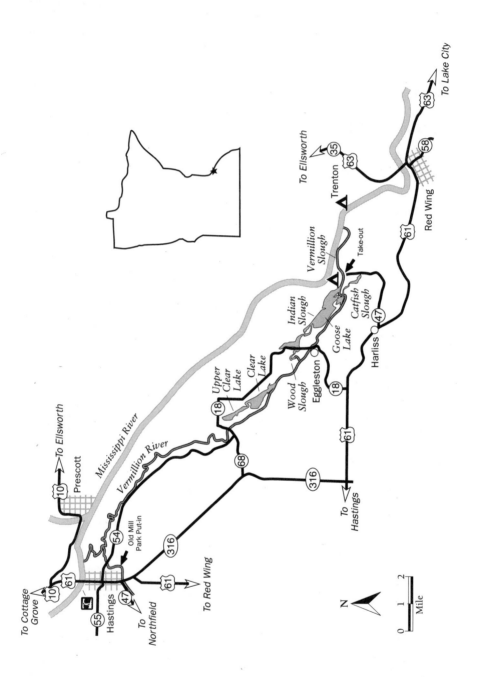

Instead of taking out at Vermillion Slough, it's possible to paddle down the slough to the Mississippi and continue your trip through the main channel or other backwaters of the big river.

Access: The **Old Mill Park put-in** is located next to the 18th Street Bridge. Carry in along the footpath. The **Vermillion Slough take-out** is located about 5 miles northwest of Red Wing (as the crow flies). From the intersection of U.S. Highway 61 and Minnesota Highway 316, drive east 6 miles on US 61 to the tiny community of Harliss. As US 61 heads south, drive east and then north 4 miles on CR 47 to the put-in.

The boat ramp near Truedale Slough pretty nearly bisects this trip. It is located on County Route 54 about 5 miles east-southeast of Hastings.

Shuttle: 20 miles one way. About one hour. Using Truedale Slough as a take-out shortens the shuttle to about 5 miles, one way.

ADDITIONAL HELP

MA&G: 34, A2–4.
Camping: A water-accessible campsite sits on the Mississippi River channel immediately north of the take-out. Camp by car at Frontenac State Park or Afton State Park.
Food, gas, and lodging: Hastings, Red Wing.
For more information: MDNR area wildlife managers 612-496-7686 and 507-332-4133.

108 Whitewater River

Character: The Whitewater, a racing coldwater stream, offers the chance for canoeing, wildlife watching, and trout fishing.
Length: 18 miles.
Average run time: Six to nine hours.
Class: I.
Skill level: Beginner.
Optimal flow: Estimated at 200 cfs on USGS gauge near Beaver. Check website.
Average gradient: 3.4 feet per mile.
Hazards: Watch for deadfalls and remnants of an old rock weir downstream from County Route 30.
Maps: MDNR *Zumbro River, Whitewater River: A Canoe & Boating Guide.*

The paddling: The crystalline North, Middle, and South branches of the Whitewater slide through riffles and cut against limestone cliffs. Excellent trout streams, they are generally too small for canoeing. Near the town of Elba they join. From there downstream to the Mississippi, the Whitewater provides plenty of depth for a float trip.

108 Whitewater River

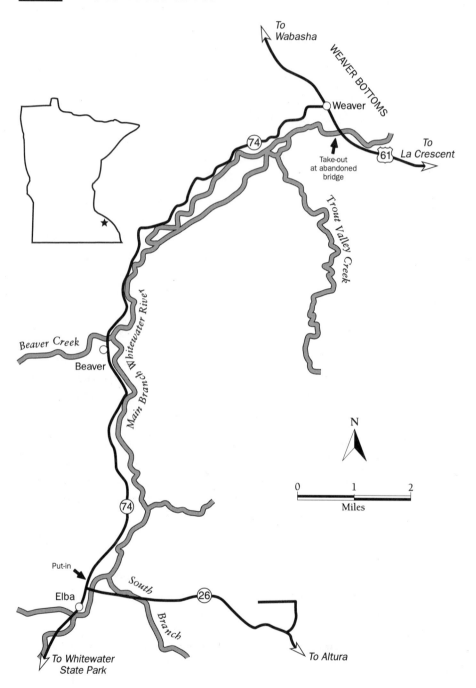

Below Elba, the river races through the bottomlands of the Whitewater Wildlife Management Area, tumbling occasionally through fast, class I chutes and easing through long, quiet pools. Watch out for deadfalls, some of which are left in place to provide habitat for fish. Though the largely sandy river doesn't support the number of trout that are found upstream, some large trout do lurk in the deep pools and runs.

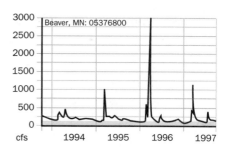

200 cfs = estimated minimum for good paddling

Just downstream from the County Route 30 bridge, Beaver Creek, another trout stream, joins from the left (west). Near the confluence lies the former site of the valley farming community known as Beaver. During the late 1800s and early 1900s, as farmers cleared the hardwood forest and plowed the hillsides, floods increased in frequency and severity throughout the area. Silt washed out of the hills, muddying streams and covering farms and communities in the valleys below. In 1938 the town of Beaver flooded 28 times. Today, the town site lies buried in sediment. In the decades since, better farm and forestry practices have reduced erosion and flooding.

Two miles downstream, the Whitewater splits into two channels. The channel to the right, which has been channelized, is kept clear to be passable and carry away floodwaters. Unfortunately, the dredged channel has little character or value to fish and other animals. Plans call for the old channel to be restored soon to benefit wildlife.

The bottomland forest harbors a variety of bird life, including various species of owls, hawks, woodpeckers, and songbirds. Game birds such as ruffed grouse and wild turkeys are abundant. Pools have been created in the river bottoms to the benefit of wetland species such as ducks, Canada geese, great egrets, great blue herons, ospreys, and kingfishers.

The take-out at an abandoned bridge lies about a mile upstream from the Whitewater's confluence with the Mississippi River.

Access: Elba put-in: From town, drive east about a quarter mile on County Route 26 to the bridge over the main stem of the Whitewater and the access. **U.S. Highway 61 take-out:** The access is located next to an abandoned bridge just upstream of the US 61 bridge over the Whitewater.

Alternate access is possible at three places along Minnesota Highway 74, which parallels the stream.

Shuttle: About 13 miles one way. About 45 minutes.

ADDITIONAL HELP

MA&G: 26, A3; 35, E9.
Camping: No camping is allowed along this stretch of the Whitewater in Whitewater WMA. Camp by car in Whitewater or Carley State Park.
Food, gas, and lodging: Elba, Rochester, Wabasha, Winona.
For more information: MDNR Information Center.

ZUMBRO RIVER

The Zumbro River reaches across the landscape of southeastern Minnesota with many long, crooked fingers. In geological terms, the pattern of the Zumbro and its tributaries form a classic dendritic pattern, with one stream splitting into two, and each of those splitting again, until they form an intricate web. The sheer number of streams complicates the naming of them: North Fork, North Branch of the Middle Fork, South Branch of the Middle Fork, South Branch, and so on. The name of the main stem is confusing enough. It stems from the French *Rivière des Embarras,* meaning river of difficulties or obstacles, in reference most likely to the downed trees on the smaller reaches and tributaries of the river. Put on your best French accent and the result is something like "de Zombara." For the English-speaking settlers, Zumbro was close enough.

The many forks and branches of the Zumbro begin on the plowed and planted plateau along the western edge of the watershed. All are, for the most part, lazily meandering streams with occasional riffles, bounded by low banks, woods, and farmland. Only the larger streams are described here. Others, such as the North Branch of the Middle Fork west of Pine Island and the Middle Fork down to Shady Lake, are canoeable in high water but are likely to be blocked by snags. As these tributaries join one by one to form the main stem of the Zumbro, the river begins to dig deep into the old limestone geology of the southeast, winding past cliffs and outcrops.

109 North Fork

Character: The North Fork is a small stream that courses through woodland and pasture.
Length: 23 miles, including 7.5 miles on the main stem of the Zumbro to the take-out at Zumbro Falls.
Average run time: Seven to ten hours.
Class: I.
Skill level: Beginner.
Optimal flow: Above 1 foot on the gauge on the Minnesota Highway 58 bridge in Zumbrota.
Average gradient: 5.7 feet per mile.
Hazards: Watch for downed trees blocking the channel.
Maps: MDNR *Zumbro River, Whitewater River: A Canoe & Boating Guide.*

109 North Fork

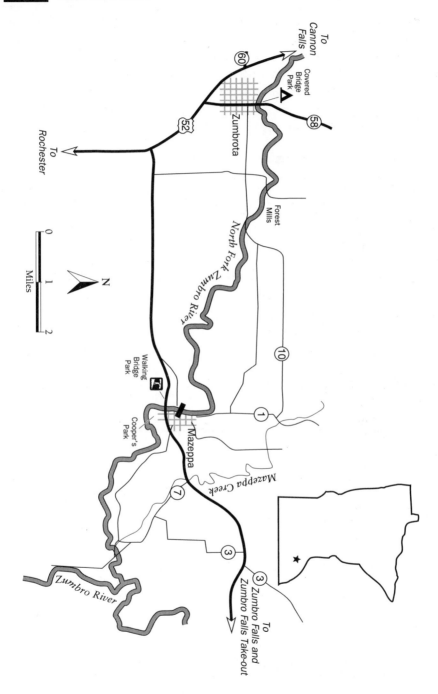

317

The paddling: Put in at Covered Bridge Park in Zumbrota. The river winds primarily through cropland and pasture. In Mazeppa, the river spills over an 18-foot-high dam. Wabasha County plans to demolish and remove the dam. In the meantime, paddlers can pull out on river left about a quarter mile upstream and portage across the bridge over the dam to river right and put back in there. Many paddlers opt simply to begin or end their trip at Mazeppa to avoid the portage. Below town, the river runs through riffles as the valley grows deeper, with higher bluffs, and more wooded. Mazeppa Creek (also known as Trout Brook), a major tributary and designated trout stream, joins the North Branch just upstream from the County Route 7 bridge. In another mile, the North Fork joins the much larger main stem of the Zumbro. The main stem runs through occasional easy rapids to the take-out at Zumbro Falls.

Fishing is generally poor above Mazeppa. Downstream from town are small-mouth bass, walleye, sauger, and channel catfish.

Access: Zumbrota put-in: Covered Bridge Park in Zumbrota at the MN 58 bridge. Zumbro Falls take-out: In Zumbro Falls next to the U.S. Highway 63 bridge. An alternate access is available in Mazeppa at Walking Bridge Park, about a quarter mile downstream of the dam.

Shuttle: 15 miles one way. About 45 minutes.

ADDITIONAL HELP

MA&G: 34, D3–5.
Camping: Canoe camping is possible at Covered Bridge Park in Zumbrota. A state forest campground is located at Dumfries.
Food, gas, and lodging: Zumbrota, Rochester.
For more information: MDNR Information Center.

110 South Branch of the Middle Fork

Character: The South Branch is a small, wooded farmland river with quick current in the riffles and long, slow pools.
Length: 24.5 miles, including 1.5 miles on Zumbro Lake.
Average run time: 8 to 12 hours.
Class: I.
Skill level: Beginner.
Optimal flow: Over 0.5 foot on the gauge on the County Route 3 bridge, located about 3 miles upstream from Shady Lake.
Average gradient: 4.9 feet per mile, including a 20-foot drop at the Shady Lake Dam.
Hazards: Watch out for deadfalls and farm fences strung across the channel.
Maps: MDNR *Zumbro River, Whitewater River: A Canoe & Boating Guide.*

The paddling: The run begins at Oxbow County Park, a locally popular recreational area with camping and picnic areas. The South Branch Valley provides a

110 South Branch of the Middle Fork

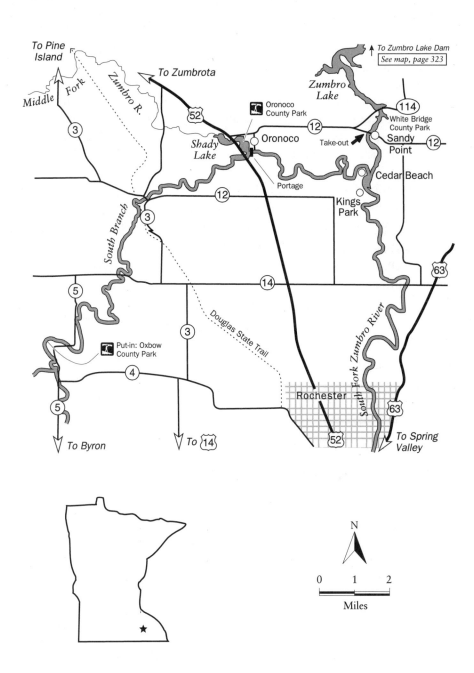

To Pine Island

Middle Fork

Zumbro R.

To Zumbrota

3

52

Shady Lake

Oronoco County Park

Oronoco

Zumbro Lake

To Zumbro Lake Dam
See map, page 323

114

White Bridge County Park

12

Take-out

Sandy Point

12

Portage

South Branch

12

Cedar Beach

Kings Park

3

5

14

63

Douglas State Trail

Put-in: Oxbow County Park

3

South Fork Zumbro River

4

5

Rochester

63

52

To Byron

To 14

To Spring Valley

N

0   1   2
Miles

wooded oasis in an area that is otherwise heavily farmed. High bluffs with occasional outcrops flank the river. The stream alternates between short, easy riffles and long, slow pools as it passes the small town of Genoa and passes under the Douglas State Trail, a 12.5-mile, nonmotorized route between Rochester and Pine Island for hiking, biking, and horseback riding. Rocky stretches of the South Branch harbor smallmouth bass.

The South Branch flows into Shady Lake, a shallow, murky reservoir formed by the 20-foot-high dam at Oronoco. Take out here, or portage the dam 200 yards to continue down the stream (which is now the Middle Fork) to Sandy Point on Zumbro Lake, another reservoir. This section of river runs through easy rapids and provides fishing for smallmouth bass. Unfortunately, because of the sorry condition of Shady Lake, the stream is always turbid.

For a historical treat, tour the town of Mantorville (several miles upstream of the put-in), a former stagecoach stop whose entire downtown is on the National Register of Historic Places. Many of the restored buildings date to the 1850s.

Access: Oxbow Park put-in: From Byron, drive north 3 miles on County Route 5. As County Route 5 turns west, continue north on County Road 105 to the park. **Sandy Point take-out** on Zumbro Lake: From Rochester, drive north about 10 miles on U.S. Highway 63 to County Route 12 to the access. Alternate access: A carry-in canoe access is located in Oronoco on Shady Lake. A boat ramp is located about a half mile to the south near the portage around the dam.

Shuttle: 20 miles one way. About one hour.

ADDITIONAL HELP

MA&G: 25, A7; 34, E4–5.
Camping: Oxbow County Park. Private campgrounds are located at Shady Lake, Zumbro Lake Dam, and Zumbro Falls.
Food, gas, and lodging: Rochester, Mantorville.
For more information: MDNR Information Center.

111 South Fork

Character: The small, gentle South Fork follows a wooded valley from Rochester north to Zumbro Lake.
Length: 14.5 miles, including a 1.5-mile paddle on Zumbro Lake.
Average run time: Five to seven hours.
Class: I.
Skill level: Beginner.
Optimal flow: The estimated minimum for good paddling is about 150 cfs (check the USGS website) or about 52.6 feet on the gauge on the 37th Street Bridge in Rochester.
Average gradient: 3 feet per mile.
Hazards: Snags and jams block the channel. Watch out in high water.
Maps: MDNR *Zumbro River, Whitewater River: A Canoe & Boating Guide.*

111 South Fork

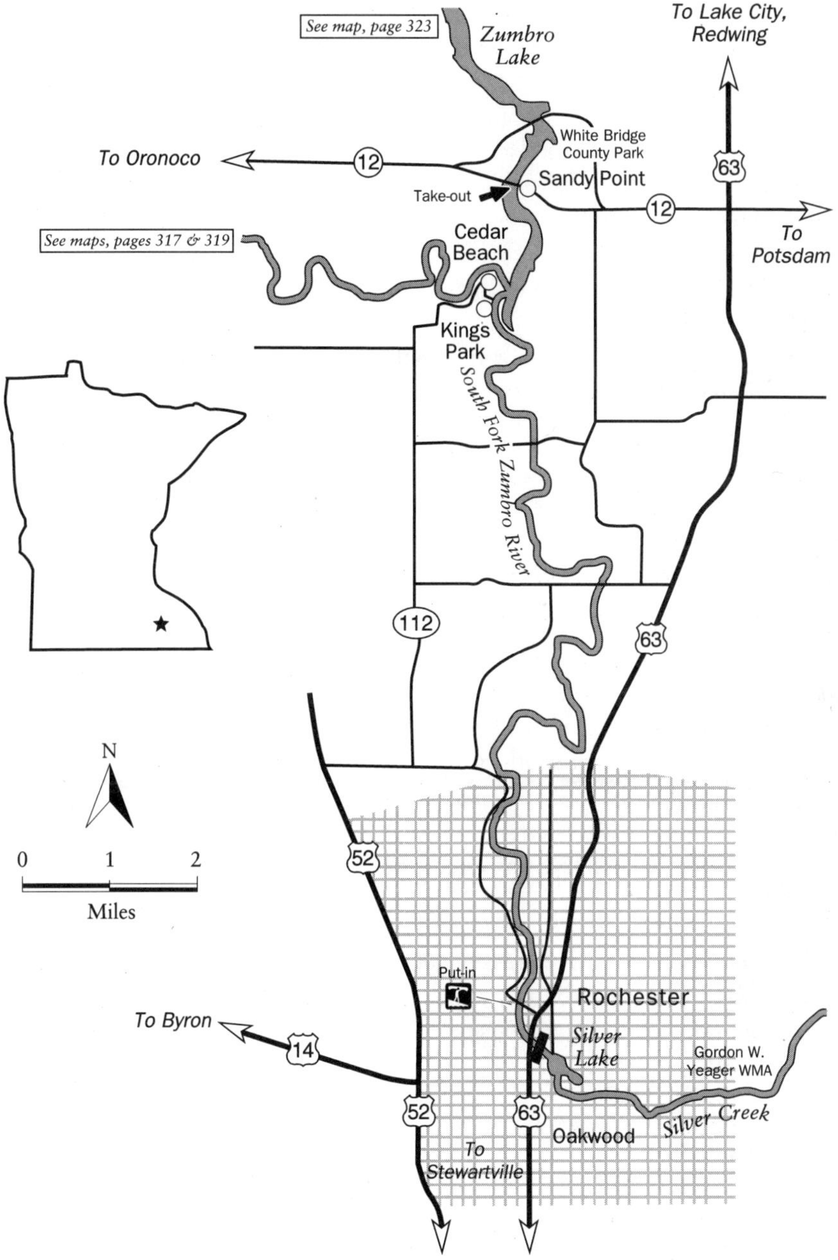

See map, page 323
Zumbro Lake
To Lake City, Redwing
To Oronoco
12
White Bridge County Park
63
Sandy Point
Take-out
12
To Potsdam
See maps, pages 317 & 319
Cedar Beach
Kings Park
South Fork Zumbro River
112
63
N
0
1
2
Miles
52
Put-in
Rochester
To Byron
14
Silver Lake
Gordon W. Yeager WMA
52
63
Oakwood
Silver Creek
To Stewartville

The paddling: The South Fork begins in hills far south of Rochester. South of town, the stream is large enough to paddle, but several dams and riprapped areas make the stretch unappealing. Instead, begin your trip at the access just north of Silver Lake. The riverside is pretty and wooded in places, and lined with suburban homes in others. There are a few outcrops and riffles along the way. Once you reach Zumbro Lake, paddle north to the Sandy Point access.

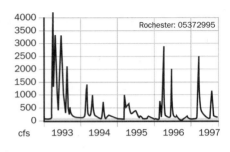

150 cfs = estimated minimum
for good paddling

Fishing can be good, especially for smallmouth bass and walleye.

Access: Rochester put-in: North of Silver Lake next to the Elton Hills Drive bridge. **Sandy Point take-out** on Zumbro Lake: From Rochester, drive north about 10 miles on U.S. Highway 63 to County Route 12, then west about a mile to the access.

Shuttle: 12 miles one way. About 30 minutes.

ADDITIONAL HELP

MA&G: 25, A9; 34, E5.
Camping: No canoe campsites on this stretch. Car camp at Oxbow County Park north of Byron, Carley State Park south of Plainview, or Whitewater State Park. Private campgrounds are located at Shady Lake, Zumbro Lake Dam, and Zumbro Falls.
Food, gas, and lodging: Rochester.
For more information: MDNR Information Center.

112 Zumbro Lake Dam to Millville

Character: A broad, riffly stream, the main stem of the Zumbro is good for canoeing and fishing.
Length: 26.3 miles.
Average run time: 9 to 13 hours.
Class: I.
Skill level: Beginner.
Optimal flow: Above 7 feet on the USGS gauge in Zumbro Falls (about 400 cfs).
Average gradient: 3.8 feet per mile.
Hazards: Watch for snags, especially on the outside of bends.
Maps: MDNR *Zumbro River, Whitewater River: A Canoe & Boating Guide.*

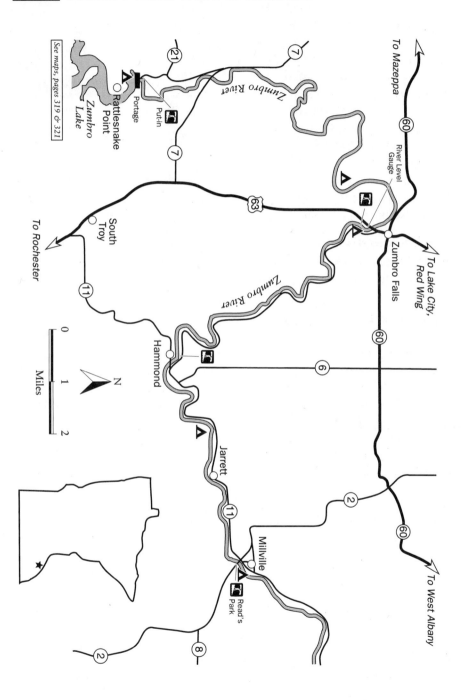

See maps, pages 319 & 321

Zumbro Lake

Rattlesnake Point

Put-in

Portage

21

7

Zumbro River

To Mazeppa

60

River Level Gauge

7

63

South Troy

To Rochester

11

Zumbro Falls

To Lake City, Red Wing

60

Zumbro River

Hammond

6

0 1 2

Miles

N

Jarrett

11

2

Millville

60

To West Albany

Read's Park

8

2

The paddling: By the time the Zumbro spills from the 30-foot-high dam at Zumbro Lake, it has become a broad stream. The valley, too, has become large, with high hills and rocky bluffs standing at the edge of the floodplain. The current is lively and races through frequent but easy rapids. After 4 miles, the river grows substantially as it gathers in the waters of the North Fork. For the next

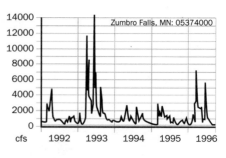

400 cfs = minimum for good paddling

several miles, the river winds past wooded bluffs with only limited development and gives the impression of flowing far out into wild country.

Unfortunately, the sound of traffic brings paddlers back to reality. County Route 11 follows the river from Zumbro Falls to Millville (and for some distance beyond). Zumbro Falls began as a railway village. The low falls for which it was named has eroded to become a stretch of rapids.

The Zumbro continues to run through easy riffles. With every mile, the valley grows deeper. The river often runs up against limestone cliffs, which cast deep shadows over the water. Limestone hilltops stand up to 300 feet above the river. Below Jarrett the floodplain broadens and the bluffs move back from the river.

An abundance of songbirds flit through the riverside forest. Kingfishers chatter and swoop low over the river. Hawks and turkey vultures soar on rising thermals.

Fishing, especially for smallmouth bass, can be excellent in this stretch of the Zumbro. Fish deep, rocky water, especially on the outside of river bends. Other game species include channel catfish and walleye.

Access: Zumbro Lake Dam put-in: From Rochester, drive north 12 miles on U.S. Highway 63 to South Troy. Turn west on an unnumbered county road to County Road 80. Jog north a half mile and then turn west on another unnumbered road to the access. **Millville take-out:** Read's Park on County Route 11.

You can also gain access to the river at Zumbro Falls and across the river from Hammond.

Shuttle: 13 miles one way. About 45 minutes.

ADDITIONAL HELP

MA&G: 34, 35, D5–6.

Camping: Canoe campsites are located on state forest land 2 miles downstream from Hammond on river right and at Read's Park. In low water, the river's sandbars make pleasant picnic and camping sites, but be prepared to move if rain raises the water level. Camp by car at the Snake Creek Unit and Kruger Unit of Richard J. Dorer Memorial Hardwood State Forest. (State forest maps are available from the MDNR.) Private campgrounds are located at Shady Lake, Zumbro Lake Dam, and Zumbro Falls.

Food, gas, and lodging: Rochester, Zumbrota, Zumbro Falls.

For more information: MDNR Information Center.

113 Millville to Kellogg

Character: Lofty outcrops and wooded bluffs tower above the placid lower Zumbro.

Length: 30.7 miles.

Average run time: 10 to 15 hours. With several campsites available, this stretch makes a good overnight trip.

Class: I.

Skill level: Beginner.

Optimal flow: Over 27 feet at the USGS gauge at Theilman.

Average gradient: 3.3 feet per mile.

Hazards: Watch for downed trees, especially in high water.

Maps: MDNR *Zumbro River, Whitewater River: A Canoe & Boating Guide.*

The paddling: Below Millville, the streambed is made up largely of sand. Gone are the rapids and rocky shallows that characterized the previous section of river. On the plus side, the Zumbro digs ever deeper into its valley. Bluffs and cliffs are loftier and more impressive than ever. A thick, bottomland forest flanks the river.

Several miles below Millville, the river and highway wander their separate ways. The canoeist is rewarded with a greater sense of solitude. Large holdings of state forestland below Theilman protect the riverside forest. The combination of grassy and forested floodplain provides excellent habitat for the threatened wood turtle. Other turtle species you might see include snapping, painted, and map turtles, and two species of soft-shelled turtle, the smooth and the spiny. This is also a good area to spot wild turkeys, a valued game bird that has become increasingly common in southern Minnesota.

The last access on the Zumbro is located at the town of Kellogg. Most paddlers will probably opt to take out here. Downstream, the river has been channelized and diked. It cuts through a broad plain of farmland. If you choose to run this stretch, you'll have to take out on the Mississippi, several miles upstream or downstream from the mouth of the river (see Site 58).

Because the streambed is made up largely of shifting sand, game fish are less plentiful and harder to find than in the rockier upper reaches of the Zumbro. There are, however, some saugers, channel cats, and some northern pike; look for them in deep holes with woody cover.

113 Millville to Kellogg

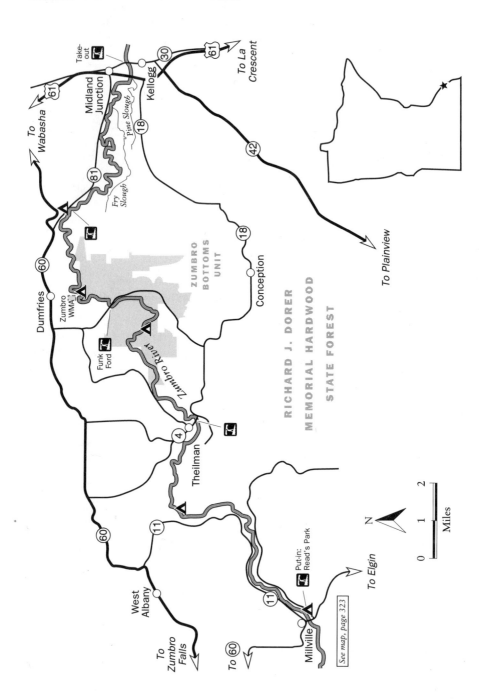

Access: **Millville put-in:** Read's Park on County Route 11. **Kellogg take-out:** County Route 30 bridge on the north edge of town.

Shuttle: 27 miles one way. About 1.25 hours.

ADDITIONAL HELP

MA&G: 35, D7–10.

Camping: Riverside campsites are located in Read's Park in Millville, about 3 miles above Theilman on river right, at two locations in the Zumbro Bottoms Unit of Richard J. Dorer Memorial Hardwood State Forest, and in the Kruger Unit of the forest. Camp by car at the Snake Creek Unit and Kruger Unit of Richard J. Dorer Memorial Hardwood State Forest. (State forest maps are available from the MDNR.)

Food, gas, and lodging: Wabasha, Rochester.

For more information: MDNR Information Center.

Southwest

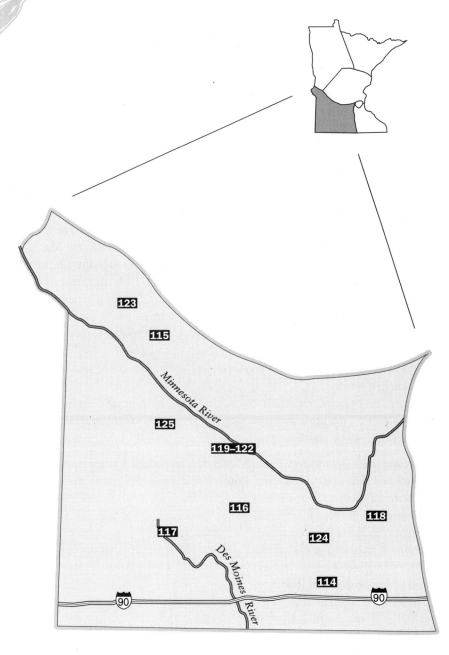

123

115

Minnesota River

125

119–122

116

117

Des Moines River

124

118

114

90

90

114 Blue Earth River

Character: In medium to high water, the Blue Earth provides a quick, fun run down one of the most beautiful valleys in southwestern Minnesota.

Length: 12.3 miles.

Average run time: Four to six hours.

Class: I.

Skill level: Beginner to intermediate.

Optimal flow: Check the USGS website for at least 200 cfs on the gauge near Rapidan.

Average gradient: 4.9 feet per mile.

Hazards: Watch for deadfalls.

Maps: MDNR *Minnesota River Canoe Route 3* also shows the Blue Earth.

The paddling: The Blue Earth River, named for a deposit of earth the Dakota used as pigment and French explorer Pierre Le Sueur erroneously believed to be copper., flows quickly through a deep, wooded valley to join the Minnesota River at Mankato.

The Blue Earth heads up far to the south of Mankato, near the Iowa border. In high water, you can start your trip at the County Route 13 bridge west of Good Thunder, the U.S. Highway 169 bridge at Vernon Center, or the Minnesota Highway 30 bridge west of Amboy. But the most reliable water levels, best rapids, and most impressive scenery begin just downstream of the Rapidan Dam at a private park. You'll have to pay a small fee to launch. The current is lively, dropping through frequent class I rapids. Large boulders in the streambed make canoeing difficult in low water.

Fishing can be good, especially below the dam and in other deep holes below rapids. Catfish are the principal game fish, but you can also find smallmouth bass, northern pike, walleye, and sauger.

Access: Rapidan Dam put-in: From Mankato, drive south 5 miles on Minnesota Highway 66; turn west on County Route 9 and drive 3 miles to the river. The **Mankato take-out** lies at the confluence of the Blue Earth and Minnesota Rivers on the west side of Mankato. A boat ramp sits on the west side of the Blue Earth in Dakota Wakiksuye Makoce Park, but a fee is charged for landing there; a canoe carry-in lies across the Blue Earth in Sibley Municipal Park.

Shuttle: 9 miles one way. About 30 minutes.

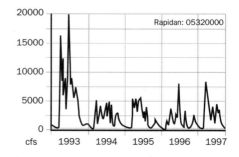

200 cfs = estimated minimum for good paddling

114 Blue Earth River

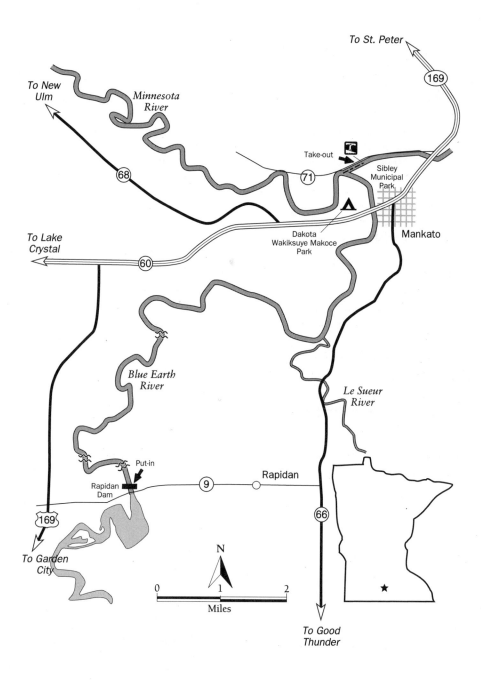

To St. Peter

169

To New Ulm

Minnesota River

68

Take-out

Sibley Municipal Park

71

Dakota Wakiksuye Makoce Park

Mankato

To Lake Crystal

60

Blue Earth River

Le Sueur River

Put-in

Rapidan

9

Rapidan Dam

66

169

To Garden City

N

0   1   2

Miles

★

To Good Thunder

ADDITIONAL HELP

MA&G: 22–23; 32, E1.

Camping: Riverside camping is possible at Dakota Wakiksuye Makoce Park in Mankato. Minneopa State Park, about 5 miles west of Mankato, has a campground for car camping.

Food, gas, and lodging: Mankato.

For more information: MDNR Information Center.

115 Chippewa River

Character: The Chippewa River provides a pleasant run through southwestern Minnesota's farmland.

Length: 33.2 miles.

Average run time: One to two days.

Class: I.

Skill level: Beginner.

Optimal flow: Check USGS website for flow greater than 200 cfs on gauge near Mitan. The MDNR doesn't take water level readings on the Chippewa.

Average gradient: 2.4 feet per mile.

Hazards: Watch out for the dam at Watson.

Maps: MDNR *Minnesota River Canoe Route 1 of 4*, PRIM *Willmar*.

The paddling: Begin your trip at the city park at Benson. The Chippewa River provides a wooded retreat in the farmland of southwestern Minnesota. Most of the route is heavily wooded. Bluffs rise above the river, making for pleasant vistas as you look downstream. A few class I rapids mark the route.

With some marshes and lakes in its headwaters, the Chippewa tends to hold its water well into the summer.

Just upstream of Watson, a dam diverts much of the Chippewa's flow from the natural river channel westward through Watson Sag to the Minnesota River. Pull out at the park on the left, upstream from the dam. Without a good flush of current to clear out obstructions, the natural channel tends to collect a lot of downed trees. For that reason, the stretch from Watson to Montevideo is less often traveled by canoe than the upper reach.

When the flow of water is adequate, the Chippewa provides some exciting fishing for medium-sized northern pike and, in spring, for walleye.

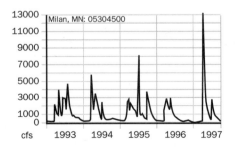

200 cfs = estimated minimum
for good paddling

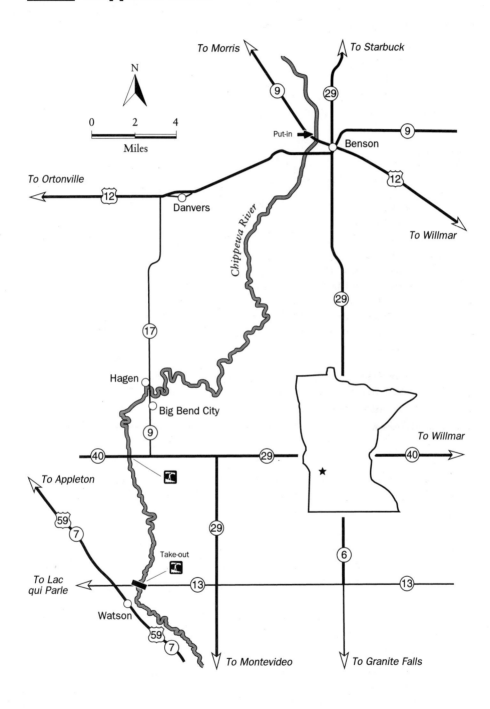

Access: The **Benson put-in** is located in town at the city park northeast of Minnesota Highway 9. The **Watson take-out** is located at a park on the east side of the river, just upstream of the dam and the County Route 13 bridge.

Access is also possible at several county roads and a developed access at Minnesota Highway 40.

Shuttle: 31 miles one way. About 1.25 hours.

ADDITIONAL HELP

MA&G: 37.
Camping: River camping is possible at the Benson city park.
Food, gas, and lodging: Benson, Montevideo.
For more information: MDNR, Trails and Waterway, New London office, 320-354-4940.

116 Cottonwood River

Character: The Cottonwood provides a quick run down a narrow, wooded corridor.
Length: 23.8 miles.
Average run time: 9 to 13 hours.
Class: I.
Skill level: Beginner to intermediate.
Optimal flow: Check USGS website for flows greater than 200 cfs on the gauge near New Ulm.
Average gradient: 5.7 feet per mile.
Hazards: Watch for downed trees.
Maps: MDNR *Minnesota River Canoe Route 3.*

The paddling: In a landscape otherwise planted in corn and soybeans, the Cottonwood forms a long, wooded oasis as it flows eastward to join the Minnesota River at New Ulm. Start your trip at the Minnesota Highway 4 access south of Sleepy Eye or several miles downstream at the County Route 11 access. The river runs through several stretches of swift water but no real whitewater. Depending on the amount of streambank erosion, you may also have to maneuver around some snags, especially in the stream's upper reaches. The Cottonwood cuts down through deep "drift" deposited

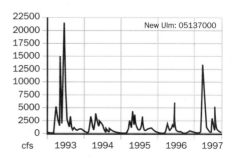

200 cfs = estimated minimum for good paddling (1.9 feet on gauge)

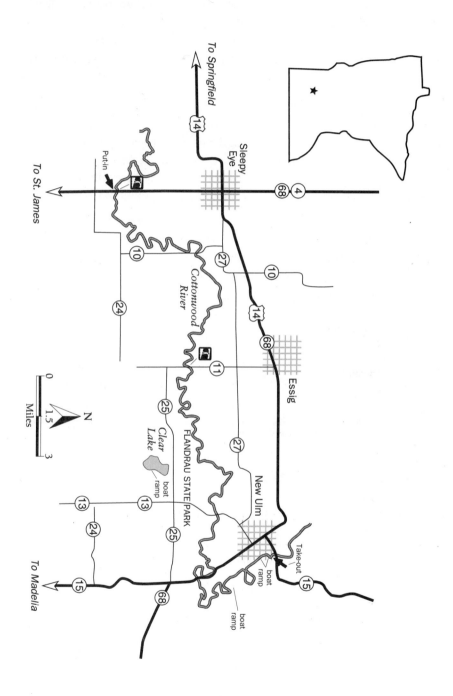

by glaciers that covered southern Minnesota more than 10,000 years ago. The meandering river has created a broad floodplain, in places up to a half mile wide. Some gravel pits are located on sand deposits along the river and bluffs. By the time the stream reaches Flandrau State Park, it has created a valley more than 100 feet deep. The steep slopes next to the floodplain are covered with maple, basswood, and hackberry. Oak and red cedar grow on sunny slopes. Prairie plants such as big bluestem, butterfly weed, and blazing star cover exposed knolls.

Depression-era workers built a dam on the Cottonwood to provide a swimming pond and beach at Flandrau. Flood waters destroyed dams at the site three times, most recently in 1969. Since then, the river has been left to flow freely.

The Cottonwood Street access in New Ulm is located 3 miles from the river's mouth. If you wish, you can continue downstream to the confluence with the Minnesota and several miles downstream to the access south of Courtland.

Access: The **MN 4 put-in** is located 4 miles south of Sleepy Eye. The **New Ulm take-out** is located at the Cottonwood Street bridge, near Minnesota Highway 15. An alternate access to start or end a trip is located at the County Route 11 bridge about 6 miles east of Sleepy Eye as the crow flies.

Shuttle: 20 miles one way. About one hour.

ADDITIONAL HELP

MA&G: 31, D6-8.
Camping: River camp sites aren't available, but you can camp by car in Flandrau State Park.
Food, gas, and lodging: New Ulm.
For more information: MDNR Information Center.

117 Des Moines River

Character: The Des Moines offers a leisurely canoe trip along a wooded valley in the midst of prime farmland.
Length: 65 miles.
Average run time: Three to four days. Many shorter trips are possible. A good one-day trip is from Windom to Jackson through Kilen Woods State Park.
Class: Quiet, with a few class I riffles.
Skill level: Beginner.
Optimal flow: 4.0 feet or higher on the USGS gauge in Jackson, or more than 200 cfs on gauge at Jackson (check USGS website).
Average gradient: 1.9 feet per mile.
Hazards: Avoid dams at Talcot Lake, Windom, and Jackson.
Maps: MDNR *Des Moines River Canoe Route.*

The paddling: The Des Moines is a placid farmland river that offers respite from southwestern Minnesota's unrelenting agricultural horizon. It provides a refuge for woodland wildlife, including many kinds of songbirds and species such as kingfishers and great blue herons. Look also for mammals such as white-tailed deer, raccoons, and red fox.

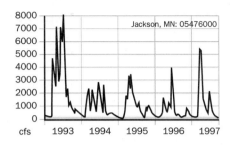

200 cfs = estimated minimum for good paddling

The trip begins at Talcot Lake. Put in at the access below the dam, or at the boat ramp at the south end of the lake to look for wildlife. If you do start on the lake, portage the dam at the outlet. Talcot Lake lies at the center of a 4,000-acre state wildlife management area composed of marshes, bottomlands, uplands, and farmland. Nesting species include American bitterns, sora and Virginia rails, common yellowthroats, northern cardinals, indigo buntings, bobolinks, northern harriers, and several species of sparrows. Large flocks of Canada geese use the lake in fall. Beavers and muskrats make their homes on the lake.

From Talcot Lake to Windom, the Des Moines travels through flat farmland with few trees. One small oasis is Pat's Grove County Park, located on the Heron Lake Outlet, a half mile upstream from the Des Moines. Heron Lake, once a legendary waterfowl lake, fell on hard times in recent decades. Farm runoff, fluctuating water levels, and infestations of carp caused the loss of many aquatic plants that attracted and fed waterfowl. Recent efforts to protect the lakeshore, reduce polluted runoff, and replant wild celery have helped restore some of the luster to this waterfowl oasis.

The river valley gradually deepens below Windom. Willow, green ash, and slippery elm line the river banks. As the river approaches Kilen Woods State Park, the floodplain narrows and bluffs rise to more than 100 feet. On the steep slopes grow the prairie bush clover, one of the Midwest's rarest plants. The park also contains meadows and limestone fens, a kind of wetland. An oak savanna, an uncommon grassland with widely scattered trees, is found on the west bank of the river. Savannas once covered large acreages in Minnesota, but became overgrown when wildfires were controlled. The riverside forest elsewhere in Kilen Woods harbors pileated woodpeckers. You're also likely to see deer, beavers, muskrats, weasels, mink, great blue herons, and many species of songbirds.

From Kilen Woods to Jackson, high hills continue to flank the Des Moines. From Jackson to the state line, however, the river again flows through a shallow, almost treeless valley that is intensely farmed.

117 Des Moines River

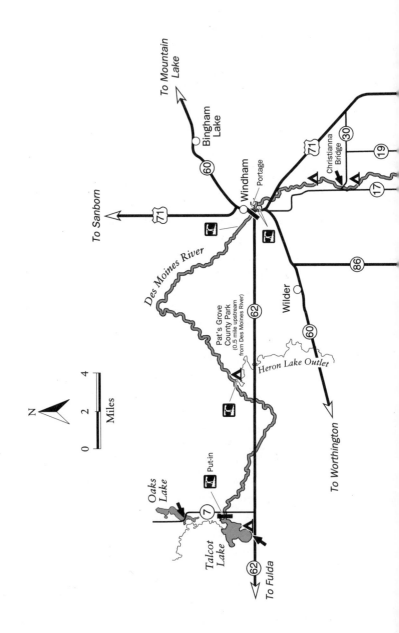

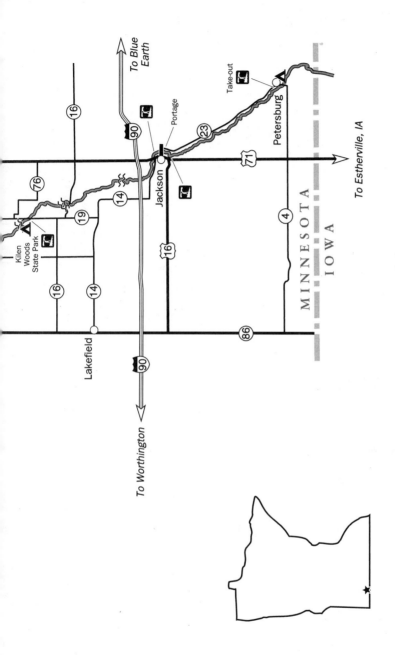

The Des Moines is not renowned for fishing, but it does harbor northern pike, walleye, crappies, channel catfish, and black bullheads.

Access: Talcot Lake put-in: From Fulda, drive east 8.5 miles on Minnesota Highway 62 then 2 miles north on County Route 7 to the bridge and access. **Petersburg take-out:** From Jackson, drive southeast 8 miles on County Route 23, just past the bridge over the Des Moines.

Additional accesses are located at Pat's Grove County Park, Windom, Christianna Bridge (County Route 30), Kilen Woods State Park, and Jackson.

Shuttle: 46 miles one way. About two hours.

ADDITIONAL HELP

MA&G: 20–21.
Camping: Canoe campsites are located about 1.5 miles upstream from the Christianna Bridge and a mile downstream. Campgrounds which can be used by canoe campers or auto campers are located at the county park at Talcot Lake, Pat's Grove County Park, Kilen Woods State Park, and Petersburg.
Food, gas, and lodging: Windom, Jackson.
For more information: MDNR Information Center.

118 Le Sueur River

Character: An intimate stream with lively current and wooded valley, the Le Sueur makes a good day trip when water is up.
Length: 22 miles.
Average run time: 7 to 11 hours.
Class: I.
Skill level: Beginner to intermediate.
Optimal flow: A USGS gauge is located near Rapidan. The MDNR hasn't had much of a track record with this gauge, but it appears a reading above 2 feet guarantees enough water for canoeing. Otherwise, check the USGS website for at least 200 cfs on the gauge near Rapidan.
Average gradient: 7.7 feet per mile.
Hazards: Watch for downed trees.
Maps: MDNR *Minnesota River Canoe Route 3.*

The paddling: The Le Sueur River, named for French explorer Pierre Le Sueur, scribes a twisting path over the agricultural plateau overlooking the Minnesota River Valley. The wooded corridor provides good bird watching for songbirds, waterfowl, and shorebirds.

Begin the trip at Wildwood County Park. Several class I rapids mark the river's course. Many of the banks are eroded, so watch for downed trees that have fallen

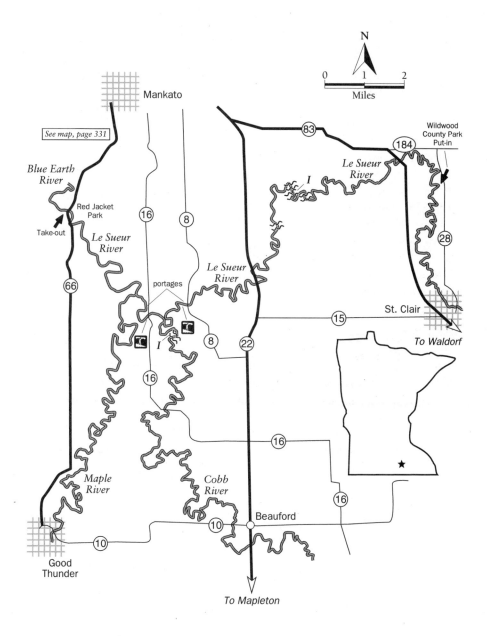

N

0   1   2
Miles

Mankato

See map, page 331

Blue Earth
River

Red Jacket
Park

Take-out

Le Sueur
River

66

16

8

portages

Le Sueur
River

I

16

8

22

15

Le Sueur
River

I

83

184

Wildwood
County Park
Put-in

28

St. Clair

To Waldorf

16

16

Maple
River

Cobb
River

16

Beauford

10

10

Good
Thunder

To Mapleton

★

or lodged in the river channel. These sorts of obstructions are especially hazardous when the water is very high and fast.

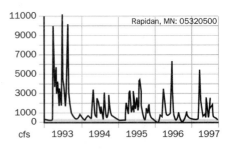

200 cfs = estimated minimum for good paddling

Mile by mile the valley of the Le Sueur becomes deeper. As the Cobb River and then the Maple River (see below) join the Le Sueur due south of Mankato, the river valley grows dramatically. Bluffs rise 200 feet above the narrow floodplain.

The take-out for this trip is the Red Jacket Park landing, located at an old railroad trestle next to the Minnesota Highway 66 bridge. If you want, continue down the Le Sueur about 1.5 miles to the Blue Earth River and then about 3.5 miles down the Blue Earth to the take-out at Mankato.

Two tributaries to the Le Sueur also provide good paddling when the water is up.

Put in on the **Cobb River** at the Minnesota Highway 22 bridge or County Route 10 bridge near Beauford. The stream is narrow, quick, and sinuous, flowing through some class I stretches. The run from the County Route 10 bridge to the confluence with the Le Sueur totals 14 miles and drops an average of 10 feet per mile through several class I rapids. About a half mile after the confluence with the Le Sueur, take out at the County Route 16 access. Like the Le Sueur, the Cobb is shown on the MDNR Minnesota River Canoe Route map (3 of 4).

Put in on the **Maple River** at the County Route 10 access in Good Thunder. The Maple, too, is a twisting, narrow stream with a screen of woods separating paddlers from the farm fields just over the banks. The run from Good Thunder to the confluence with the Le Sueur is 13 miles, dropping 10 feet per mile through several class I stretches. Once you reach the confluence, paddle down the Le Sueur about 4 miles to the access at Red Jacket Park.

Access: Wildwood County Park put-in: From Mankato drive east 4 miles on Minnesota Highway 83 to County Road 184. As MN 83 turns south, turn left on CR 184 to continue east about 1.5 miles to County Route 28. Turn south (right) on County Route 28 about 1 mile to the park. The **Red Jacket Park take-out** is located about 3 miles south of Mankato, where MN 66 crosses the Le Sueur River.

Alternate accesses to begin or end your trip are located at County Route 8 and County Route 16, both south of Mankato.

Shuttle: 15 miles one way. About 45 minutes.

MA&G: 23, A6–8; 32, E2.

Camping: Riverside camping is possible at the private park at Rapidan Dam and at Dakota Wakiksuye Makoce Park in Mankato. Minneopa State Park, located about 5 miles west of Mankato, has a campground.

Food, gas, and lodging: Mankato.

For more information: MDNR Information Center.

MINNESOTA RIVER

119 Big Stone to Lac qui Parle

Character: The marshy river and lakes heading up the Minnesota River offer great opportunities for watching wildlife.

Length: 40 miles. Rather than run the length of this stretch, you'll probably want to paddle the shorelines of a lake and return to your put-in.

Average run time: Varies. See above.

Class: Quiet.

Skill level: Beginner.

Optimal flow: Not applicable.

Average gradient: Virtually none except for the vertical drop associated with the dams.

Hazards: Avoid dams just downstream from Big Stone Lake (about 1,000 feet west of U.S. Highway 12), at U.S. Highway 75, and at the outlets of Marsh Lake and Lac qui Parle.

Maps: MDNR *Minnesota River Canoe Route 1.*

The paddling: The Minnesota River begins at Big Stone Lake, an aptly named body of water along Minnesota's border with South Dakota. The shores are marked by big boulders and occasional outcrops. The lake lies in a long, impressively wide, and often windswept valley. The lake is known for good walleye fishing.

The river trip begins just downstream of the lake and dam, south of Ortonville. Paddle through the tangled channel that loops and curves through Big Stone National Wildlife Refuge. The 10,000-acre wildlife area provides a variety of landforms including a reservoir, native prairie, floodplain forest, marshes, and granite outcrops. The vegetation is similarly diverse and includes a forest of elm, ash, maple, and oak, and prairie plants such as prickly pear and big bluestem. Big Stone NWR is one of the rare breeding grounds for the snowy egret in Minnesota. Other wildlife you might see in the river and surrounding marshes are western grebes, great blue herons, white pelicans, various ducks, bald eagles, and many owls and hawks. The rock outcrop hiking trail in the refuge takes you through

119 Big Stone to Lac qui Parle

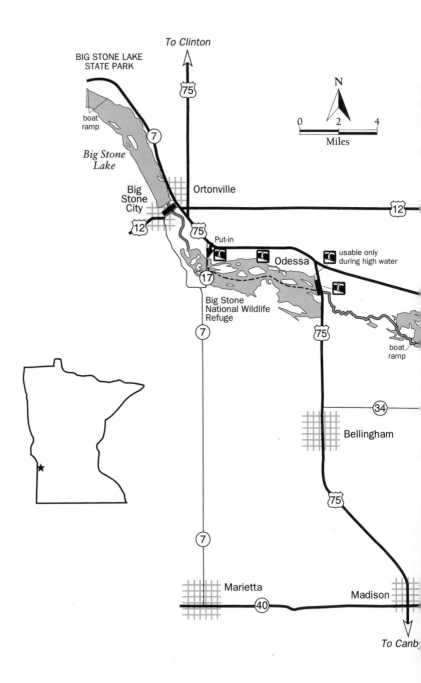

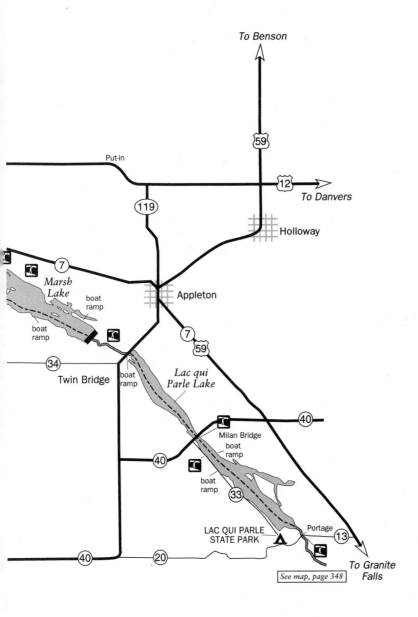

To Benson

To Danvers

Put-in

119

59

12

Holloway

7

Marsh
Lake

boat
ramp

boat
ramp

Appleton

7

59

34

Twin Bridge

boat
ramp

Lac qui
Parle Lake

40

40

Milan Bridge
boat
ramp

boat
ramp

33

LAC QUI PARLE
STATE PARK

Portage

13

40

20

See map, page 348

To Granite
Falls

The shoreline of Big Stone Lake, part of Lac qui Parle State Park. MINNESOTA
OFFICE OF TOURISM

various habitats and plant communities. The river runs through marsh for several miles. Past Odessa the stream enters a reservoir formed by the dam at US 75.

Below the US 75 dam, the river enters a wooded channel for several miles before spreading into Marsh Lake, another reservoir. Below the dam that forms Marsh Lake, the Minnesota River runs through a distinct channel before spreading once again into a lake, this time Lac qui Parle. This entire area, from US 75 to the southeastern end of Lac qui Parle, lies within the boundaries of Lac qui Parle Wildlife Management Area, whose 31,000 acres form one of the state's most diverse wildlife areas. The state's largest concentration of nesting white pelicans belongs to Lac qui Parle. You can spot colonies at Marsh Lake near Appleton and Lac qui Parle near Watson. As many as 150,000 Canada geese stop during fall migration. Other migrating species include tundra swans, snow geese, sandhill cranes, and up to 50 bald eagles. You might also spot river otters, which have been reintroduced to the area.

Be aware that hunting is allowed at Lac qui Parle. The stretch of the lake from Minnesota Highway 40 downstream to the dam is closed to the public from September 20 to December 1. No canoeing is allowed on that stretch during that time.

Access: Access is possible at several boat ramps and carry-in sites along the lake and river shores. See the map for locations.

Shuttle: 40 miles one way for the whole section. About 1.75 hours.

ADDITIONAL HELP

MA&G: 36–37.
Camping: No canoe campsites are located on this stretch. There's a campground at Lac qui Parle State Park at the southeast end of the Lac qui Parle.
Food, gas, and lodging: Ortonville, Appleton, Montevideo.
For more information: MDNR Information Center.

120 Lac qui Parle to North Redwood

Character: A small stream in a big valley, this stretch of the Minnesota provides a leisurely ride with a few easy rapids and pleasant scenery.
Length: 72 miles. Several shorter trips are possible.
Average run time: Three to four days for the whole stretch.
Class: I.
Skill level: Beginner.
Optimal flow: Above 3 feet on the USGS gauge at Montevideo, or above 2 feet on the gauge in Upper Sioux Agency State Park. Check the USGS website for more than 300 cfs on Montevideo gauge.
Average gradient: 1.5 feet per mile.
Hazards: Portage dams in Granite Falls and 2 miles downstream from Granite Falls.
Maps: MDNR *Minnesota River Canoe Route 1 and 2.*

120 Lac qui Parle to North Redwood

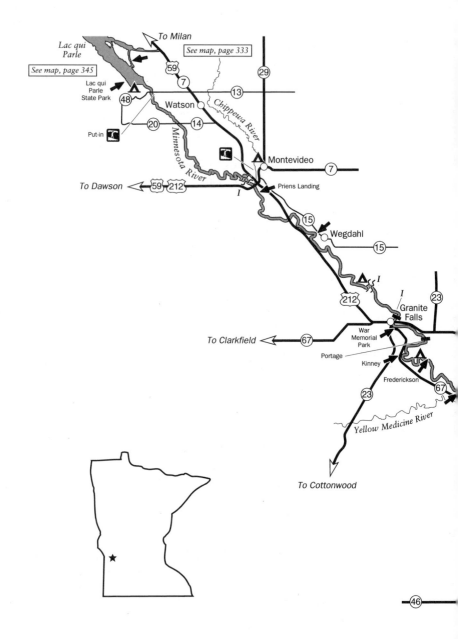

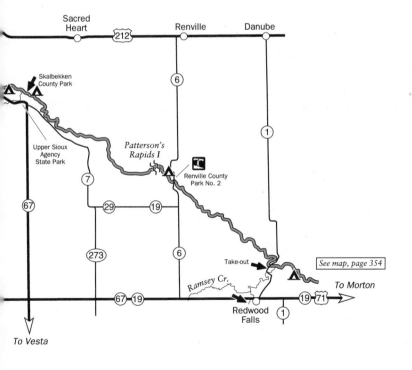

N

0   4   8
Miles

Sacred
Heart   212   Renville   Danube

Skalbekken
County Park

6

Upper Sioux
Agency
State Park

Patterson's
Rapids I

1

Renville County
Park No. 2

7

67   29   19

273   6

Take-out   See map, page 354

Ramsey Cr.

67   19   19   71
                          To Morton

Redwood
Falls   1

To Vesta

The paddling: Below Lac qui Parle, the Minnesota River resumes its riverine appearance— this time for keeps. It flows down a narrow channel down a very broad valley. In geological terms, the river is "underfit," a puny inheritor of the vast trench carved by the mighty Glacial River Warren, which drained mammoth Glacial Lake Agassiz to what is now the Mississippi Valley. This torrent carved a vast, broad valley until about 9,000 years ago, when Agassiz was drained away and Glacial River Warren had shrunk to a trickle. As a consequence, lofty bluffs lie at times a mile or more from the present-day Minnesota. In places the valley is more than 5 miles wide and more than 300 feet deep.

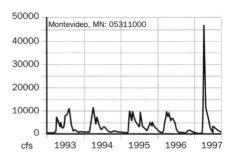

300 cfs = estimated minimum for good paddling (3.0 feet on gauge)

The geologic history of the Minnesota River is notable for another reason: bedrock underlying the basin includes some of the oldest rocks known on earth, dating back more than 3.6 billion years. Some of this material, known as Montevideo and Morton gneisses, for its location in the Minnesota River Valley, forms outcrops along the river. Outcrops become more prevalent downstream from Montevideo. Outcrops and lofty, rocky domes covered with cedar and oak flank the river as far south as North Redwood and are periodically interrupted by expanses of fertile farmland.

The name *Minnesota* is a Dakota word, translated variously as "clear water" or "cloudy water." While some turbidity was probably natural from the fine soils in the basin, clearly the water quality of the river has suffered during the last 150 years, since the first white settlers tore away the prairie sod with steel plows. Agricultural runoff is the greatest source of sediment and pollution in the river today.

The river flows through several short, easy rapids. A class I drop lies just above Montevideo. Others occur just upstream from Granite Falls. **Patterson's Rapids,** which rates class I, lies just upstream from Renville County Park Number 2, where the river falls about 5 feet in a third of a mile over many boulders. The rapids was named for Charles Patterson, an early trader who in 1783 established a trading post at the rapids. Nearby Sacred Heart Creek and the town of Sacred Heart also owe their name to Patterson. The trader wore a hat made from the skin and fur of a bear, which was sacred to the Dakota Indians, who called Patterson "Sacred Hat Man." The area near the rapids was the site of a short-lived gold rush in the 1890s. The gold, discovered in 1894, soon played out, leaving newly founded Springville a ghost town.

In Granite Falls, watch for the dam that lies just downstream of a sharp bend to the right. Portage right about 250 yards. A second dam lies about 3 miles downstream. Portage that dam on the right, about 200 yards.

Anglers can catch walleye, northern pike, and smallmouth bass in the deep water above and below rapids and dams. Slower sections of the river are good for flathead and channel catfish.

Several sites along the Minnesota River played a role in the often fractious relationship between the Dakota Indians and early white settlers. Lac qui Parle Mission, which overlooks the put-in to this trip, occupies the long-time location of a Wahpeton Dakota village. The mission began as a trading post built in 1826 by explorer and trader Joseph Renville, whose mother was Dakota and father was French. Renville invited missionaries to Lac qui Parle. The missionaries sought not only to convert the Indians to Christianity, but to to make farmers of them as well. Relations between the Dakota and missionaries, often filled with distrust and misunderstanding, deteriorated once the highly respected Renville died in 1846. The missionaries left in 1854. Nonetheless, many present Indian Congregational and Presbyterian congregations trace their origins to the Lac qui Parle Mission.

Upper Sioux Agency, located at the confluence of the Minnesota and Yellow Medicine Rivers, was established in 1853 to convert the Dakota Indians to the ways of the white settlers. The Dakota, once hunters, had conveyed all their land in Minnesota under the treaties of Traverse des Sioux and Mendota except for a strip 10 miles wide on either side of the Minnesota River. Though many Dakota opposed the work of the mission, others learned European styles of agriculture and carpentry. By 1861, 145 families cultivated more than 1,000 acres at the mission. Much of the success of the agency could be attributed to Joseph R. Brown, the most respected and capable of the agents to run the Upper Sioux Agency and the Lower Sioux Agency, 30 miles downstream. The inflexibility of Brown's successor, Thomas J. Galbraith, aggravated white-Dakota discord and may have contributed to the U.S.–Dakota War of 1862.

Access: The **Lac qui Parle put-in** is located at the southeast end of the lake, just downstream from the dam at the County Route 13 bridge. The **North Redwood take-out** is located just north of town next to the County Route 1/101 bridge.

Take a shorter trip by using any of several accesses at Montevideo, Wegdahl, Granite Falls, two locations just downstream from Granite Falls, two sites near Upper Sioux Agency State Park, and Renville County Park Number 2.

Shuttle: 65 miles one way. About 2.5 hours.

ADDITIONAL HELP

MA&G: 37, C–E 6–9; 29, A9; 30 A–B 1–3.

Camping: River campsites are located 3 miles upstream of Montevideo, 3 miles upstream from Granite Falls, just downstream from Granite Falls, at the access on river left 8 miles downstream from Granite Falls, and at the accesses near Upper Sioux Agency State Park, and Renville County Park Number 2. Campgrounds are located at Lac qui Parle and Upper Sioux Agency State Park.

Food, gas, and lodging: Montevideo, Granite Falls, Redwood Falls.

For more information: MDNR Information Center.

121 North Redwood to Mankato

Character: Slow and meandering, the Minnesota follows a wooded corridor and wide valley.

Length: 94 miles. Several shorter trips are possible.

Average run time: Three to five days for the whole stretch.

Class: Quiet.

Skill level: Beginner.

Optimal flow: Above 12 feet on the USGS gauge in New Ulm, or above 5 feet on the USGS gauge in Mankato (about 1,500 cfs on USGS Mankato gauge).

Average gradient: 0.8 foot per mile.

Hazards: No particular hazards.

Maps: MDNR *Minnesota River Canoe Route 3.*

The paddling: Once past North Redwood, the Minnesota River becomes more sinuous. At the put-in and for several miles downstream, the Minnesota flows by the broad, marshy floodplain of the Honner State Wildlife Management Area, an excellent place to spot waterfowl and shorebirds. Although the river has grown larger, it is still woefully inadequate to fill the broad valley. In places, bluffs rise several hundred yards back from the river. A bottomland forest of silver maple, cottonwoods, elm, and ash screen the river from the farmland beyond the corridor.

The slow and rather featureless river channel doesn't provide much habitat for most game fish, but the river does provide notable fishing for large flathead and channel catfish. Use live or cut bait to fish in deep holes with woody cover such as downed trees.

Many sites along this stretch of river were landmarks in the brief but bloody skirmish of Dakota Indians against white settlers and U.S. soldiers in the summer of 1862. The war, often called the Sioux Uprising, was the culmination of long-simmering Dakota resentment over loss of their land and frustration with the government's failure to make timely annuity payments.

By the 1850s, the Dakota had signed treaties forcing them onto reservations along the Minnesota River, where the U.S. government tried to remake them into full-time farmers. Crops failed in 1861, and by the next year, many Dakota were starving. They gathered at Upper and Lower Sioux Agency to await federal payments to buy food. Promised by treaty and due in June, the annuities still had not arrived by mid-August.

When the agent in charge of Lower Sioux Agency near Morton refused to release food from a warehouse until the payments arrived, the Dakotas' rage finally exploded. On August 18, warriors attacked the agency, a thriving town of about 100 white and mixed-blood settlers. The Indians broke into the warehouse and took food. The Dakota killed many of the 40 soldiers sent from nearby Fort Ridgely to restore order. During the next week, the militants among the Indians—according to all evidence, in the vast minority—killed dozens of settlers in the countryside.

The war quickly spread throughout much of the Minnesota River Valley. The Dakota laid siege to Fort Ridgely, an unfortified outpost built on a nearly indefensible site flanked on three sides by wooded ravines. Nonetheless, a force of about 400 Dakota failed in its efforts to overrun the 180 soldiers defending the fort. Today the Minnesota Historical Society operates an interpretive center on the grounds of the old fort. Few buildings remain, but exhibits at the fort's restored commissary tell the story of the fort and the Dakota war.

After fighting began, Dakota looted and burned the Upper Sioux Agency near Granite Falls. John Other Day, a Dakota chief, like many Indians of the Upper Sioux Agency, refused to take part in the fighting and led many whites from the agency to safety. Today, the site of the annuity center is marked by the foundation and bricks from the original building in Upper Sioux Agency State Park.

The Minnesota River near New Ulm. MINNESOTA OFFICE OF TOURISM

121 North Redwood to Mankato

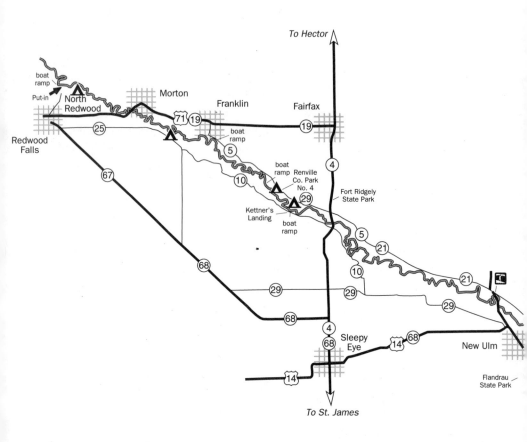

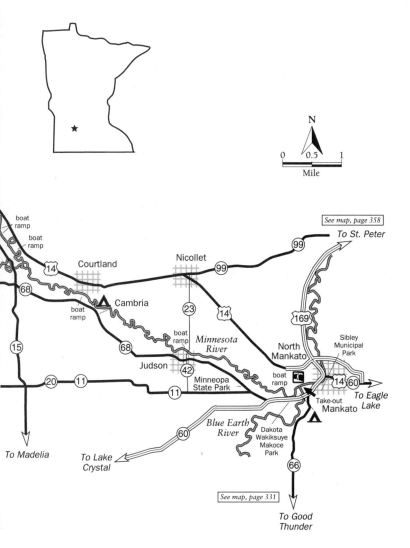

N

0   0.5   1
Mile

boat ramp

boat ramp

14 Courtland

Nicollet

99 To St. Peter

See map, page 358

68

15

68

23

14

169

boat ramp

Cambria

boat ramp

Minnesota River

North Mankato

Sibley Municipal Park

20   11

Judson

42

Minneopa State Park

boat ramp

14 60

To Eagle Lake

11

Take-out Mankato

60 Blue Earth River

Dakota Wakiksuye Makoce Park

66

To Madelia

To Lake Crystal

See map, page 331

To Good Thunder

After the war, more than 300 Dakota were sentenced to death and taken to Mankato. President Abraham Lincoln commuted the sentences of the 265 convicts who were determined to have been simple combatants. The remaining 38, convicted of murder or rape, were hanged on a single scaffold to the cheers of a vengeful crowd of farmers and townsfolk.

Access: The **North Redwood put-in** is located just north of town next to the County Route 1/101 bridge. The **Mankato take-out** lies at the confluence of the Blue Earth and Minnesota rivers on the west side of Mankato at the west end of Mound Avenue. A boat ramp sits on the west side of the Blue Earth in Dakota Wakiksuye Makoce Park (fee charged); a canoe carry-in lies across the Blue Earth in Sibley Municipal Park.

Plenty of alternate accesses exist to make for a shorter trip: Franklin, Renville County Park Number 4, Kettner's Landing, a site 3 miles upstream from New Ulm, three sites at New Ulm, Courtland, and Judson.

Shuttle: 72 miles one way. About 2.75 hours.

ADDITIONAL HELP

MA&G: 30–31; 32, E1.

Camping: River campsites are located about 2 miles downstream from North Redwood, about 5 miles downstream from Morton, Renville County Park Number 4, Kettner's Landing, across the river from Cambria, Sibley Municipal Park. Camp by car at Fort Ridgely, Flandrau, and Minneopa State Parks.

Food, gas, and lodging: Redwood Falls, New Ulm, Mankato.

For more information: MDNR Information Center.

122 Mankato to Fort Snelling

Character: A large, winding, and muddy river with a deep, wooded valley, the Minnesota provides easy canoeing. It also offers the possibility of catching huge catfish.

Length: 116 miles. Many shorter trips are possible.

Average run time: Three to six days for the entire stretch.

Class: Quiet.

Skill level: Beginner.

Optimal flow: *Below* 12 feet on the USGS gauge near Jordan. This section of river floods badly and can carry paddlers into deadfalls, bridges, and other obstructions. It's never so low as to be unrunnable by canoe.

Average gradient: 0.5 foot per mile.

Hazards: Obstructions in high water. Tugs and barges operate in the lower 22 miles of the river.

Maps: MDNR *Minnesota River Canoe Route 3 and 4.* Also check the *Metro Area Rivers Guide*, published by the MDNR.

The paddling: At Mankato, the Minnesota bends sharply northward, like an elbow reaching across the waist of Minnesota. At the same time, it takes in the flow of several tributaries, notably the Blue Earth River, and has grown in width. The bluffs are still a long way off. At times, the views of the valley are truly majestic. With its low gradient and soft, shifting streambed, this section of the Minnesota has no rapids. For the

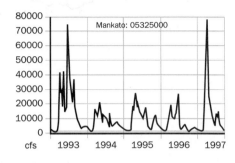

1500 cfs = minimum for good paddling
(5.0 feet on gauge)

same reason, it offers little habitat for most game fish; however, large channel and flathead catfish lie in deep holes protected by log jams. To catch them, fish on the bottom with live fish or cut bait.

As the Minnesota winds northwards, it passes woodlands and farm fields planted in the bottoms. Several small local parks are also located on the river's banks.

Downstream from St. Peter, the Minnesota passes Traverse des Sioux City Park. Dakota Indians forded the river at this site to travel from the hardwood forests of the east to their buffalo-hunting grounds to the west. The Treaty Site History Center, operated by the Nicollet County Historical Society, depicts Indians and early traders and explorers, including French cartographer Joseph Nicollet, who admired the Indians' descriptive geographic names and tried to preserve them in original or translated form. Another prominent resident was the Dakota chief, Mazasha, who adapted some white ways, planting crops, including wheat, and building a log cabin and barn. He was one of 35 Dakota chiefs who signed the treaty at Traverse des Sioux in 1851, opening 24 million acres of southern Minnesota, Iowa, and South Dakota to white settlement. French Canadian Louis Provençalle, who ran a trading post at Traverse des Sioux, kept his ledger in a self-styled hieroglyphics—reportedly so it could be read by trader and Indian alike. Historian William E. Lass is less charitable. Provençalle "epitomized the old order," writes Lass, "He entered the trade as an illiterate young man and left it as an illiterate old man."

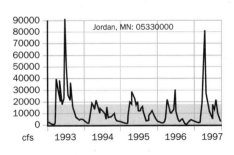

18000 cfs = flood stage

Downstream from Le Sueur, the Minnesota is flanked by several large parcels of public land that protect the extensive marshes and bottomlands

122 Mankato to Fort Snelling

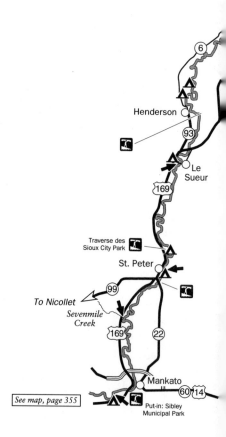

Henderson

Le Sueur

Traverse des
Sioux City Park

St. Peter

To Nicollet

Sevenmile
Creek

Mankato

See map, page 355

Put-in: Sibley
Municipal Park

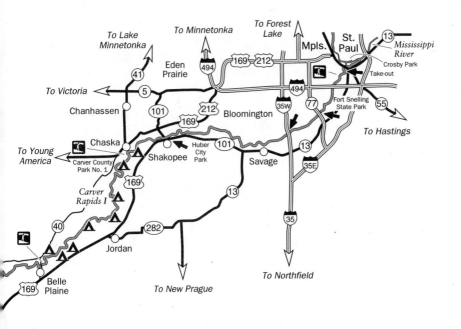

To Lake Minnetonka

To Minnetonka

To Forest Lake

Mpls.

St. Paul

13

Mississippi River

Crosby Park

Take-out

Eden Prairie

169 — 212

494

41

To Victoria

5

494

35W

77

55

Chanhassen

101

212

Bloomington

Fort Snelling State Park

To Hastings

Chaska

169

To Young America

Carver County Park No. 1

Shakopee

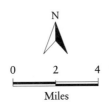

Huber City Park

101

Savage

13

35E

Carver Rapids I

169

13

40

35

282

Jordan

169

Belle Plaine

To New Prague

To Northfield

N

0   2   4

Miles

The skyline of Bloomington rises above the Minnesota River backwater. MINNESOTA OFFICE OF TOURISM

that lie along the river channel. The Minnesota Valley State Recreation Area provides hiking, camping, canoeing, horseback riding, and fishing at several locations along the Minnesota River between Le Sueur and Shakopee. Intertwined with the state lands are units of the Minnesota Valley National Wildlife Refuge.

Starting just downstream from Belle Plaine are the headquarters and Lawrence unit (the state recreation unit is made up of several separate units). Located several hundred yards off the river is the lone remaining building from the 1850s town of St. Lawrence. There is also a campground and more than 20 miles of trail for hiking, mountain biking, and horseback riding.

Next, lying just north of Jordan, is the Carver Rapids–Louisville Swamp unit of the national wildlife refuge. Located at the site of class I **Carver Rapids,** the only rapids on the lower river, this unit has 7 miles of hiking trials. Another attraction of the unit is the Historic Jabs Farm, which unfortunately is located well back from the river.

The Gifford Lake and Nyseen's Lake units of the state recreation area lie near Chaska. Public land flanks the river all the way to Shakopee.

Just downstream from Shakopee, start to keep an eye out for tugboats and tows of barges. If you see one coming, move out of the way and expect a large wake.

Between Shakopee and Savage, the Wilke–Rice Lake unit of the national wildlife refuge flanks the south side of the river for 4 miles.

In its final 8 miles, the Minnesota passes through Fort Snelling State Park, 3,300 acres encompassing wooded uplands, savanna, bottomland forest, backwaters, and spring-fed lakes. Hiking and biking trails lace the area. The park offers interpretive programs and guided tours to explain the geology, wildlife, vegetation, and rivers and lakes. Fort Snelling is a major wildlife area in the metro area, with white-tailed deer, red and gray foxes, woodchucks, badgers, and various herons, egrets, American bittern, waterfowl, and songbirds.

If you paddle to the confluence of the Minnesota and Mississippi, you'll be able to look back upstream at the walls of Fort Snelling, built in 1819 to protect the new nation's interest in the wilderness. One might argue it is the state's most important historic site, not only for its importance to "Minnesotans," but also to the Dakota who preceded them. The fort sits at *Bdo-te,* the sacred confluence of two rivers of major importance to the Indians.

The fort was never attacked. Yet it provided a strong offense in a figurative sense: Fort Snelling served as the vanguard of white civilization, with the state's first hospital, school, and library. The state's first Protestant church, located at the fort, served as a social hall. Indians came to the fort to receive payments owed them under the treaty by which the land was purchased. Even then, one duty of the Indian agent at the fort was to transform the Indians to the white way of life. Writes historian William E. Lass, "The American government recognized the transitory nature of the fur trade and the inevitable aftermath of settlement, and it tried to prepare the Indians for the future."

Standing at the head of steamboat navigation on the Mississippi, Fort Snelling had many prominent visitors, especially as a tour of the river, through the heart of the unsettled West, became fashionable adventure. Among these were British novelist Frederick Marryat and Swedish author Frederika Bremer. President Zachary Taylor served as post commander early in his career.

Fort Snelling served as a prison camp for the Dakota in the aftermath of the U.S.–Dakota War of 1862. As Minneapolis and St. Paul grew, the fort waned in importance. Today it is operated by the Minnesota Historical Society and has been restored to its 1827 appearance. Soldier look-alikes in the uniforms of the 1820s engage visitors in the small talk of the time, run through drills, and fire the cannon.

Access: The **Mankato put-in** lies at the confluence of the Blue Earth and Minnesota rivers on the west side of Mankato. A boat ramp sits on the west side of the Blue Earth in Dakota Wakiksuye Makoce Park (fee charged); a canoe carry-in lies across the Blue Earth in Sibley Municipal Park. The **Fort Snelling take-out** is located in Fort Snelling State Park. To reach the park, take the Post Road exit from Minnesota Highway 5.

Many other accesses are available to break this route into shorter segments, including Sevenmile Creek north of Mankato, three in or near St. Peter, Le Sueur, two near Henderson, Belle Plaine, Jordan, Chaska, Shakopee, Interstate 35, Minnesota Highway 77, and two in Fort Snelling.

Shuttle: 80 miles one way. About 3 hours.

ADDITIONAL HELP

MA&G: 32; 40, E5; 41, E6–8.

Camping: River campsites and campgrounds are located at several sites along the river, including St. Peter, Traverse des Sioux City Park, Le Sueur, two sites just downstream of Henderson, several sites between Belle Plaine and Shakopee. No campsites are located downstream from Shakopee.

Food, gas, and lodging: Mankato, St. Peter, Le Sueur, Shakopee, Minneapolis, and St. Paul.

For more information: MDNR Information Center.

123 Pomme de Terre River

Character: The Pomme de Terre River scribes a narrow, wooded route through land that is heavily farmed.
Length: 21.2 miles.
Average run time: Seven to ten hours.
Class: I.
Skill level: Beginner.
Optimal flow: Check the USGS website for at least 100 cfs at the station of Appleton (about 4.2 feet on gauge).
Average gradient: 4.1 feet per mile.
Hazards: Portage the dam at Appleton. Watch for farm fences strung across the river.
Maps: PRIM *Big Stone Lake, Willmar.*

The paddling: In a region of Minnesota that is devoted almost completely to agriculture, the Pomme de Terre provides a pleasant oasis. The stream runs past low bluffs and a mix of woods, pasture, and some farmland. Look for white-tailed deer, mink, songbirds, and water-loving birds such as kingfishers and great blue herons.

Start your trip at the developed access at County Route 20. The river, screened by a fringe of woods, meanders across its floodplain.

In Appleton, portage the dam. The failing structure is unable to hold back water and is slated to be removed soon.

Below Appleton, the Pomme de Terre runs through several easy rapids as it drops to meet the Minnesota River at Marsh Lake.

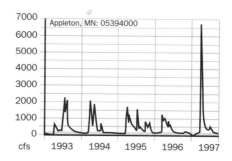

100 cfs = estimated minimum for good paddling (4.2 feet on gauge)

123 Pomme de Terre River

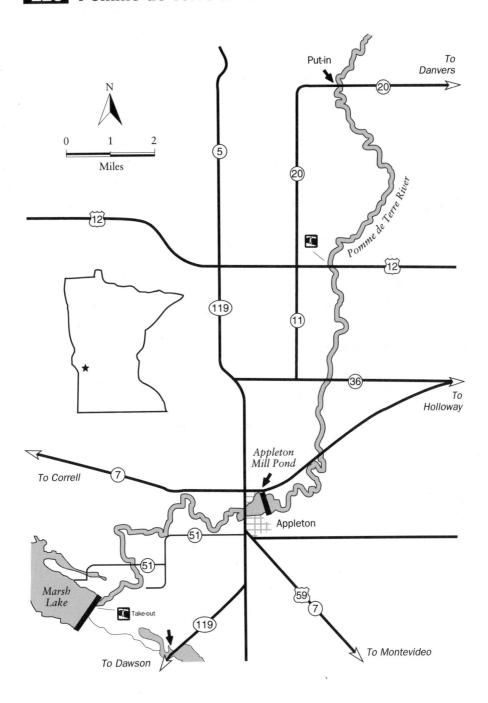

Access: County Route 20 put-in: From Appleton 2 miles north on Minnesota Highway 119, 1.5 miles east on County Road 36, 7 miles north on County Route 11, which turns into County Route 20. County Route 20 turns east and goes 1 mile to the river. The **Marsh Lake take-out** is located next to the dam at Marsh Lake. From Appleton, follow County Road 51 west to an unnumbered township road which leads to an access about 1 mile upstream from the river's mouth at Marsh Lake.

Access is also possible at several county roads, at U.S. Highway 12, and at MN 119 in Appleton.

Shuttle: 18 miles one way. About 50 minutes.

ADDITIONAL HELP

MA&G: 43, E9; 36, A5.
Camping: River camping is possible at the US 12 landing.
Food, gas, and lodging: Appleton, Willmar, Marshall.
For more information: MDNR Information Center.

124 Watonwan River

Character: The Watonwan provides a good route for watching wildlife and finding wooded seclusion in a region that otherwise is heavily farmed.
Length: 22 miles.
Average run time: 7 to 11 hours.
Class: I.
Skill level: Beginner to intermediate.
Optimal flow: The MDNR doesn't have much information about the USGS gauge in Garden City to determine minimum runnable levels. Readings above 1.2 feet (about 100 cfs on the USGS gauge near Garden City—check the website) appear adequate.
Average gradient: 3.6 feet per mile.
Hazards: Watch for downed trees.
Maps: MDNR *Minnesota River Canoe Route 3.*

The paddling: Put in at Watona Park in Madelia. In stark contrast to the farmland all around, the Watonwan offers a secluded wooded valley. Bluffs of 50 to 75 feet, some nearly vertical, flank the river. The river flows quickly at times, but the only real rapids are class I stretches near the confluence with the Blue Earth River.

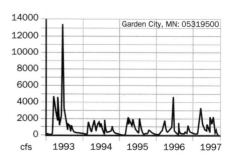

100 cfs = estimated minimum for good paddling (1.2 feet on gauge)

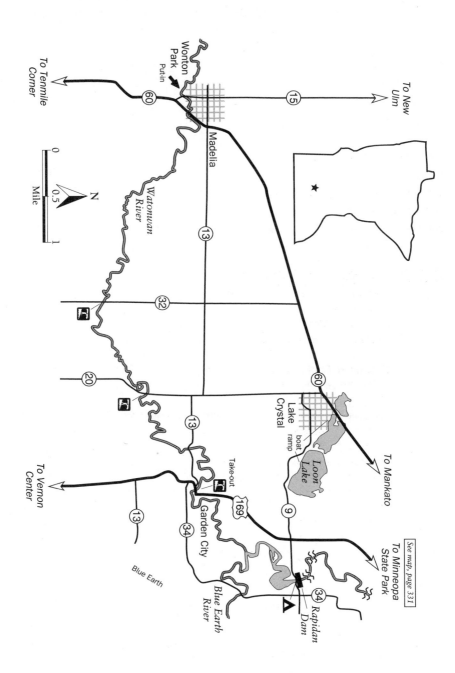

As you paddle, keep an eye out for various woodland wildlife, including white-tailed deer and wild turkeys.

You can follow the Watonwan downstream from Garden City to the confluence with the Blue Earth and the reservoir formed by the Rapidan Dam. Pull out at the county park just upstream of the dam.

Access: The **Madelia put-in** is located in town, just upstream from the Minnesota Highway 15 bridge. The **Garden City take-out** is located in town near the U.S. Highway 169 bridge. Boat ramps are also located at the county fairgrounds on the east edge of town. Make a shorter trip by using either of the accesses at the County Route 32 bridge or County Route 20 bridge.

Shuttle: 14 miles one way. About 45 minutes.

ADDITIONAL HELP

MA&G: 22, A3–5.

Camping: River sites aren't available, but you can camp by car in Minneopa State Park.

Food, gas, and lodging: Madelia, Mankato.

For more information: MDNR Information Center.

125 Yellow Medicine River

Character: Yikes—whitewater in the prairies and farmland of southwestern Minnesota!

Length: 19 miles.

Average run time: Six to nine hours.

Class: II.

Skill level: Intermediate.

Optimal flow: The Yellow Medicine is flashy—quick to go up, quick to come down. Look to run this stream in late April or May, when the water is high, but not in flood. Check the USGS website for at least 200 cfs on the gauge near Granite Falls.

Average gradient: 7.7 feet per mile.

Hazards: Watch for snags.

Maps: PRIM *Montevideo*.

The paddling: For much of its length, the Yellow Medicine River flows slowly over the relatively flat farmland and prairie of southwestern Minnesota. Several miles past Hanley Falls, the pace picks up as the land slopes toward the Minnesota River. As the Yellow Medicine races to meet the larger stream, it passes frequently through short, steep, bouldery rapids. You'll need to dodge boulders and trains of standing waves. High, steep bluffs flank the river.

The final 2 miles of the stream are flanked on both sides by Upper Sioux Agency State Park. Important archaeological artifacts have been found in the park.

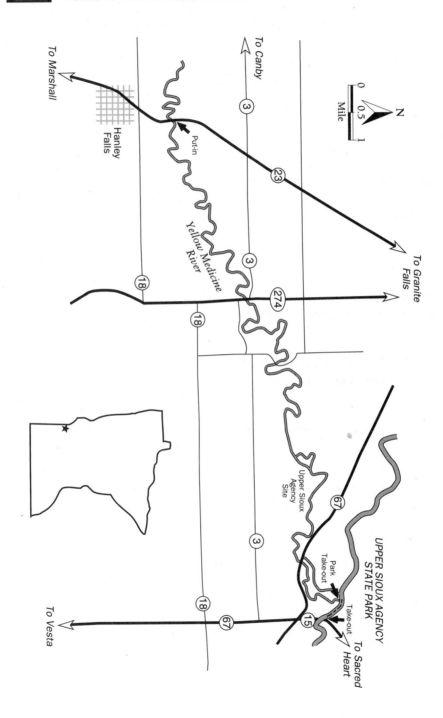

More than 1,000 years ago, an un-known Plains Indian tribe lived in a village on the floodplain along the Yellow Medicine. The river is named for the yellow root of the moonseed plant, used by the Dakota as a me-dicinal herb. The peninsula between the converging Yellow Medicine and Minnesota Rivers contains many more recent graves, most likely of Dakota Indians.

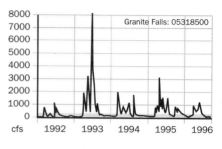

200 cfs = estimated minimum for good paddling (3.3 feet on gauge)

It is possible to take out at the state park at the confluence of the two rivers. Otherwise, continue down the Minnesota River to the access at the County Route 15 bridge.

Fishing can be good for walleye, northern pike, and smallmouth bass, espe-cially in the spring.

Access: The **Hanley Falls put-in** is located on the north edge of town, where Minnesota Highway 23 crosses the Yellow Medicine. **Minnesota River take-out:** The picnic area in Upper Sioux Agency State Park; otherwise, from the park drive 2 miles east to County Route 15; turn north and drive across the Minnesota River to the access.

Shuttle: 12 miles one way. About 40 minutes.

ADDITIONAL HELP

MA&G: 29, A8–9.
Camping: No river camping is available. Camp by car at Upper Sioux Agency State Park.
Food, gas, and lodging: Appleton, Wilmar, Marshall.
For more information: MDNR Information Center.

Information Index

Further details on most of the following waterways are available from the Minnesota
Department of Natural Resources Information Center

500 Lafayette Road
St. Paul, MN 55155-4040;
612-296-6157 or 800-766-6000 (toll free in Minnesota)

NORTHEAST

Bigfork River
Cloquet River
Little Fork River
St. Louis River: Aurora to Forbes; Forbes to Floodwood; Floodwood to Cloquet;
Scanlon to Thomson Reservoir; Thomson Dam to Swinging Bridge; and MN
23 to Duluth Harbor
Sturgeon River
Vermilion River

LAKE SUPERIOR AND NORTH SHORE

Baptism River
Brule River
Two Harbors to Cook County Line

NORTHWEST

Glendalough State Park
Otter Tail River

MISSISSIPPI RIVER

All sections

CENTRAL

Crow Wing River
Kettle River
Lower Tamarack River
North Fork of the Crow River
Pine River
Rum River
Sauk River
Snake River
St. Croix River

MINNEAPOLIS-ST. PAUL

Minneapolis Chain of Lakes

SOUTHWEST

Blue Earth River
Cannon River
Cottonwood River
Des Moines River
Le Seuer River
Minnesota River
Pomme de Terre River
Root River
Straight River
Watonwan River
Whitewater River
Yellow Medicine River
Zumbro River

Other sources of information are listed beside waterways below

NORTHEAST

Birch Lake: Superior National Foresr, Kawishiwi District, Ely, MN 55731 (218) 720-5440.

Boundary Waters Canoe Area Wilderness: Superior National Forest, P. O. Box 338, Duluth, MN 55801 (877) 550-6777.

Rainy River: MDNR Fisheries office in International Falls 218-286-5220, or Baudette (218) 634-2522.

Rice River: Chippewa National Forest, Marcell Ranger District, Box 155, Marcell, MN 56657 (218) 832-3161.

St. Louis River: Round Lake to Aurora: Superior National Forest, Laurentian Ranger District, Aurora, MN 55705 (218) 229-8800.

St. Louis River: Thomson Reservoir to Swinging Bridge, University of Minnesota-Duluth, Outdoor Center (218) 726-6177.

Sturgeon River: Side Lake to County Road 923 - Superior National Forest, LaCroix Ranger District, Cook, MN 55723 (218) 666-0021, TTY (218) 666-0021.

Timber-Frear Loop: Superior National Forest, Tofte Ranger District, Tofte, MN (218) 663-7981.

Twin Lake Loop: Superior National Forest, Gunflint Ranger District, Grand Marais, MN (218) 387-1750.

Vermilion River: Superior National Forest, Gunflint Ranger District, see Twin Lake Loop above.

Voyageurs National Park: Superintendent, Voyageurs National Park, 3131 Highway 53, International Falls, MN 56649-8904; (218) 283-2103. Lake States Interpretive Association, 3131 Highway 53, International Falls, MN 56649-8904 (218) 283-2103.

Whiteface River: Whiteface Reservoir to Cotton - MDNR Forestry, Cloquet Valley State Forest.

LAKE SUPERIOR AND NORTH SHORE

Baptism River: Cascade Kayaks, P.O. Box 215, Grand Marais, MN 55604; (800) 720-2809. Website: www.boreal.org\ckayaks. E-mail: cascadekayaks@ boreal.org.

Brule River: Cascade Kayaks see above.

Two Harbors to Tettegouche State Park: Cascade Kayaks see above.

The Susie Islands: The Nature Conservancy; Grand Portage Band; Cascade Kayaks see above.

NORTHWEST

Boy River: Chippewa National Forest, Forest Supervisor's Office; (218) 335-8600; TTY (218) 335-8632 or Walker Ranger District, HCR 73, Box 15, Walker, MN 56484 (218) 547-1044.

Glendalough State Park: P.O. Box 358, Battle Lake, MN 56515 (218) 864-0110.

Pike Bay Connection: Chippewa National Forest, Supervisor's Office (218) 335-8600; TTY (218) 335-8632 or Cass Lake Ranger District, Route 3, Box 219, Cass Lake, MN 56633 (218) 335-2283.

Red Lake River: Thief River Falls Municipal Power Plant, (218) 681-3506. U.S. Army Corps of Engineers web page, www.mvp.usace.army.mil.

Red River of the North: U.S. Army Corps of Engineers web page, see Red Lake River above.

Turtle River: Chippewa National Forest, Cass Lake Ranger District: see Pike Bay Connection above.

MISSISSIPPI RIVER

Mississippi River: Coon Rapids Dam to Iowa: U.S. Army Corps of Engineers web page, see Red Lake River above.

CENTRAL

Lower Tamarack River: MDNR Area Forester, P.O. Box 74, Hinckley, MN 55037 (320) 384-6146.

Platte River: Two Rivers Park; (320) 584-5125.

Sauk River: Stearns County Park Department, 425 South 72nd Avenue, St. Cloud, MN 56301 (320) 255-6172.

St. Croix River: Superintendent, St. Croix National Scenic Riverway, P.O. Box 708, St.Croix Falls, WI 54024 (715) 483-3284.

Upper Tamarack River: MDNR Area Forester, P.O. Box 74, Hinckley, MN 55037 (320) 384-6146.

MINNEAPOLIS-ST. PAUL

Minneapolis Chain of Lakes: Minneapolis Park & Recreation Board, 200 Grain Exchange Building, 400 South Fourth Street, Minneapolis, MN 55415-1400 or MDNR Information Center, see above.

Minnehaha Creek: Minnehaha Creek Watershed District (612) 471-0590.

Rice Creek: Ramsey County Parks and Recreation, 2015 Van Dyke Street, Maplewood, MN 55109; (651) 748-2500. Anoka County Parks and Recreation, 550 NW Bunker Lake Boulevard, Andover, MN 55304 (612) 757-3920.

SOUTHWEST

Vermillion: Hastings Parks and Recreation, (651) 437-4127.

About the Author

An avid paddler for more than 30 years. Greg Breining has kayaked the whitewater streams of the North Shore, canoe-camped in the Boundary Waters Canoe Area Wilderness, and float-fished streams throughout the state. He recently paddled his sea kayak around Lake Superior to write about Minnesota's biggest lake. He has written several books about travel and the outdoors, including *Return of the Eagle*. His articles have appeared in *Sports Illustrated, Audubon, Islands, National* and *International Wildlife,* and *Minnesota Monthly.* For many years he has been the managing editor of the *Minnesota Conservation Volunteer,* bimonthly magazine of the Minnesota Department of Natural Resources.

Greg Breining and daughter Kate Breining-Hill.

MINNESOTA CONSERVATION VOLUNTEER

Catch the next issue

Illustration by Jeff Tolbert

Join the people who read *Minnesota Conservation Volunteer*—Minnesota's premiere outdoor magazine featuring award-winning stories and beautiful color photography.

Use the convenient form below to subscribe and mail your subscription donation—today! Thank you.

Mail to *Minnesota Conservation Volunteer*, DNR, 500 Lafayette Road, St. Paul, MN 55155-4035.

✓Yes, I am supporting the *Volunteer* with a tax-deductible check made payable to *Minnesota Conservation Volunteer*.

subscription number on mailing label (if you already subscribe)

name

address

city   **state**   **ZIP + 4**

phone

☐ **This is an address change or correction**   ☐ **New subscriber**

☐ **VISA**   ☐ **MasterCard**   ☐ **Discover**

card number   **expiration date**

signature

The amount of my donation is:

*Sponsor ☐ **$100 or more**   ***Corporate/Foundation** ☐ **$250 or more**
*Patron ☐ **$50–$99**   ****Other** ☐
Supporter ☐ **$20–$49**   *Will be acknowledged in the magazine*   ☐ *Please do not list my name*
PM99   ***Out-of-state residents pay a minimum of $20 per subscription*